FIXED INCOME ANALYSIS WORKBOOK

CFA Institute is the premier association for investment professionals around the world, with over 85,000 members in 129 countries. Since 1963 the organization has developed and administered the renowned Chartered Financial Analyst® Program. With a rich history of leading the investment profession, CFA Institute has set the highest standards in ethics, education, and professional excellence within the global investment community, and is the foremost authority on investment profession conduct and practice.

Each book in the CFA Institute Investment Series is geared toward industry practitioners along with graduate-level finance students and covers the most important topics in the industry. The authors of these cutting-edge books are themselves industry professionals and academics and bring their wealth of knowledge and expertise to this series.

FIXED INCOME ANALYSIS WORKBOOK

Second Edition

Frank J. Fabozzi, PhD, CFA

BICENTENNIAL
1807
WILEY
2007
BICENTENNIAL

John Wiley & Sons, Inc.

CONTENTS

PART I

LEARNING OUTCOMES, SUMMARY OVERVIEW, AND PROBLEMS

CHAPTER 1

FEATURES OF DEBT SECURITIES

LEARNING OUTCOMES

After reading Chapter 1 you should be able to:

- describe the basic features of a bond (e.g., maturity, par value, coupon rate, bond redeeming provisions, currency denomination, issuer or investor granted options).
- describe affirmative and negative covenants.
- identify the various coupon rate structures, such as fixed rate coupon bonds, zero-coupon bonds, step-up notes, deferred coupon bonds, floating-rate securities.
- describe the structure of floating-rate securities (i.e., the coupon formula, interest rate caps and floors).
- define accrued interest, full price, and clean price.
- describe the provisions for redeeming bonds, including the distinction between a nonamortizing bond and an amortizing bond.
- explain the provisions for the early retirement of debt, including call and refunding provisions, prepayment options, and sinking fund provisions.
- differentiate between nonrefundable and noncallable bonds.
- explain the difference between a regular redemption price and a special redemption price.
- identify embedded options (call option, prepayment option, accelerated sinking fund option, put option, and conversion option) and indicate whether each benefits the issuer or the bondholder.
- explain the importance of options embedded in a bond issue.
- identify the typical method used by institutional investors to finance the purchase of a security (i.e., margin or repurchase agreement).

SUMMARY OVERVIEW

- A fixed income security is a financial obligation of an entity (the issuer) who promises to pay a specified sum of money at specified future dates.
- Fixed income securities fall into two general categories: debt obligations and preferred stock.
- The promises of the issuer and the rights of the bondholders are set forth in the indenture.
- The par value (principal, face value, redemption value, or maturity value) of a bond is the amount that the issuer agrees to repay the bondholder at or by the maturity date.
- Bond prices are quoted as a percentage of par value, with par value equal to 100.

- The interest rate that the issuer agrees to pay each year is called the coupon rate; the coupon is the annual amount of the interest payment and is found by multiplying the par value by the coupon rate.
- Zero-coupon bonds do not make periodic coupon payments; the bondholder realizes interest at the maturity date equal to the difference between the maturity value and the price paid for the bond.
- A floating-rate security is an issue whose coupon rate resets periodically based on some formula; the typical coupon formula is some reference rate plus a quoted margin.
- A floating-rate security may have a cap, which sets the maximum coupon rate that will be paid, and/or a floor, which sets the minimum coupon rate that will be paid.
- A cap is a disadvantage to the bondholder while a floor is an advantage to the bondholder.
- A step-up note is a security whose coupon rate increases over time.
- Accrued interest is the amount of interest accrued since the last coupon payment; in the United States (as well as in many countries), the bond buyer must pay the bond seller the accrued interest.
- The full price (or dirty price) of a security is the agreed upon price plus accrued interest; the price (or clean price) is the agreed upon price without accrued interest.
- An amortizing security is a security for which there is a schedule for the repayment of principal.
- Many issues have a call provision granting the issuer an option to retire all or part of the issue prior to the stated maturity date.
- A call provision is an advantage to the issuer and a disadvantage to the bondholder.
- When a callable bond is issued, if the issuer cannot call the bond for a number of years, the bond is said to have a deferred call.
- The call or redemption price can be either fixed regardless of the call date or based on a call schedule or based on a make-whole premium provision.
- With a call schedule, the call price depends on when the issuer calls the issue.
- A make-whole premium provision sets forth a formula for determining the premium that the issuer must pay to call an issue, with the premium designed to protect the yield of those investors who purchased the issue.
- The call prices are regular or general redemption prices; there are special redemption prices for debt redeemed through the sinking fund and through other provisions.
- A currently callable bond is an issue that does not have any protection against early call.
- Most new bond issues, even if currently callable, usually have some restrictions against refunding.
- Call protection is much more absolute than refunding protection.
- For an amortizing security backed by a pool of loans, the underlying borrowers typically have the right to prepay the outstanding principal balance in whole or in part prior to the scheduled principal payment dates; this provision is called a prepayment option.
- A sinking fund provision requires that the issuer retire a specified portion of an issue each year.
- An accelerated sinking fund provision allows the issuer to retire more than the amount stipulated to satisfy the periodic sinking fund requirement.
- A putable bond is one in which the bondholder has the right to sell the issue back to the issuer at a specified price on designated dates.
- A convertible bond is an issue giving the bondholder the right to exchange the bond for a specified number of shares of common stock at a specified price.

- The presence of embedded options makes the valuation of fixed income securities complex and requires the modeling of interest rates and issuer/borrower behavior in order to project cash flows.
- An investor can borrow funds to purchase a security by using the security itself as collateral.
- There are two types of collateralized borrowing arrangements for purchasing securities: margin buying and repurchase agreements.
- Typically, institutional investors in the bond market do not finance the purchase of a security by buying on margin; rather, they use repurchase agreements.
- A repurchase agreement is the sale of a security with a commitment by the seller to repurchase the security from the buyer at the repurchase price on the repurchase date.
- The borrowing rate for a repurchase agreement is called the repo rate and while this rate is less than the cost of bank borrowing, it varies from transaction to transaction based on several factors.

PROBLEMS

1. Consider the following two bond issues.

   Bond A: 5% 15-year bond
   Bond B: 5% 30-year bond
   Neither bond has an embedded option. Both bonds are trading in the market at the same yield.

   Which bond will fluctuate *more* in price when interest rates change? Why?

2. Given the information in the first and third columns, complete the table in the second and fourth columns:

Quoted price	Price per $1 of par value	Par value	Dollar price
96 1/4		$1,000	
102 7/8		$5,000	
109 9/16		$10,000	
68 11/32		$100,000	

3. A floating-rate issue has the following coupon formula:

   1-year Treasury rate + 30 basis points with a cap of 7% and a floor of 4.5%

   The coupon rate is reset every year. Suppose that at the reset date the 1-year Treasury rate is as shown below. Compute the coupon rate for the next year:

	1-year Treasury rate	Coupon rate
First reset date	6.1%	?
Second reset date	6.5%	?
Third reset date	6.9%	?
Fourth reset date	6.8%	?
Fifth reset date	5.7%	?
Sixth reset date	5.0%	?
Seventh reset date	4.1%	?
Eighth reset date	3.9%	?
Ninth reset date	3.2%	?
Tenth reset date	4.4%	?

4. An excerpt from the prospectus of a $200 million issue by Becton, Dickinson and Company 7.15% Notes due October 1, 2009:

> *OPTIONAL REDEMPTION* We may, at our option, redeem all or any part of the notes. If we choose to do so, we will mail a notice of redemption to you not less than 30 days and not more than 60 days before this redemption occurs. The redemption price will be equal to the greater of: (1) 100% of the principal amount of the notes to be redeemed; and (2) the sum of the present values of the Remaining Scheduled Payments on the notes, discounted to the redemption date on a semiannual basis, assuming a 360-day year consisting of twelve 30-day months, at the Treasury Rate plus 15 basis points.

   a. What type of call provision is this?
   b. What is the purpose of this type of call provision?

5. An excerpt from Cincinnati Gas & Electric Company's prospectus for the 10 ⅛% First Mortgage Bonds due in 2020 states,

> The Offered Bonds are redeemable (though CG&E does not contemplate doing so) prior to May 1, 1995 through the use of earnings, proceeds from the sale of equity securities and cash accumulations other than those resulting from a refunding operation such as hereinafter described. The Offered Bonds are not redeemable prior to May 1, 1995 as a part of, or in anticipation of, any refunding operation involving the incurring of indebtedness by CG&E having an effective interest cost (calculated to the second decimal place in accordance with generally accepted financial practice) of less than the effective interest cost of the Offered Bonds (similarly calculated) or through the operation of the Maintenance and Replacement Fund.

   What does this excerpt tell the investor about provisions of this issuer to pay off this issue prior to the stated maturity date?

6. An assistant portfolio manager reviewed the prospectus of a bond that will be issued next week on January 1 of 2000. The call schedule for this $200 million, 7.75% coupon 20-year issue specifies the following:

> The Bonds will be redeemable at the option of the Company at any time in whole or in part, upon not fewer than 30 nor more than 60 days' notice, at the following redemption prices (which are expressed in percentages of principal amount) in each case together with accrued interest to the date fixed for redemption:
> If redeemed during the 12 months beginning January 1,

2000 through 2005	104.00%
2006 through 2010	103.00%
2011 through 2012	101.00%
from 2013 on	100.00%

> provided, however, that prior to January 1, 2006, the Company may not redeem any of the Bonds pursuant to such option, directly or indirectly, from or in anticipation of the proceeds of the issuance of any indebtedness for money borrowed having an interest cost of less than 7.75% per annum.

The prospectus further specifies that

> The Company will provide for the retirement by redemption of $10 million of the principal amount of the Bonds each of the years 2010 to and including

2019 at the principal amount thereof, together with accrued interest to the date of redemption. The Company may also provide for the redemption of up to an additional $10 million principal amount . . . annually, . . . such optional right being non-cumulative.

The assistant portfolio manager made the following statements to a client after reviewing this bond issue. Comment on each statement. *(When answering this question, remember that the assistant portfolio manager is responding to statements just before the bond is issued in 2000.)*

a. "My major concern is that if rates decline significantly in the next few years, this issue will be called by the Company in order to replace it with a bond issue with a coupon rate less than 7.75%."

b. "One major advantage of this issue is that if the Company redeems it *for any reason* in the first five years, investors are guaranteed receiving a price of 104, a premium over the initial offering price of 100."

c. "A beneficial feature of this issue is that it has a sinking fund provision that reduces the risk that the Company won't have enough funds to pay off the issue at the maturity date."

d. "A further attractive feature of this issue is that the Company can accelerate the payoff of the issue via the sinking fund provision, reducing the risk that funds will not be available at the maturity date."

e. In response to a client question about what will be the interest and principal that the client can depend on if $5 million par value of the issue is purchased, the assistant portfolio manager responded: "I can construct a schedule that shows every six months for the next 20 years the dollar amount of the interest and the principal repayment. It is quite simple to compute—basically it is just multiplying two numbers."

7. There are some securities that are backed by a pool of loans. These loans have a schedule of interest and principal payments every month and give each borrower whose loan is in the pool the right to payoff their respective loan at any time at par. Suppose that a portfolio manager purchased one of these securities. Can the portfolio manager rely on the schedule of interest and principal payments in determining the cash flow that will be generated by such securities (assuming no borrowers default)? Why or why not?

8. a. What is an accelerated sinking fund provision?
   b. Why can an accelerated sinking fund provision be viewed as an embedded call option granted to the issuer?

9. The importance of knowing the terms of bond issues, especially those relating to redemption, cannot be emphasized. Yet there have appeared numerous instances of investors, professional and others, who acknowledge that they don't read the documentation. For example, in an Augusts 14, 1983 article published in *The New York Times* titled "The Lessons of a Bond Failure," the following statements were attributed to some stockbrokers: "But brokers in the field say they often don't spend much time reading these [official] statements," "I can be honest and say I never look at the prospectus. . . . Generally, you don't have time to do that," and "There are some clients who really don't know what they buy. . . . They just say, 'That's a good interest rate.' "
   Why it is important to understand the redemption features of a bond issue?

10. What is meant by an embedded option?

11. a. What is the typical arrangement used by institutional investors in the bond market: bank financing, margin buying, or repurchase agreement?
    b. What is the difference between a term repo and an overnight repo?

CHAPTER 2

RISKS ASSOCIATED WITH INVESTING IN BONDS

LEARNING OUTCOMES

After reading Chapter 2 you should be able to:

- explain the various risks associated with investing in bonds (e.g, interest rate risk, call and prepayment risk, yield curve risk, reinvestment risk, credit risk, liquidity risk, exchange-rate risk, inflation risk, volatility risk, and event risk).
- explain why there is an inverse relationship between changes in interest rates and bond prices.
- identify the relationships among a bond's coupon rate, yield required by the market, and price relative to par value (i.e., discount, premium, or par value).
- explain how features of a bond (maturity, coupon, and embedded options) affect its interest rate risk.
- identify the relationship among the price of a callable bond, the price of an option-free bond, and the price of the embedded call option.
- explain how the yield level impacts the interest rate risk of a bond.
- explain the interest rate risk of a floating-rate security and why its price may differ from par value.
- compute the duration of a bond given its price changes when interest rates change.
- interpret the meaning of the duration of a bond.
- use duration to approximate the percentage price change of a bond and calculate the new price if interest rates change.
- explain yield curve risk and explain why duration does not account for yield curve risk for a portfolio of bonds.
- explain key rate duration.
- identify the factors that affect the reinvestment risk of a security.
- explain the disadvantages of a callable and prepayable security to an investor.
- explain why prepayable amortizing securities expose investors to greater reinvestment risk than nonamortizing securities.
- describe the types of credit risk: default risk, credit spread risk, and downgrade risk.
- explain a rating transition matrix.
- distinguish between investment grade bonds and noninvestment grade bonds.
- explain what a rating agency does and what is meant by a rating upgrade and a rating downgrade.

- explain why liquidity risk is important to investors even if they expect to hold a security to the maturity date.
- describe the exchange rate risk an investor faces when a bond makes payments in a foreign currency.
- explain inflation risk.
- explain yield volatility, how it affects the price of a bond with an embedded option, and how changes in volatility affect the value of a callable bond and a putable bond.
- describe the various forms of event risk.
- describe the components of sovereign risk.

SUMMARY OVERVIEW

- The price of a bond changes inversely with a change in market interest rates.
- Interest rate risk refers to the adverse price movement of a bond as a result of a change in market interest rates; for the bond investor typically it is the risk that interest rates will rise.
- A bond's interest rate risk depends on the features of the bond—maturity, coupon rate, yield, and embedded options.
- All other factors constant, the longer the bond's maturity, the greater is the bond's price sensitivity to changes in interest rates.
- All other factors constant, the lower the coupon rate, the greater the bond's price sensitivity to changes in interest rates.
- The price of a callable bond is equal to the price of an option-free bond minus the price of any embedded call option.
- When interest rates rise, the price of a callable bond will not fall by as much as an otherwise comparable option-free bond because the price of the embedded call option decreases.
- The price of a putable bond is equal to the price of an option-free bond plus the price of the embedded put option.
- All other factors constant, the higher the level of interest rate at which a bond trades, the lower is the price sensitivity when interest rates change.
- The price sensitivity of a bond to changes in interest rates can be measured in terms of (1) the percentage price change from initial price or (2) the dollar price change from initial price.
- The most straightforward way to calculate the percentage price change is to average the percentage price change due to the same increase and decrease in interest rates.
- Duration is a measure of interest rate risk; it measures the price sensitivity of a bond to interest rate changes.
- Duration can be interpreted as the approximate percentage price change of a bond for a 100 basis point change in interest rates.
- The computed duration is only as good as the valuation model used to obtain the prices when interest rates are shocked up and down by the same number of basis points.
- There can be substantial differences in the duration of complex bonds because valuation models used to obtain prices can vary.
- Given the duration of a bond and its market value, the dollar price change can be computed for a given change in interest rates.
- Yield curve risk for a portfolio occurs when, if interest rates increase by different amounts at different maturities, the portfolio's value will be different than if interest rates had increased by the same amount.

- A portfolio's duration measures the sensitivity of the portfolio's value to changes in interest rates assuming the interest rates for all maturities change by the same amount.
- Any measure of interest rate risk that assumes interest rates change by the same amount for all maturities (referred to as a "parallel yield curve shift") is only an approximation.
- One measure of yield curve risk is rate duration, which is the approximate percentage price change for a 100 basis point change in the interest rate for one maturity, holding all other maturity interest rates constant.
- Call risk and prepayment risk refer to the risk that a security will be paid prior to the scheduled principal payment dates.
- Reinvestment risk is the risk that interest and principal payments (scheduled payments, called proceeds, or prepayments) available for reinvestment must be reinvested at a lower interest rate than the security that generated the proceeds.
- From an investor's perspective, the disadvantages to call and prepayment provisions are (1) the cash flow pattern is uncertain, (2) reinvestment risk increases because proceeds received will have to be reinvested at a relatively lower interest rate, and (3) the capital appreciation potential of a bond is reduced.
- Reinvestment risk for an amortizing security can be significant because of the right to prepay principal and the fact that interest and principal are repaid monthly.
- A zero-coupon bond has no reinvestment risk but has greater interest rate risk than a coupon bond of the same maturity.
- There are three forms of credit risk: default risk, credit spread risk, and downgrade risk.
- Default risk is the risk that the issuer will fail to satisfy the terms of indebtedness with respect to the timely payment of interest and principal.
- Credit spread risk is the risk that the price of an issuer's bond will decline due to an increase in the credit spread.
- Downgrade risk is the risk that one or more of the rating agencies will reduce the credit rating of an issue or issuer.
- There are three rating agencies in the United States: Standard & Poor's Corporation, Moody's Investors Service, Inc., and Fitch.
- A credit rating is an indicator of the potential default risk associated with a particular bond issue that represents in a simplistic way the credit rater's assessment of an issuer's ability to pay principal and interest in accordance with the terms of the debt contract.
- A rating transition matrix is prepared by rating agencies to show the change in credit ratings over some time period.
- A rating transition matrix can be used to estimate downgrade risk and default risk.
- Liquidity risk is the risk that the investor will have to sell a bond below its indicated value.
- The primary measure of liquidity is the size of the spread between the bid and ask price quoted by dealers.
- A market bid-ask spread is the difference between the highest bid price and the lowest ask price from among dealers.
- The liquidity risk of an issue changes over time.
- Exchange rate risk arises when interest and principal payments of a bond are not denominated in the domestic currency of the investor.
- Exchange rate risk is the risk that the currency in which the interest and principal payments are denominated will decline relative to the domestic currency of the investor.
- Inflation risk or purchasing power risk arises from the decline in value of a security's cash flows due to inflation, which is measured in terms of purchasing power.

- Volatility risk is the risk that the price of a bond with an embedded option will decline when expected yield volatility changes.
- For a callable bond, volatility risk is the risk that expected yield volatility will increase; for a putable bond, volatility risk is the risk that expected yield volatility will decrease.
- Event risk is the risk that the ability of an issuer to make interest and principal payments changes dramatically and unexpectedly because of certain events such as a natural catastrophe, corporate takeover, or regulatory changes.
- Sovereign risk is the risk that a foreign government's actions cause a default or an adverse price decline on its bond issue.

PROBLEMS

1. For each of the following issues, indicate whether the price of the issue should be par value, above par value, or below par value:

	Issue	Coupon rate	Yield required by market
a.	A	5 ¼%	7.25%
b.	B	6 ⅝%	7.15%
c.	C	0%	6.20%
d.	D	5 ⅞%	5.00%
e.	E	4 ½%	4.50%

2. Explain why a callable bond's price would be expected to decline less than an otherwise comparable option-free bond when interest rates rise?

3. a. Short-term investors such as money market mutual funds invest in floating-rate securities having maturities greater than 1 year. Suppose that the coupon rate is reset everyday. Why is the interest rate risk small for such issues?

   b. Why would it be improper to say that a floating-rate security whose coupon rate resets every day has no interest rate risk?

4. John Smith and Jane Brody are assistant portfolio managers. The senior portfolio manager has asked them to consider the acquisition of one of two option-free bond issues with the following characteristics:

   > Issue 1 has a lower coupon rate than Issue 2
   > Issue 1 has a shorter maturity than Issue 2

   Both issues have the same credit rating.

   Smith and Brody are discussing the interest rate risk of the two issues. Smith argues that Issue 1 has greater interest rate risk than Issue 2 because of its lower coupon rate. Brody counters by arguing that Issue 2 has greater interest rate risk because it has a longer maturity than Issue 1.

   a. Which assistant portfolio manager is correct with respect their selection to the issue with the greater interest rate risk?

   b. Suppose that you are the senior portfolio manager. How would you suggest that Smith and Brody determine which issue has the greater interest rate risk?

5. A portfolio manager wants to estimate the interest rate risk of a bond using duration. The current price of the bond is 82. A valuation model found that if interest rates decline by

30 basis points, the price will increase to 83.50 and if interest rates increase by 30 basis points, the price will decline to 80.75. What is the duration of this bond?

6. A portfolio manager purchased $8 million in market value of a bond with a duration of 5. For this bond, determine the estimated change in its market value for the change in interest rates shown below:

   a. 100 basis points
   b. 50 basis points
   c. 25 basis points
   d. 10 basis points

7. A portfolio manager of a bond fund is considering the acquisition of an extremely complex bond issue. It is complex because it has multiple embedded options. The manager wants to estimate the interest rate risk of the bond issue so that he can determine the impact of including it in his current portfolio. The portfolio manager contacts the dealer who created the bond issue to obtain an estimate for the issue's duration. The dealer estimates the duration to be 7. The portfolio manager solicited his firm's in-house quantitative analyst and asked her to estimate the issue's duration. She estimated the duration to be 10. Explain why there is such a dramatic difference in the issue's duration as estimated by the dealer's analysts and the firm's in-house analyst?

8. Duration is commonly used as a measure of interest rate risk. However, duration does not consider yield curve risk. Why?

9. What measure can a portfolio manager use to assess the interest rate risk of a portfolio to a change in the 5-year yield?

10. For the investor in a callable bond, what are the two forms of reinvestment risk?

11. Investors are exposed to credit risk when they purchase a bond. However, even if an issuer does not default on its obligation prior to its maturity date, there is still a concern about how credit risk can adversely impact the performance of a bond. Why?

12. Using the hypothetical rating transition matrix shown in Exhibit 4 of the chapter, answer the following questions:

   a. What is the probability that a bond rated BBB will be downgraded?
   b. What is the probability that a bond rated BBB will go into default?
   c. What is the probability that a bond rated BBB will be upgraded?
   d. What is the probability that a bond rated B will be upgraded to investment grade?
   e. What is the probability that a bond rated A will be downgraded to noninvestment grade?
   f. What is the probability that a AAA rated bond will *not* be downgraded at the end of one year?

13. Suppose that the bid and ask prices of five dealers for Issue XYX is 96 plus the number of 32nds shown:

	Dealer				
	1	2	3	4	5
Bid price	14	14	15	15	13
Ask price	18	17	18	20	19

What is the market bid-ask spread for Issue XYX?

14. A portfolio manager is considering the purchase of a new type of bond. The bond is extremely complex in terms of its embedded options. Currently, there is only one dealer making a market in this type of bond. In addition, the manager plans to finance the purchase of this bond by using the bond as collateral. The bond matures in five years and the manager plans to hold the bond for five years. Because the manager plans to hold the bond to its maturity, he has indicated that he is not concerned with liquidity risk. Explain why you agree or disagree with the manager's view that he is not concerned with liquidity risk.

15. Identify the difference in the major risks associated with the following investment alternatives:

    a. For an investor who plans to hold a security for one year, purchasing a Treasury security that matures in one year versus purchasing a Treasury security that matures in 30 years.

    b. For an investor who plans to hold an investment for 10 years, purchasing a Treasury security that matures in 10 years versus purchasing an AAA corporate security that matures in 10 years.

    c. For an investor who plans to hold an investment for two years, purchasing a zero-coupon Treasury security that matures in one year versus purchasing a zero-coupon Treasury security that matures in two years.

    d. For an investor who plans to hold an investment for five years, purchasing an AA sovereign bond (with dollar denominated cash flow payments) versus purchasing a U.S. corporate bond with a B rating.

    e. For an investor who plans to hold an investment for four years, purchasing a less actively traded 10-year AA rated bond versus purchasing a 10-year AA rated bond that is actively traded.

    f. For a U.S. investor who plans to hold an investment for six years, purchasing a Treasury security that matures in six years versus purchasing an Italian government security that matures in six years and is denominated in lira.

16. Sam Stevens is the trustee for the Hole Punchers Labor Union (HPLU). He has approached the investment management firm of IM Associates (IMA) to manage its $200 million bond portfolio. IMA assigned Carol Peters as the portfolio manager for the HPLU account. In their first meeting, Mr. Stevens told Ms. Peters:

    > "We are an extremely conservative pension fund. We believe in investing in only investment grade bonds so that there will be minimal risk that the principal invested will be lost. We want at least 40% of the portfolio to be held in bonds that will mature within the next three years. I would like your thoughts on this proposed structure for the portfolio."

    How should Ms. Peters respond?

17. a. A treasurer of a municipality with a municipal pension fund has required that its in-house portfolio manager invest all funds in the highest investment grade securities that mature in one month or less. The treasurer believes that this is a safe policy. Comment on this investment policy.

    b. The same treasurer requires that the in-house portfolio municipality's operating fund (i.e., fund needed for day-to-day operations of the municipality) follow the same investment policy. Comment on the appropriateness of this investment policy for managing the municipality's operating fund.

18. In January 1994, General Electric Capital Corporation (GECC) had outstanding $500 million of Reset Notes due March 15, 2018. The reset notes were floating-rate securities. In January 1994, the bonds had an 8% coupon rate for three years that ended March 15, 1997. On January 26, 1994, GECC notified the noteholders that it would redeem the issue on March 15th at par value. This was within the required 30 to 60 day prior notice period. Investors who sought investments with very short-term instruments (e.g., money market investors) bought the notes after GECC's planned redemption announcement. The notes were viewed as short-term because they would be redeemed in six weeks or so. In early February, the Federal Reserve started to boost interest rates and on February 15th, GECC canceled the proposed redemption. Instead, it decided to reset the new interest rate based on the indenture at 108% of the three-year Treasury rate in effect on the tenth day preceding the date of the new interest period of March 15th. *The Wall Street Journal* reported that the notes dropped from par to 98 ($1,000 to $980 per note) after the cancellation of the proposed redemption.*

     Why did the price decline?

19. A British portfolio manager is considering investing in Japanese government bonds denominated in yen. What are the major risks associated with this investment?

20. Explain how certain types of event risk can result in downgrade risk.

21. Comment on the following statement: "Sovereign risk is the risk that a foreign government defaults on its obligation."

---

*To complete this story, investors were infuriated and they protested to GECC. On March 8th the new interest rate of 5.61% was announced in the financial press. On the very next day GECC announced a tender offer for the notes commencing March 17th. It would buy them back at par plus accrued interest on April 15th. This bailed out many investors who had faith in GECCs original redemption announcement.

CHAPTER 3

OVERVIEW OF BOND SECTORS AND INSTRUMENTS

LEARNING OUTCOMES

After reading Chapter 3 you should be able to:

- explain how a country's bond market sectors are classified.
- describe a sovereign bond and explain the credit risk associated with investing in a sovereign bond.
- list the different methods used by central governments to issue bonds.
- identify the types of securities issued by the U.S. Department of the Treasury.
- outline how stripped Treasury securities are created.
- describe a semi-government or government agency bond.
- for the U.S. bond market, explain the difference between federally related institutions and government sponsored enterprises.
- describe a mortgage-backed security and identify the cash flows for a mortgage-backed security.
- define prepayment and explain prepayment risk.
- distinguish between a mortgage passthrough security and a collateralized mortgage obligation and explain the motivation for creating a collateralized mortgage obligation.
- identify the types of securities issued by municipalities in the United States.
- summarize the bankruptcy process and bondholder rights.
- list the factors considered by rating agencies in assigning a credit rating to corporate debt.
- describe secured debt, unsecured debt, and credit enhancements for corporate bonds.
- describe a medium-term note and explain the differences between a corporate bond and a medium-term note.
- describe a structured note and explain the motivation for their issuance by corporations.
- describe commercial paper and identify the different types of issuers.
- describe the different types of bank obligations.
- describe an asset-backed security.
- summarize the role of a special purpose vehicle in an asset-backed securities transaction.
- explain the motivation for a corporation to issue an asset-backed security.
- explain a collateralized debt obligation.
- describe the structure of the primary and secondary market for bonds.

SUMMARY OVERVIEW

- The bond market of a country consists of an internal bond market (also called the national bond market) and an external bond market (also called the international bond market, the offshore bond market, or, more popularly, the Eurobond market).
- A country's national bond market consists of the domestic bond market and the foreign bond market.
- Eurobonds are bonds which generally have the following distinguishing features: (1) they are underwritten by an international syndicate, (2) at issuance they are offered simultaneously to investors in a number of countries, (3) they are issued outside the jurisdiction of any single country, and (4) they are in unregistered form.
- Sovereign debt is the obligation of a country's central government.
- Sovereign credits are rated by Standard & Poor's and Moody's.
- There are two ratings assigned to each central government: a local currency debt rating and a foreign currency debt rating.
- Historically, defaults have been greater on foreign currency denominated debt.
- There are various methods of distribution that have been used by central governments when issuing securities: regular auction cycle/single-price system; regular auction cycle/multiple-price system, ad hoc auction system, and the tap system.
- In the United States, government securities are issued by the Department of the Treasury and include fixed-principal securities and inflation-indexed securities.
- The most recently auctioned Treasury issue for a maturity is referred to as the on-the-run issue or current coupon issue; off-the-run issues are issues auctioned prior to the current coupon issue.
- Treasury discount securities are called bills and have a maturity of one year or less.
- A Treasury note is a coupon-bearing security which when issued has an original maturity between two and 10 years; a Treasury bond is a coupon-bearing security which when issued has an original maturity greater than 10 years.
- The Treasury issues inflation-protection securities (TIPS) whose principal and coupon payments are indexed to the Consumer Price Index.
- Zero-coupon Treasury instruments are created by dealers stripping the coupon payments and principal payment of a Treasury coupon security.
- Strips created from the coupon payments are called coupon strips; those created from the principal payment are called principal strips.
- A disadvantage for a taxable entity investing in Treasury strips is that accrued interest is taxed each year even though interest is not received.
- The bonds of an agency or organization established by a central government are called semi-government bonds or government agency bonds and may have either a direct or implied credit guarantee by the central government.
- In the U.S. bond market, federal agencies are categorized as either federally related institutions or government sponsored enterprises.
- Federally related institutions are arms of the U.S. government and, with the exception of securities of the Tennessee Valley Authority and the Private Export Funding Corporation, are backed by the full faith and credit of the U.S. government.
- Government sponsored enterprises (GSEs) are privately owned, publicly chartered entities that were created by Congress to reduce the cost of capital for certain borrowing sectors of the economy deemed to be important enough to warrant assistance.
- A mortgage loan is a loan secured by the collateral of some specified real estate property.

- Mortgage loan payments consist of interest, scheduled principal payment, and prepayments.
- Prepayments are any payments in excess of the required monthly mortgage payment.
- Prepayment risk is the uncertainty about the cash flows due to prepayments.
- Loans included in an agency issued mortgage-backed security are conforming loans—loans that meet the underwriting standards established by the issuing entity.
- For a mortgage passthrough security the monthly payments are passed through to the certificate holders on a pro rata basis.
- In a collateralized mortgage obligation (CMO), there are rules for the payment of interest and principal (scheduled and prepaid) to the bond classes (tranches) in the CMO.
- The payment rules in a CMO structure allow for the redistribution of prepayment risk to the tranches comprising the CMO.
- In the U.S. bond market, municipal securities are debt obligations issued by state governments, local governments, and entities created by state and local governments.
- There are both tax-exempt and taxable municipal securities, where "tax-exempt" means that interest is exempt from federal income taxation; most municipal securities that have been issued are tax-exempt.
- There are basically two types of municipal security structures: tax-backed debt and revenue bonds.
- Tax-backed debt obligations are instruments secured by some form of tax revenue.
- Tax-backed debt includes general obligation debt (the broadest type of tax-backed debt), appropriation-backed obligations, and debt obligations supported by public credit enhancement programs.
- Revenue bonds are issued for enterprise financings that are secured by the revenues generated by the completed projects themselves, or for general public-purpose financings in which the issuers pledge to the bondholders the tax and revenue resources that were previously part of the general fund.
- Insured bonds, in addition to being secured by the issuer's revenue, are backed by insurance policies written by commercial insurance companies.
- Prerefunded bonds are supported by a portfolio of Treasury securities held in an escrow fund.
- In the United States, the Bankruptcy Reform Act of 1978 as amended governs the bankruptcy process.
- Chapter 7 of the bankruptcy act deals with the liquidation of a company; Chapter 11 of the bankruptcy act deals with the reorganization of a company.
- In theory, creditors should receive distributions based on the absolute priority rule to the extent assets are available; this rule means that senior creditors are paid in full before junior creditors are paid anything.
- Generally, the absolute priority rule holds in the case of liquidations and is typically violated in reorganizations.
- In analyzing a corporate bond, a credit analyst must consider the four C's of credit—character, capacity, collateral, and covenants.
- Character relates to the ethical reputation as well as the business qualifications and operating record of the board of directors, management, and executives responsible for the use of the borrowed funds and their repayment.
- Capacity deals with the ability of an issuer to pay its obligations.
- Collateral involves not only the traditional pledging of assets to secure the debt, but also the quality and value of unpledged assets controlled by the issuer.
- Covenants impose restrictions on how management operates the company and conducts its financial affairs.

- A corporate debt issue is said to be secured debt if there is some form of collateral pledged to ensure payment of the debt.
- Mortgage debt is debt secured by real property such as land, buildings, plant, and equipment.
- Collateral trust debentures, bonds, and notes are secured by financial assets such as cash, receivables, other notes, debentures or bonds, and not by real property.
- Unsecured debt, like secured debt, comes in several different layers or levels of claim against the corporation's assets.
- Some debt issues are credit enhanced by having other companies guarantee their payment.
- One of the important protective provisions for unsecured debt holders is the negative pledge clause which prohibits a company from creating or assuming any lien to secure a debt issue without equally securing the subject debt issue(s) (with certain exceptions).
- Investors in corporate bonds are interested in default rates and, more importantly, default loss rates or recovery rates.
- There is ample evidence to suggest that the lower the credit rating, the higher the probability of a corporate issuer defaulting.
- Medium-term notes are corporate debt obligations offered on a continuous basis and are offered through agents.
- The rates posted for medium-term notes are for various maturity ranges, with maturities as short as nine months to as long as 30 years.
- MTNs have been issued simultaneously with transactions in the derivatives market to create structured MTNs allowing issuers greater flexibility in creating MTNs that are attractive to investors who seek to hedge or take a market position that they might otherwise be prohibited from doing.
- Common structured notes include: step-up notes, inverse floaters, deleveraged floaters, dual-indexed floaters, range notes, and index amortizing notes.
- Commercial paper is a short-term unsecured promissory note issued in the open market that is an obligation of the issuing entity.
- Commercial paper is sold on a discount basis and has a maturity less than 270 days.
- Bank obligations in addition to the traditional corporate debt instruments include certificates of deposits and bankers acceptances.
- Asset-backed securities are securities backed by a pool of loans or receivables.
- The motivation for issuers to issue an asset-backed security rather than a traditional debt obligation is that there is the opportunity to reduce funding cost by separating the credit rating of the issuer from the credit quality of the pool of loans or receivables.
- The separation of the pool of assets from the issuer is accomplished by means of a special purpose vehicle or special purpose corporation.
- In obtaining a credit rating for an asset-backed security, the rating agencies require that the issue be credit enhanced; the higher the credit rating sought, the greater the credit enhancement needed.
- There are two general types of credit enhancement structures: external and internal.
- A collateralized debt obligation is a product backed by a pool of one or more of the following types of fixed income securities: bonds, asset-backed securities, mortgage-backed securities, bank loans, and other CDOs.
- The asset manager in a collateralized debt obligation is responsible for managing the portfolio of assets (i.e., the debt obligations backing the transaction) and there are restrictions imposed on the activities of the asset manager.
- The funds to purchase the underlying assets in a collateral debt obligation are obtained from the CDO issuance with ratings assigned by a rating agency.

- Collateralized debt obligations are categorized as either arbitrage transactions or balance sheet transactions, the classification being based on the motivation of the sponsor of the transaction.
- Bonds have traditionally been issued via an underwriting as a firm commitment or on a best efforts basis; bonds are also underwritten via a bought deal or an auction process.
- A bond can be placed privately with an institutional investor rather than issued via a public offering.
- In the United States, private placements are now classified as Rule 144A offerings (underwritten by an investment bank) and non-Rule 144A offerings (a traditional private placement).
- Bonds typically trade in the over-the-counter market.
- The two major types of electronic trading systems for bonds are the dealer-to-customer systems and the exchange systems.

PROBLEMS

1. Explain whether you agree or disagree with each of the following statements:

   a. "The foreign bond market sector of the Japanese bond market consists of bonds of Japanese entities that are issued outside of Japan."
   b. "Because bonds issued by central governments are backed by the full faith and credit of the issuing country, these bonds are not rated."
   c. "A country's semi-government bonds carry the full faith and credit of the central government."
   d. "In the United States, all federal agency bonds carry the full faith and credit of the U.S. government."

2. Why do rating agencies assign two types of ratings to the debt of a sovereign entity?
3. When issuing bonds, a central government can select from several distribution methods.

   a. What is the difference between a single-price auction and a multiple-price auction?
   b. What is a tap system?

4. Suppose a portfolio manager purchases $1 million of par value of a Treasury inflation protection security. The real rate (determined at the auction) is 3.2%.

   a. Assume that at the end of the first six months the CPI-U is 3.6% (annual rate). Compute the (i) inflation adjustment to principal at the end of the first six months, (ii) the inflation-adjusted principal at the end of the first six months, and (iii) the coupon payment made to the investor at the end of the first six months.
   b. Assume that at the end of the second six months the CPI-U is 4.0% (annual rate). Compute the (i) inflation adjustment to principal at the end of the second six months, (ii) the inflation-adjusted principal at the end of the second six months, and (iii) the coupon payment made to the investor at the end of the second six months.

5. a. What is the measure of the rate of inflation selected by the U.S. Treasury to determine the inflation adjustment for Treasury inflation protection securities?
   b. Suppose that there is deflation over the life of a Treasury inflation protection security resulting in an inflation-adjusted principal at the maturity date that is less than the

initial par value. How much will the U.S. Treasury pay at the maturity date to redeem the principal?

   c. Why is it necessary for the U.S. Treasury to report a daily index ratio for each TIPS issue?

6. What is a U.S. federal agency debenture?

7. Suppose that a 15-year mortgage loan for $200,000 is obtained. The mortgage is a level-payment, fixed-rate, fully amortized mortgage. The mortgage rate is 7.0% and the monthly mortgage payment is $1,797.66.

   a. Compute an amortization schedule for the first six months.
   b. What will the mortgage balance be at the end of the 15th year?
   c. If an investor purchased this mortgage, what will the timing of the cash flow be assuming that the borrower does not default?

8. a. What is a prepayment?
   b. What do the monthly cash flows of a mortgage-backed security consist of?
   c. What is a curtailment?

9. What is prepayment risk?

10. a. What is the difference between a mortgage passthrough security and a collateralized mortgage obligation?
   b. Why is a collateralized mortgage obligation created?

11. Name two U.S. government-sponsored enterprises that issue mortgage-backed securities.

12. What is the difference between a limited and unlimited general obligation bond?

13. What is a moral obligation bond?

14. What is an insured municipal bond?

15. a. What is a prefunded bond?
   b. Why does a properly structured prefunded municipal bond have no credit risk?

16. a. What is the difference between a liquidation and a reorganization?
   b. What is the principle of absolute priority?
   c. Comment on the following statement: "An investor who purchases a mortgage bond issued by a corporation knows that should the corporation become bankrupt, mortgage bondholders will be paid in full before the stockholders receive any proceeds."

17. a. What is a subordinated debenture corporate bond?
   b. What is negative pledge clause?

18. a. Why is the default rate alone not an adequate measure of the potential performance of corporate bonds?
   b. One study of default rates for speculative grade corporate bonds has found that one-third of all such issues default. Other studies have found that the default rate is between 2.15% and 2.4% for speculative grade corporate bonds. Why is there such a difference in these findings for speculative grade corporate bonds?
   c. Comment on the following statement: "Most studies have found that recovery rates are less than 15% of the trading price at the time of default and the recovery rate does not vary with the level of seniority."

19. a. What is the difference between a medium-term note and a corporate bond?
   b. What is a structured note?
   c. What factor determines the principal payment for an index amortizing note and what is the risk of investing in this type of structured note?

20. a. What is the risk associated with investing in a negotiable certificate of deposit issued by a U.S. bank?
   b. What is meant by "1-month LIBOR"?

21. What are the risks associated with investing in a bankers acceptance?
22. A financial corporation with a BBB rating has a consumer loan portfolio. An investment banker has suggested that this corporation consider issuing an asset-backed security where the collateral for the security is the consumer loan portfolio. What would be the advantage of issuing an asset-backed security rather than a straight offering of corporate bonds?
23. What is the role played by a special purpose vehicle in an asset-backed security structure?
24. a. What are the various forms of external credit enhancement for an asset-backed security?
    b. What is the disadvantage of using an external credit enhancement in an asset-backed security structure?
25. a. What is a collateralized debt obligation?
    b. Explain whether you agree or disagree with the following statement: "The asset manager in a collateralized debt obligation is free to manage the portfolio as aggressively or passively as he or she deems appropriate."
    c. What distinguishes an arbitrage transaction from a balance sheet transaction?
26. What is a bought deal?
27. How are private placements classified?
28. Explain the two major types of electronic bond trading systems.

CHAPTER 4

UNDERSTANDING YIELD SPREADS

LEARNING OUTCOMES

After reading Chapter 4 you should be able to:

- identify the interest rate policy tools used by the U.S. Federal Reserve Board.
- explain the Treasury yield curve and describe the various shapes of the yield curve.
- describe the term structure of interest rates.
- describe the three theories of the term structure of interest rates: pure expectations theory, liquidity preference theory, and market segmentation theory.
- for each theory of the term structure of interest rates, explain the implication that the shape of the yield curve suggests regarding the market's expectation about future interest rates.
- define a Treasury spot rate.
- define a spread product and a spread sector.
- explain the different types of yield spread measures (absolute yield spread, relative yield spread, and yield ratio) and how to calculate yield spread measures given the yields for two securities.
- distinguish between intermarket and intramarket sector spreads.
- describe an issuer's on-the-run yield curve.
- describe a credit spread and the suggested relationship between credit spreads and the well being of the economy.
- identify the relationship between embedded options and yield spreads.
- define a nominal spread.
- explain an option-adjusted spread.
- explain how the liquidity of an issue affects its yield spread.
- explain the relationship between the yield on Treasury securities and the yield on tax-exempt municipal securities.
- calculate the after-tax yield of a taxable security and the tax-equivalent yield of a tax-exempt security.
- define LIBOR and why it is an important measure to funded investors who borrow short term.
- describe an interest rate swap, the swap rate, the swap spread, and the swap spread curve.
- explain how an interest rate swap can be used to create synthetic fixed-rate assets or floating-rate assets.

- describe the factors that determine the swap spread.
- discuss the observed relationship between swap spreads and credit spreads.

SUMMARY OVERVIEW

- The interest rate offered on a particular bond issue depends on the interest rate that can be earned on risk-free instruments and the perceived risks associated with the issue.
- The U.S. Federal Reserve Board is the policy making body whose interest rate policy tools directly influence short-term interest rates and indirectly influence long-term interest rates in the United States.
- The Fed's most frequently employed interest rate policy tools are open market operations and changing the discount rate; less frequently used tools are changing bank reserve requirements and verbal persuasion to influence how bankers supply credit to businesses and consumers
- Because Treasury securities have no credit risk, market participants look at the interest rate or yield offered on an on-the-run Treasury security as the minimum interest rate required on a non-Treasury security with the same maturity.
- The Treasury yield curve shows the relationship between yield and maturity of on-the-run Treasury issues.
- The typical shape for the Treasury yield curve is upward sloping—yield increases with maturity—which is referred to as a normal yield curve.
- Inverted yield curves (yield decreasing with maturity) and flat yield curves (yield roughly the same regardless of maturity) have been observed for the yield curve.
- Two factors complicate the relationship between maturity and yield as indicated by the Treasury yield curve: (1) the yield for on-the-run issues is distorted since these securities can be financed at cheaper rates and, as a result, offer a lower yield than in the absence of this financing advantage and (2) on-the-run Treasury issues and off-the-run issues have different interest rate reinvestment risks.
- The yields on Treasury strips of different maturities provide a superior relationship between yield and maturity compared to the on-the-run Treasury yield curve.
- The yield on a zero-coupon or stripped Treasury security is called the Treasury spot rate.
- The term structure of interest rates is the relationship between maturity and Treasury spot rates.
- Three theories have been offered to explain the shape of the yield curve: pure expectations theory, liquidity preference theory, and market segmentation theory.
- The pure expectations theory asserts that the market sets yields based solely on expectations for future interest rates.
- According to the pure expectations theory: (1) a rising term structure reflects an expectation that future short-term rates will rise, (2) a flat term structure reflects an expectation that future short-term rates will be mostly constant, and (3) a falling term structure reflects an expectation that future short-term rates will decline.
- The liquidity preference theory asserts that market participants want to be compensated for the interest rate risk associated with holding longer-term bonds.
- The market segmentation theory asserts that there are different maturity sectors of the yield curve and that each maturity sector is independent or segmented from the other maturity sectors. Within each maturity sector, the interest rate is determined by the supply and demand for funds.

- According to the market segmentation theory, any shape is possible for the yield curve.
- Despite the imperfections of the Treasury yield curve as a benchmark for the minimum interest rate that an investor requires for investing in a non-Treasury security, it is common to refer to a non-Treasury security's additional yield over the nearest maturity on-the-run Treasury issue as the "yield spread."
- The yield spread can be computed in three ways: (1) the difference between the yield on two bonds or bond sectors (called the absolute yield spread), (2) the difference in yields as a percentage of the benchmark yield (called the relative yield spread), and (3) the ratio of the yield relative to the benchmark yield (called the yield ratio).
- An intermarket yield spread is the yield spread between two securities with the same maturity in two different sectors of the bond market.
- The most common intermarket sector spread calculated is the yield spread between the yield on a security in a non-Treasury market sector and a Treasury security with the same maturity.
- An intramarket sector spread is the yield spread between two issues within the same market sector.
- An issuer specific yield curve can be computed given the yield spread, by maturity, for an issuer and the yield for on-the-run Treasury securities.
- The factors other than maturity that affect the intermarket and intramarket yield spreads are (1) the relative credit risk of the two issues; (2) the presence of embedded options; (3) the relative liquidity of the two issues; and, (4) the taxability of the interest.
- A credit spread or quality spread is the yield spread between a non-Treasury security and a Treasury security that are "identical in all respects except for credit rating."
- Some market participants argue that credit spreads between corporates and Treasuries change systematically because of changes in economic prospects—widening in a declining economy ("flight to quality") and narrowing in an expanding economy.
- Generally investors require a larger spread to a comparable Treasury security for issues with an embedded option favorable to the issuer, and a smaller spread for an issue with an embedded option favorable to the investor.
- For mortgage-backed securities, one reason for the increased yield spread relative to a comparable Treasury security is exposure to prepayment risk.
- The option-adjusted spread of a security seeks to measure the yield spread after adjusting for embedded options.
- A yield spread exists due to the difference in the perceived liquidity of two issues.
- One factor that affects liquidity (and therefore the yield spread) is the size of an issue—the larger the issue, the greater the liquidity relative to a smaller issue, and the greater the liquidity, the lower the yield spread.
- Because of the tax-exempt feature of municipal bonds, the yield on municipal bonds is less than that on Treasuries with the same maturity.
- The difference in yield between tax-exempt securities and Treasury securities is typically measured in terms of a yield ratio—the yield on a tax-exempt security as a percentage of the yield on a comparable Treasury security.
- The after-tax yield is computed by multiplying the pre-tax yield by one minus the marginal tax rate.
- In the tax-exempt bond market, the benchmark for calculating yield spreads is a generic AAA general obligation bond with a specified maturity.
- Technical factors having to do with temporary imbalances between the supply of and demand for new issues affect yield spreads.

- The same factors that affect yield spreads in the United States affect yield spreads in other countries and between countries.
- Major non-U.S. bond markets have government benchmark yield curves similar to the U.S. Treasury yield curve.
- Because of the important role of the German bond market, nominal spreads in the European bond market are typically computed relative to German government bonds.
- Funded investors who borrow short term typically measure the relative value of a security using borrowing rates rather than the Treasury rate.
- The most popular borrowing cost reference rate is the London interbank offered rate (LIBOR), which is the interest rate banks pay to borrow funds from other banks in the London interbank market.
- Funded investors typically pay a spread over LIBOR and seek to earn a spread over that funding cost when they invest the borrowed funds.
- In an interest rate swap, two parties agree to exchange periodic interest payments with the dollar amount of the interest payments exchanged based on a notional principal (also called a notional amount).
- In a typical interest rate swap, one party (the fixed-rate payer) agrees to pay to the counterparty fixed interest payments at designated dates for the life of the contract and the counterparty (the fixed-rate receiver) agrees to make interest rate payments that float with some reference rate.
- In an interest rate swap, the fixed rate paid by the fixed-rate payer is called the swap rate.
- The most common reference rate used in a swap is LIBOR.
- The swap spread is the spread that the fixed-rate payer agrees to pay above the Treasury yield with the same term to maturity as the swap.
- The swap rate is the sum of the yield of a Treasury with the same maturity as the swap plus the swap spread.
- Institutional investors can use an interest rate swap to convert a fixed-rate asset (or liability) into a floating-rate asset (or liability) and vice versa.
- The swap spread is viewed by market participants throughout the world as the appropriate spread measure for valuation and relative value analysis.
- The swap spread is the spread of the global cost of short-term borrowing over the Treasury rate.
- There is a high correlation between swap spreads and credit spreads in various sectors of the bond market.
- A swap spread curve shows the relationship between the swap rate and swap maturity for a given country.

PROBLEMS

1. The following statement appears on page 2 of the August 2, 1999 issue of Prudential Securities' *Spread Talk*.

   > The market appears to be focusing all of its energy on predicting whether or not the Fed will raise rates again at the August and/or October FOMC [Federal Open Market Committee] meetings.

   How do market observers try to predict "whether or not the Fed will raise rates"?

2. Ms. Peters is a financial advisor. One of her clients called and asked about a recent change in the shape of the yield curve from upward sloping to downward sloping. The client told

Ms. Peters that she thought that the market was signaling that interest rates were expected to decline in the future. What should Ms. Peters' response be to her client?

3. How does the liquidity preference theory differ from the pure expectations theory?

4. According to the pure expectations theory, what does a humped yield curve suggest about the expectations of future interest rates?

5. Assume the following information pertaining to federal agency spreads was reported:

Agency Spreads versus Benchmark Treasury (basis points)

		Last 12 months		
	Yield spread	High	Low	Average
Noncallable				
3-year	70	70	28	44.1
5-year	80	80	32	55.4
10-year	95	95	45	71.2
Callable				
3-year (NC1)	107	107	50	80.2
5-year (NC1)	145	145	77	112.1
5-year (NC2)	132	132	65	96.9
5-year (NC3)	124	124	—	33.6
10-year (NC3)	178	178	99	132.9
10-year (NC5)	156	156	79	112.5

		Last 12 months		
	Yield spread	High	Low	Average
Callable OAS (volatility = 14%)				
3-year (NC1)	75	75	20	50.0
5-year (NC1)	100	100	20	63.8
5-year (NC2)	100	100	23	60.7
5-year (NC3)	100	100	29	59.6
10-year (NC3)	115	115	34	77.0
10-year (NC5)	115	115	36	77.4

Note: NCX = X-year deferred call; — = not available

a. Relative to the previous 12 months, what does the yield spread data above indicate about yield spreads?

b. Explain what causes the yield spread relationship between callable and noncallable issues for a given maturity?

c. Explain what causes the yield spread relationship among the different callable issues for a given maturity?

d. Why are the yield spreads shown in the second panel referred to as nominal spreads?

e. Explain what causes the yield spread relationship between the callable yield spread and the callable OAS for a given maturity and given deferred call?

6. Comment on the following statement by a representative of an investment management firm who is working with a client in selecting sectors in which the manager for the account will be permitted to invest:

Mortgage-backed securities give our managers the opportunity to increase yield because these securities offer a higher yield than comparable Treasury securities. In particular, our managers prefer Ginnie Mae mortgage-backed securities because they have no credit risk since they are backed by the full faith and credit of the U.S. government. Therefore, our managers can pick up additional yield with no additional credit risk. While Ginnie Mae mortgage-backed securities may not be as liquid as U.S. Treasury securities, the yield spread is more than adequate to compensate for the lesser liquidity.

7. a. Why is the yield spread between a bond with an embedded option and an otherwise comparable Treasury security referred to as a "nominal spread"?
   b. What is an option-adjusted spread and why is it superior to a nominal spread as a yield spread measure for a bond with an embedded option?

8. Suppose that the yield on a 10-year noncallable corporate bond is 7.25% and the yield for the on-the-run 10-year Treasury is 6.02%. Compute the following:

   a. the absolute yield spread
   b. the relative yield spread
   c. the yield ratio

9. Following is a quote that appeared in the May 19, 1999 *Global Relative Value* by Lehman Brothers (COR-1):

   > As we have written in the past, percent yield spreads (spread as a percent of Treasury yields) are still cheap on an historical basis. As an illustration, the average single A 10-year industrial percent yield spread was 17% on April 30 compared to a 10 year monthly average of 12%.

   a. What is another name for the yield spread measure cited in the quote?
   b. Why would the analysts at Lehman Brothers focus on "percent yield spreads" rather than absolute yield spread?

10. If proposals are being considered by Congress to reduce tax rates and the market views that passage of such legislation is likely, what would you expect to happen to municipal bond yields?

11. a. Why isn't the Treasury yield curve used as a benchmark in measuring yield spreads between different sectors of the municipal bond market?
    b. What benchmark is used?

12. a. What is the after-tax yield for an investor in the 40% tax bracket if the taxable yield is 5%?
    b. What is the taxable-equivalent yield for an investor in the 39% tax bracket if the tax-exempt yield on an investment is 3.1%?

13. Why are funded investors who borrow short term interested in a LIBOR yield curve rather than the Treasury yield curve?

14. If the swap spread for a 5-year interest rate swap is 120 basis points and the yield on the 5-year Treasury is 4.4%, what is the swap rate?

15. Why is the swap spread an important spread measure?

16. Suppose that an institutional investor has entered into an interest rate swap, as the fixed-rate payer, with the following terms:

Term of swap:	2 years
Frequency of payments:	quarterly
Notional amount:	$10 million
Reference rate:	3-month LIBOR
Swap spread:	100 basis points

At the time of the swap, the Treasury yield curve is as follows:

3-month rate:	4.0%	3-year rate:	6.5%
6-month rate:	4.4%	4-year rate:	7.1%
1-year rate:	4.9%	5-year rate:	7.8%
2-year rate:	5.8%		

a. What is the swap rate?
b. What is the dollar amount of the quarterly payment that will be made by the fixed-rate payer?
c. Complete the following table showing the quarterly payment that will be received by the fixed-rate payer, based on 3-month LIBOR:

If 3-month LIBOR is	Annual dollar amount	Amount of payment
5.00%		
5.50%		
6.00%		
6.50%		
7.00%		
7.50%		
8.00%		
8.50%		

d. Complete the following table showing the quarterly net payment that the fixed-rate payer must make, based on 3-month LIBOR:

If 3-month LIBOR is	Floating-rate received	Net payment by fixed-rate payer
5.00%		
5.50%		
6.00%		
6.50%		
7.00%		
7.50%		
8.00%		
8.50%		

17. An investor has purchased a floating-rate security with a 5-year maturity. The coupon formula for the floater is 6-month LIBOR plus 200 basis points and the interest payments are made *semiannually*. The floater is not callable. At the time of purchase, 6-month LIBOR is 7.5%. The investor borrowed the funds to purchase the floater by issuing a 5-year note at par value with a fixed coupon rate of 7%.

a. Ignoring credit risk, what is the risk that this investor faces?
b. Explain why an interest rate swap can be used to offset this risk?
c. Suppose that the investor can enter into a 5-year interest rate swap in which the investor pays LIBOR (i.e., the investor is the fixed-rate receiver). The swap rate is 7.3% and the frequency of the payments is *semiannual*. What annual income spread can the investor lock in?

CHAPTER 5

INTRODUCTION TO THE VALUATION OF DEBT SECURITIES

LEARNING OUTCOMES

After reading Chapter 5 you should be able to:

- describe the fundamental principles of bond valuation.
- explain the steps in the valuation process (i.e., estimate expected cash flows, determine an appropriate discount rate or rates, and compute the present value of the cash flows).
- define a bond's cash flows.
- describe the difficulties of estimating the expected cash flows for some types of bonds.
- compute the value of a bond, given the expected cash flows and the appropriate discount rates.
- explain how the value of a bond changes if the discount rate increases or decreases.
- explain how the price of a bond changes as the bond approaches its maturity date.
- compute the value of a zero-coupon bond.
- compute the value of a bond that is between coupon payments.
- explain the deficiency of the traditional approach to bond valuation.
- explain the arbitrage-free bond valuation approach and the role of Treasury spot rates in the valuation process.
- explain how the process of stripping and reconstitution forces the price of a bond towards its arbitrage-free value.
- demonstrate how a dealer can generate an arbitrage profit if a bond is mispriced.
- compute the price of the bond given the term structure of default free spot rates and the term structure of credit spreads.
- explain the basic features common to models used to value bonds with embedded options.

SUMMARY OVERVIEW

- Valuation is the process of determining the fair value of a financial asset.
- The fundamental principle of valuation is that the value of any financial asset is the present value of the expected cash flows, where a cash flow is the amount of cash expected to be received at some future periods.

- The valuation process involves three steps: (1) estimating the expected cash flows, (2) determining the appropriate interest rate or interest rates to be used to discount the cash flows, and (3) calculating the present value of the expected cash flows.
- For any fixed income security which neither the issuer nor the investor can alter the payment of the principal before its contractual due date, the cash flows can easily be determined assuming that the issuer does not default.
- The difficulty in determining cash flows arises for securities where either the issuer or the investor can alter the cash flows, or the coupon rate is reset by a formula dependent on some reference rate, price, or exchange rate.
- On-the-run Treasury yields are viewed as the minimum interest rate an investor requires when investing in a bond.
- The risk premium or yield spread over the interest rate on a Treasury security investors require reflects the additional risks in a security that is not issued by the U.S. government.
- For a given discount rate, the present value of a single cash flow received in the future is the amount of money that must be invested today that will generate that future value.
- The present value of a cash flow will depend on when a cash flow will be received (i.e., the timing of a cash flow) and the discount rate (i.e., interest rate) used to calculate the present value
- The sum of the present values for a security's expected cash flows is the value of the security.
- The present value is lower the further into the future the cash flow will be received.
- The higher the discount rate, the lower a cash flow's present value and since the value of a security is the sum of the present value of the cash flows, the higher the discount rate, the lower a security's value.
- The price/yield relationship for an option-free bond is convex.
- The value of a bond is equal to the present value of the coupon payments plus the present value of the maturity value.
- When a bond is purchased between coupon periods, the buyer pays a price that includes accrued interest, called the full price or dirty price.
- The clean price or simply price of a bond is the full price minus accrued interest.
- In computing accrued interest, day count conventions are used to determine the number of days in the coupon payment period and the number of days since the last coupon payment date.
- The traditional valuation methodology is to discount every cash flow of a security by the same interest rate (or discount rate), thereby incorrectly viewing each security as the same package of cash flows.
- The arbitrage-free approach values a bond as a package of cash flows, with each cash flow viewed as a zero-coupon bond and each cash flow discounted at its own unique discount rate.
- The Treasury zero-coupon rates are called Treasury spot rates.
- The Treasury spot rates are used to discount the cash flows in the arbitrage-free valuation approach.
- To value a security with credit risk, it is necessary to determine a term structure of credit rates.
- Adding a credit spread for an issuer to the Treasury spot rate curve gives the benchmark spot rate curve used to value that issuer's security.
- Valuation models seek to provide the fair value of a bond and accommodate securities with embedded options.
- The common valuation models used to value bonds with embedded options are the binomial model and the Monte Carlo simulation model.

- The binomial model is used to value callable bonds, putable bonds, floating-rate notes, and structured notes in which the coupon formula is based on an interest rate.
- The Monte Carlo simulation model is used to value mortgage-backed and certain asset-backed securities.
- The user of a valuation model is exposed to modeling risk and should test the sensitivity of the model to alternative assumptions.

PROBLEMS

1. Compute the value of a 5-year 7.4% coupon bond that pays interest annually assuming that the appropriate discount rate is 5.6%.

2. A 5-year amortizing security with a par value of $100,000 and a coupon rate of 6.4% has an expected cash flow of $23,998.55 per year assuming no prepayments. The annual cash flow includes interest and principal payment. What is the value of this amortizing security assuming no principal prepayments and a discount rate of 7.8%.

3. a. Assuming annual interest payments, what is the value of a 5-year 6.2% coupon bond when the discount rate is (i) 4.5%, (ii) 6.2%, and (iii) 7.3%?

   b. Show that the results obtained in part a are consistent with the relationship between the coupon rate, discount rate, and price relative to par value.

4. A client is reviewing a year-end portfolio report. Since the beginning of the year, market yields have increased slightly. In comparing the beginning-of-the-year price for the bonds selling at a discount from par value to the end-of-year prices, the client observes that all the prices are higher. The client is perplexed since he expected that the price of all bonds should be lower since interest rates increased. Explain to the client why the prices of the bonds in the portfolio selling at discount have increased in value.

5. A 4-year 5.8% coupon bond is selling to yield 7%. The bond pays interest annually. One year later interest rates decrease from 7% to 6.2%.

   a. What is the price of the 4-year 5.8% coupon bond selling to yield 7%?

   b. What is the price of this bond one year later assuming the yield is unchanged at 7%?

   c. What is the price of this bond one year later if instead of the yield being unchanged the yield decreases to 6.2%?

   d. Complete the following:
      Price change attributable to moving to maturity
         (no change in discount rate)
      Price change attribute to an increase in the
         discount rate from 7% to 6.2%
      Total price change   _____

6. What is the value of a 5-year 5.8% annual coupon bond if the appropriate discount rate for discounting each cash flow is as follows:

Year	Discount rate
1	5.90%
2	6.40%
3	6.60%
4	6.90%
5	7.30%

7. What is the value of a 5-year 7.4% coupon bond selling to yield 5.6% assuming the coupon payments are made semiannually?

8. What is the value of a zero-coupon bond paying semiannually that matures in 20 years, has a maturity of $1 million, and is selling to yield 7.6%.

9. Suppose that a bond is purchased between coupon periods. The days between the settlement date and the next coupon period is 115. There are 183 days in the coupon period. Suppose that the bond purchased has a coupon rate of 7.4% and there are 10 semiannual coupon payments remaining.

   a. What is the dirty price for this bond if a 5.6% discount rate is used?
   b. What is the accrued interest for this bond?
   c. What is the clean price?

10. Suppose that the prevailing Treasury spot rate curve is the one shown in Exhibit 5.

   a. What is the value of a 7.4% 8-year Treasury issue?
   b. Suppose that the 7.4% 8-year Treasury issue is priced in the market based on the on-the-run 8-year Treasury yield. Assume further that yield is 5.65%, so that each cash flow is discounted at 5.65% divided by 2. What is the price of the 7.4% 8-year Treasury issue based on a 5.65% discount rate?
   c. Given the arbitrage-free value found in part a and the price in part b, what action would a dealer take and what would the arbitrage profit be if the market priced the 7.4% 8-year Treasury issue at the price found in part b?
   d. What process assures that the market price will not differ materially from the arbitrage-free value?

11. Suppose that the prevailing Treasury spot rate curve is the one shown in Exhibit 5.

   a. What is the value of a 4% 8-year Treasury issue?
   b. Suppose that the 4% 8-year Treasury issue is priced in the market based on the on-the-run 8-year Treasury yield. Assume further that yield is 5.65%, so that each cash flow is discounted at 5.65% divided by 2. What is the price of the 4% 8-year Treasury issue based on a 5.65% discount rate?
   c. Given the arbitrage-free value found in part a and the price in part b, what action would a dealer take and what would the arbitrage profit be if the market priced the 4% 8-year Treasury issue at the price found in part b?
   d. What process assures that the market price will not differ materially from the arbitrage-free value?

CHAPTER 6

YIELD MEASURES, SPOT RATES, AND FORWARD RATES

LEARNING OUTCOMES

After reading Chapter 6 you should be able to:

- explain the sources of return from investing in a bond (coupon interest payments. capital gain/loss, and reinvestment income).
- compute the traditional yield measures for fixed-rate bonds (current yield, yield to maturity, yield to first call, yield to first par call date, yield to refunding, yield to put, yield to worst, and cash flow yield).
- explain the assumptions underlying traditional yield measures and the limitations of the traditional yield measures.
- calculate the reinvestment income required to generate the yield computed at the time of purchase.
- explain the factors affecting reinvestment risk.
- calculate the spread for life and discount margin measure for a floating-rate security and explain the limitations of both.
- calculate the yield on a discount basis for a Treasury bill and explain its limitations.
- compute using the method of bootstrapping the theoretical Treasury spot rate curve given the Treasury yield curve derived from the on-the-run Treasury issues.
- explain the limitations of the nominal spread.
- describe and compute a zero-volatility spread given a spot rate curve.
- explain why the zero-volatility spread will diverge from, and is superior to, the nominal spread.
- explain an option-adjusted spread for a bond with an embedded option and explain what is meant by the option cost.
- explain why the nominal spread hides the option risk for bonds with embedded options.
- define a forward rate and compute forward rates from spot rates.
- demonstrate the relationship between short-term forward rates and spot rates.
- explain why valuing a bond using spot rates and forward rates produces the same value.
- calculate the forward discount factor from forward rates.
- calculate the value of a bond given forward rates.

SUMMARY OVERVIEW

- The sources of return from holding a bond to maturity are the coupon interest payments, any capital gain or loss, and reinvestment income.
- Reinvestment income is the interest income generated by reinvesting coupon interest payments and any principal payments from the time of receipt to the bond's maturity.
- The current yield relates the annual dollar coupon interest to the market price and fails to recognize any capital gain or loss and reinvestment income.
- The yield to maturity is the interest rate that will make the present value of the cash flows from a bond equal to the price plus accrued interest.
- The market convention to annualize a semiannual yield is to double it and the resulting annual yield is referred to as a bond-equivalent yield.
- When market participants refer to a yield or return measure as computed on a bond-equivalent basis it means that a semiannual yield or return is doubled.
- The yield to maturity takes into account all three sources of return but assumes that the coupon payments and any principal repayments can be reinvested at an interest rate equal to the yield to maturity.
- The yield to maturity will only be realized if the interim cash flows can be reinvested at the yield to maturity and the bond is held to maturity.
- Reinvestment risk is the risk an investor faces that future reinvestment rates will be less than the yield to maturity at the time a bond is purchased.
- Interest rate risk is the risk that if a bond is not held to maturity, an investor may have to sell it for less than the purchase price.
- The longer the maturity and the higher the coupon rate, the more a bond's return is dependent on reinvestment income to realize the yield to maturity at the time of purchase.
- The yield to call is the interest rate that will make the present value of the expected cash flows to the assumed call date equal to the price plus accrued interest.
- Yield measures for callable bonds include yield to first call, yield to next call, yield to first par call, and yield to refunding.
- The yield to call considers all three sources of potential return but assumes that all cash flows can be reinvested at the yield to call until the assumed call date, the investor will hold the bond to the assumed call date, and the issuer will call the bond on the assumed call date.
- For a putable bond a yield to put is computed assuming that the issue will be put on the first put date.
- The yield to worst is the lowest yield from among all possible yield to calls, yield to puts, and the yield to maturity.
- For mortgage-backed and asset-backed securities, the cash flow yield based on some prepayment rate is the interest rate that equates the present value of the projected principal and interest payments to the price plus accrued interest.
- The cash flow yield assumes that all cash flows (principal and interest payments) can be reinvested at the calculated yield and that the assumed prepayment rate will be realized over the security's life.
- For amortizing securities, reinvestment risk is greater than for standard coupon nonamortizing securities because payments are typically made monthly and include principal as well as interest payments.
- For floating-rate securities, instead of a yield measure, margin measures (i.e., spread above the reference rate) are computed.
- Two margin measures commonly used are spread for life and discount margin.

- The discount margin assumes that the reference rate will not change over the life of the security and that there is no cap or floor restriction on the coupon rate.
- The theoretical spot rate is the interest rate that should be used to discount a default-free cash flow.
- Because there are a limited number of on-the-run Treasury securities traded in the market, interpolation is required to obtain the yield for interim maturities; hence, the yield for most maturities used to construct the Treasury yield curve are interpolated yields rather than observed yields.
- Default-free spot rates can be derived from the Treasury yield curve by a method called bootstrapping.
- The basic principle underlying the bootstrapping method is that the value of a Treasury coupon security is equal to the value of the package of zero-coupon Treasury securities that duplicates the coupon bond's cash flows.
- The nominal spread is the difference between the yield for a non-Treasury bond and a comparable-maturity Treasury coupon security.
- The nominal spread fails to consider the term structure of the spot rates and the fact that, for bonds with embedded options, future interest rate volatility may alter its cash flows.
- The zero-volatility spread or Z-spread is a measure of the spread that the investor will realize over the entire Treasury spot rate curve if the bond is held to maturity, thereby recognizing the term structure of interest rates.
- Unlike the nominal spread, the Z-spread is not a spread off one point on the Treasury yield curve but is a spread over the entire spot rate curve.
- For bullet bonds, unless the yield curve is very steep, the nominal spread will not differ significantly from the Z-spread; for securities where principal is paid over time rather than just at maturity there can be a significant difference, particularly in a steep yield curve environment.
- The option-adjusted spread (OAS) converts the cheapness or richness of a bond into a spread over the future possible spot rate curves.
- An OAS is said to be option adjusted because it allows for future interest rate volatility to affect the cash flows.
- The OAS is a product of a valuation model and, when comparing the OAS of dealer firms, it is critical to check on the volatility assumption (and other assumptions) employed in the valuation model.
- The cost of the embedded option is measured as the difference between the Z-spread and the OAS.
- Investors should not rely on the nominal spread for bonds with embedded options since it hides how the spread is split between the OAS and the option cost.
- OAS is used as a relative value measure to assist in the selection of bonds with embedded options.
- Using arbitrage arguments, forward rates can be extrapolated from the Treasury yield curve or the Treasury spot rate curve.
- The spot rate for a given period is related to the forward rates; specifically, the spot rate is a geometric average of the current 6-month spot rate and the subsequent 6-month forward rates.

PROBLEMS

1. What are the sources of return any yield measure should incorporate?

2. a. Suppose a 10-year 9% coupon bond is selling for $112 with a par value of $100. What is the current yield for the bond?

   b. What is the limitation of the current yield measure?

3. Determine whether the yield to maturity of a 6.5% 20-year bond that pays interest semiannually and is selling for $90.68 is 7.2%. 7.4%, or 7.8%.

4. The following yields and prices were reported in the financial press. Are any of them incorrect assuming that the reported price and coupon rate are correct? If so, explain why? (No calculations are needed to answer this question.)

Bond	Price	Coupon rate	Current yield	Yield to maturity
A	100	6.0%	5.0%	6.0%
B	110	7.0%	6.4%	6.1%
C	114	7.5%	7.1%	7.7%
D	95	4.7%	5.2%	5.9%
E	75	5.6%	5.1%	4.1%

5. Comment on the following statement: "The yield to maturity measure is a useless measure because it doubles a semiannual yield (calling the annual yield a bond-equivalent yield) rather than computing an effective annual yield. This is the major shortcoming of the yield-to-maturity measure."

6. a. Suppose that an investor invests $108.32 in a 5-year certificate of deposit that pays 7% annually (on a bond-equivalent basis) or 3.5% semiannually and the interest payments are semiannual. What are the total future dollars of this investment at the end of 5 years (i.e., ten 6-month periods)?

   b. How much total interest is generated from the investment in this certificate of deposit?

   c. Suppose an investor can purchase any investment for $108.32 that offers a 7% yield on a bond-equivalent basis and pays interest semiannually. What is the total future dollars and the total dollar return from this investment?

   d. Suppose an investor can purchase a 5-year 9% coupon bond that pays interest semiannually and the price of this bond is $108.32. The yield to maturity for this bond is 7% on a bond-equivalent basis. What is the total future dollars and the total dollar return that will be generated from this bond if it is to yield 7%?

   e. Complete the following for this bond:

   coupon interest   =
   capital gain/loss   =
   reinvestment income = _____

   total dollar return   =

   f. What percentage of the total dollar return is dependent on reinvestment income?

   g. How is the reinvestment income in part e realized?

7. a. Which of the following three bonds has the greatest dependence on reinvestment income to generate the computed yield? Assume that each bond is offering the same yield to maturity. (No calculations are needed to answer this question.)

Bond	Maturity	Coupon rate
X	25 years	0%
Y	20 years	7%
Z	20 years	8%

   b. Which of the three bonds in part a has the least dependence on reinvestment income to generate the computed yield? Assume that each bond is offering the same yield to maturity. (No calculations are needed to answer this question.)

8. What is the reinvestment risk and interest rate risk associated with a yield to maturity measure?

9. a. If the yield to maturity on an annual-pay bond is 5.6%, what is the bond-equivalent yield?

   b. If the yield of a U.S. bond issue quoted on a bond-equivalent basis is 5.6%, what is the yield to maturity on an annual-pay basis?

10. Suppose that a 10% 15-year bond has the following call structure:

   not callable for the next 5 years
   first callable in 5 years at $105
   first par call date is in 10 years
   The price of the bond is $127.5880.

   a. Is the yield to maturity for this bond 7.0%, 7.4%, or 7.8%?
   b. Is the yield to first call for this bond 4.55%, 4.65%, or 4.85?
   c. Is the yield to first par call for this bond 6.25%, 6.55%, or 6.75%?

11. Suppose a 5% coupon 6-year bond is selling for $105.2877 and is putable in four years at par value. The yield to maturity for this bond is 4%. Determine whether the yield to put is 3.38%, 3.44% or 3.57%.

12. Suppose that an amortizing security pays interest monthly. Based on the projected principal payments and interest, suppose that the monthly interest rate that makes the present value of the cash flows equal to the price of the security is 0.41%. What is the cash flow yield on a bond-equivalent basis?

13. Two portfolio managers are discussing the investment characteristics of amortizing securities. Manager A believes that the advantage of these securities relative to nonamortizing securities is that since the periodic cash flows include principal payments as well as coupon payments, the manager can generate greater reinvestment income. In addition, the payments are typically monthly so even greater reinvestment income can be generated. Manager B believes that the need to reinvest monthly and the need to invest larger amounts than just coupon interest payments make amortizing securities less attractive. Who do you agree with and why?

14. An investor is considering the purchase of a 5-year floating-rate note that pays interest semiannually. The coupon formula is equal to 6-month LIBOR plus 30 basis points. The current value for 6-month LIBOR is 5% (annual rate). The price of this note is 99.1360. Is the discount margin 40 basis points, 50 basis points, or 55 basis points?

15. How does the discount margin handle any cap on a floater and the fact that the reference rate may change over time?

16. a. A Treasury bill with 105 days from settlement to maturity is selling for $0.989 per $1 of maturity value. What is the yield on a discount basis?

   b. A Treasury bill with 275 days from settlement to maturity is quoted as having a yield on a discount basis of 3.68%. What is the price of this Treasury bill?

   c. What are the problems with using the yield on a discount basis as measure of a Treasury bill's yield?

17. Explain how a Treasury yield curve is constructed even though there are only a limited number of on-the-run Treasury issues available in the market.

18. Suppose that the annual yield to maturity for the 6-month and 1-year Treasury bill is 4.6% and 5.0%, respectively. These yields represent the 6-month and 1-year spot rates. Also assume the following Treasury yield curve (i.e., the price for each issue is $100) has been estimated for 6-month periods out to a maturity of 3 years:

Years to maturity	Annual yield to maturity (BEY)
1.5	5.4%
2.0	5.8%
2.5	6.4%
3.0	7.0%

Compute the 1.5-year, 2-year, 2.5-year, and 3-year spot rates.

19. Given the spot rates computed in the previous question and the 6-month and 1-year spot rates, compute the arbitrage-free value of a 3-year Treasury security with a coupon rate of 8%.

20. What are the two limitations of the nominal spread as a measure of relative value of two bonds?

21. Suppose that the Treasury spot rate curve is as follows:

Period	Years to maturity	Spot rate
1	0.5	5.0%
2	1.0	5.4
3	1.5	5.8
4	2.0	6.4
5	2.5	7.0
6	3.0	7.2
7	3.5	7.4
8	4.0	7.8

Suppose that the market price of a 4-year 6% coupon non-Treasury issue is $91.4083 Determine whether the zero-volatility spread (Z-spread) relative to the Treasury spot rate curve for this issue is 80 basis points, 90 basis points, or 100 basis points.

22. The Prestige Investment Management Company sent a report to its pension client. In the report, Prestige indicated that the yield curve is currently flat (i.e., the yield to maturity for each maturity is the same) and then discussed the nominal spread for the corporate bonds held in the client's portfolio. A trustee of the pension fund was concerned that Prestige focused on the nominal spread rather than the zero-volatility spread or option-adjusted spread for these bond issues. Joan Thomas is Prestige's employee who is the contact person for this account. She received a phone call from the trustee regarding his concern. How should she respond regarding the use of nominal spread rather than zero-volatility spread and option-adjusted spread as a spread measure for corporate bonds?

23. John Tinker is a a junior portfolio manager assigned to work for Laura Sykes, the manager of the corporate bond portfolio of a public pension fund. Ms. Sykes asked Mr. Tinker to construct a portfolio profile that she could use in her presentation to the trustees. One of the measures Ms. Sykes insisted that Mr. Tinker include the option-adjusted spread of each issue. In preparing the portfolio profile, Mr. Tinker encountered the following situations that he did not understand. Provide Mr. Tinker with an explanation.

a. Mr. Tinker checked with several dealer firms to determine the option-adjusted spread for each issue. For several of the issues, there were substantially different option-adjusted spreads reported. For example, for one callable issue one dealer reported an OAS of 100 basis points, one dealer reported 170 basis points, and a third dealer 200 basis points. Mr. Tinker could not understand how the dealers could have substantially different OAS values when in fact the yield to maturity and nominal spread values for each of the issues did not differ from dealer to dealer.

b. The dealers that Mr. Tinker checked with furnished him with the nominal spread and the Z-spread for each issue in addition to the OAS. For all the bond issues where there were no embedded options, each dealer reported that the Z-spread was equal to the OAS. Mr. Tinker could not understand why.

c. One dealer firm reported an option cost for each issue. There were positive, negative, and zero values reported. Mr. Tinker observed that for all the bond issues that were putable, the option cost was negative. For all the option-free bond issues, the reported value was zero.

24. Max Dumas is considering the purchase of a callable corporate bond. He has available to him two analytical systems to value the bond. In one system, System A, the vendor uses the on-the-run Treasury issues to construct the theoretical spot rate that is used to construct a model to compute the OAS. The other analytical system, System B, uses the on-the-run issue for the particular issuer in constructing a model to compute the OAS.

   a. Suppose that using System A, Mr. Dumas finds that the OAS for the callable corporate he is considering is 50 basis points. How should he interpret this OAS value?

   b. Suppose that using System B, Mr. Dumas finds that the OAS computed is 15 basis points. How should he interpret this OAS value?

   c. Suppose that a dealer firm shows Mr. Dumas another callable corporate bond of the same credit quality and duration with an OAS of 40 basis points. Should Mr. Dumas view that this bond is more attractive or less attractive than the issue he is considering for acquisition?

25. Assume the following Treasury spot rates:

Period	Years to maturity	Spot rate
1	0.5	5.0%
2	1.0	5.4
3	1.5	5.8
4	2.0	6.4
5	2.5	7.0
6	3.0	7.2
7	3.5	7.4
8	4.0	7.8

Compute the following forward rates:

a. the 6-month forward rate six months from now.
b. the 6-month forward rate one year from now.
c. the 6-month forward rate three years from now.
d. the 2-year forward rate one year from now.
e. the 1-year forward rate two years from now.

26. For the previous question, demonstrate that the 6-month forward rate six month from now is the rate that will produce at the end of one year the same future dollars as investing either (1) at the current 1-year spot rate of 5.4% or (2) at the 6-month spot rate of 5.0% and reinvesting at the 6-month forward rate six months from now.

27. Two sales people of analytical systems are making a presentation to you about the merits of their respective systems. One sales person states that in valuing bonds the system first constructs the theoretical spot rates and then discounts cash flows using these rates. The other sales person interjects that his firm takes a different approach. Rather than using spot rates, forward rates are used to value the cash flows and he believes this is a better approach to valuing bonds compared to using spot rates. How would you respond to the second sales person's comment about his firm's approach?

28. a. Given the following 6-month forward rates, compute the forward discount factor for each period

Period	Annual forward rate (BEY)
1	4.00%
2	4.40
3	5.00
4	5.60
5	6.00
6	6.40

    b. Compute the value of a 3-year 8% coupon bond using the forward rates.

CHAPTER 7

INTRODUCTION TO THE MEASUREMENT OF INTEREST RATE RISK

LEARNING OUTCOMES

After reading Chapter 7 you should be able to:

- distinguish between the full valuation and the duration/convexity approaches for measuring interest rate risk.
- compute the interest rate risk exposure of a bond position for a given scenario.
- explain the advantage of using the full valuation approach compared to the duration/convexity approach.
- state the price volatility characteristics for option-free bonds when interest rates change (including the concept of "positive convexity").
- state the price volatility characteristics of callable bonds and prepayable securities (including the concept of "negative convexity").
- diagram the relationship between price and yield for an option-free bond and show why duration is effective in estimating price changes for small changes in yield but is not as effective for a large change in yield.
- diagram the relationship between price and yield for a callable and prepayable security and show what is meant by negative convexity.
- compute the effective duration of a bond given information about how the price will increase and decrease for a given shock in interest rates.
- compute the approximate percentage price change for a bond given its effective duration and a specified change in yield.
- diagram the relationship between price and yield for a putable bond.
- explain how the interest rate shocks used to compute duration may affect the duration calculation.
- differentiate between modified duration and effective (or option-adjusted) duration.
- explain why effective duration should be used for bonds with embedded options.
- explain the relationship between modified duration and Macaulay duration and the limitations of using either for measuring the interest rate risk for bonds with embedded options.
- compute the duration of a portfolio given the duration of the bonds comprising the portfolio and the limitations of portfolio duration.

- compute the convexity adjustment to the duration estimate of a bond's percentage price change for a given change in yield.
- compute the estimated percentage price change for a bond for a given change in yield using the bond's duration and convexity adjustment.
- explain the difference between a modified convexity adjustment and an effective convexity adjustment.
- compute the price value of a basis point ("dollar value of an 01") of a bond.
- state the relationship between duration and the price value of a basis point.
- explain the importance of yield volatility when measuring the exposure of a bond position to interest rate risk.

SUMMARY OVERVIEW

- To control interest rate risk, a manager must be able to quantify what will occur from an adverse change in interest rates.
- A valuation model is used to determine the value of a position after an interest rate movement and therefore, if a reliable valuation model is not used, there is no way to measure interest rate risk exposure.
- There are two approaches to measure interest rate risk: full valuation approach and duration/convexity approach.
- The full valuation approach involves revaluing a bond position (every position in the case of a portfolio) for a scenario of interest rate changes.
- The advantage of the full valuation approach is its accuracy with respect to interest rate exposure for a given interest rate change scenario—accurate relative to the valuation model used—but its disadvantage for a large portfolio is having to revalue each bond for each scenario.
- The characteristics of a bond that affect its price volatility are (1) maturity, (2) coupon rate, and (3) presence of any embedded options.
- The shape of the price/yield relationship for an option-free bond is convex.
- The price sensitivity of a bond to changes in the required yield can be measured in terms of the dollar price change or percentage price change.
- One property of an option-free bond is that although its price moves in the opposite direction of a change in yield, the percentage price change is not the same for all bonds.
- A second property of an option-free bond is that for small changes in the required yield, the percentage price change for a given bond is roughly the same whether the yield increases or decreases.
- A third property of an option-free bond is that for a large change in yield, the percentage price change for an increase in yield is not the same for a decrease in yield.
- A fourth property of an option-free bond is that for a large change in yield, the price of an option-free bond increases more than it decreases.
- "Negative convexity" means that for a large change in interest rates, the amount of the price appreciation is less than the amount of the price depreciation.
- Option-free bonds exhibit positive convexity.
- "Positive convexity" means that for a large change in interest rates, the amount of the price appreciation is greater than the amount of the price depreciation.
- A callable bond exhibits positive convexity at high yield levels and negative convexity at low yield levels where "high" and "low" yield levels are relative to the issue's coupon rate.
- At low yield levels (low relative to the issue's coupon rate), the price of a putable bond is basically the same as the price of an option-free bond because the value of the put option

is small; as rates rise, the price of a putable bond declines, but the price decline is less than that for an option-free bond.

- Duration is a first approximation of a bond's price or a portfolio's value to interest rate changes.
- To improve the estimate provided by duration, a convexity adjustment can be used.
- Using duration combined with a convexity adjustment to estimate the percentage price change of a bond to changes in interest rates is called the duration/convexity approach to interest rate risk measurement.
- Duration does a good job of estimating the percentage price change for a small change in interest rates but the estimation becomes poorer the larger the change in interest rates.
- In calculating duration, it is necessary to shock interest rates (yields) up and down by the same number of basis points to obtain the values when rates change.
- In calculating duration for option-free bonds, the size of the interest rate shock is unimportant for reasonable changes in yield.
- For bonds with embedded options, the problem with using a small shock to estimate duration is that divergences between actual and estimated price changes are magnified by dividing by a small change in rate in the denominator of the duration formula; in addition, small rate shocks that do not reflect the types of rate changes that may occur in the market do not permit the determination of how prices can change because expected cash flows may change.
- For bonds with embedded options, if large rate shocks are used the asymmetry caused by convexity is encountered; in addition, large rate shocks may cause dramatic changes in the expected cash flows for bonds with embedded options that may be far different from how the expected cash flows will change for smaller rate shocks.
- Modified duration is the approximate percentage change in a bond's price for a 100 basis point change in yield assuming that the bond's expected cash flows do not change when the yield changes.
- In calculating the values to be used in the numerator of the duration formula, for modified duration the cash flows are not assumed to change and therefore, the change in the bond's price when the yield is changed is due solely to discounting at the new yield levels.
- Effective duration is the approximate percentage change in a bond's price for a 100 basis point change in yield assuming that the bond's expected cash flows do change when the yield changes.
- Modified duration is appropriate for option-free bonds; effective duration should be used for bonds with embedded options.
- The difference between modified duration and effective duration for bonds with an embedded option can be quite dramatic.
- Macaulay duration is mathematically related to modified duration and is therefore a flawed measure of the duration of a bond with an embedded option.
- Interpretations of duration in temporal terms (i.e.s, some measure of time) or calculus terms (i.e., first derivative of the price/yield relationship) are operationally meaningless and should be avoided.
- The duration for a portfolio is equal to the market-value weighted duration of each bond in the portfolio.
- In applying portfolio duration to estimate the sensitivity of a portfolio to changes in interest rates, it is assumed that the yield for all bonds in the portfolio change by the same amount.
- The duration measure indicates that regardless of whether interest rates increase or decrease, the approximate percentage price change is the same; however, this is not a property of a bond's price volatility for large changes in yield.
- A convexity adjustment can be used to improve the estimate of the percentage price change obtained using duration, particularly for a large change in yield.

- The convexity adjustment is the amount that should be added to the duration estimate for the percentage price change in order to obtain a better estimate for the percentage price change.
- The same distinction made between modified duration and effective duration applies to modified convexity adjustment and effective convexity adjustment.
- For a bond with an embedded option that exhibits negative convexity at some yield level, the convexity adjustment will be negative.
- The price value of a basis point (or dollar value of an 01) is the change in the price of a bond for a 1 basis point change in yield.
- The price value of a basis point is the same as the estimated dollar price change using duration for a 1 basis point change in yield.
- Yield volatility must be recognized in estimating the interest rate risk of a bond and a portfolio.
- Value-at-risk is a measure that ties together the duration of a bond and yield volatility.

PROBLEMS

1. Explain why you agree or disagree with the following statement:

   The disadvantage of the full valuation approach to measuring interest rate risk is that it requires a revaluation of each bond in the portfolio for each interest rate scenario. Consequently, you need a valuation model. In contrast, for the duration/convexity approach there is no need for a valuation model because the duration and convexity adjustment can be obtained without a valuation model.

2. Explain why you agree or disagree with the following statement:

   The problem with both the full valuation approach and the duration/convexity approach is that they fail to take into account how the change in the yield curve can affect a portfolio's value.

3. Explain why you agree or disagree with the following statement:

   If two bonds have the same duration, then the percentage change in price of the two bonds will be the same for a given change in interest rates.

4. James Smith and Donald Robertson are assistant portfolio managers for Micro Management Partners. In a review of the interest rate risk of a portfolio, Smith and Robertson discussed the riskiness of two Treasury securities. Following is the information about these two Treasuries:

Bond	Price	Modified duration
A	90	4
B	50	6

   Smith noted that Treasury bond B has more price volatility because of its higher modified duration. Robertson disagreed noting that Treasury bond A has more price volatility despite its lower modified duration. Which manager is correct?

5. At its quarterly meeting, the trustees of the National Baggage Handlers Pension Fund reviewed the status of its bond portfolio. The portfolio is managed by William Renfro of Wiser and Wiser Management Company. The portfolio consists of 20% Treasury bonds,

10% corporate bonds that are noncallable for the life of the bonds, 30% callable corporate bonds, and 40% mortgage-backed securities. The report provided by Wiser and Wiser includes the following information for each bond in the portfolio: (1) modified duration and (2) effective duration. The portfolio's modified duration and effective duration were reported to be 5 and 3, respectively. Renfro attended the board meeting to answer any questions that the trustees might have. Nancy Weston, one of the trustee for the fund, prepared the following list of questions:

a. What does the duration of a bond mean and how should the board interpret the portfolio duration?
b. Why is the modified duration and effective duration for each Treasury bond and noncallable corporate bond the same?
c. What is the appropriate duration measure, effective duration or modified duration?
d. How were the effective duration measures obtained?
e. What are the limitations in using duration?

The minutes of the board meeting indicated the following response by Mr. Renfro to each of these questions:

a. Duration is a measure of the approximate weighted average life of a bond or a bond portfolio. For example, a portfolio duration of 5 means that the fund will realize the return of the amount invested (in present value terms) in about 5 years.
b. Because the Treasury bonds in the portfolio are noncallable, modified duration is the same as effective duration. The same is true for the corporate bonds that are noncallable for life.
c. The appropriate measure is the effective duration since it takes into account the option embedded in the bonds held in the portfolio.
d. We obtained the effective duration from various sources—dealers firms and commercial vendors. There is a standard formula that all of these sources use to obtain the effective duration. Sometimes, a source may provide an effective duration that is not logical and we override the value by using the modified duration. For example, for some of the collateralized mortgage obligations, one vendor reported an effective duration of 40. This value was obviously wrong since the underlying collateral is 30-year loans; therefore, the duration cannot exceed 30. Moreover, for some of the CMOs, the duration is negative and this is obviously wrong. Again, in such instances we use the modified duration.
e. Duration is only a good measure for small changes in yield and assumes that the yield curve will shift in a parallel fashion. However, if these assumptions are satisfied, two portfolios with the same duration will perform in exactly the same way.

You are employed by Pension Consultants, a consultant to the labor union. You have been given the minutes of the meeting of the board of trustees with the responses of Mr. Renfro to the questions of Ms. Weston. Prepare a report indicating whether you agree or disagree with Mr. Renfro's responses.

6. Lewis Marlo, an assistant portfolio manager, was reviewing a potential buy list of corporate bonds. The list provided information on the effective duration and effective convexity adjustment assuming a 200 basis point change in interest rates for each corporate bond on the list. The senior portfolio manager, Jane Zorick, noticed that Mr. Marlo crossed

out each bond with a negative convexity adjustment. When Ms. Zorick asked Mr. Marlo why, he responded that a negative value meant that the particular corporate bond was unattractive. How do you think Ms. Zorick should respond?

7. A client is reviewing information about the portfolio. For one of the issues in the portfolio the client sees the following:

Issue	Maturity	Duration
X	10 years	13

The client has questioned you as to whether or not the reported duration of 13 is correct. The client's concern is that he has heard that duration is some measure of time for a bond and as such cannot exceed the maturity of the security. Yet, the duration of Issue X exceeds its maturity. What explanation do you give to the client?

8. Suppose that you are given the following information about two callable bonds of the same issuer that can be called immediately:

	Estimated percentage change in price if interest rates change by:	
	−50 basis points	+ 50 basis points
Bond ABC	+2%	−5%
Bond XYZ	+11%	−8%

You are told that both bonds have about the same maturity and the coupon rate of one bond is 7% and the other 13%. Suppose that the yield curve for this issuer is flat at 8%. Based on this information, which bond is the lower coupon bond and which is the higher coupon bond? Explain why.

9. a. Why is modified duration an inappropriate measure for a high-coupon callable bond?
   b. What would be a better measure than modified duration?

10. Suppose that a 7% coupon corporate bond is immediately callable. Also suppose that if this issuer issued new bonds the coupon rate would be 12%. Why would the modified duration be a good approximation of the effective duration for this bond?

Questions 11–15 are based on the following price information for four bonds and assuming that all four bonds are trading to yield 5%:

Yield	Coupon maturity	5.0% 4	5.0% 25	8.0% 4	8.0% 25
3.00%		107.4859	134.9997	118.7148	187.4992
4.00%		103.6627	115.7118	114.6510	162.8472
4.50%		101.8118	107.4586	112.6826	152.2102
4.75%		100.9011	103.6355	111.7138	147.2621
4.90%		100.3593	101.4324	111.1374	144.4042
5.00%		100.0000	100.0000	110.7552	142.5435
5.10%		99.6423	98.5959	110.3746	140.7175
5.25%		99.1085	96.5416	109.8066	138.0421
5.50%		98.2264	93.2507	108.8679	133.7465
6.00%		96.4902	87.1351	107.0197	125.7298
7.00%		93.1260	76.5444	103.4370	111.7278

Percentage price change based on an initial yield of 5%

Yield	Coupon maturity	5.0% 4	5.0% 25	8.0% 4	8.0% 25
3.00%		7.49%	35.00%	7.19%	31.54%
4.00%		3.66%	15.71%	3.52%	14.24%
4.50%		1.81%	7.46%	1.74%	6.78%
4.75%		0.90%	3.64%	0.87%	3.31%
4.90%		0.36%	1.43%	0.35%	1.31%
5.00%		0.00%	0.00%	0.00%	0.00%
5.10%		−0.36%	−1.40%	−0.34%	−1.28%
5.25%		−0.89%	−3.46%	−0.86%	−3.16%
5.50%		−1.77%	−6.75%	−1.70%	−6.17%
6.00%		−3.51%	−12.86%	−3.37%	−11.80%
7.00%		−6.87%	−23.46%	−6.61%	−21.62%

11. Assuming all four bonds are selling to yield 5%, compute the following for each bond:

    a. duration based on a 25 basis point rate shock ($\Delta y = 0.0025$)
    b. duration based on a 50 basis point rate shock ($\Delta y = 0.0050$)

12. Assuming all four bonds are selling to yield 5%, compute the value for C in the convexity equation for each bond using a 25 basis point rate shock ($\Delta y = 0.0025$).

13. a. Using the duration computed in question 11a, compute the approximate percentage price change using duration for the two 8% coupon bonds assuming that the yield changes by 10 basis points ($\Delta y_* = 0.0010$).

    b. How does the estimated percentage price change compare to the actual percentage price change?

14. a. Using the duration computed in question 11a, compute the approximate percentage price change using duration for the two 8% coupon bonds assuming that the yield changes by 200 basis points ($\Delta y_* = 0.02$).

    b. How does the estimated percentage price change compare to the actual percentage price change?

15. a. Using the value for C computed in question 12, compute the convexity adjustment for the two 25-year bonds assuming that the yield changes by 200 basis points ($\Delta y_* = 0.02$).

    b. Compute the estimated percentage price change using duration (as computed in question 11a) and convexity adjustment if yield changes by 200 basis points.

    c. How does the estimated percentage price change using duration and convexity adjustment compare to the actual percentage price change for a 200 basis point change in yield?

16. a. Given the information below for a 6.2% 18-year bond compute the price value of a basis point:

    price $= 114.1338$ yield $= 5\%$ price if yield is $5.01\% = 114.0051$

   b. If the duration of the 6.2% 18-year bond is 11.28, what is the estimated price change for a 1 basis point change in yield.

17. Why is information about a bond's duration and convexity adjustment insufficient to quantify interest rate risk exposure?

TERM STRUCTURE AND VOLATILITY OF INTEREST RATES

LEARNING OUTCOMES

After reading Chapter 8 you should be able to:

- illustrate and explain parallel and nonparallel shifts in the yield curve, a yield curve twist, and a change in the curvature of the yield curve (i.e., butterfly shift).
- describe and explain the factors that have been observed to drive zero-coupon U.S. Treasury returns and discuss the relative importance of each factor.
- explain the various universes of Treasury securities that are used to construct the theoretical spot rate curve, and discuss their advantages and disadvantages.
- explain the swap rate curve (LIBOR curve) and discuss the reasons that market participants have increasingly used the swap rate curve as a benchmark rather than a government bond yield curve.
- explain the various theories of the term structure of interest rates (i.e., pure expectations theory, liquidity preference theory, preferred habitat theory, and market segmentation) and the implications of each theory for the shape of the yield curve.
- compute the effects of how to measure the yield curve risk of a security or a portfolio using key rate duration.
- compute and interpret the yield volatility given historical yields.
- differentiate between historical yield volatility and implied yield volatility.
- explain how yield volatility is forecasted.

SUMMARY OVERVIEW

- Historically, four shapes have been observed for the yield curve: (1) normal or positively sloped (i.e., the longer the maturity, the higher the yield), (2) flat (i.e., the yield for all maturities is approximately equal), (3) inverted or negatively sloped (i.e., the longer the maturity, the lower the yield), and (4) a humped yield curve.
- The spread between long-term Treasury yields and short-term Treasury yields is referred to as the steepness or slope of the yield curve.

- Some investors define the slope of the yield curve as the spread between the 30-year yield and the 3-month yield and others as the spread between the 30-year yield and the 2-year yield.
- A shift in the yield curve refers to the relative change in the yield for each Treasury maturity.
- A parallel shift in the yield curve refers to a shift in which the change in the yield for all maturities is the same; a nonparallel shift in the yield curve means that the yield for all maturities does not change by the same number of basis points.
- Historically, the two types of nonparallel yield curve shifts that have been observed are a twist in the slope of the yield curve and a change in the curvature of the yield curve.
- A flattening of the yield curve means that the slope of the yield curve has decreased; a steepening of the yield curve means that the slope has increased.
- A butterfly shift is the other type of nonparallel shift—a change in the curvature or humpedness of the yield curve.
- Historically, the factors that have been observed to drive Treasury returns are a (1) shift in the level of interest rates, (2) a change in the slope of the yield curve, and (3) a change in the curvature of the yield curve.
- The most important factor driving Treasury returns is a shift in the level of interest rates. Two other factors, in decreasing importance, include changes in the yield curve slope and changes in the curvature of the yield curve.
- The universe of Treasury issues that can be used to construct the theoretical spot rate curve is (1) on-the-run Treasury issues, (2) on-the-run Treasury issues and selected off-the-run Treasury issues, (3) all Treasury coupon securities and bills, and (4) Treasury strips.
- There are three methodologies that have been used to derive the theoretical spot rate curve: (1) bootstrapping when the universe is on-the-run Treasury issues (with and without selected off-the-run issues), (2) econometric modeling for all Treasury coupon securities and bills, and (3) simply the observed yields on Treasury coupon strips.
- The problem with using Treasury coupon strips is that the observed yields may be biased due to a liquidity premium or an unfavorable tax treatment.
- The swap rate is the rate at which fixed cash flows can be exchanged for floating cash flows.
- In a LIBOR-based swap, the swap curve provides a yield curve for LIBOR.
- A swap curve can be constructed that is unique to a country where there is a swap market.
- The swap spread is primarily a gauge of the credit risk associated with a country's banking sector.
- The advantages of using a swap curve as the benchmark interest rate rather than a government bond yield curve are (1) there is almost no government regulation of the swap market making swap rates across different markets more comparable, (2) the supply of swaps depends only on the number of counterparties that are seeking or are willing to enter into a swap transaction at any given time, (3) comparisons across countries of government yield curves is difficult because of the differences in sovereign credit risk, and (4) there are more maturity points available to construct a swap curve than a government bond yield curve.
- From the swap yield curve a LIBOR spot rate curve can be derived using the bootstrapping methodology and the LIBOR forward rate curve can be derived.
- The three forms of the expectations theory (the pure expectations theory, the liquidity preference theory, and the preferred habitat theory) assume that the forward rates in current long-term bonds are closely related to the market's expectations about future short-term rates.
- The three forms of the expectations theory differ on whether or not other factors also affect forward rates, and how.

- The pure expectations theory postulates that no systematic factors other than expected future short-term rates affect forward rates.
- Because forward rates are not perfect predictors of future interest rates, the pure expectations theory neglects the risks (interest rate risk and reinvestment risk) associated with investing in Treasury securities.
- The broadest interpretation of the pure expectations theory suggests that investors expect the return for any investment horizon to be the same, regardless of the maturity strategy selected.
- The local expectations form of the pure expectations theory suggests that the return will be the same over a short-term investment horizon starting today and it is this narrow interpretation that economists have demonstrated is the only interpretation that can be sustained in equilibrium.
- Two interpretations of forward rates based on arbitrage arguments are that they are (1) "break-even rates" and (2) rates that can be locked in.
- Advocates of the pure expectations theory argue that forward rates are the market's consensus of future interest rates.
- Forward rates have not been found to be good predictors of future interest rates; however, an understanding of forward rates is still extremely important because of their role as break-even rates and rates that can be locked in.
- The liquidity preference theory and the preferred habitat theory assert that there are other factors that affect forward rates and these two theories are therefore referred to as biased expectations theories.
- The liquidity preference theory states that investors will hold longer-term maturities only if they are offered a risk premium and therefore forward rates should reflect both interest rate expectations and a liquidity risk premium.
- The preferred habitat theory, in addition to adopting the view that forward rates reflect the expectation of the future path of interest rates as well as a risk premium, argues that the yield premium need not reflect a liquidity risk but instead reflects the demand and supply of funds in a given maturity range.
- A common approach to measure yield curve risk is to change the yield for a particular maturity of the yield curve and determine the sensitivity of a security or portfolio to this change holding all other key rates constant.
- Key rate duration is the sensitivity of a portfolio's value to the change in a particular key rate.
- The most popular version of key rate duration uses 11 key maturities of the spot rate curve (3 months, 1, 2, 3, 5, 7, 10, 15, 20, 25, and 30 years).
- Variance is a measure of the dispersion of a random variable around its expected value.
- The standard deviation is the square root of the variance and is a commonly used measure of volatility.
- Yield volatility can be estimated from daily yield observations.
- The observation used in the calculation of the daily standard deviation is the natural logarithm of the ratio of one day's and the previous day's yield.
- The selection of the time period (the number of observations) can have a significant effect on the calculated daily standard deviation.
- A daily standard deviation is annualized by multiplying it by the square root of the number of days in a year.
- Typically, either 250 days, 260 days, or 365 days are used to annualize the daily standard deviation.
- Implied volatility can also be used to estimate yield volatility based on some option pricing model.

- In forecasting volatility, it is more appropriate to use an expectation of zero for the mean value.
- The simplest method for forecasting volatility is weighting all observations equally.
- A forecasted volatility can be obtained by assigning greater weight to more recent observations.
- Autoregressive conditional heteroskedasticity (ARCH) models can be used to capture the time series characteristic of yield volatility in which a period of high volatility is followed by a period of high volatility and a period of relative stability appears to be followed by a period that can be characterized in the same way.

PROBLEMS

1. What are the four types of shapes observed for the yield curve?
2. How is the slope of the yield curve defined and measured?
3. Historically, how has the slope of the long end of the yield curve differed from that of the short end of the yield curve at a given point in time?
4. a. What are the three factors that have empirically been observed to affect Treasury returns?
   b. What has been observed to be the most important factor in affecting Treasury returns?
   c. Given the most important factor identified in part b, justify the use of duration as a measure of interest rate risk.
   d. What has been observed to be the second most important factor in affecting Treasury returns?
   e. Given the second most important factor identified in part d, justify the use of a measure of interest rate risk in addition to duration.
5. a. What are the limitations of using just the on-the-run Treasury issues to construct the theoretical spot rate curve?
   b. Why if all Treasury bills and Treasury coupon securities are used to construct the theoretical spot rate curve is it not possible to use the bootstrapping method?
6. a. What are the problems with using the yield on Treasury strips to construct the theoretical spot rate curve?
   b. Why, even if a practitioner decides to use the yield on Treasury strips to construct the theoretical spot rate curve despite the problems identified in part a, will the practitioner restrict the analysis to Treasury coupon strips?
7. What are the advantages of using the swap curve as a benchmark of interest rates relative to a government bond yield curve?
8. How can a spot rate curve be constructed for a country that has a liquid swap market?
9. a. What is a swap spread?
   b. What is the swap spread indicative of?
10. a. What is the pure expectations theory?
    b. What are the shortcomings of the pure expectations theory?
11. Based on the broadest interpretation of the pure expectations theory, what would be the difference in the 4-year total return if an investor purchased a 7-year zero-coupon bond or a 15-year zero-coupon bond?
12. Based on the local expectations form of the pure expectations theory, what would be the difference in the 6-month total return if an investor purchased a 5-year zero-coupon bond or a 2-year zero-coupon bond?

13. Comment on the following statement made by a portfolio manager to a client:

> Proponents of the unbiased expectations theory argue that the forward rates built into the term structure of interest rates are the market's consensus of future interest rates. We disagree with the theory because studies suggest that forward rates are poor predictors of future interest rates. Therefore, the position that our investment management firm takes is that forward rates are irrelevant and provide no information to our managers in managing a bond portfolio.

14. Based on arbitrage arguments give two interpretations for each of the following three forward rates:

   a. The 1-year forward rate seven years from now is 6.4%.
   b. The 2-year forward rate one year from now is 6.2%.
   c. The 8-year forward rate three years from now is 7.1%.

15. There are two forms of the "biased" expectations theory. Why are these two forms referred to as "biased" expectations?
16. You are the financial consultant to a pension fund. After your presentation to the trustees of the fund, you asked the trustees if they have any questions. You receive the two questions below. Answer each one.

   a. "The yield curve is upward-sloping today. Doesn't this suggest that the market consensus is that interest rates are expected to increase in the future and therefore you should reduce the interest rate risk exposure for the portfolio that you are managing for us?"
   b. "I am looking over one of the pages in your presentation that shows spot rates and I am having difficulty in understanding it. The spot rates at the short end (up to three years) are increasing with maturity. For maturities greater than three years but less than eight years, the spot rates are declining with maturity. finally, for maturities greater than eight years the spot rates are virtually the same for each maturity. There is simply no expectations theory that would explain that type of shape for the term structure of interest rates. Is this market simply unstable?"

17. Below are the key rate durations for three portfolios of U.S. Treasury securities all with the same duration for a parallel shift in the yield curve.

   (a) For each portfolio describe the type of portfolio (barbell, ladder, or bullet).

Key rate maturity	Portfolio A	Portfolio B	Portfolio C
3-month	0.04	0.04	0.03
1-year	0.06	0.29	0.07
2-year	0.08	0.67	0.31
3-year	0.28	0.65	0.41
5-year	0.38	0.65	1.90
7-year	0.65	0.64	0.35
10-year	3.38	0.66	0.41
15-year	0.79	0.67	0.70
20-year	0.36	0.64	1.95
25-year	0.12	0.62	0.06
30-year	0.06	0.67	0.01

b. Which portfolio will benefit the most if the spot rate for the 10-year decreases by 50 basis points while the spot rate for all other key maturities change very little?

c. What is the duration for a parallel shift in the yield curve for the three portfolios?

18. Compute the 10-day daily standard deviation of the percentage change in yield assuming continuous compounding assuming the following daily yields.

t	y_t
0	5.854
1	5.843
2	5.774
3	5.719
4	5.726
5	5.761
6	5.797
7	5.720
8	5.755
9	5.787
10	5.759

19. For the daily yield volatility computed in the previous question, what is the annual yield volatility assuming the following number of days in the year:

(a) 250 days?
(b) 260 days?
(c) 365 days?

20. Comment on the following statement: "Two portfolio managers with the same set of daily yields will compute the same historical annual volatility."

21. Suppose that the annualized standard deviation of the 2-year Treasury yield based on daily yields is 7% and the current level of the 2-year Treasury yield is 5%. Assuming that the probability distribution for the percentage change in 2-year Treasury yields is approximately normally distributed, how would you interpret the 7% annualized standard deviation?

22. a. What is implied volatility?
b. What are the problems associated with using implied volatility as a measure of yield volatility?

23. a. In forecasting yield volatility, why would a manager not want to weight each daily yield change equally?
b. In forecasting yield volatility, what is recommended for the sample mean in the formula for the variance or standard deviation?

CHAPTER 9

VALUING BONDS WITH EMBEDDED OPTIONS

LEARNING OUTCOMES

After reading Chapter 9 you should be able to:

- explain the importance of the benchmark interest rates in interpreting spread measures.
- explain the binomial interest rate modeling strategy.
- explain the backward induction valuation methodology within the binomial interest rate tree framework.
- compute the value of a callable bond from an interest rate tree given the call schedule and the rule for calling a bond.
- explain how the value of an embedded option is determined.
- explain the relationship among the values of a bond with an embedded option, the corresponding option-free bond, and the embedded option.
- explain the effect of volatility on the arbitrage-free value of a bond with an embedded option.
- calculate an option-adjusted spread using the binomial model and interpret an option-adjusted spread with respect to the benchmark interest rates.
- calculate effective duration and effective convexity using the binomial model.
- compute the value of a putable bond using the binomial model.
- describe the basic features of a convertible bond.
- compute and explain the meaning of the following for a convertible bond: conversion value, straight value, market conversion price, market conversion premium per share, market conversion premium ratio, premium payback period, and premium over straight value.
- discuss the components of a convertible bond's value that must be included in an option-based valuation approach.
- compare the risk/return characteristics of a convertible bond's value to the risk/return characteristics of the underlying common stock.

SUMMARY OVERVIEW

- The potential benchmark interest rates that can be used in bond valuation are those in the Treasury market, a specific bond sector with a given credit rating, or a specific issuer.

- Benchmark interest rates can be based on either an estimated yield curve or an estimated spot rate curve.
- Yield spread measures are used in assessing the relative value of securities.
- Relative value analysis is used to identify securities as being overpriced ("rich"), underpriced ("cheap"), or fairly priced relative to benchmark interest rates.
- The interpretation of a spread measure depends on the benchmark used.
- The option-adjusted spread is a spread after adjusting for the option risk.
- Depending on the benchmark interest rates used to generate the interest rate tree, the option-adjusted spread may or may not capture credit risk.
- The option-adjusted spread is not a spread off of one maturity of the benchmark interest rates; rather, it is a spread over the forward rates in the interest rate tree that were constructed from the benchmark interest rates.
- A valuation model must produce arbitrage-free values; that is, a valuation model must produce a value for each on-the-run issue that is equal to its observed market price.
- There are several arbitrage-free models that can be used to value bonds with embedded options but they all follow the same principle—they generate a tree of interest rates based on some interest rate volatility assumption, they require rules for determining when any of the embedded options will be exercised, and they employ the backward induction methodology.
- A valuation model involves generating an interest rate tree based on (1) benchmark interest rates, (2) an assumed interest rate model, and (3) an assumed interest rate volatility.
- The assumed volatility of interest rates incorporates the uncertainty about future interest rates into the analysis.
- The interest rate tree is constructed using a process that is similar to bootstrapping but requires an iterative procedure to determine the interest rates that will produce a value for the on-the-run issues equal to their market value.
- At each node of the tree there are interest rates and these rates are effectively forward rates; thus, there is a set of forward rates for each year.
- Using the interest rate tree the arbitrage-free value of any bond can be determined.
- In valuing a callable bond using the interest rate tree, the cash flows at a node are modified to take into account the call option.
- The value of the embedded call option is the difference between the value of an option-free bond and the value of the callable bond.
- The volatility assumption has an important impact on the arbitrage-free value.
- The option-adjusted spread is the constant spread that when added to the short rates in the binomial interest rate tree will produce a valuation for the bond (i.e., arbitrage-free value) equal to the market price of the bond.
- The interpretation of the OAS, or equivalently, what the OAS is compensating an investor for, depends on what benchmark interest rates are used.
- The required values for calculating effective duration and effective convexity are found by shifting the on-the-run yield curve, calculating a new binomial interest rate tree, and then determining the required values after adjusting the tree by adding the OAS to each short rate.
- For a bond with any embedded option or options, application of the binomial model requires that the value at each node of the tree be adjusted based on whether or not the option will be exercised; the binomial model can be used to value bonds with multiple or interrelated embedded options by determining at each node of the tree whether or not one of the options will be exercised.

- With a putable bond, the option will be exercised if the value at a node is less than the price at which the bondholder can put the bond to the issuer.
- The value of a putable bond is greater than the value of an otherwise option-free bond.
- The binomial model can be used to value a single step-up callable note or a multiple step-up callable note.
- To value a floating-rate note that has a cap, the coupon at each node of the tree is adjusted by determining whether or not the cap is reached at a node; if the rate at a node does exceed the cap, the rate at the node is the capped rate rather than the rate determined by the floater's coupon formula.
- For a floating-rate note, the binomial method must be adjusted to account for the fact that a floater pays in arrears; that is, the coupon payment is determined in a period but not paid until the next period.
- Convertible and exchangeable securities can be converted into shares of common stock.
- The conversion ratio is the number of common stock shares for which a convertible security may be converted.
- Almost all convertible securities are callable and some are putable.
- The conversion value is the value of the convertible bond if it is immediately converted into the common stock.
- The market conversion price is the price that an investor effectively pays for the common stock if the convertible security is purchased and then converted into the common stock.
- The premium paid for the common stock is measured by the market conversion premium per share and market conversion premium ratio.
- The straight value or investment value of a convertible security is its value if there was no conversion feature.
- The minimum value of a convertible security is the greater of the conversion value and the straight value.
- A fixed income equivalent (or a busted convertible) refers to the situation where the straight value is considerably higher than the conversion value so that the security will trade much like a straight security.
- A common stock equivalent refers to the situation where the conversion value is considerably higher than the straight value so that the convertible security trades as if it were an equity instrument.
- A hybrid equivalent refers to the situation where the convertible security trades with characteristics of both a fixed income security and a common stock instrument.
- While the downside risk of a convertible security usually is estimated by calculating the premium over straight value, the limitation of this measure is that the straight value (the floor) changes as interest rates change.
- An advantage of buying the convertible rather than the common stock is the reduction in downside risk.
- The disadvantage of a convertible relative to the straight purchase of the common stock is the upside potential give-up because a premium per share must be paid.
- An option-based valuation model is a more appropriate approach to value convertible securities than the traditional approach because it can handle multiple embedded options.
- There are various option-based valuation models: one-factor and multiple-factor models.
- The most common convertible bond valuation model is the one-factor model in which the one factor is the stock price movement.

PROBLEMS

1. Comment on the following statement:

   "There are several arbitrage-free models for valuing callable bonds. These models differ significantly in terms of how interest rates may change in the next period. There are models that allow the rate in the next period to take on only one of two values. Such a model is called a binomial model. There are models that allow the rate in the next period to take on more than two possible values. For example, there is model that allows the rate in the next period to take on three possible values. Such a model is called a trinomial model. All these models represent a significantly different approach to valuation and involve different procedures for obtaining the arbitrage-free value."

2. Why is the procedure for valuing a bond with an embedded option called "backward induction"?

3. Why is the value produced by a binomial model and any similar models referred to as an "arbitrage-free value"?

4. a. When valuing an option-free bond, short-term forward rates can be used. When valuing a bond with an embedded option, there is not one forward rate for a period but a set of forward rates for a given period. Explain why.

   b. Explain why the set of forward rates for a given period depend on the assumed interest rate volatility.

5. The on-the-run issue for the Inc.Net Company is shown below:

Maturity (years)	Yield to maturity (%)	Market price
1	7.5	100
2	7.6	100
3	7.7	100

   Using the bootstrapping methodology, the spot rates are:

Maturity (years)	Spot rate (%)
1	7.500
2	7.604
3	7.710

   Assuming an interest rate volatility of 10% for the 1-year rate, the binomial interest rate tree for valuing a bond with a maturity of up to three years is shown below:

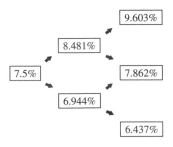

   a. Demonstrate using the 2-year on-the-run issue that the binomial interest rate tree
      above is in fact an arbitrage-free tree.
   b. Demonstrate using the 3-year on-the-run issue that the binomial interest rate tree
      above is in fact an arbitrage-free tree.
   c. Using the spot rates given above, what is the arbitrage-free value of a 3-year 8.5%
      coupon issue of Inc.Net Company?
   d. Using the binomial tree, determine the value of an 8.5% 3-year option-free bond.
   e. Suppose that the 3-year 8.5% coupon issue is callable starting in Year 1 at par (100)
      (that is, the call price is 100). Also assume that the following call rule is used: if the
      price exceeds 100 the issue will be called. What is the value of this 3-year 8.5% coupon
      callable issue?
   f. What is the value of the embedded call option for the 3-year 8.5% coupon callable
      issue?

6. In discussing the approach taken by its investment management firm in valuing bonds, a
   representative of the firm made the following statement:

   > "Our managers avoid the use of valuation methodologies such as the binomial
   > model or other fancier models because of the many assumptions required to
   > determine the value. Instead, our managers are firm believers in the concept of
   > option-adjusted spread."

   Comment on this statement.

7. A portfolio manager must mark a bond position to market. One issue, a callable issue, has
   not traded in the market recently. So to obtain a price that can be used to mark a position
   to market, the manager requested a bid from a dealer and a value from a pricing service.
   The dealer bid's price was 92. The pricing service indicated a bid price of 93 would be a
   fair value. The manager could not understand the reason for the 1 point difference in the
   bid prices.

   Upon questioning the trader at the dealer firm that gave a bid of 92, the manager
   found that the trader based the price on the dealer's valuation model. The model used is
   the binomial model and the benchmark interest rates the model uses are the on-the-run
   Treasury issues. The manager then contacted a representative from the pricing service and
   asked what type of valuation model it used. Again, the response was that the binomial
   model is used and that the on-the-run Treasury issues are used as the benchmark interest
   rates.

   The manager is puzzled why there is a 1 point difference even though the dealer and the
   pricing service used the same model and the same benchmark interest rates. The manager
   has asked you to explain why. Provide an explanation to the manager.

8. The manager of an emerging market bond portfolio is approached by a broker about
   purchasing a new corporate bond issue in Brazil. The issue is callable and the broker's
   firm estimates that the option-adjusted spread is 220 basis points. What questions would
   you ask the broker with respect to the 220 basis points OAS?

9. In explaining the option-adjusted spread to a client, a manager stated the following: "The
   option-adjusted spread measures the yield spread using the Treasury on-the-run yield
   curve as benchmark interest rates." Comment on this statement.

10. a. Explain why the greater the assumed interest rate volatility the lower the value of a
       callable bond?
    b. Explain why the greater the assumed interest rate volatility the higher the value of a
       putable bond?

11. An assistant portfolio manager described the process for valuing a bond that is both callable and putable using the binomial model as follows:

   "The process begins by first valuing one of the embedded options, say the call option. Then the model is used to value the put option. The value of the corresponding option-free bond is then computed. Given the value of the call option, the value of the put option, and the value of the option-free bond, the value of the bond that is callable and putable is found by adding to the value of the option-free bond the value of the put option and then subtracting the value of the call option."

   Explain why you agree or disagree with this assistant portfolio manager's description of the process for valuing a bond that is both callable and putable.

12. Explain why, when the binomial model is used to obtain the values to be used in the formula for computing duration and convexity, the measures computed are an effective duration and effective convexity.

13. An assistant portfolio manager is trying to find the duration of a callable bond of FeedCo Corp. One vendor of analytical systems reported that the duration for the issue is 5.4. A dealer firm reported that the duration is 4.5. The assistant portfolio manager was confused by the difference in the reported durations for the FeedCo Corp. issue. He discussed the situation with the senior portfolio manager. In the discussion, the assistant portfolio manager commented: "I don't understand how such a difference could occur. After all, there is a standard formula for computing any duration." How should the senior portfolio manager respond?

14. In computing the effective duration and convexity of a bond with an embedded option, what assumption is made about the option-adjusted spread when rates change?

15. Four portfolio managers are discussing the meaning of option-adjusted spread. Here is what each asserted:

   Manager 1: "The option-adjusted spread is a measure of the value of the option embedded in the bond. That is, it is the compensation for accepting option risk."

   Manager 2: "The option-adjusted spread is a measure of the spread relative to the Treasury on-the-run yield curve and reflects compensation for credit risk."

   Manager 3: "The option-adjusted spread is a measure of the spread relative to the Treasury on-the-run yield curve and reflects compensation for credit risk and liquidity risk."

   Manager 4: "The option-adjusted spread is a measure of the spread relative to the issuer's on-the-run yield curve and reflects compensation for credit risk and liquidity risk."

   Comment on each manager's interpretation of OAS.

16. Suppose that a callable bond is valued using as the benchmark interest rates the on-the-run yield curve of the issuer and that the yield for the 10-year issue is 6%. Suppose further that the option-adjusted spread computed for a 10-year callable bond of this issuer is 20 basis points. Is it proper to interpret the OAS as meaning that the 10-year callable bond is offering a spread of 20 basis point over the 6% yield on the 10-year on-the run-issue? If not, what is the proper interpretation of the 20 basis point OAS?

17. Suppose that a callable bond has an option-adjusted spread of zero. Does that mean the corporate bond is being overvalued in the market (i.e., trading rich)?

18. In valuing a floating rate note, it is necessary to make a modification to the backward induction method.

    a. Why is the adjustment necessary?
    b. What adjustment is made?
    c. If the floating rate note has a cap, how is that handled by the backward induction method?

19. a. In what sense does a convertible bond typically have multiple embedded options?
    b. Why is it complicated to value a convertible bond?

20. In the October 26, 1992 prospectus summary of The Staples 5% convertible subordinated debentures due 1999 the offering stated: "Convertible into Common Stock at a conversion price of $45 per share . . . " Since the par value is $1,000, what is the conversion ratio?

21. Consider the convertible bond by Miser Electronics:

    par value = $1,000
    coupon rate = 8.5%
    market price of convertible bond = $900
    conversion ratio = 30
    estimated straight value of bond = $700
    Assume that the price of Miser Electronics common stock is $25 and that the dividend per share is $1 per annum.

    Calculate each of the following:

    a. conversion value
    b. market conversion price
    c. conversion premium per share
    d. conversion premium ratio
    e. premium over straight value
    f. yield advantage of bond
    g. premium payback period

22. Suppose that the price of the common stock of Miser Electronics whose convertible bond was described in the previous question increases from $25 to $54.

    a. What will be the approximate return realized from investing in the convertible bond if an investor had purchased the convertible for $900?
    b. What would be the return realized if $25 had been invested in the common stock?
    c. Why would the return be higher by investing in the common stock directly rather than by investing in the convertible bond?

23. Suppose that the price of the common stock declines from $25 to $10.

    a. What will be the approximate return realized from investing in the convertible bond if an investor had purchased the convertible for $900 *and* the straight value does not change?
    b. What would be the return realized if $25 had been invested in the common stock?
    c. Why would the return be higher by investing in the convertible bond rather than by investing in the common stock directly?

24. The following excerpt is taken from an article entitled "Caywood Looks for Convertibles," that appeared in the January 13, 1992 issue of *BondWeek*, p. 7:

Caywood Christian Capital Management will invest new money in its $400 million high-yield portfolio in "busted convertibles," double-and triple-B rated convertible bonds of companies whose stock . . . , said James Caywood, CEO. Caywood likes these convertibles as they trade at discounts and are unlikely to be called, he said.

    a. What is a "busted convertible"?
    b. What is the premium over straight value that these bonds would trade?
    c. Why does Mr. Caywood seek convertibles with higher investment grade ratings?
    d. Why is Mr. Caywood interested in call protection?

25. Explain the limitation of using premium over straight value as a measure of the downside risk of a convertible bond?
26. a. The valuation of a convertible bond using an options approach requires a two-factor model. What is meant by a two-factor model and what are the factors?
    b. In practice, is a two-factor model used to value a convertible bond?

CHAPTER 10

MORTGAGE-BACKED SECTOR OF THE BOND MARKET

LEARNING OUTCOMES

After reading Chapter 10 you should be able to:

- describe a mortgage loan and explain the cash flow characteristics of a fixed-rate, level payment, fully amortized mortgage loan.
- describe prepayments and how they result in prepayment risk.
- explain the importance of prepayments to the estimation of the cash flow of a mortgage-backed security.
- compare and contrast the single monthly mortality rate, conditional prepayment, and the Public Securities Association (PSA) prepayment benchmark that are used to set assumed prepayment rates, including their relationship to each other.
- explain why the average life of a mortgage-backed security is a more relevant measure than the security's legal maturity.
- discuss the factors that affect prepayments.
- explain contraction and extension prepayment risks and why they occur.
- explain why and how a collateralized mortgage obligation is created and how a CMO distributes prepayment risk among tranches so as to create products that provide a better matching of assets and liabilities for institutional investors.
- distinguish among sequential-pay tranche, accrual tranche, planned amortization class tranche, and support tranche in a CMO with respect to the risk characteristics and the relative performance of each, given changes in prepayment rates due to changes in interest rates.
- explain the investment characteristics of principal-only and interest-only mortgage strips.
- compare and contrast agency and nonagency mortgage-backed securities.
- differentiate credit risk analysis of commercial mortgage-backed securities from residential nonagency mortgage-backed securities.
- explain the features of a commercial mortgage loan and provisions for protecting the lender against prepayment risk.

SUMMARY OVERVIEW

- The basic mortgage-backed security is the mortgage passthrough security created from a pool of mortgage loans.

63

- Agency passthrough securities are those issued/guaranteed by Ginnie Mae, Fannie Mae, and Freddie Mac.
- The cash flow of a passthrough includes net interest, scheduled principal repayments (i.e., scheduled amortization), and prepayments.
- Any amount paid in excess of the required monthly mortgage payment is a prepayment; the cash flow of a mortgage-backed security is unknown because of prepayments.
- A projection of prepayments is necessary to project the cash flow of a passthrough security.
- The single monthly mortality (SMM) rate is the ratio of the amount of prepayments divided by the amount available to prepay (i.e., outstanding mortgage balance at the beginning of the month minus the scheduled principal payment for the month).
- The PSA prepayment benchmark is a series of conditional prepayment rates and is simply a market convention that describes in general the pattern of prepayments.
- A measure commonly used to estimate the life of a passthrough is its average life.
- The prepayment risk associated with investing in mortgage passthrough securities can be decomposed into contraction risk and extension risk.
- Prepayment risk makes passthrough securities unattractive for certain financial institutions to hold from an asset/liability perspective.
- The three factors that affect prepayments are (1) the prevailing mortgage rate, (2) normal housing turnover, and (3) characteristics of the underlying mortgage pool.
- Collateralized mortgage obligations are bond classes created by redirecting the interest and principal from a pool of passthroughs or whole loans.
- The creation of a CMO cannot eliminate prepayment risk; it can only transfer the various forms of this risk among different classes of bonds called tranches.
- From a fixed-rate CMO tranche, a floating-rate tranche and an inverse floating-rate tranche can be created.
- A notional interest-only tranche (also called a structured IO) can be created from the excess interest available from other tranches in the structure; excess interest is the difference between the collateral's coupon rate and a tranche's coupon rate.
- The amortization schedule for a planned amortization class is structured based on a lower PSA prepayment assumption and an upper PSA prepayment assumption—called the initial PAC collar.
- A planned amortization class (PAC) tranche has reduced average life variability, the better prepayment protection provided by the support tranches.
- If the collateral from which a PAC bond is created pays at a constant PSA rate that is anywhere within the initial PAC collar, the amortization schedule will be satisfied.
- Over time, the prepayment collar that will be able to support the PAC tranches (i.e., provide the prepayment protection) changes as the amount of the support tranches change.
- The effective collar is the lower and upper PSA prepayment rates that can occur in the future and still be able to satisfy the amortization schedule for the PAC tranche.
- The key to the prepayment protection for the PAC tranches is the support tranches.
- The support tranches are exposed to the greatest prepayment risk of all the tranches in a CMO structure and greater prepayment risk than the collateral (i.e., passthrough securities) from which a deal is created.
- Support tranches with a PAC schedule can be created from the support tranches; these tranches are still support tranches but they have better prepayment protection than other support tranches in the structure that do not have a schedule.
- A stripped mortgage-backed security is a derivative mortgage-backed security that is created by redistributing the interest and principal payments to two different classes.

- A principal-only mortgage strip (PO) benefits from declining interest rates and fast prepayments.
- An interest-only mortgage strip (IO) benefits from rising interest rates and a slowing of prepayments; if rates fall instead, the investor in an interest-only security may not realize the amount invested even if the security is held to maturity.
- Nonagency securities are not backed by any federal government agency guarantee.
- The underlying loans for nonagency securities are nonconforming mortgage loans—loans that do not qualify for inclusion in mortgage pools that underlie agency mortgage-backed securities.
- Credit enhancement is needed to support nonagency mortgage-backed securities.
- Credit enhancement levels are determined relative to a specific rating desired for a security and there are two general types of credit enhancement structures—external and internal.
- Commercial mortgage-backed securities are backed by a pool of commercial mortgage loans-loans on income-producing property
- Unlike residential mortgage loans where the lender relies on the ability of the borrower to repay and has recourse to the borrower if the payment terms are not satisfied, commercial mortgage loans are nonrecourse loans, and as a result the lender can only look to the income-producing property backing the loan for interest and principal repayment.
- Two measures that have been found to be key indicators of the potential credit performance of a commercial mortgage loan are the debt-to-service coverage ratio (i.e., the property's net operating income divided by the debt service) and the loan-to-value ratio.
- The degree of call protection available to a CMBS investor is a function of (1) call protection available at the loan level and (2) call protection afforded from the actual CMBS structure.
- At the commercial loan level, call protection can be in the form of a prepayment lockout, defeasance, prepayment penalty points, or yield maintenance charges.
- Many commercial loans backing CMBS transactions are balloon loans that require substantial principal payment at the end of the balloon term and therefore the investor faces balloon risk—the risk that the loan will extend beyond the scheduled maturity date.

PROBLEMS

1. a. Complete the following schedule for a 30-year fully amortizing mortgage loan with a mortgage rate of 7.25% where the amount borrowed is $150,000. The monthly mortgage payment is $1,023.26.

Month	Beginning mortgage	Mortgage payment	Interest	Sch. Prin repayment	End of month balance
1	150,000.00	1,023.26			
2		1,023.26			
3		1,023.26			
4		1,023.26			
5		1,023.26			
6		1,023.26			
7		1,023.26			
8		1,023.26			
9		1,023.26			
10		1,023.26			
11		1,023.26			
12		1,023.26			
13		1,023.26			
14		1,023.26			

b. Complete the following schedule for the mortgage loan in part a given the following information:

Month	Beginning mortgage	Mortgage payment	Interest	Sch. Prin repayment	End of month balance
357	4,031.97	1,023.26			
358		1,023.26			
359		1,023.26			
360		1,023.26			

2. a. Suppose that the servicing fee for a mortgage loan is 0.5%. Complete the following schedule for the mortgage loan in the previous question. The column labeled "Servicing Fee" is the dollar amount of the servicing fee for the month. The column labeled "Net Interest" is the monthly interest after the servicing fee for the month.

Month	Beginning mortgage	Mortgage payment	Servicing fee	Net interest	Sch. Prin repayment	End of month balance
1						
2						
3						
4						
5						
6						

b. Determine for the first six months the cash flow for an investor who purchases this mortgage loan after the servicing fee is paid.

3. Explain why you agree or disagree with the following statement: "Since mortgage passthrough securities issued by Ginnie Mae are guaranteed by the full faith and credit of the U.S. government, there is no uncertainty about the cash flow for the security."

4. Consider the following mortgage pool.

Loan	Outstanding mortgage balance	Mortgage rate	Months remaining
1	$215,000	6.75%	200
2	$185,000	7.75%	185
3	$125,000	7.25%	192
4	$100,000	7.00%	210
5	$200,000	6.50%	180
Total	$825,000		

a. What is the weighted average coupon rate for this mortgage pool?
b. What is the weighted average maturity for this mortgage pool?

5. Mr. Jamison is looking at the historical prepayment for a passthrough security. He finds the following:

mortgage balance in month 42	=	$260,000,000
scheduled principal payment in month 42	=	$1,000,000
prepayment in month 42	=	$2,450,000

a. What is the SMM for month 42?
b. How should Mr. Jamison interpret the SMM computed?

c. What is the CPR for month 42?

d. How should Mr. Jamison interpret the CPR computed?

6. Using the Public Securities Association Prepayment benchmark, complete the following table:

Month	PSA	CPR	SMM
5	100		
15	80		
20	175		
27	50		
88	200		
136	75		
220	225		

7. Explain why 30 months after the origination of a mortgage pool, discussing prepayments in terms of one CPR and a PSA are identical.

8. Suppose that in month 140 the mortgage balance for a mortgage pool underlying a passthrough security is $537 million and that the scheduled principal repayment for month 140 is $440,000. Assuming 175 PSA, what is the amount of the prepayment for month 140?

9. Comment on the following statement: "The PSA model is a prepayment model."

10. Robert Reed is an assistant portfolio manager who has been recently given the responsibility of assisting Joan Soprano, the portfolio manager for the mortgage-backed securities portfolio. Ms. Soprano gave Mr. Reed a copy of the a Prudential Securities publication for November 1999 entitled *Mortgage and Asset-Backed Prepayment and Issuance*. An excerpt from the publication is given below:

GNMA 30 Year		Projected PSA				
		Dec	Jan	Feb	One year	Long term
6.0	1998	73	68	60	60	65
6.5	1998	113	102	92	91	90
7.0	1998	154	137	124	126	116
7.5	1993	181	166	150	155	138
8.0	1996	220	211	181	185	159
8.5	1994	283	272	223	205	173
9.0	1986	269	263	232	209	195

The mortgage rate at the time of the report was 8.13%.

Mr. Reed asks the following questions about the information in the above excerpt. Respond to each question.

a. What does "GNMA 30 YEAR" mean?

b. What does "8.5 1994" mean?

c. What do the numbers under "PROJECTED" mean?

d. Do the prepayment rates for "7.5 1993" apply to all GNMA issues in the market?

e. Why are the projected prepayments for "one year" and "long term" such that they increase with the coupon rate?

11. Suppose that you are analyzing prepayments of a passthrough security that was issued more than 15 years ago. The weighted average coupon (WAC) for the underlying mortgage pool was 13%. Suppose that the mortgage rate over the year of the analysis declined from 8% to 7% but prepayments for this mortgage pool you are analyzing did not increase. Explain why there is no increase in prepayments despite the lower mortgage rate relative to 13% being paid by borrowers and the decline in the mortgage rates over the year.

12. What type of prepayment risk is an investor interested in a short-term security concerned with when purchasing a mortgage-backed security?

13. Suppose that a portfolio manager is considering a collateralized mortgage obligation structure KMF-01. This structure has three tranches. The deal is a simple sequential pay and was issued several years ago. The tranches are A, B, and C with a coupon rate paid to each tranche each month and principal payments are made first to tranche A, then to tranche B, and finally to tranche C. Here is the status of the deal as of the time of the analysis:

Tranche	Coupon rate	Par amount outstanding
A	6%	$3 million
B	7%	8 million
C	8%	30 million

Based on some prepayment rate, the projected principal payments (prepayments plus scheduled principal repayment) for the next four years for the collateral underlying this deal are as follows:

Month	Sch. principal repayment + prepayments	Month	Sch. principal repayment + prepayments
1	520,000	25	287,000
2	510,000	26	285,000
3	490,000	27	283,000
4	450,000	28	280,000
5	448,000	29	278,000
6	442,000	30	275,000
7	410,000	31	271,000
8	405,000	32	270,000
9	400,000	33	265,000
10	396,000	34	260,000
11	395,000	35	255,000
12	390,000	36	252,000
13	388,000	37	250,000
14	385,000	38	245,000
15	380,000	39	240,000
16	377,000	40	210,000
17	375,000	41	200,000
18	370,000	42	195,000
19	369,000	43	190,000
20	366,000	44	185,000
21	300,000	45	175,000
22	298,000	46	170,000
23	292,000	47	166,000
24	290,000	48	164,000

    a. Compute the principal, interest, and cash flow for tranche A for the 48 months.

    b. Compute the principal, interest, and cash flow for tranche B for the 48 months.

    c. Compute the principal, interest, and cash flow for tranche C for the 48 months.

    d. Compute the average life for tranche A.

14. Suppose that in the previous CMO structure, KMF-01, that tranche C is an accrual tranche that accrues coupon interest monthly. We will refer to this new CMO structure as KMF-02.

    a. What is the principal repayment, interest, and cash flow for tranche A in KMF-02?

    b. What is the principal balance for tranche C for the first five months?

    c. What is the average life for tranche A in KMF-02 and contrast this with the average life for tranche A in KMF-01?

15. Explain why it is necessary to have a cap for the floater when a fixed-rate tranche is split into a floater and an inverse floater.

16. Suppose that a tranche from which a floater and an inverse floater are created has an average life of six years. What will be the average life of the floater and the inverse floater?

17. How does a CMO alter the cash flow from mortgages so as to redistribute the prepayment risk across various tranches in a deal?

18. "By creating a CMO, an issuer eliminates the prepayment risk associated with the underlying mortgages loans." Explain why you agree or disagree with this statement?

19. Ellen Morgan received a phone call from the trustee of a pension fund. Ms. Morgan is the portfolio manager for the pension fund's bond portfolio. The trustee expressed concerns about the inclusion of CMOs in the portfolio. The trustee's concern arose after reading several articles in the popular press where the CMO market was characterized as the sector of the mortgage-backed securities market with the greatest prepayment risk and the passthrough sector as the safest sector in terms of prepayment risk. What should Ms. Morgan say to this trustee regarding such statements made in the popular press?

20. What is the role of a support tranche in a CMO structure?

21. Suppose that the manager of a savings & loan association portfolio has decided to invest in mortgage-backed securities and is considering the following two securities: (i) a Fannie Mae passthrough security with a WAM of 310 months or (ii) a PAC tranche of a Fannie Mae CMO issue with an average life of 2 years. Which mortgage-backed security would probably be better from an asset/liability perspective?

22. Suppose that a PAC bond is created using prepayment speeds of 90 PSA and 240 PSA and the average life is 5 years. Will the average life for this PAC tranche be shorter than, longer than, or equal to 5 years if the collateral pays at 140 PSA over its life? Explain your answer.

23. Suppose that $1 billion of passthroughs are used to create a CMO structure, KMF-05. This structure includes a PAC tranche with a par value of $650 million and a support tranche with a par value of $350 million.

    a. Which of the following will have the least average life variability: (i) the collateral, (ii) the PAC tranche, or (iii) the support tranche? Why?

    b. Which of the following will have the greatest average life variability: (i) the collateral, (ii) the PAC tranche, or (iii) the support tranche? Why?

24. Suppose that the $1 billion of collateral in the CMO structure KMF-05 in the previous question was divided into a PAC tranche with a par value of $800 million and a support

tranche with a par value of $200 million (instead of $650 million and $350 million). The new structure is KMF-06. Will the PAC tranche in KMF-06 have more or less protection than the PAC tranche in KMF-05?

25. Suppose that $500 million of passthroughs are used to create a CMO structure with a PAC tranche with a par value of $350 million (PAC I), a support tranche with a schedule (PAC II) with a par value of $100 million, and a support tranche without a schedule with a par value of $200 million.

   a. Will the PAC I or PAC II have less average life variability? Why?
   b. Will the support tranche without a schedule or the PAC II have the greater average life variability? Why?

26. In a CMO structure with several PAC tranches that pay off sequentially, explain what the structure effectively becomes once all the support tranches are paid off.

27. Suppose that for the first four years of a CMO, prepayments are well below the initial upper PAC collar and within the initial lower PAC collar. What will happen to the effective upper collar?

28. Consider the following CMO structure backed by 8% collateral:

Tranche	Par amount	Coupon rate
A	$400,000,000	6.25%
B	$200,000,000	6.75%
C	$225,000,000	7.50%
D	$175,000,000	7.75%

Suppose that the structurer of this CMO wants to create a notional IO tranche with a coupon rate of 8%. Calculate the notional amount for this notional IO tranche.

29. An issuer is considering the following two CMO structures:
Structure I:

Tranche	Par amount	Coupon rate
A	$150 million	6.50%
B	100 million	6.75%
C	200 million	7.25%
D	150 million	7.75%
E	100 million	8.00%
F	500 million	8.50%

Tranches A-E are a sequence of PAC Is and F is the support tranche.
Structure II:

Tranche	Par amount	Coupon rate
A	$150 million	6.50%
B	100 million	6.75%
C	200 million	7.25%
D	150 million	7.75%
E	100 million	8.00%
F	200 million	8.25%
G	300 million	?????

Tranches A-E are a sequence of PAC Is, F is a PAC II, and G is a support tranche without a schedule.

   a. In Structure II tranche G is created from tranche F in Structure I. What is the coupon rate for tranche G assuming that the combined coupon rate for tranches F and G in Structure II should be 8.5%?

   b. What is the effect on the value and average life of tranches A-E by including the PAC II in Structure II?

   c. What is the difference in the average life variability of tranche G in Structure II and tranche F in Structure I?

30. What is a broken or busted PAC?

31. Assume that in FJF-01 in the chapter (see Exhibit 5 in the chapter), tranche C had been split to create a floater with a principal of $80,416,667 and an inverse floater with a principal of $16,083,333.

   a. What would be the cap rate for the inverse floater if the coupon rate for the floater is 1-month LIBOR plus 1%?

   b. Assuming that (1) the coupon formula for the floater is 1-month LIBOR plus 1% and (2) a floor is imposed on the inverse floater of zero, what would be the cap rate on the floater?

32. a. In assessing the prepayment protection offered by a seasoned PAC tranche, explain why the initial collars may provide limited insight?

   b. What measure provides better information about the prepayment protection offered by a seasoned PAC tranche?

33. a. For a mortgage loan, is a higher or lower loan-to-value ratio an indication of greater credit risk? Explain why.

   b. What is the empirical relationship between defaults and loan-to-value ratio observed by studies of residential mortgage loans?

34. a. What is a principal-only mortgage strip and an interest-only mortgage strip?

   b. How does an interest-only mortgage strip differ with respect to the certainty about the cash flow from a Treasury strip created from the coupon interest?

   c. How is the price of an interest-only mortgage strip expected to change when interest rates change?

35. a. An investor purchased $10 million par value of a 7% Ginnie Mae passthrough security agreeing to pay 102. The pool factor is 0.72. How much does the investor pay to the seller?

   b. Why would an investor who wants to purchase a principal-only mortgage strip not want to do so on a TBA basis?

36. Why can't all residential mortgage loans be securitized by either Ginnie Mae, Fannie Mae, or Freddie Mac?

37. Why is credit enhancement needed for a nonagency mortgage-backed security?

38. With respect to a default by the borrower, how does a residential mortgage loan differ from a commercial mortgage loan?

39. Why is the debt-to-service coverage ratio used to assess the credit risk of a commercial mortgage loan?
40. a. What types of provisions are usually included in a commercial loan to protect the lender against prepayment risk?
    b. In a commercial mortgage-backed securities deal, explain why the investor in a security may be afforded prepayment protection at the deal level.
41. What is balloon risk and how is it related to extension risk?

CHAPTER 11

ASSET-BACKED SECTOR OF THE BOND MARKET

LEARNING OUTCOMES

After reading Chapter 11 you should be able to:

- describe the basic structural features of and parties to a securitization transaction.
- explain prepayment tranching and credit tranching in a securitization transaction.
- differentiate between the payment structure of a securitization backed by amortizing assets and non-amortizing assets.
- explain the different types of credit enhancement (internal and external).
- explain the different conventions for measuring prepayments for asset-backed securities (conditional prepayment rate, absolute prepayment rate, and prospectus prepayment curve).
- describe the cash flow and prepayment characteristics for securities backed by home equity loans, manufactured housing loans, automobile loans, student loans, SBA loans, and credit card receivables.
- describe what a collateralized debt obligation is and the different types (cash and synthetic).
- explain the motivation of sponsors for creating a collateralized debt obligation: arbitrage and balance sheet transactions.

SUMMARY OVERVIEW

- An entity that wants to raise funds via a securitization will sell assets to a special purpose vehicle and is referred to as the "seller" in the transaction.
- The buyer of assets in a securitization is a special purpose vehicle and this entity, referred to as the issuer or trust, raises funds to buy the assets via the sale of securities (the asset-backed securities).
- There will be an entity in a securitization that will be responsible for servicing the loans or receivables.
- Third party entities in the securitization are attorneys, independent accountants, trustee, rating agencies, servicer, and possibly a guarantor.
- The waterfall of a transaction describes how the distribution of the cash flow will be distributed to the bond classes after fees are paid.
- In a securitization structure, the bond classes issued can consist of a senior bond that is tranched so as to redistribute prepayment risk and one or more subordinate bonds; the creation of the subordinate bonds provides credit tranching for the structure.

- The collateral for an asset-backed security can be either amortizing assets (e.g., auto loans and closed-end home equity loans) or nonamortizing assets (e.g., credit card receivables).
- For amortizing assets, projection of the cash flow requires projecting prepayments.
- For non-amortizing assets, prepayments by an individual borrower do not apply since there is no schedule of principal repayments.
- When the collateral is amortizing assets, typically the principal repayments are distributed to the security holders.
- When the collateral consists of non-amortizing assets, typically there is a lockout period, a period where principal repayments are reinvested in new assets; after the lockout period, principal repayments are distributed to the security holders.
- A structure where there is a lockout for principal repayments is called a revolving structure.
- One factor that may affect prepayments is the prevailing level of interest rates relative to the interest rate on the loan.
- Since a default is a prepayment (an involuntary prepayment), prepayment modeling for an asset-backed security backed by amortizing assets requires a model for projecting the amount that will be recovered and when it will be recovered.
- Cash flow analysis can be performed on a pool level or a loan level.
- The expected final maturity of an asset-backed security is the maturity date based on expected prepayments at the time of pricing of a deal; the legal final maturity can be two or more years after the expected final maturity.
- Average life is commonly used as a measure for the length of time an asset-backed security will be outstanding.
- With an asset-backed security, due to prepayments a bond that is expected to have a bullet maturity may have an actual maturity that differs from that specified in the prospectus and is therefore referred to as a soft bullet.
- Asset-backed securities are credit enhanced; that is, there must be support from somewhere to absorb a certain amount of defaults.
- Credit enhancement levels are determined relative to a specific rating desired for a security.
- There are two general types of credit enhancement structures: external and internal.
- External credit enhancements come in the form of third-party guarantees that provide for first loss protection against losses up to a specified level.
- External credit enhancement includes insurance by a monoline insurer, a guarantee by the seller of the assets, and a letter of credit.
- The most common forms of internal credit enhancements are reserve funds and senior/subordinate structures.
- The senior/subordinated structure is the most widely used internal credit support structure with a typical structure having a senior tranche and one or more non-senior tranches.
- For mortgage-related asset-backed securities and nonagency mortgage-backed securities there is a concern that prepayments will erode the protection afforded by the non-senior (i.e., subordinated) tranches after the deal closes.
- A shifting interest structure is used to protect against a deterioration in the senior tranche's credit protection due to prepayments by redistributing the prepayments disproportionately from the non-senior tranches to the senior tranche according to a specified schedule.
- With an asset-backed security, one of the following call provisions may be granted to the trustee: (1) percent of collateral call, (2) percent of bonds, (3) percent of tranche, (4) call on or after specified date, (5) latter of percent or date, or (6) auction call.
- The collateral for a home equity loan is typically a first lien on residential property and the loan fails to satisfy the underwriting standards for inclusion in a loan pool of Ginnie Mae,

Fannie Mae, or Freddie Mac because of the borrower's impaired credit history or too high a payment-to-income ratio.

- Typically, a home equity loan is used by a borrower to consolidate consumer debt using the current home as collateral rather than to obtain funds to purchase a new home.
- Home equity loans can be either closed end (i.e., structured the same way as a fully amortizing residential mortgage loan) or open end (i.e., homeowner given a credit line).
- The monthly cash flow for a home equity loan-backed security backed by closed-end HELs consists of (1) net interest, (2) regularly scheduled principal payments, and (3) prepayments.
- Several studies by Wall Street firms have found that the key difference between the prepayment behavior of HELs and traditional residential mortgages is the important role played by the credit characteristics of the borrower.
- Studies strongly suggests that borrower credit quality is the most important determinant of prepayments, with the sensitivity of refinancing to interest rates being greater the higher the borrower's credit quality.
- The prospectus of an HEL offering contains a base case prepayment assumption regarding the initial speed and the amount of time until the collateral is expected to season.
- A prospectus prepayment curve is a multiple of the base case prepayments assumed in the prospectus (i.e., base case is equal to 100% PPC).
- Typically, home equity loan-backed securities are securitized by both closed-end fixed-rate and adjustable-rate (or variable-rate) HELs.
- Unlike a typical floater which has a cap that is fixed throughout the security's life, the available funds cap of a HEL floater is variable and depends on the amount of funds generated by the net coupon on the principal, less any fees.
- To provide stability to the average life of a senior tranche, closed-end home equity loan transactions will include either a non-accelerating senior (NAS) tranche or a planned amortization class (PAC) tranche.
- A NAS tranche receives principal payments according to a schedule based not on a dollar amount for a given month, but instead on a schedule that specifies for each month the share of pro rata principal that must be distributed to the NAS tranche.
- For a PAC tranche a schedule of the dollar amount for each month is specified.
- The structure of residential mortgage-backed securities outside the United States is similar to that of the nonagency mortgage market; there are internal and external credit enhancements.
- Auto loan-backed securities are issued by the financial subsidiaries of auto manufacturers, commercial banks, and independent finance companies and small financial institutions specializing in auto loans.
- The cash flow for auto loan-backed securities consists of regularly scheduled monthly loan payments (interest and scheduled principal repayments), and any prepayments.
- Prepayments on auto loans are not sensitive to interest rates.
- Prepayments on auto loan-backed securities are measured in terms of the absolute prepayment speed (denoted ABS) which measures monthly prepayments relative to the original collateral amount.
- Manufactured housing-backed securities are backed by loans on manufactured homes (i.e., homes built at a factory and then transported to a site).
- Manufactured housing-backed securities are issued by Ginnie Mae and private entities, the former being guaranteed by the full faith and credit of the U.S. government.
- A manufactured housing loan's cash flow consists of net interest, regularly scheduled principal, and prepayments.

- Prepayments are more stable for manufactured housing-backed securities because they are not sensitive to interest rate changes.
- SLABS are asset-backed securities backed by student loans.
- The student loans most commonly securitized are those that are made under the Federal Family Education Loan Program (FFELP) whereby the government makes loans to students via private lenders and the government guaranteeing up to 98% of the principal plus accrued interest.
- Alternative loans are student loans that are not part of a government guarantee program and are basically consumer loans.
- In contrast to government guaranteed loans, the lender's decision to extend an alternative loan is based on the ability of the applicant to repay the loan.
- Student loans involve three periods with respect to the borrower's payments—deferment period, grace period, and loan repayment period.
- Prepayments typically occur due to defaults or a loan consolidation (i.e, a loan to consolidate loans over several years into a single loan).
- Issuers of SLABs include the Student Loan Marketing Association (Sallie Mae), traditional corporate entities, and non-profit organizations.
- Student loan-backed securities offer a floating rate; for some issues the reference rate is the 3-month Treasury bill rate but for most issues the reference rate is LIBOR.
- Small Business Administration (SBA) loans are backed by the full faith and credit of the U.S. government.
- Most SBA loans are variable-rate loans where the reference rate is the prime rate with monthly payments consisting of interest and principal repayment.
- Voluntary prepayments can be made by the SBA borrower without any penalty.
- Factors contributing to the prepayment speed of a pool of SBA loans are (1) the maturity date of the loan (it has been found that the fastest speeds on SBA loans and pools occur for shorter maturities), (2) the purpose of the loan, and (3) whether or not there is a cap on the loan.
- Credit card receivable-backed securities are backed by credit card receivables for credit cards issued by banks, retailers, and travel and entertainment companies.
- Credit card deals are structured as a master trust.
- For a pool of credit card receivables, the cash flow consists of finance charges collected, fees, and principal.
- The principal repayment of a credit card receivable-backed security is not amortized; instead, during the lockout period, the principal payments made by credit card borrowers are retained by the trustee and reinvested in additional receivables and after the lockout period (the principal-amortization period), the principal received by the trustee is no longer reinvested but paid to investors.
- There are provisions in credit card receivable-backed securities that require early amortization of the principal if certain events occur.
- Since for credit card receivable-backed securities the concept of prepayments does not apply, participants look at the monthly payment rate (MPR) which expresses the monthly payment (which includes interest, finance charges, and any principal) of a credit card receivable portfolio as a percentage of debt outstanding in the previous month.
- The MPR for credit card receivable-backed securities is important because (1) if it reaches an extremely low level, there is a chance that there will be extension risk with respect to the principal payments and (2) if the MPR is very low, there is a chance that there will not be sufficient cash flows to pay off principal (which can trigger early amortization of the principal).

- To assess the performance of the portfolio of credit card receivables and the ability of the issuer to meet its interest obligation and repay principal as scheduled, an investor must analyze the gross portfolio yield (which includes finance charges collected and fees), charge-offs (which represents the accounts charged off as uncollectible), the net portfolio yield, gross portfolio yield minus charge-offs, and delinquencies (the percentage of receivable that are past due as specified number of months).

- There are three amortization structures that have been used in credit card receivable-backed security structures: (1) passthrough structure, (2) controlled-amortization structure, and (3) bullet-payment structure.

- A collateralized debt obligation is an asset-backed security backed by a diversified pool of debt obligations (high-yield corporate bonds, structured financial products, emerging market bonds, bank loans, and special situation loans and distressed debt).

- A collateralized bond obligation is a CDO in which the underlying pool of debt obligations consists of bond-type instruments (high-yield corporate and emerging market bonds).

- A collateralized loan obligation is a CDO in which the underlying pool of debt obligations consists of bank loans.

- In a CDO there is an asset manager responsible for managing the portfolio of assets.

- The tranches in a CDO include senior tranches, mezzanine tranches, and subordinate/equity tranche.

- The senior and mezzanine tranches are rated and the subordinate/equity tranche is unrated.

- The proceeds to meet the obligations to the CDO tranches (interest and principal repayment) can come from (1) coupon interest payments of the underlying assets, (2) maturing assets in the underlying pools, and (3) sale of assets in the underlying pool.

- CDOs are categorized based on the motivation of the sponsor of the transaction—arbitrage and balance sheet transactions.

- The motivation in an arbitrage transaction is for the sponsor to earn the spread between the yield offered on the debt obligations in the underlying pool and the payments made to the various tranches in the structure.

- In a balance sheet transaction the motivation of the sponsor is to remove debt instruments (primarily loans) from its balance sheet.

- The key as to whether or not it is economic to create an arbitrage transaction is whether or not a structure can offer a competitive return to the subordinated/equity tranche.

- Arbitrage transactions are classified as either cash flow CDOs or market value CDOs depending on where the primary source of the proceeds from the underlying asset is to come from to satisfy the obligation to the tranches.

- In a cash flow CDO the primary source is the interest and maturing principal from the underlying assets; in a market value CDO the proceeds to meet the obligations depends heavily on the total return generated from the portfolio.

- The three relevant periods in a CDO are the ramp up period, the reinvestment period or revolving period, and the final period where the portfolio assets are sold and the debt holders are paid off.

- In a CDO transaction, senior tranches are protected against a credit deterioration by coverage tests; a failure of coverage tests results in the paying off of the senior tranches until the coverage tests are satisfied.

- The tests imposed in a cash flow structure are quality tests (e.g., minimum asset diversity score, a minimum weighted average rating, and maturity restrictions) and coverage tests.

- Coverage tests are tests to ensure that the performance of the collateral is sufficient to make payments to the various tranches and include par value tests and interest coverage ratio.

- In market value structures the focus is on monitoring of the assets and their price volatility by the frequent marking to market of the assets.
- In a synthetic CDO a credit derivative instrument is used is to allow the CDO issuer to transfer the economic risk, but not the legal ownership of a reference asset.
- In a synthetic CDO, the credit derivative used is a credit default swap and this instrument allows the "protection buyer" (the asset manager in a synthetic CDO) to protect against default risk on a reference asset; the protection sellers are the tranches in the junior section of the CDO.
- In a synthetic CDO, the return to the junior note holders is based on the return from a portfolio of high-quality debt instruments plus the premium received in the credit default swap, reduced by the payment that must be made as a result of a credit event.
- There are synthetic balance sheet CDO transactions and synthetic arbitrage CDO transactions.

PROBLEMS

1. Caterpillar Financial Asset Trust 1997-A is a special purpose vehicle. The collateral (i.e., assets) for the trust is a pool of fixed-rate retail installment sales contracts that are secured by new and used machinery manufactured primarily by Caterpillar Inc. The retail installment sales contracts were originated by the Caterpillar Financial Funding Corporation, a wholly-owned subsidiary of Caterpillar Financial Services Corporation. Caterpillar Financial Services Corporation is a wholly-owned subsidiary of Caterpillar Inc. The prospectus for the trust states that:

   "THE NOTES REPRESENT OBLIGATIONS OF THE ISSUER ONLY AND DO NOT REPRESENT OBLIGATIONS OF OR INTERESTS IN CATERPILLAR FINANCIAL FUNDING CORPORATION, CATERPIL-LAR FINANCIAL SERVICES CORPORATION, CATERPILLAR INC. OR ANY OF THEIR RESPECTIVE AFFILIATES."

   The servicer of the retail installment sales contracts is Caterpillar Financial Services Corporation, a wholly-owned finance subsidiary of Caterpillar Inc. and is referred to as the servicer in the prospectus. For servicing the collateral, Caterpillar Financial Services Corporation receives a servicing fee of 100 basis points of the outstanding loan balance.

   The securities were issued on May 19, 1997 and had a par value of $337,970,000. In the prospectus the securities are referred to as "asset-backed notes." There were four rated bond classes are:

Bond class	Par value
Class A-1	$88,000,000
Class A-2	$128,000,000
Class A-3	$108,100,000
Class B	$13,870,000

   a. In the prospectus, the term "Seller" is used. Who in this transaction would be the "Seller" and why?
   b. In the prospectus, the term "Issuer" is used. Who in this transaction would be the "Issuer" and why?
   c. Despite not having the waterfall for this structure, which bond classes do you think are the senior bonds?

   d. Despite not having the waterfall for this structure, which bond classes do you think are the subordinate bonds?

   e. Despite not having the waterfall for this structure, explain why there appears to be credit and prepayment tranching in this structure?

2. In the securitization process, what is the role played by the (a) attorneys and (b) independent accountants?

3. How are principal repayments from the collateral used by the trustee in a securitization transaction?

4. Suppose that the collateral for an asset-backed securities structure has a gross weighted average coupon of 8.6%. The servicing fee is 50 basis points. The tranches issued have a weighted average coupon rate of 7.1%. What is the excess servicing spread?

5. Suppose that the structure for an asset-backed security transaction is as follows:

senior tranche	$220 million
subordinate tranche 1	$50 million
subordinate tranche 2	$30 million

   and that the value of the collateral for the structure is $320 million. Subordinate tranche 2 is the first loss tranche.

   a. How much is the overcollateralization in this structure?

   b. What is the amount of the loss for each tranche if losses due to defaults over the life of the structure total $15 million?

   c. What is the amount of the loss for each tranche if losses due to defaults over the life of the structure total $35 million?

   d. What is the amount of the loss for each tranche if losses due to defaults over the life of the structure total $85 million?

   e. What is the amount of the loss for each tranche if losses due to defaults over the life of the structure total $110 million?

6. a. Explain why individual loans that are of a non-amortizing type are not subject to prepayment risk.

   b. Explain why securities backed by collateral consisting of non-amortizing assets may expose an investor to prepayment risk.

7. An asset-backed security has been credit enhanced with a letter of credit from a bank with a single A credit rating. If this is the only form of credit enhancement, explain why this issue is unlikely to receive a triple A credit rating.

8. Why is it critical for monoline insurance companies that provide insurance for asset-backed security transactions to maintain a triple A credit rating?

9. What is the difference between a cash reserve fund and an excess servicing spread account?

10. Why is the assumption about how defaults may occur over the life of an asset-backed security transaction important in assessing the effectiveness of excess servicing spread as a form of internal credit enhancement?

11. a. Explain why a senior-subordinate structure is a form of internal credit enhancement.

    b. Explain the need for a shifting interest mechanism in a senior-subordinate structure when the underlying assets are subject to prepayments.

12. a. What is meant by the "senior prepayment percentage" in a shifting interest mechanism of a senior-subordinate structure?

    b. Why does a shifting interest mechanism affect the cash flow of the senior tranche and increase the senior tranche's exposure to contraction risk?

13. What is a "latter of percent or call date" call provision?

14. a. What is the cash flow of a closed-end home equity loan?

    b. Indicate whether you agree or disagree with the following statement: "Typically, closed-end home equity loans are loans to borrowers of the highest credit quality."

15. The Izzobaf Home Equity Loan Trust 2000–1 is backed by fixed-rate closed-end home equity loans. The base case prepayment for this deal is specified in the prospectus as follows:

> The model used with respect to the loans (the "prepayment ramp") assumes that the home equity loans prepay at a rate of 5% CPR in the first month after origination, and an additional 1.8% each month thereafter until the 12th month. Beginning in the 12th month and each month thereafter, the prepayment ramp assumes a prepayment rate of 24.8% CPR.

What is the CPR assuming 200% PPC for the following months

Month	CPR	Month	CPR	Month	CPR
1		11		30	
2		12		125	
3		13		150	
4		14		200	
5		15		250	
6		16		275	
7		17		300	
8		18		325	
9		19		350	
10		20		360	

16. James Tellmen is an assistant portfolio manager for a mortgage-backed securities portfolio. Mr. Tellmen's responsibility is to analyze agency mortgage-backed securities. Recently, the portfolio manager has been given authorization to purchase closed-end home equity loan-backed securities. Mr. Tellmen is analyzing his first structure in this sector of the asset-backed securities market. Upon reading the prospectus he finds that the base case prepayment is specified and believes that this prepayment assumption is the benchmark used in all closed-end home equity loan-backed securities. Explain why you agree or disagree with Mr. Tellmen.

17. Why is there is an available funds cap in an asset-backed security in which the collateral is adjustable-rate home equity loans?

18. Suppose that the base case shifting interest percentage schedule for a closed-end home equity loan-backed security is as follows:

Years after issuance	Senior prepayment percentage
1–4	100%
5	90%
6	80%
7	50%
8	20%
after year 8	0%

    a. If there are prepayments in month 36 of $100,000, how much of the prepayments is paid to the senior tranche? How much is paid to the subordinate tranches?

    b. If there are prepayments in the 8th year after issuance of $100,000, how much of the prepayments is paid to the senior tranche? How much is paid to the subordinate tranches?

    c. If there are prepayments in the 10th year after issuance of $100,000, how much of the prepayments is paid to the senior tranche? How much is paid to the subordinate tranches?

19. Larry Forest is an analyst reviewing for the first time a closed-end home equity loan-backed structure in order to determine whether or not to purchase the deal's senior tranche. He understands how the shifting interest percentage schedule is structured so as to provide the senior tranches with protection after the deal is closed. However, he is concerned that the schedule in the prospectus will not be adequate if the collateral's performance deteriorates (i.e., there is considerably greater losses for the collateral than expected). Explain to Mr. Forest what provision is included in the prospectus for protecting the senior tranches if the performance of the collateral deteriorates.

20. How is a non-accelerating senior tranche provided protection to reduce contraction risk and extension risk?

21. a. What are the components of the cash flow for a manufactured housing-backed security?

    b. What are the reasons why prepayments due to refinancing are not significant for manufactured housing loans?

22. Why are residential mortgage-backed securities outside the United States structured more like transactions in the nonagency U.S. market than the agency market.

23. a. What are the components of the cash flow for an auto loan-backed security?

    b. How important are prepayments due to refinancing for auto loans?

24. What is the difference between a single monthly mortality rate and an absolute prepayment speed?

25. a. If the ABS for a security is 1.5% at month 21, what is the corresponding SMM?

    b. If the SMM for a security is 1.9% at month 11, what is the corresponding ABS?

26. A trustee for a pension fund is working with a consultant to develop investment guidelines for the fund's bond portfolio. The trustee states that the fund should be able to invest in securities backed by student loans because the loans are fully guaranteed by the U.S. government. How should the consultant respond?

27. For a student loan-backed security, what is the difference between the deferment period and the grace period?

28. a. What are the components of the cash flow for a Small Business Administration-backed security?

    b. What reference rate is used for setting the coupon interest and how often is the coupon rate reset?

29. a. What is the cash flow for a credit card receivable-backed security during the lockout or revolving period?

    b. How is the principal received from credit card borrowers handled during the lockout or revolving period?

    c. Explain why you agree or disagree with the following statement: "After the lockout period, the principal is paid to bondholders in one lump sum amount at the maturity date of the security."

30. A manager of a corporate bond portfolio is considering the purchase of a credit card receivable-backed security. The manager believes that an advantage of such securities is

that there is no contraction risk and no extension risk. Explain why you agree or disagree with this view.

31. a. What is meant by the monthly payment rate for a credit card deal?
    b. What is the significance of the monthly payment rate?
    c. How is the net portfolio yield determined for a credit card deal?

32. What is a typical cash CDO structure?

33. Explain why you agree or disagree with the following statement: "The asset manager for a CDO is free to actively manage the portfolio without any constraints."

34. Explain why you agree or disagree with the following statement: "By using an interest rate swap, the asset manager for a CDO increases the risk associated with meeting the obligations that must be paid to the senior tranche."

35. What is the key factor in determining whether or not an arbitrage CDO can be issued?

36. Consider the following CDO transaction:

    1. The CDO is a $200 million structure. That is, the assets purchased will be $200 million.
    2. The collateral consists of bonds that all mature in 8 years and the coupon rate for every bond is the 8-year Treasury rate plus 600 basis points.
    3. The senior tranche comprises 75% of the structure ($150 million) and pays interest based on the following coupon formula: LIBOR plus 90 basis points.
    4. There is only one junior tranche ($30 million) with a coupon rate that is fixed. The coupon rate is the 8-year Treasury rate plus 300 basis points.
    5. The asset manager enters into an agreement with counterparty in which it agrees to pay the counterparty a fixed rate each year equal to the 8-year Treasury rate plus 120 basis points and receive LIBOR. The notional amount of the agreement is $150 million.

    a. How much is the equity tranche in this CDO?
    b. Assume that the 8-year Treasury rate at the time the CDO is issued is 6%. Assuming no defaults, what is the cash flow for each year and how is it distributed?
    c. Ignoring the asset management fee, what is the amount available each year for the equity tranche?

37. What are the elements of the return for the junior note holders in a synthetic CDO structure?

38. Why have banks issued synthetic balance sheet CDOs?

CHAPTER 12

VALUING MORTGAGE-BACKED AND ASSET-BACKED SECURITIES

LEARNING OUTCOMES

After reading Chapter 12 you should be able to:

- discuss the computation, use, and limitations of the cash flow yield, nominal spread, and zero-volatility spread for a mortgage-backed security and an asset-backed security.
- discuss the inputs, calibration, assumptions, appropriate discount factors, representative paths, and interest rate path present values for the Monte Carlo simulation model for valuing a mortgage-backed security.
- discuss path dependency in passthrough securities and the implications for valuation models.
- determine and interpret theoretical value, option-adjusted spread, and option cost to judge whether a mortgage-backed security is rich, cheap, or fairly priced.
- calculate and interpret effective duration, cash flow duration, and coupon curve duration.
- analyze the interest rate risk of a security given the security's effective duration and effective convexity.
- discuss the merits and limitations as well as the assumptions of effective duration, cash flow duration, modified duration, coupon curve duration, and empirical duration.
- determine whether the nominal spread, zero-volatility spread, or the option-adjusted spread should be used to evaluate a specific fixed income security.

SUMMARY OVERVIEW

- The cash flow yield is the interest rate that makes the present value of the projected cash flow for a mortgage-backed or asset-backed security equal to its market price plus accrued interest.
- The convention is to compare the yield on mortgage-backed and asset-backed securities to that of a Treasury coupon security by calculating the security's bond-equivalent yield. This measure is found by computing an effective semiannual rate and doubling it.
- The cash flow yield is based on three assumptions that thereby limit its use as a measure of relative value: (1) a prepayment assumption and default/recovery assumption, (2) an

assumption that the cash flows will be reinvested at the computed cash flow yield, and (3) an assumption that the investor will hold the security until the last loan in the pool is paid off.

- The nominal spread is commonly computed as the difference between the cash flow yield and the yield on a Treasury security with the same maturity as the mortgage-backed or asset-backed security's average life.

- The nominal spread masks the fact that a portion of the spread is compensation for accepting prepayment risk.

- An investor or portfolio manager who buys solely on the basis of nominal spread fails to determine whether or not that nominal spread offers an adequate compensation for prepayment risk.

- An investor or portfolio manager needs a measure that indicates the potential compensation after adjusting for prepayment risk and this measure is the option-adjusted spread.

- The zero-volatility spread is a measure of the spread that the investor would realize over the entire Treasury spot rate curve if the mortgage-backed or asset-backed security is held to maturity.

- The zero-volatility spread is not a spread off one point on the Treasury yield curve, as is the nominal spread, but a spread that will make the present value of the cash flows from the mortgage-backed or asset-backed security when discounted at the Treasury spot rate plus the spread equal to the market price of the security plus accrued interest.

- The binomial model and other similar models that use the backward induction method can be used to value securities where the decision to exercise a call option is not dependent on how interest rates evolved over time—that is, the decision of an issuer to call a bond will depend on the level of the rate at which the issue can be refunded relative to the issue's coupon rate, and not the path interest rates took to get to that rate.

- Mortgage-backed securities and some types of asset-backed securities are products where the periodic cash flows are "interest rate path-dependent"—meaning that the cash flow received in one period is determined not only by the current interest rate level, but also by the path that interest rates took to get to the current level.

- The Monte Carlo simulation model for valuing mortgage-backed securities involves generating a set of cash flows based on simulated future mortgage refinancing rates, which in turn imply simulated prepayment rates.

- In the Monte Carlo simulation model there is nothing to assure that the simulated interest rates will generate arbitrage-free values of the benchmark securities used in the valuation process; consequently, the simulated interest rates must be adjusted so as to produce arbitrage-free values.

- The present value of a given interest rate path can be thought of as the theoretical value of a security if that path was actually realized.

- The theoretical value of a mortgage-backed security can be determined by calculating the average of the theoretical values of all the interest rate paths.

- In the Monte Carlo simulation model, the option-adjusted spread is the spread that when added to all the spot rates on all interest rate paths will make the average present value of the paths equal to the observed market price (plus accrued interest).

- The OAS is measured relative to the benchmark interest rates that were used to generate the interest rate paths and to adjust the interest rate paths to make them arbitrage free.

- Since typically for a mortgage-backed security the benchmark interest rates are the on-the-run Treasury rates, the OAS measures the average spread over the Treasury spot rate curve, not the Treasury yield curve.

- Depending on the mortgage product being valued, the OAS reflects credit risk, liquidity risk, and modeling risk.
- The OAS is superior to the nominal spread which gives no recognition to the prepayment risk.
- The implied cost of the option embedded in a mortgage-backed or an asset-backed security can be obtained by calculating the difference between the option-adjusted spread at the assumed interest rate volatility and the zero-volatility spread.
- The option cost measures the prepayment (or option) risk embedded in the security and is a byproduct of the option-adjusted spread analysis, not valued explicitly with some option pricing model.
- In valuation modeling of collateralized mortgage obligations, the objective is to figure out how the value and risks of the collateral get transmitted to the tranches in a deal.
- There are several duration measures for mortgage-backed securities that are used in practice—effective duration, cash flow duration, coupon curve duration, and empirical duration.
- For bonds with embedded options such as mortgage-backed securities, the appropriate measure is effective duration and to capture negative convexity, effective convexity should be computed.
- Effective duration is computed using Monte Carlo simulation by shocking the short-term interest rates for each interest rate path generated up and down and obtaining the new value for the security; the new values determined when rates are shocked up and down are used in the duration formula.
- There are differences in the effective duration reported for a given mortgage-backed security by dealers and vendors of analytical systems primarily due to differences in: (1) the amount of the rate shock used, (2) the prepayment model used, (3) the option-adjusted spread computed, and (4) the relationship between short-term interest rates and refinancing rates assumed.
- Cash flow duration and coupon curve duration measures are forms of effective duration in that they do recognize that the values that should be used in the duration formula should take into account how the cash flows may change due to changes in prepayments when interest rates change.
- Cash flow duration is based on an initial cash flow yield and initial prepayment rate and computes the new values when rates are shocked (i.e., when the cash flow yield is shocked) allowing the cash flow to change based on a new prepayment rate as determined by a prepayment model.
- Cash flow duration is superior to modified duration (which assumes that cash flows do not change when rates are shocked) but inferior to effective duration as computed using the Monte Carlo simulation model.
- The coupon curve duration begins with the coupon curve of prices for similar mortgage-backed securities and uses values in the duration formula found by rolling up and down the coupon curve of prices.
- Empirical duration is a duration measure that is computed statistically using regression analysis based on observed market prices and yields.
- Empirical duration imposes no structure on the embedded option.
- A limitation of empirical duration and coupon curve duration is that they are difficult to apply to CMOs because of a lack of valid market price data.
- The zero-volatility spread added to the spot rates can be used to value an asset-backed security if either (1) the security does not have a prepayment option or (2) the borrower

has the right to prepay but it has been observed that the borrower does not tend to exercise that option if interest rates decline below the loan rate.

- The option-adjusted spread approach to valuation using the Monte Carlo simulation model is used for an asset-backed security if the borrower does have the right to prepay and it has been observed that the borrower does tend to refinance when interest rates decline below the loan rate.
- For any fixed income security, the valuation approaches that can be employed are the zero-volatility spread approach and the option-adjusted spread approach.
- For option-free bonds, the zero-volatility spread approach should be used.
- The choice of whether to use the binomial model (or a similar "nomial" model that uses the backward induction method) or the Monte Carlo simulation model for a security with an embedded option depends on the characteristics of the security.
- For corporate and agency debentures with an embedded option the binomial model or its equivalent should be used for valuation.
- For securities such as mortgage-backed and asset-backed securities (those where it is observed that borrowers do exercise the prepayment option) the Monte Carlo simulation model should be used since the cash flows are typically interest rate path dependent.

PROBLEMS

1. Suppose that based on a prepayment assumption of 200 PSA the cash flow yield for a specific agency passthrough security is 7.5% and the stated maturity is 15 years. Suppose further that the average life of this security is 8 years. Assume the following yield curve for Treasuries:

Maturity	Yield
6-year	6.2%
8-year	6.3%
10-year	6.4%
15-year	6.6%

   a. What is the nominal spread for this agency passthrough security?
   b. What must occur over the life of this agency passthrough security for the cash flow yield of 7.5% to be realized?

2. Suppose that the monthly cash flow yield is 0.74%. What is the cash flow yield on a bond-equivalent basis?

3. Jane Howard is a corporate bond analyst. Recently she has been asked to extend her responsibilities to mortgage-backed securities. In researching the methodology for valuing mortgage-backed securities she read that these securities are valued using the Monte Carlo simulation model. She was unfamiliar with this approach to valuation because in valuing callable corporate bonds she used the binomial model. Explain to Ms. Howard why the Monte Carlo simulation method is used to value mortgage-backed securities rather than the binomial method.

4. The following questions have to do with the Monte Carlo simulation model.

   a. What assumption must be made in generating the path of short-term interest rates?
   b. Why must the paths of short-term interest rates be adjusted?
   c. In determining the path of refinancing rates, what assumption must be made?

5. Nat Hawthorne, a portfolio manager, discussed the valuation of a particular mortgage-backed security with his broker, Steven Ruthledge. Mr. Hawthorne is considering the purchase of the security and asked what valuation model the brokerage firm used. Mr. Ruthledge responded that the Monte Carlo simulation model was used. Mr. Hawthorne then asked about what prepayment assumption is used in the Monte Carlo simulation model. Mr. Ruthledge responded that for the particular security Mr. Hawthorne is considering, 175 PSA was assumed. Mr. Hawthorne was confused by the response because he did not believe that a particular PSA assumption was made in the Monte Carlo simulation model. Is Mr. Hawthorne correct? Explain your answer.

6. What interest rates are used to value a mortgage-backed security on each interest rate path when using the Monte Carlo simulation model?

7. Juan Rodriquez is the manager of a portfolio containing mortgage passthrough securities. He is reviewing output of his firm's analytical system for several passthrough securities that are in the portfolio. Below is a portion of the report for three passthrough securities:

| Passthrough | Price based on an assumed interest rate volatility of | | | |
	11%	13%	15%	16%
Security 1	100	98	95	93
Security 2	92	90	88	87
Security 3	102	104	106	107

Mr. Rodriquez believes that there is an error in the analytical system. Why does he suspect that there is an error?

8. Suppose that the pool of passthroughs used as collateral for a collateralized mortgage obligation is selling at a premium. Also suppose that one tranche in the deal, Tranche X, is selling at a discount and another tranche, Tranche Y, is selling at a premium.

   a. Explain why a slowdown in prepayments will tend to increase the value of the collateral?

   b. Explain why a slowdown in prepayments will not affect the value of Tranches X and Y in the same way.

9. Assume for simplicity that only ten interest rate paths are used in the Monte Carlo simulation model to a value Tranche W of a CMO deal. Suppose further that based on a spread of 70 basis points, the present value of the interest rate paths is as follows:

Interest rate path	1	2	3	4	5	6	7	8	9	10
PV for path	80	90	84	88	94	92	86	91	99	87

Based on the Monte Carlo simulation model and assuming a spread required by the market of 70 basis points, what is the theoretical value of Tranche W.

10. Jane Hubert is using an analytical system purchased by her firm to analyze mortgage-backed securities. The analytical system uses the Monte Carlo simulation model for valuation. She is given a choice when using the system to use either the "full Monte Carlo analysis" or "16 representative interest rate paths."

   a. What is meant by "16 representative interest path paths"?

   b. How is the theoretical value of a mortgage-backed security determined when representative paths are used?

   c. What is the trade-off when using representative interest rate paths versus using the full Monte Carlo analysis?

11. A portfolio manager is using an analytical system to value Tranche K of a CMO deal. The Monte Carlo simulation model uses eight representative interest rate paths. The present value of each of the representative interest rate paths and the weight of each path are shown below:

Representative path	1	2	3	4	5	6	7	8
Weight of representative path	20%	18%	16%	12%	12%	12%	6%	4%
PV of representative path	70	82	79	68	74	86	91	93

   What is the theoretical value of Tranche K?

12. Mr. Wacker is a bond analyst whose primary responsibility has been to manage the corporate bond portfolio. Recently, his firm's analyst responsible for the mortgage-backed securities portfolio left. Mr. Wacker was asked to monitor the mortgage-backed securities portfolio until an new analyst is hired. The portfolio contains only Ginnie Mae mortgage products. In reviewing the Ginnie Mae portfolio and the option-adjusted spread (OAS) for each security, he was troubled by the values he observed. He was told that the benchmark interest rates used in the calculation of the OAS are Treasury rates. Below are two questions raised by Mr. Wacker. Respond to each one.

   a. "I don't understand why the Ginnie Mae securities in my portfolio have a positive OAS. These securities are backed by the full faith and credit of the U.S. government, so there is no credit risk. Why is there a positive OAS?"

   b. "There are different types of Ginnie Mae mortgage products in the portfolio. There are passthroughs, sequential-pay CMO tranches, planned amortization class CMO tranches, and support CMO tranches. Why do they have different OASs?"

13. Suppose that 10 representative paths are used in the Monte Carlo simulation model and that each path has a weight of 10%. The present value for each representative path is based on discounting the cash flows on an interest rate path by the short-term interest rates on that path plus a spread. For the different spreads used, the present value of each representative path is shown below for Tranche L in a CMO deal:

Representative path	Present value if the spread used is			
	70 bps	75 bps	80 bps	85 bps
1	77	72	70	68
2	82	80	77	72
3	86	84	81	78
4	89	86	83	81
5	74	70	68	65
6	88	86	82	80
7	96	92	88	86
8	92	90	86	84
9	74	71	67	65
10	68	64	61	59

   a. Suppose that the market price of Tranche L is 79.5. What is the option-adjusted spread?

b. Suppose instead of a market price for Tranche L of 79.5 the market price is 73.8. What is the option-adjusted spread?

14. Below are the results of a Monte Carlo simulation analysis using eight representative paths for two tranches of a CMO deal, Tranches M and N:

Representative path	1	2	3	4	5	6	7	8
PV of path for:								
Tranche M	60	55	90	105	110	50	48	70
Tranche N	86	85	89	91	84	92	87	86

One of the tranches is a PAC tranche and the other is a support tranche. Which tranche is probably the PAC tranche and which is probably the support tranche?

15. An analysis of an agency CMO structure using the Monte Carlo simulation model based on 12% volatility found the following:

	OAS (basis points)	Z-spread (basis points)	Effective duration
Collateral	90	130	8.0
Tranche			
PAC I A	50	60	1.5
PAC I B	70	80	3.0
PAC I C	30	120	5.0
PAC I D	30	150	9.0
PAC II A	80	150	4.0
PAC II B	20	280	6.0
Support S1	35	165	11.0
Support S2	50	190	14.0

a. What is the option cost for PAC IA, PAC II A, and Support S1?
b. Which of the PAC tranches appears to be expensive in the deal on a relative value basis?
c. PAC II tranches are support tranches with schedules. The four support tranches in the deal are therefore PAC II A, PAC II B, Support S1, and Support S2. Which of the support tranches appears to be expensive on a relative value basis?
d. Despite its low OAS of 20 basis points, why might a yield buyer be induced to purchase PAC II B?

16. How is the effective duration and effective convexity of a mortgage-backed security computed using the Monte Carlo simulation model? Be sure to explain what assumption is made regarding the option-adjusted spread when computing the effective duration and effective convexity.

17. Joel Winters is a junior portfolio manager of a corporate bond portfolio. A decision has been made to include mortgage-backed securities in the portfolio. Mr. Winters is considering the purchase of a CMO tranche called a support bond. Before he buys this tranche, he wants to know its effective duration. Because he does not have the use of an analytical system to compute effective duration, Mr. Winters contacts three dealers and inquires as to the effective duration for this tranche. He is given the following effective duration from the three dealer firms:

Dealer	1	2	3
Effective duration	8.1	4.6	11.6

Mr. Winters is puzzled by the significant variation in the effective durations, especially since all the dealers indicated that the Monte Carlo simulation model was used. In his experience with corporate bonds with embedded options he has never observed such a significant variation in the effective duration from dealer firm to dealer firm.

Explain to Mr. Winters why there is such a significant variation in the effective durations. Be sure to clearly identify the reasons for the variation in the effective durations.

18. Explain why you agree or disagree with the following statement: "If the collateral for a CMO deal has negative convexity, then all the tranches in the deal must have negative convexity. The only difference is the degree of negative convexity from one tranche to another."

19. a. What is the cash flow duration of a mortgage-backed security?
    b. What are the limitations of cash flow duration as a measure of the price sensitivity of a mortgage-backed security to changes in interest rates?

20. Suppose that the coupon curve of prices for a passthrough security for some month is as follows:

Coupon	Price
7%	94.00
8%	97.06
9%	99.50
10%	102.60
11%	105.25
12%	106.19

What is the coupon curve duration for the 9% coupon passthrough?

21. Karen Brown is considering alternative measures for estimating the duration of some complex CMO tranches. One measure she is considering is empirical duration. Explain to Ms. Brown the difficulties of using empirical duration for complex CMO tranches.

22. Thomas Larken is a portfolio manager who is considering investing in the asset-backed securities market. In particular, Mr. Larken is considering investing in either credit card receivables, auto loan-backed securities, or prime home equity loan-backed securities. Examination of the nominal spreads in these three sectors of the market indicates that the largest nominal spread for AAA and AA issues is home equity loan-backed securities. Based on this analysis, Mr. Larken believes that the best sector in which to invest is in home equity loan-backed securities because it offers the greatest relative value as measured by the nominal spread. Explain whether or not you agree with Mr. Larken's assessment of the relative attractiveness of home equity loan-backed securities.

23. An investment banker has created an asset-backed security in which the collateral is the future royalties of a song writer. Which valuation approach do you think should be used to value this security, the zero-volatility spread or the option-adjusted spread?

24. Suppose that empirical evidence on prepayments for manufactured housing loans suggests that borrowers do not take advantage of refinancing when interest rates decline. Explain whether the zero-volatility spread approach or OAS approach is appropriate for valuing securities backed by manufacturing housing loans.

25. Evidence by Wall Street firms on home equity loans strongly suggests that high quality borrowers do take advantage of a decline in interest rates to refinance a loan. In contrast, low quality borrowers tend not to take advantage of a decline in interest rates to refinance.

    a. What is the appropriate valuation approach (option-adjusted spread approach or zero-volatility spread approach) to value home equity loan-backed securities where the underlying pool of loans are those of high quality borrowers? Explain why.
    b. What is the appropriate valuation approach (option-adjusted spread approach or zero-volatility spread approach) to value home equity loan-backed securities where the underlying pool of loans are those of low quality borrowers? Explain why.

CHAPTER 13

INTEREST RATE DERIVATIVE INSTRUMENTS

LEARNING OUTCOMES

After reading Chapter 13 you should be able to:

- discuss the characteristics of interest rate futures and forward contracts.
- calculate the implied repo rate for an acceptable to-deliver bond for a Treasury futures contract and demonstrate how this rate is used to choose the cheapest-to-deliver issue.
- contrast (1) interest rate options and interest rate futures, (2) exchange-traded-options and over-the-counter options, and (3) futures options on fixed income securities and options on fixed income securities.
- characterize the change in the value of an interest rate swap for each counterparty when interest rates change.
- compare the position of (1) the counterparties in an interest rate swap to the counterparties in an interest rate futures and (2) the counterparties in an interest rate swap to the counterparties in a floating rate bond purchased by borrowing on a fixed-rate basis.
- demonstrate how both a cap and a floor are packages of (1) options on interest rates and (2) options on fixed income instruments.
- compute the payoff for a cap and a floor and explain how a collar is created.

SUMMARY OVERVIEW

- A futures contract is an agreement between a buyer (seller) and an established exchange or its clearinghouse in which the buyer (seller) agrees to take (make) delivery of something at a specified price at the end of a designated period of time.
- A forward contract is an agreement for the future delivery of something at a specified price at a designated time, but differs from a futures contract in that it is usually non-standardized and traded in the over-the-counter market.
- An investor who takes a long futures position realizes a gain when the futures price increases; an investor who takes a short futures position realizes a gain when the futures price decreases.
- The parties to a futures contract are required to satisfy margin requirements.
- Parties to over-the-counter interest rate contracts are exposed to counterparty risk which is the risk that the counterparty will not satisfy its contractual obligations.

- For the Treasury bond futures contract the underlying instrument is $100,000 par value of a hypothetical 20-year 6% coupon Treasury bond.
- Conversion factors are used to adjust the invoice price of a Treasury bond futures contract to make delivery equitable to both parties.
- The short in a Treasury bond futures contract has several delivery options: quality option (or swap option), timing option, and wildcard option.
- For all the issues that may be delivered to satisfy a Treasury futures contract, a rate of return can be computed in a cash and carry trade; the rate of return is called the implied repo rate.
- For all the issues that may be delivered to satisfy a Treasury futures contract, the cheapest-to-deliver issue is the one with the highest implied repo rate.
- By varying the yield on Treasury bonds, it can be determined which issue will become the new cheapest-to-deliver issue.
- There are futures contracts in which the underlying is a Fannie Mae and Freddie Mac debenture.
- An option is a contract in which the writer of the option grants the buyer of the option the right, but not the obligation, to purchase from or sell to the writer something at a specified price within a specified period of time (or at a specified date).
- The option buyer pays the option writer (seller) a fee, called the option price (or premium).
- A call option allows the option buyer to purchase the underlying from the option writer at the strike price; a put option allows the option buyer to sell the underlying to the option writer at the strike price.
- Interest rate options include options on fixed income securities and options on interest rate futures contracts; the latter, called futures options, are the preferred exchange-traded vehicle for implementing investment strategies.
- Because of the difficulties of hedging particular fixed income securities, some institutional investors have found over-the-counter options more useful.
- An interest rate swap is an agreement specifying that the parties exchange interest payments at designated times, with a generic or vanilla swap calling for one party to make fixed-rate payments and the other to make floating-rate payments based on a notional principal.
- The swap rate is the interest rate paid by the fixed-rate payer.
- The swap spread is the spread paid by the fixed-rate payer over the on-the-run Treasury rate with the same maturity as the swap agreement.
- The convention in quoting swaps is to quote the payments made by the floating-rate payer flat (that is, without a spread) and the fixed-rate payer payments as a spread to the on-the-run Treasury with the same maturity as the swap (the swap spread)
- A swap position can be interpreted as either a package of forward/futures contracts or a package of cash flows from buying and selling cash market instruments.
- An interest rate cap specifies that one party receive a payment if the reference rate is above the cap rate; an interest rate floor specifies that one party receive a payment if a reference rate is below the floor rate.
- The terms of a cap and floor set forth the reference rate, the strike rate, the length of the agreement, the frequency of reset, and the notional amount.
- In an interest rate cap and floor, the buyer pays an upfront fee, which represents the maximum amount that the buyer can lose and the maximum amount that the seller of the agreement can gain.
- Buying a cap is equivalent to buying a package of puts on a fixed income security and buying a floor is equivalent to buying a package of calls on a fixed income security.

- If an option is viewed as one in which the underlying is an interest rate, then buying a cap is equivalent to buying a package of calls on interest rates and buying a floor is equivalent to buying a package of puts on interest rates.
- An interest collar is created by buying an interest rate cap and selling an interest rate floor.
- Forward contracts and swaps expose the parties to bilateral counterparty risk while buyers of OTC options, caps, and floors face unilateral counterparty risk.

PROBLEMS

1. What is the counterparty risk associated with a derivative instrument?
2. Explain why you agree or disagree with the following statement: "One difference between futures and forward contracts is that futures contracts are marked to market while forward contracts are not."
3. Explain why you agree or disagree with the following statement: "Futures and forward contracts expose the parties to the same degree of counterparty risk."
4. Eileen Morris is the manager of a bond portfolio and has recently received authorization to use Treasury futures contracts. The chief investment officer of her firm, Rita Gomez, advised Ms. Morris to be sure to keep sufficient cash available to satisfy any contingency payments that must be made as a result of the futures positions. Ms. Morris was not clear as to why any contingency payments must be made. She has asked you to explain why. What is your response?
5. George Salvich is an equity portfolio manager who uses stock index futures. He is considering managing a balanced fund (i.e., a fund that includes both equities and bonds). He would like to use Treasury bond futures in managing the bond component of the fund. He was told by a broker that the underlying for a Treasury bond futures contract is $100,000 par value of a 20-year 6% coupon Treasury bond. The broker noted that no such Treasury bond exists. Mr. Salvich responded that the contract was probably a cash settlement contract because there is no deliverable. How should the broker respond?
6. a. Why is it necessary to have conversion factors for a Treasury futures contract?
   b. How is the converted price of an issue that is acceptable for delivery for a Treasury futures contract computed?
7. Suppose that the June 200X futures contract settles at 105–08 and the issue delivered has a conversion factor of 1.21. Assume that the accrued interest for the issue delivered is $5,300 per $100,000 par value. What is the invoice price the buyer must pay the seller?
8. Calculate the implied repo rate for a hypothetical issue that is deliverable for a Treasury bond futures contract assuming the following for the deliverable issue and the futures contract:

   Futures contract

   Futures price = $102

   days to futures delivery date $(days_1)$ = 114 days

   Deliverable issue

   price of issue = $96

   accrued interest paid = $3.2219

   coupon rate = 8%

   days remaining before interim coupon made = 79 days

interim coupon = $4.00

number of days between when the interim coupon payment is received
 and the actual delivery date of the futures contract (day_2) = 35 days

conversion factor = 0.9305

accrued interest received at futures settlement date = $1.7315

Other information:

35-day term repo rate = 5%

9. a. What is the implied repo rate for a deliverable Treasury issue?
    b. What is meant by the cheapest-to-deliver issue?
10. Suppose that a government bond futures contract of some country has the same delivery requirements as the U.S. Treasury bond futures contract. Suppose further that there are four possible issues that are acceptable for delivery and the short has the choice of which to deliver. These issues and information about them are shown in the table below. Each of the issues that may be delivered has no accrued interest and the next coupon payment is six months from now. The futures price for the government bond contract that settles in six months (just when each of the five issues matures) is 99.50. (Note: the futures price and the prices of each issue in this question are in decimal form, not $^1\!/_{32}$.)

Issue	Market price ($)	Coupon rate (%)	Conversion factor
1	$79.48	4.0%	0.8215
2	86.54	5.7	0.8942
3	104.77	9.0	1.0544
4	109.22	9.6	1.1123

Determine the cheapest-to-deliver issue?

11. Describe the following delivery options granted to the seller of the Treasury bond futures contract.

    a. quality or swap option
    b. timing option
    c. wild card option

12. What is the maximum amount the buyer of an option can lose?
13. Suppose an investor purchases a call option on a Treasury bond futures contract with a strike price of $91.

    a. If at the expiration date the price of the Treasury bond futures contract is $96, will the investor exercise the call option and, if so, what will the investor and the writer of the call option receive?
    b. If at the expiration date the price of the Treasury bond futures contract is $89, will the investor exercise the call option and, if so, what will the investor and the writer of the call option receive?

14. Suppose an investor purchases a put option on a Treasury bond futures contract with a strike price of $97.

    a. If at the expiration date the price of the Treasury bond futures contract is $99, will the investor exercise the put option and, if so, what will the investor and the writer of the put option receive?
    b. If at the expiration date the price of the Treasury bond futures contract is $91, will the investor exercise the put option and, if so, what will the investor and the writer of the put option receive?

15. a. What is the motivation for the purchase of an over-the-counter option by an institutional investor?
     b. Does it make sense for an investor who wants to speculate on interest rate movements to purchase an over-the-counter option versus exchange-traded options?
16. In an interest rate swap what is meant by the swap rate and the swap spread?
17. Suppose that Ted Munson, a portfolio manager, enters into a 3-year interest rate swap with a commercial bank that is a swap dealer. The notional amount for the swap is $40 million and the reference rate is 3-month LIBOR. Suppose that the payments are made quarterly. The swap rate that Mr. Munson agrees to pay is 5.6%.

     a. Who is the fixed-rate payer and who is the fixed-rate receiver in this swap?
     b. What are the payments that must be made by the fixed-rate payer every quarter?
     c. Suppose for the first floating-rate payment 3-month LIBOR is 3.6%. What is the amount of the first floating-rate payment that must be made by the fixed-rate receiver?

18. Give two interpretations of an interest rate swap and explain why an interest rate swap can be interpreted in each way.
19. Suppose that interest rates decrease subsequent to the inception of an interest rate swap.

     a. What is the effect on the value of the swap from the perspective of the fixed-rate payer?
     b. What is the effect on the value of the swap from the perspective of the fixed-rate receiver?

20. Why is the fixed-rate payer in an interest rate swap said to be "short the bond market"?
21. Suppose that a 1-year cap has a cap rate of 8% and a notional amount of $10 million. The frequency of settlement is quarterly and the reference rate is 3-month LIBOR. Assume that 3-month LIBOR for the next four quarters is as shown below. What is the payoff for each quarter?

Period	3-month LIBOR
1	8.7%
2	8.0%
3	7.8%
4	8.2%

22. Suppose that a 1-year floor has a floor rate of 4% and a notional amount of $20 million. The frequency of settlement is quarterly and the reference rate is 3-month LIBOR. Assume that 3-month LIBOR for the next four quarters is as shown below. What is the payoff for each quarter?

Period	3-month LIBOR
1	4.7%
2	4.4%
3	3.8%
4	3.4%

23. What counterparty risk is the seller of an interest rate floor exposed to?
24. a. What is an interest rate cap or floor equivalent to?
    b. What is a caplet and a floorlet?

CHAPTER 14

VALUATION OF INTEREST RATE DERIVATIVE INSTRUMENTS

LEARNING OUTCOMES

After reading Chapter 14 you should be able to:

- compute the profit or loss generated in a cash and carry trade and in a reverse cash and carry trade using futures.
- compute the theoretical price of an interest rate futures contract.
- explain how the theoretical price of a Treasury bond futures contract is affected by the delivery options.
- explain the complications in extending the standard arbitrage pricing model to the valuation of Treasury bond and Treasury note futures contracts.
- compute the floating-rate payments in an interest rate swap given the futures price of a Eurodollar CD futures contract.
- justify the appropriate interest rate to use in calculating the present value of the payments in an interest rate swap.
- calculate the forward discount factor used to discount the swap payments given the forward rates.
- explain how the swap rate and swap spread are determined.
- explain how the value of a swap is determined.
- calculate the swap rate, swap spread, and value of a swap.
- compute the new floating-rate payments and value for a swap if interest rates change.
- discuss the factors that affect the value of an option, or options on futures, for a fixed income instrument.
- explain the limitations of applying the Black-Scholes model to valuing options on bonds.
- compute the value of an option on a bond using the arbitrage-free binomial model.
- discuss the Black model for valuing options on futures.
- explain how to measure the sensitivity of an option to changes in the factors that affect its value.
- compare the roles of delta and duration in approximating price changes.
- compute the value of each caplet and the value of a cap and a floor given a binomial interest rate tree.

SUMMARY OVERVIEW

- A cash and carry trade and a reverse cash and carry trade can be used to determine the arbitrage profit available from a futures strategy.
- A cash and carry trade and a reverse cash and carry trade can be used to determine the theoretical price of a futures contract.
- The theoretical price of a futures contract is equal to the cash or spot price plus the cost of carry.
- The cost of carry is equal to the cost of financing the position less the cash yield on the underlying security.
- The shape of the yield curve affects the cost of carry.
- The "cash and carry" arbitrage model must be modified to take into consideration the nuances of a particular futures contract.
- For a Treasury bond futures contract, the delivery options granted to the seller reduce the theoretical futures price below the theoretical futures price suggested by the "cash and carry" arbitrage model.
- To compute the payments for both parties to an interest rate swap, the number of days in the payment period must be determined.
- The first floating-rate swap payment is determined by the current value of the reference rate.
- In a swap where the reference rate is 3-month LIBOR, the Eurodollar CD futures contract provides the forward rate for locking in future floating-rate payments, as well as the forward rates that should be used for discounting all swap payments.
- In determining the present value of swap payments, care must be exercised in determining exactly when the payments will occur.
- The forward rates obtained from Eurodollar CD futures contracts are used to compute the forward discount factor.
- The forward discount factor for a period multiplied by the swap payment for a period determines the present value of the swap payment.
- At the inception of a swap, the present value of the floating-rate payments must equal the present value of the fixed-rate payments to prevent arbitrage.
- The swap rate is the rate that will produce fixed-rate payments such that the present value of these payments is equal to the present value of the floating-rate payments.
- The swap spread is the difference between the swap rate and the rate on a selected benchmark.
- When interest rates change in the market, the future floating-rate payments will change, but the fixed-rate payments do not change.
- When interest rates change in the market, the forward rates change and therefore the present value of the swap payments changes.
- The value of a swap is the difference in the present value of the swap payments for a party to a swap—that is, the difference between the present value of the payments to be received and the present value of the payments to be paid.
- The value of an option is equal to its intrinsic value plus its time value.
- The six factors that affect the value of an option are the price of the underlying security, the strike price of the option, the time to expiration of the option, the expected interest rate volatility over the life of the option, the short-term risk-free interest rate over the life of the option, and the coupon interest payment over the life of the option.
- Several assumptions underlying the Black-Scholes model limit its use in pricing options on bonds.

- The arbitrage-free binomial model is the proper model to value options on bonds since it takes into account the yield curve.
- The most common option pricing model for bonds is the Black-Derman-Toy model.
- The Black model is the most common model for valuing options on bond futures.
- Money managers need to know how sensitive an option's value is to changes in the factors that affect the value of an option.
- The delta of an option measures how sensitive the option price is to changes in the price of the underlying bond and varies from minus one (for put options deep in the money) to zero (for call options deep out of the money) to one (for call options deep in the money).
- The gamma of an option measures the rate of change of delta as the price of the underlying bond changes.
- The theta of an option measures the change in the option price as the time to expiration decreases.
- The kappa of an option measures the change in the price of the option for a 1% change in expected interest rate volatility.
- The arbitrage binomial method can be used to value a cap or a floor.
- The valuation of a cap (floor) involves first determining the value of each caplet (floorlet).
- The value of a cap (or floor) is the sum of the values of all the caplets (floorlets).

PROBLEMS

1. a. Suppose that the price of a bond futures contract that settles in four months is $101 and the price of the underlying bond is $98. The underlying bond has a coupon rate of 9%, par value of $100, and the next coupon payment is to be made in six months. The borrowing rate is 7.2% per annum. If an investor implemented a cash and carry trade, what would the arbitrage profit be?
   b. Suppose that instead of a futures price of $101, the futures price is $96. If an investor implemented a reverse cash and carry trade, what would the arbitrage profit be?
   c. What is the theoretical futures price?
   d. Demonstrate using a cash and carry trade that the theoretical futures price computed in part c will produce no arbitrage profit.
2. a. Suppose that the underlying bond for a futures contract has a coupon rate of 6%, par value of $100, and the next coupon payment is to be made in six months. Suppose further that the cash market price for this bond is 94. What is the theoretical futures price for a contract that settles in five months if the borrowing rate is 4.6% per annum?
   b. Suppose that the futures price is $93.25. Given your answer to a, is there an arbitrage opportunity and, if so, what strategy will generate that arbitrage profit?
   c. Suppose that instead of a single financing rate of 4.6%, there is a borrowing rate of 4.7% and a lending rate of 4.3%. If the futures price is $93.25, is there an arbitrage opportunity available?
3. Explain what the effect of delivery options for the Treasury bond futures contract are on its theoretical futures price and why these delivery options affect the theoretical futures price.
4. Mr. Robert Thompson is an investment manager. Recently, he attended a conference on opportunities in futures markets. Based on the information presented at the conference, he believes that he can enhance returns by exploiting mispriced Treasury bond futures contracts. He saw how a mispriced futures contracts can be exploited to lock in an arbitrage profit by either a cash and carry trade or a reverse cash and carry trade.

   According to the material distributed at the conference, the theoretical price of a futures contract is determined by the cash market price and the cost of carry. Material distributed at the conference provided a general formula for the theoretical price of any futures contract (e.g., stock index futures contracts, foreign exchange futures contracts, commodity futures contracts). When Mr. Thompson applied the general formula for the theoretical futures price to the Treasury bond futures contract he found that the price of the futures contract in the market was always above that of the theoretical futures price given by the general formula. Based on this observation, Mr. Thompson told his clients that there was ample mispricing in the Treasury bond futures market and requested that they give him authorization to trade Treasury bond futures contracts to enhance portfolio returns.

Do you believe that Mr. Thompson can exploit arbitrage opportunities based on his observation of the mispricing of the Treasury bond futures contract?

5. Consider the following interest rate swap:

   - swap starts today, January 1 of year 1 (swap settlement date)
   - the floating-rate payments are made quarterly based on "actual/360"
   - the reference rate is 3-month LIBOR
   - the notional amount of the swap is $40 million
   - the term of the swap is three years

   a. Suppose that today 3-month LIBOR is 5.7%. What will the fixed-rate payer for this interest rate swap receive on March 31 of year 1 (assuming that year 1 is not a leap year)?

   b. Assume the Eurodollar CD futures price for the next seven quarters are as shown below:

Quarter starts	Quarter ends	No. of days in quarter	3-month Eurodollar CD futures price
April 1 year 1	June 30 year 1	91	94.10
July 1 year 1	Sept 30 year 1	92	94.00
Oct 1 year 1	Dec 31 year 1	92	93.70
Jan 1 year 2	Mar 31 year 1	90	93.60
April 1 year 2	June 30 year 2	91	93.50
July 1 year 2	Sept 30 year 2	92	93.20
Oct 1 year 2	Dec 31 year 2	92	93.00

   Compute the forward rate for each quarter and the floating-rate payment at the end of each quarter.

   c. What is the present value of the floating-rate payment at the end of each quarter for this interest rate swap?

6. a. Assume that the swap rate for an interest rate swap is 7% and that the fixed-rate swap payments are made quarterly on an "actual/360 basis." If the notional amount of a 2-year swap is $20 million, what is the fixed-rate payment at the end of each quarter assuming the following number of days in each quarter:

Period quarter	Days in quarter
1	92
2	92
3	90
4	91
5	92
6	92
7	90
8	91

b. Assume that the swap in part a requires payments semiannually rather than quarterly. What is the semiannual fixed-rate payment?

c. Suppose that the notional amount for the 2-year swap is not the same in both years. Suppose instead that in year 1 the notional amount is $20 million, but in year 2 the notional amount is $12 million. What is the fixed-rate payment every six months?

7. Given the current 3-month LIBOR and the five CD Eurodollar CD futures prices shown in the table below, compute the forward rate and the forward discount factor for each period.

Period	Days in quarter	Current 3-month LIBOR	3-month Eurodollar CD CD futures price
1	90	5.90%	
2	91		93.90
3	92		93.70
4	92		93.45
5	90		93.20
6	91		93.15

8. a. Suppose at the inception of a 5-year interest rate swap in which the reference rate is 3-month LIBOR the present value of the floating-rate payments is $16,555,000. The fixed-rate payments are assumed to be semiannual. Assume also that the following is computed for the fixed-rate payments (using the notation in the chapter):

$$\sum_{t=1}^{10} \text{notional amount} \times \frac{\text{Days}_t}{360} \times \text{FDF}_t = \$236,500,000$$

What is the swap rate for this swap?

b. Suppose that the 5-year yield from the on-the-run Treasury yield curve is 6.4%. What is the swap spread?

9. An interest rate swap had an original maturity of five years. Today, the swap has two years to maturity. The present value of the fixed-rate payments for the remainder of the term of the swap is $910,000. The present value of the floating-rate payments for the remainder of the swap is $710,000.

a. What is the value of this swap from the perspective of the fixed-rate payer?

b. What is the value of this swap from the perspective of the fixed-rate receiver?

10. Suppose that an interest rate swap has one year remaining. The notional amount of the swap is $50 million and all payments (fixed rate and floating rate) are quarterly based on an "actual/360" day count basis. The reference rate is 3-month LIBOR.

a. Complete the following table for the forward rate, period forward rate, and forward discount factor given the information below:

Period	Days in quarter	Current 3-month LIBOR	3-month Eurodollar CD futures price	Forward rate	Period forward rate	Forward discount factor
1	90	5.90%				
2	91		93.90			
3	92		93.70			
4	92		93.45			

b. Complete the following table for the floating-rate payment given the period forward rate in part a:

Period	Days in quarter	Period forward rate	Floating-rate payment
1	90		
2	91		
3	92		
4	92		

c. If the swap rate is 8%, compute the following:

Period	Days in quarter	Fixed-rate payment based on swap rate
1	90	
2	91	
3	92	
4	92	

d. What is the value of this 1-year swap given the values computed in parts a, b, and c from the perspective of the fixed-rate payer?

e. What is the value of this 1-year swap given the values computed in parts a, b, and c from the perspective of the fixed-rate receiver?

11. Complete the table below for the six options specified in the first column. Assume that the bond's price in the third column means the price of the underlying bond and that each option expires in one year:

Type of option	Strike price	Bond's price	Option price	In, at, or out of the money	Intrinsic value	Time value
call	94	90	7			
call	102	104	6			
call	88	88	3			
put	106	110	5			
put	92	92	9			
put	95	89	11			

12. After a period of extreme interest rate volatility that saw interest rates increase, an investor observed that the price of both put and call options on bond futures increased even though bond prices decreased. The investor was confused because he thought that a rise in rates resulting in a decline in the price of a bond would adversely affect the price of call options, not increase their price. Explain to this investor why the call options increased in price.

13. Herman Mills is a bond portfolio manager who is just learning about options on bonds. In college, he learned about options on common stock and he was introduced to the Black-Scholes option pricing model. Mr. Mills has asked you whether or not it is appropriate to apply the Black-Scholes option pricing model to valuing options on bonds. What is your response?

14. Use the following arbitrage-free binomial interest rate tree to answer the questions that follow:

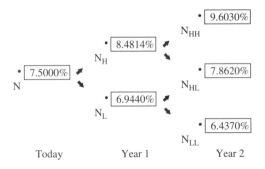

a. What is the value of a 3-year Treasury bond with a 9% coupon rate?
b. What is the value of a 2-year call option on a bond that currently has three years to maturity and coupon rate of 9% if the strike price is 98? Assume in this calculation that the current price of the 3-year Treasury bond is the value found in part a.
c. What is the value of a 2-year put option on a bond that currently has three years to maturity and coupon rate of 9% if the strike price is 105? Assume in this calculation that the current price of the 3-year Treasury bond is the value found in part a.

15. a. What is the most common model for valuing options on Treasury bond futures contracts?
    b. What are the limitations of this model?
16. Assume the following:

$$
\begin{array}{ll}
\text{Price of a call option} & = \$1.70 \\
\text{Price of underlying bond} & = 70 \\
\text{Strike price for call option} & = 115 \\
\text{Time to expiration} & = 2 \text{ years}
\end{array}
$$

Without doing any calculations, explain what you believe the value of the delta of this call option is?

17. The duration and convexity measure of a bond are used to approximate the change in the price of a bond if interest rates change. What two measures play a similar role in trying to estimate the price of an option if the price of the underlying bond changes?
18. a. Would the buyer of an option prefer a high or low theta?
    b. If an investor anticipates a rise in expected interest rate volatility that is currently not priced into an option, would this investor prefer an option on a bond with a high or low kappa?
19. Answer the following questions based on the following binomial interest rate tree:

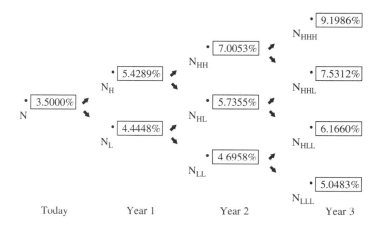

Consider a 3-year cap with a cap rate of 4% and the payoff for the cap is annual. Suppose that the notional amount of the cap is $25 million.

a. What is the value of the Year 1 caplet?
b. What is the value of the Year 2 caplet?
c. What is the value of the Year 3 caplet?
d. What is the value of the 3-year cap?

20. Using the binomial interest rate tree from the previous question, answer the following questions for a 3-year floor with a floor rate of 5.5% where the payoff is annual. Assume that the notional amount of the floor is $50 million.

a. What is the value of the Year 1 floorlet?
b. What is the value of the Year 2 floorlet?
c. What is the value of the Year 3 floorlet?
d. What is the value of the 3-year floor?

CHAPTER 15

GENERAL PRINCIPLES OF CREDIT ANALYSIS

LEARNING OUTCOMES

After reading Chapter 15 you should be able to:

- distinguish among default risk, credit spread risk, and downgrade risk.
- describe the meaning of credit ratings, rating watches, and rating outlooks.
- explain how credit analysis encompasses assessing the borrower's character (including the quality of management) and capacity to repay (including sources of liquidity), and the issue's underlying collateral and covenants.
- compute the key ratios used by credit analysts to assess the ability of a company to satisfy its debt obligations and explain the limitations of these ratios.
- evaluate the credit quality of an issuer of a corporate bond, given such data as key financial ratios for the issuer and the industry.
- evaluate the credit quality of an asset-backed, non-agency mortgage-backed security, municipal bond, or sovereign bond, given information about the issuer.
- describe corporate governance ratings.
- discuss why and how cash flow from operations is used to assess the ability of an issuer to service its debt obligations and to assess the financial flexibility of a company.
- describe the various covenants and discuss their importance in assessing credit risk for both investment grade and non-investment grade companies.
- explain the typical elements of the debt structure of a high-yield issuer, the interrelationships among these elements, and the impact of these elements on the risk position of the lender.
- explain the importance of the corporate structure of a high-yield issuer that has a holding company.
- explain why some investors advocate using an equity perspective when analyzing the creditworthiness of high-yield issues.
- discuss the factors considered by rating agencies in rating asset-backed securities (i.e., collateral credit quality, seller/servicer quality, cash flow stress and payment structure, and legal structure).
- explain how the creditworthiness of municipal bonds is assessed, and contrast the analysis of tax-backed debt with the analysis of revenue obligations.
- discuss the key economic and political risks considered by Standard & Poor's in assigning sovereign ratings.
- explain why two ratings are assigned to each national government and discuss the key factors emphasized by Standard & Poor's for each rating.

- contrast the credit analysis required for corporate bonds with that required for: (1) asset-backed securities, (2) municipal securities, and (3) sovereign debt.
- describe what a credit scoring model is and its limitations in predicting corporate bankruptcy.
- explain structural and reduced form credit risk models and compare these two types of models.

SUMMARY OVERVIEW

- There are three types of credit risk: default risk, credit spread risk, and downgrade risk.
- Default risk is the risk that the issuer will fail to meet its obligation to make timely payment of interest and principal.
- Credit spread risk is the risk that the spread that the market demands for an issue will increase or widen, resulting in inferior performance of an issue relative to other issues.
- Downgrade risk is the risk that the issue will be downgraded, resulting in an increase in the credit spread demanded by the market.
- For long-term debt obligations, a credit rating is a forward-looking assessment of (1) the probability of default and (2) the relative magnitude of the loss should a default occur. For short-term debt obligations (i.e., obligations with initial maturities of one year or less), a credit rating is a forward-looking assessment of the probability of default.
- A rating agency monitors the credit quality of the issuer and can reassign a different credit rating to its bonds (an upgrade or a downgrade).
- Before an issue's rating is changed, typically a rating agency will place on rating watch or credit watch that it is reviewing the issue with the potential for upgrade or downgrade.
- Rating agencies issue rating outlooks, a projection as to whether an issue in the long term is likely to be upgraded, downgraded, or maintain its current rating.
- A credit analyst must consider the four C's of credit—character, capacity, collateral, and covenants.
- Character relates to the ethical reputation as well as the business qualifications and operating record of the board of directors, management, and executives responsible for the use of the borrowed funds and its repayment.
- Capacity deals with the ability of an issuer to repay its obligations.
- Collateral involves not only the traditional pledging of assets to secure the debt, but also the quality and value of those unpledged assets controlled by the issuer.
- Covenants are important because they impose restrictions on how management operates the company and conducts its financial affairs.
- The statement of cash flows is used in the analysis of an entity's ability to repay its financial obligations and to gain insight into an entity's financing methods, capital investment strategies, and dividend policy.
- To assess the ability of a company to meet its financial obligations, an analyst looks at profitability ratios that help explain the underlying causes of a change in the company's earnings.
- One of the best ways an analyst can predict future downward earnings is through a careful analysis of accounts receivable and inventories; two signs that can indicate problems are a larger than average accounts receivable balance situation and/or a bloated inventory.
- There are three sets of ratios that are used by credit analysts as indicators to assess the ability of a firm to satisfy its debt obligations: (1) short-term solvency ratios which assess the ability of the firm to meet debts maturing over the coming year, (2) capitalization (or

financial leverage) ratios which assess the extent to which the firm relies on debt financing, and (3) coverage ratios which assess the ability of the firm to meet the fixed obligations brought about by debt financing.

- Analysts have reformatted the information from the firm's income statement and statement of cash flows to obtain what they view as a better description of the company's activities; these measures include funds from operations, operating cash flow, free operating cash flow, discretionary cash flow, and prefinancing cash flow.

- Negative covenants are covenants which require the borrower not to take certain actions; some of the more common restrictive covenants include various limitations on the company's ability to incur debt.

- There are two types of interest or fixed charge coverage tests: (1) a maintenance test which requires the borrower's ratio of earnings available for interest or fixed charges to be at least a certain minimum figure and (2) a debt incurrence test when the company wishes to do additional borrowing; in addition, there could be cash flow tests or requirements and working capital maintenance provisions.

- In assessing management quality, analysts consider the corporation's (1) strategic direction, (2) financial philosophy, (3) conservatism, (4) track record, (5) succession planning, and (6) control systems.

- Corporate financial theory helps us understand how the abuses that diminish shareholder value arise (agency problem) and the potential for mitigating the abuse.

- The corporate bylaws are the rules of governance; independent organizations have developed corporate governance ratings.

- In analyzing the credit worthiness of high-yield corporate bond issuers, the analyst will want to pay close attention to the characteristics of the debt obligations in the capital structure.

- The corporate structure is particularly important to investigate when assessing the credit worthiness of high-yield corporate bond issuers where there is a holding company structure because of potential limitations or restrictions on cash flow from operating subsidiaries to the parent company and among operating subsidiaries.

- Covenants in high-yield corporate bond issues should be reviewed in conjunction with the issuer's overall strategy.

- Some analysts believe that in assessing the credit quality of a high-yield corporate bond issuer an equity analysis approach is more informative than simply a traditional credit analysis approach.

- In analyzing the credit risk of an asset-backed security, rating companies basically look at four factors: (1) the credit quality of the collateral; (2) the quality of the seller/servicer, (3) cash flow stress test and payment (financial) structures, and (4) legal structure.

- A key factor in assessing the quality of the collateral is the amount of equity the borrower has in the asset.

- To reduce concentration risk in an asset-backed security, rating companies impose concentration limits.

- Based on their analysis of the four factors in assigning ratings, rating companies will determine the amount of credit enhancement needed for an issue to receive a particular rating.

- Fundamentally, because of the absence of operational risk, an asset-backed security transaction generally has greater certainty about the cash flow than a corporate bond issue.

- A true asset-backed security transaction involves minimal involvement by the servicer beyond administrative functions.

- In a hybrid asset-backed security transaction, the servicer has more than an administrative function; the greater the importance of the servicer, the more the transaction should be evaluated as a quasi-corporate entity.
- In assessing the credit risk of tax-backed debt, four basic informational categories should be considered: (1) information on the issuer's debt structure to determine the overall debt burden; (2) information on the issuer's ability and political discipline to maintain sound budgetary policy; (3) information on the specific local taxes and intergovernmental revenues available to the issuer; and, (4) information on the issuer's overall socioeconomic environment.
- While there are numerous security structures for revenue bonds, the underlying principle in rating is whether the project being financed will generate sufficient cash flows to satisfy the obligations due bondholders.
- The principles involved in analyzing the credit risk of a revenue bond are the same as for a corporate bond.
- In assessing the credit risk for revenue bonds, the trust indenture and legal opinion should provide legal comfort in the following bond-security areas: (1) the limits of the basic security, (2) the flow-of-funds structure, (3) the rate, or user-charge, covenant, (4) the priority-of-revenue claims, (5) the additional-bonds tests, and (6) other relevant covenants.
- Sovereign credits are rated by Standard & Poor's and Moody's.
- In deriving ratings, the two general categories analyzed are economic risk (the ability to pay) and political risk (the willingness to pay).
- There are two ratings assigned to each central government: a local currency debt rating and a foreign currency debt rating.
- Historically, defaults have been greater on foreign currency denominated debt.
- In assessing the credit quality of local currency debt, rating agencies emphasize domestic government policies that foster or impede timely debt service.
- For foreign currency debt, rating agencies analyze a country's balance of payments and the structure of its external balance sheet.
- Analysts familiar with corporate credit analysis can build a structure for the analysis of quantitative and qualitative information of a sovereign issuer.
- Analysts must assess qualitative factors in assessing the credit risk of both a sovereign and corporate entity.
- A structure developed for corporate credit analysis can be developed for assessing the credit risk of a sovereign.
- Multiple discriminant analysis, a statistical classification technique, has been used by some analysts to predict corporate bankruptcies.
- Credit risk models for assessing credit risk to value corporate bonds include structural models and reduced form models.

PROBLEMS

1. Explain whether you agree or disagree with the following statement: "The credit risk of a bond is the risk that the issuer will fail to meet its obligation to make timely payment of interest and principal."
2. a. In addition to credit ratings, what other information is provided by rating agencies that investors can use to gauge the credit risk of an issuer?
   b. How do long-term credit ratings differ from short-term credit ratings?

3. What are some of the major factors considered by rating agencies in assessing the quality of management?

4. a. There are various forms of back-up credit facilities available to a corporation. What factors should an analyst consider in assessing the back-up credit facilities available to an issuer?

   b. What is a "material adverse change clause provision" in a back-up credit facility and what is its significance in terms of the strength of a back-up credit facility?

5. In 1998 there were several developments in Europe leading to the liberalization of the European telecommunication industry. In October 1998, Moody's Investors Service published a report ("Rating Methodology: European Telecoms") addressing the issues in the rating of European telecommunication companies. Below are quotes from the report followed by questions that should be answered.

   a. "We look carefully at a company's general funding strategy—the debt and equity markets the company accesses, and the sources of bank financing it arranges. ... This becomes more important the lower down the rating scale, particularly in the case of high yield issuers ..." (p. 10) Why is the funding strategy of high-yield issuers of particular concern to Moody's analysts?

   b. "As a very general rule of thumb, the larger the company's cushion of cash and assets above fixed payments due, the more able it will be to meet maturing debt obligations in potentially adverse conditions, and the higher the rating. In many cases, the size of this cushion may be less important than its predictability or sustainability. Moody's views the telecom industry as having generally very predictable revenue streams, which accounts for the relatively high level of ratings of the telecom industry compared to other industries." (p. 10) Explain why "predictability and sustainability" may be more important than size of a coverage ratio.

   c. In discussing the financial measures it uses, the report explains the importance of "cash flow to debt figures." The report stated (p. 11), "We also look at adjusted retained cash flow which includes any items which we view as non-discretionary to gauge the financial flexibility of a company, ..." What is meant by "financial flexibility of a company"?

   d. The quote in the previous part ends with "as well as adjusted debt figures which include unfunded pension liabilities and guarantees." Why would Moody's adjust debt figures for these items?

   e. In the report, Moody's looks at various measures considered in ratings such as coverage ratios and capitalization ratios, and shows these ratios for a sample of European telecom companies. In each case when discussing ratios, Moody's notes the "loose correlation" between ratings and ratios; that is, it is not necessarily the case that companies with the best ratios will always receive a better rating. Moody's noted that "inconsistencies underscore the limitations of ratio analysis." (p. 11). Explain why one might expect a loose correlation between ratios and ratings.

6. What type of information can a credit analyst obtain from an analysis of the statement of cash flows?

7. a. Using S&P's definitions, what is the relationship between free cash flow, discretionary cash, and prefinancing cash flow?

   b. What is the meaning of free cash flow, discretionary cash flow, and prefinancing cash flow?

8. a. Why is the analysis of covenants important in credit analysis?
   b. What is a negative covenant?
   c. Why is covenant analysis particularly important for assessing the credit worthiness of high-yield corporate issuers?
9. What is meant by agency risk?
10. a. What is the motivation for corporate governance ratings?
    b. What are some of the characteristics of a firm considered in assigning a corporate governance rating?
11. Explain the following two statements made by Robert Levine in "Unique Factors in Managing High-Yield Bond Portfolios," in Frank K. Reilly (ed.), *High-Yield Bonds: Analysis and Risk Assessment* (Charlottesville, VA: Association for Investment Management and Research, 1990), p. 36.

    a. "One must understand the structure because not all debt that is listed as senior is actually senior debt."
    b. "Intellectually zero-coupon bonds are troublesome when they are not at the bottom of the capital structure... From a credit standpoint, it is not desirable to have more senior debt growing faster than the subordinated cash-pay securities, thus offering less protection to the subordinated holders in bankruptcy. We prefer to see less debt that is less senior growing faster than the debt that is more senior—e.g., less above us in the event of bankruptcy."

12. Explain why an understanding of the corporate structure of a high-yield issuer that has a holding company structure is important.
13. The following statement was made by Stephen Esser in "High-Yield Bond Analysis: The Equity Perspective," in Ashwinpaul C. Sondhi (ed.), *Credit Analysis of Nontraditional Debt Securities* (Charlottesville, VA: Association for Investment Management and Research, 1995), p. 54: "An equity perspective on high-yield bond analysis can be an important edge for an active manager." Explain why.
14. In the analysis of an asset-backed security, the analysis of the collateral allows the analyst to project the cash flow from the underlying collateral under different scenarios. However, this is not sufficient to assess the credit worthiness of an asset-backed security transaction. Explain why?
15. Why is it necessary for an analyst to assess the financial condition of a servicer in an asset-backed security transaction?
16. a. Some asset-backed security transactions may be characterized as "true securitizations," while others may be more properly classified as "hybrid transactions." What is the distinguishing feature of a "true securitization" and a "hybrid transaction"?
    b. How is the credit quality of a "hybrid transaction" evaluated?
17. What are the four basic categories that are considered in assessing the credit quality of tax-backed municipal debt?
18. a. What is the underlying principle in assessing the credit worthiness of municipal revenue bonds?
    b. In a municipal revenue bond, what is a "rate covenant" and why is such a covenant included?
19. You are reviewing a publication of Moody's Investors Service entitled "Moody's Approach to Rating Regional and Local Governments in Latin America," published in August 1997. On page 3 of the publication, the following was written:

"A Moody's credit rating is an independent opinion of the relative ability and willingness of an issuer of fixed-income securities to make full and timely payments of amounts due on the security over its life."

Why in the case of a sovereign entity is the "willingness" of an issuer to pay important?

20. a. Why do rating agencies assign both a local currency debt rating and a foreign currency debt rating to the bonds of a sovereign government?

    b. How do the factors considered in deriving a local currency debt rating differ from those for a foreign currency debt rating?

21. Comment on the following statement: "The difficulty with analyzing bonds issued by foreign governments is the intangible and non-quantitative elements involved in the credit analysis. I would not encounter such complexities when analyzing the credit worthiness of domestic corporate bonds or domestic municipal bonds."

22. Krane Products Inc. is a manufacturer of ski equipment. The company has been in operation since 1997. Ms. Andrews is a credit analyst for an investment management company. She has been asked to analyze Krane Products as a possible purchase for the bond portfolio of one of her firm's accounts. At the time of the analysis, Krane Products Inc. was rated BB by S&P. The bonds of the company trade in the market with the same spread as other comparable BB bonds.

    Ms. Andrews collected financial data for Krane Products Inc. for the years 2000 and 1999 and computed several financial ratios. Information for selected ratios is given below:

Ratios	2000	1999
EBIT interest coverage	3.8	2.7
EBITDA interest coverage	5.9	4.1
Funds from operations/total debt	28.3%	24.5%
Free operating cash flow/total debt	19.2%	1.2%
Pretax return on capital	24.4%	17.1%
Operating income/sales	25.5%	19.5%
Long-term debt/capitalization	55.0%	57.4%
Total debt/capitalization	57.1%	59.5%

Based on the first three quarters of fiscal year 2001, Ms. Andrews projected the following ratios for 2001:

Ratios	2001
EBIT interest coverage	4.5
EBITDA interest coverage	6.9
Funds from operations/total debt	41.5%
Free operating cash flow/total debt	22.5%
Pretax return on capital	24.2%
Operating income/sales	25.12%
Long-term debt/capitalization	40.5%
Total debt/capitalization	45.2%

Ms. Andrews obtained from S&P information about median ratios by credit rating. These ratios are reproduced as follows:

	AAA	AA	A	BBB	BB	B
EBIT interest coverage	12.9	9.2	7.2	4.1	2.5	1.2
EBITDA interest coverage	18.7	14.0	10.0	6.3	3.9	2.3
Funds from operations/total debt	89.7	67.0	49.5	32.3	20.1	10.5
Free operating cash flow/total debt	40.5	21.6	17.4	6.3	1.0	(4.0)
Pretax return on capital	30.6	25.1	19.6	15.4	12.6	9.2
Operating income/sales	30.9	25.2	17.9	15.8	14.4	11.2
Long-term debt/capitalization	21.4	29.3	33.3	40.8	55.3	68.8
Total debt/capitalization	31.8	37.0	39.2	46.4	58.5	71.4

What do you think Ms. Andrews' recommendation will be with respect to the purchase of the bonds of Krane Products Inc.? Explain why.

23. Credit scoring models have been found to be helpful to analysts and bond portfolio managers. What are their limitations as a replacement for human judgment in credit analysis?

24. What are the two types of credit risk models used to value corporate bonds?

CHAPTER 16

INTRODUCTION TO BOND PORTFOLIO MANAGEMENT

LEARNING OUTCOMES

After reading Chapter 16 you should be able to:

- identify the activities in the investment management process (setting the investment objectives, developing and implementing a portfolio strategy, monitoring the portfolio, and adjusting the portfolio).
- explain the two types of benchmarks (liability structure and bond index) used to identify an investment objective.
- define liabilities.
- classify different types of liabilities.
- define what a funded investor is and the investment objective of a funded investor.
- identify the major broad-based bond market indexes.
- describe what performance risk is.
- identify some of the risks associated with liabilities.
- explain what the economic surplus of an entity is and how its exposure to changes in interest rates is assessed.
- define what the duration of a liability is.
- identify the types of constraints imposed on managers and/or investors.
- identify the elements in developing and implementing a portfolio strategy (writing an investment policy, selecting the type of investment strategy, formulating the inputs for portfolio construction, and constructing the portfolio).
- distinguish between active and passive strategies.
- explain how the degree of departure of a managed portfolio from the benchmark index determines the degree of active management.
- explain the role of forward rates in formulating the inputs for constructing a portfolio.
- explain what is involved in the monitoring activity phase of the investment management process.
- distinguish between performance measurement and performance evaluation.

SUMMARY OVERVIEW

- The investment management process involves the following four activities: setting the investment objectives, developing and implementing a portfolio strategy, monitoring the portfolio, and adjusting the portfolio.

- The investment objectives depend on the characteristics of the investor.
- The investment objectives are typically expressed in terms of risk and return.
- The benchmark may be either a liability structure or a bond market index.
- A manager is evaluated relative to a predetermined investable benchmark.
- Investors that have a liability structure are either (1) funded investors whose borrowing created the liability structure or (2) investors who did not borrow the funds that created the liability structure.
- For funded investors, the spread is the difference between the return on the funds invested and the cost of borrowing.
- A liability is characterized in terms of the amount of the liability and the timing of the liability.
- Liabilities can be classified according to the degree of uncertainty with regards to amount and timing.
- When there are no liabilities that must be satisfied, the investment objective is to either match or outperform a designated bond index.
- Bond market indexes can be classified as broad-based U.S. bond market indexes, specialized U.S. bond market indexes, and global and international bond market indexes.
- The Lehman index is divided into six sectors: (1) Treasury sector, (2) agency sector, (3) mortgage passthrough sector, (4) commercial mortgage-backed sector, (5) asset-backed sector, and (6) credit sector.
- The specialized U.S. bond market indexes focus on one sector or subsector of the bond market.
- For global and international bond market indexes, there are three types of indexes (unhedged and hedged for currency changes) that include non-U.S. bonds: global bond indexes (world bond indexes), international bond indexes (or ex-U.S. bond indexes), and specialized bond indexes for particular non-U.S. bond sectors.
- Specialized indexes have been created that better reflect the liability structure of defined benefit pension plans.
- Client-imposed constraints include maximum allocation of funds to a particular issuer or industry, a minimum acceptable credit rating for issues eligible for purchase, the minimum and maximum duration for the portfolio, any restrictions on leverage and shorting, and limitations on the use of derivative instruments.
- An investor must consider any regulatory constraints and tax factors that affect the portfolio.
- Performance risk is the risk that the investment objective will not be satisfied.
- One measure that allows the manager to incorporate all of the major risks associated with a portfolio relative to a benchmark index is tracking error.
- In constructing a portfolio, it is possible to predict how well the future performance of the portfolio will track the future performance of a benchmark index.
- Developing and implementing a portfolio strategy involves writing an investment policy, selecting the type of investment strategy, formulating the inputs for portfolio construction, and constructing the portfolio.
- Portfolio strategies can be classified as either active strategies or passive strategies.
- All active bond portfolio strategies are based on expectations about the factors that influence bond performance.
- Passive strategies require minimal expectational input.
- Structured portfolio strategies involve designing a bond portfolio to achieve the performance of a designated benchmark.

- Passive and active management can be distinguished in terms of the degree to which the risk characteristics of the managed portfolio differ from those of the benchmark index.
- For bond indexing, a form of passive management, the manager attempts to construct a portfolio such that the risk characteristics of the managed portfolio are identical to the risk characteristics of the benchmark index, resulting in minimal tracking error.
- In active management, the manager creates a portfolio that departs from the risk profile of the benchmark index and, as a result, tracking error is expected to be greater with increased departure from the risk profile of the benchmark index.
- When the benchmark is a liability structure, there may be a single liability or multiple liabilities.
- There are risks associated with liabilities as there are with assets.
- The economic surplus of any entity is the difference between the market value of its assets and the present value of its liabilities.
- The sensitivity of liabilities to interest rate changes can be approximated by the duration and convexity of the liabilities.
- To properly assess the interest rate sensitivity of the economic surplus of an entity it is necessary to assess the dollar duration and the convexity of both the assets and the liabilities.
- In formulating the inputs to be used in portfolio construction, a manager forecasts key factors and compare those forecasts to market-derived values (i.e., forward rates).
- A manager assesses the relative value of the universe of securities that are eligible for purchase.
- A manager monitors a portfolio in terms of the inputs used in the portfolio construction process and the performance of the portfolio.
- Performance measurement involves calculating the return achieved by a manager over a specified time period.
- Performance evaluation is concerned with determining whether the manager added value by outperforming the established benchmark and how the manager achieved the observed return.
- Return attribution analysis decomposes the performance results in order to explain why those results were achieved.
- After monitoring the portfolio, adjustments may be necessary due to changes in market conditions and/or the performance of the portfolio.

PROBLEMS

1. a. What are the two dimensions of a liability?
   b. Why is it not always simple to estimate the liability of an institution?
2. What is the economic surplus of an institution?
3. a. What is a funded investor?
   b. What is the investment objective of a funded investor?
4. What are the risks when a defined benefit pension plan uses as its benchmark the performance of a broad-based bond market index?
5. Some specialized bond indexes are based on the characteristics of liabilities of typical defined benefit pension funds. Explain why such indexes have been developed?
6. The Reliable Performance Management firm was retained by a client. The investment objective specified by the client was to outperform a broad-based bond market index by at least 50 basis points. In the first year, Reliable was able to earn more than 80

basis points over the benchmark index. However, the client was dissatisfied with the performance of Reliable because the client was not able to meet its liabilities. Ms. Florez of Reliable is responsible for client accounts. How should Ms. Florez respond to the client's dissatisfaction with the performance of Reliable?

7. Why are tax considerations important in developing an investment policy?
8. What is the difference between an active and a passive bond portfolio strategy?
9. a. What is tracking error?
   b. Explain why tracking error occurs?
10. A client retained the Conservative Management Company to manage funds on an indexed basis. The benchmark selected was the Lehman Brothers U.S. Aggregate index. In each of the first four quarters, the management company outperformed the benchmark by a minimum of 70 basis points. In its annual review, a representative of the management company stressed its company's superior performance. You are a consultant who has been retained by the client. Comment on the claim of the management company representative.
11. a. Explain why a liability may expose an institution to call risk?
    b. Why might a funded investor be exposed to cap risk?
12. Suppose that the present value of the liabilities of a British financial institution is £6 billion and the surplus is £8 billion. The duration of the liabilities is equal to 5. Suppose further that the portfolio of this financial institution includes only British government bonds and that the duration of the portfolio is 6.

    a. What is the market value of the bond portfolio?
    b. What is the dollar duration per £6 100 par value for the asset portfolio?
    c. What is the dollar duration per £6 100 par value for the liabilities?
    d. Suppose that interest rates increase by 50 basis points. What is the approximate new value for the surplus?
    e. Suppose that interest rates decrease by 50 basis points. What is the approximate new value for the surplus?

13. You and a friend are discussing the savings and loan (S&L) crisis in the United States. She states that "the whole mess started in the early 1980s. When short-term rates increased dramatically, S&Ls were adversely affected—their spread income went from positive to negative. They were borrowing short and lending long."

    a. What does she mean by "borrowing short and lending long"?
    b. Do increasing or decreasing interest rates adversely affect an institution that borrows short and lends long?
    c. How would you restate the risk exposure of S&Ls in terms of duration?

14. Why do you think a debt instrument whose interest rate is changed periodically based on a specified market interest rate (i.e., a floater) would be more suitable for a depository institution than a long-term debt instrument with a fixed interest rate?
15. In a publication by the ICFA Continuing Education, *Managing Asset/Liability Portfolios*, the following appeared in an article by Martin L. Leibowitz ("Setting the Stage"):

    The importance of surplus *[management]* differs for each type of financial intermediary.... [and] can range from being all-encompassing (as in spread banking) to almost insignificant for some highly funded corporate and public pension funds.

    a. What does Leibowitz mean by surplus management?

    b. Why is surplus management more important for banks than for highly funded pension funds (i.e., pension funds with a large surplus)?

16. a. What is the difference between performance measurement and performance evaluation?

    b. What are the two issues that performance evaluation seeks to address?

CHAPTER 17

MEASURING A PORTFOLIO'S RISK PROFILE

LEARNING OUTCOMES

After reading Chapter 17 you should be able to:

- explain why the standard deviation is used as a measure of risk and explain its limitations as a measure of risk for bonds.
- discuss the alternative measures of risk that focus on downside risk—target semivariance and shortfall risk—and the difficulties that arise when using these risk measures for bonds.
- explain why it is important to compare the risk profile of a portfolio to the risk profile of a bond market index.
- describe tracking error.
- explain the difference between actual and predicted tracking error.
- compute the duration of a portfolio and a bond market index.
- compute the contribution to portfolio duration and the contribution to benchmark index duration.
- describe yield curve risk and how it can be quantified.
- define spread duration.
- identify the different types of spread duration measures.
- compare the spread duration exposure of a portfolio with the spread duration of a benchmark index.
- describe sector risk and how it can be quantified.
- explain how call and prepayment risk can be measured.
- describe the types of prepayment risk associated with investing in mortgage-backed securities and how these risks can be measured.
- describe a multi-factor risk model and how it is used to quantify the risk exposure of a portfolio and a benchmark index.
- discuss the different types of risk in a multifactor risk model.
- explain the role of tracking error in a multifactor risk model.

SUMMARY OVERVIEW

- The standard deviation of a bond's returns can be used as a measure of the bond's risk.
- The standard deviation is a misleading measure of risk if the probability distribution of bond returns is not symmetric (i.e., if the distribution is skewed).
- Two issues that must be addressed to determine whether a historical distribution can be characterized as normal are whether data fit the values predicted by the normal distribution and whether the serial correlation of bond returns is non-zero.
- Downside risk measures focus on that portion of the return distribution that is below a specified level.
- Downside risk measures include target semivariance, shortfall probability, and value at risk.
- For the different downside risk measures, the portfolio manager must define the target return so that returns less than the target return represent adverse consequences.
- The target semivariance is a measure of the dispersion of outcomes below the target return specified by the portfolio manager.
- When a probability distribution is symmetric around the expected value, the semivariance gives the same ranking of risk as does the variance or standard deviation.
- Shortfall risk is the probability that an outcome will be less than the target return.
- A special case of shortfall risk is the risk of loss, which is based on a target return of zero.
- While theoretically the target semivariance is superior to the variance (standard deviation) as a risk measure, it is not used in bond portfolio management to any significant extent because of the ambiguity in its use, poor understanding of the statistical properties of these measures, and the difficulty of forecasting the required data.
- For the value at risk measure, the portfolio manager specifies a target probability and then computes the return such that the outcomes will not fall below the computed return with the specified probability.
- A portfolio's variance depends not only on the variance of return for each of the component bonds but also the covariances (correlations) of return for each pair of bonds.
- The two practical problems in computing a portfolio's variance are (1) the number of estimated inputs increases dramatically as the number of bonds in the portfolio or the number of bonds considered for inclusion in the portfolio increases and (2) the difficulty of obtaining meaningful historical return data for bonds.
- In managing a portfolio relative to a benchmark index, it is important to examine a portfolio's risk profile in terms of the difference in the risk profile relative to the benchmark index.
- Tracking error measures the dispersion of a portfolio's returns relative to the returns of the benchmark index.
- Tracking error is the standard deviation of the portfolio's active return (difference in the return between the portfolio and the benchmark index).
- A portfolio manager seeking to match a benchmark index should regularly have active returns close to zero, and therefore a small tracking error will be observed.
- An actively managed portfolio that takes positions substantially different from those of the benchmark index (i.e., has a different risk profile) would likely have large observed active returns, both positive and negative, and thus would have a large observed tracking error.
- The term tracking error is used in two ways—predicted tracking error and actual tracking error.

- Predicted tracking error is used in constructing a portfolio and in assessing its probable risk profile relative to a benchmark index.
- Actual tracking error is the tracking error actually realized by a portfolio.
- In constructing a portfolio and analyzing that portfolio's risk profile, one uses predicted tracking error. In evaluating the performance of the manager, one analyzes the actual tracking error.
- Duration is used to measure a portfolio's exposure to changes in the level of interest rates assuming a parallel shift in the yield curve.
- When computing portfolio duration, the appropriate measure of duration for the individual bonds in the portfolio is effective duration.
- Effective duration measures the sensitivity of a bond to changes in interest rates, allowing for changes in the cash flows that result from interest rate changes.
- The calculation of bond duration requires the use of a valuation model; the duration estimate is only as good as the valuation model.
- Portfolio duration can be computed from the effective duration of either the individual bonds or from the bond sectors in the portfolio.
- A portfolio's duration is found by computing the weighted average of the effective duration of the bonds in the portfolio where the weight assigned to each bond is the percentage of the market value of the bond relative to the market value of the portfolio.
- Contribution to portfolio duration is a better measure of exposure of an individual issue or sector to changes in interest rates than is the weight of an individual issue or sector in the portfolio.
- The contribution to portfolio duration is found by multiplying the weight of the individual issue or sector in the portfolio times the duration of the issue or sector.
- Since a bond market index is simply a portfolio of the issues in the index, the duration of a bond market index is computed in the same manner as the duration of a portfolio.
- The effect of exposure of a portfolio to twists in the shape of the yield curve can be gauged by analyzing the distribution of the present value of the cash flows and from a portfolio's key rate durations.
- A portfolio's spread duration is a measure of the exposure of the portfolio to changes in spreads—that is, it is a measure of spread risk.
- The spread can be measured in terms of nominal spread, zero-volatility spread, or option-adjusted spread; the spread duration must be interpreted accordingly.
- Spread duration for spread products is the same as effective duration when spread is measured in terms of nominal spread.
- Optionality risk exposure of a non-MBS product with an embedded option occurs because a change in interest rates changes the value of the embedded option, which, in turn, changes the value of the bond.
- One way to quantify optionality risk is to use a measure such as the delta of the securities in the portfolio and in the benchmark index, a measure commonly used in the option pricing area.
- The three major risks associated with investing in the MBS sector are sector risk, prepayment risk, and convexity risk.
- One measure of prepayment risk is prepayment sensitivity, found by calculating the basis point change in the price of an MBS for a 1% increase in prepayments.
- Multi-factor risk models can be used by a portfolio manager to quantify the risk exposure of a portfolio or a benchmark index.

- Multi-factor risk models seek to determine the major risks that contribute to the predicted tracking error.
- Decomposition of the risks in a multi-factor risk model begins with classification into two general categories, systematic risk and non-systematic risk (i.e., the risk that remains after systematic risk is removed).
- The systematic risk can be decomposed into term structure factor risk and non-term structure factor risks.
- Term structure risk is a portfolio's exposure to changes in the general level of interest rates in terms of a parallel shift in the yield curve and a nonparallel shift in the yield curve.
- Non-term structure risk factors are other systematic risks that include sector risk, quality risk, optionality risk, coupon risk, and MBS risk.
- Non-systematic risk, also called residual risk, is divided into risks that are issuer specific and those that are issue specific and is the risk resulting from exposure to specific issues and issuers that is greater than the exposure of the benchmark index.

PROBLEMS

1. Mr. Felder is a consultant to the Hole Punchers pension fund. Suppose that the bond market index selected by the trustees is a customized index, which the trustees refer to as the "HP Index." On January 1, the trustees asked Mr. Felder to assess the likelihood that, if its bond portfolio is indexed to the HP Index, the return for the year will exceed 14%. The trustees also asked Mr. Felder to determine the likelihood that the return for the year will be at least 0.5%.

   To comply with the trustees' request, Mr. Felder undertook a statistical analysis of the HP Index. He found that the annual average return of the HP Index over the past 15 years was 5% with a standard deviation of 4.5%. He also found that the distribution of the annual returns was approximately normal.

   a. What would Mr. Felder report to the trustees as to the probability that this year's return will exceed 14%?
   b. What would Mr. Felder report to the trustees as to the probability that this year's return will be at least 0.5%.

2. A trustee of a pension fund is discussing with one of the fund's portfolio managers a consultant's report regarding the probabilities that the fund will realize various returns for its bond portfolio. The trustee questions the portfolio manager as to the continual emphasis in the report on the fact that the results are based on the assumption that the "return distribution is normal" and that the results "depended on the standard deviation." The trustee also asks the portfolio manager what the implications would be for the results in the consultant's report if the standard deviation is greater than that assumed. How should the portfolio manager respond?

3. The board of directors of a bank has retained you to advise the board regarding the risk of the strategies pursued by its portfolio managers. At the current time, the board is using the standard deviation of the return of the portfolio as a measure of risk. Several board members do not feel that this measure is appropriate because it does not recognize the funding cost associated with a particular strategy and the need to obtain a minimum

spread over that funding cost. The board wants to know whether any other measures take into account the bank's funding cost and spread requirement similar to the standard deviation that can be used as a measure of risk. What would you recommend?

4. a. Why is the semivariance a better measure of risk when the return distribution is not normally distributed?

   b. Why is the semivariance not commonly used in bond portfolio management even when a return distribution is not normally distributed?

5. a. What is the relationship between shortfall risk and risk of loss?

   b. What are the limitations of the shortfall risk measure?

6. a. What are the computational difficulties encountered when using the standard deviation as a measure of risk for a bond portfolio?

   b. How does a multi-factor risk model attempt to overcome the computational difficulties discussed in part (a).

7. Suppose that the actual returns for a portfolio and the returns on the benchmark index, the Salomon Smith Barney Broad Investment Grade Index, are as shown below. Calculate the actual tracking error for this portfolio.

Month in 2001	Portfolio return (%)	Benchmark SSB BIG return (%)
Jan	0.75	1.65
Feb	0.40	0.89
March	1.79	0.52
April	−0.89	−0.47
May	0.50	0.65
June	0.72	0.33
July	3.20	2.31
Aug	1.95	1.10
Sept	0.23	1.23
Oct	1.20	2.02
Nov	−1.90	−1.38
Dec	−0.25	−0.59

8. What is the problem with using the actual tracking error of a portfolio relative to a benchmark index to assess the potential future tracking error of the portfolio.

9. In assessing historical performance of a portfolio, a portfolio manager should use forward looking tracking error. Comment.

10. a. What is the duration for the following portfolio?

Bond	Market value	Duration
1	$10 million	7.2
2	8 million	6.1
3	4 million	1.1
4	12 million	4.8

   b. What is the contribution of bond 1 to portfolio duration?

11. a. What is spread duration?

   b. Why are there different types of spread duration measures?

c. Suppose that, using an analytical system from a commercial vendor, a portfolio manager finds that the spread duration of bond K is 2. Further suppose that the portfolio manager asks a dealer for the spread duration of bond K and the dealer reports a value of 3. Explain why this discrepancy can occur.

12. Suppose that a bond market index consists of five sectors and that the effective duration and spread duration (where spread is based on OAS) for each sector are as shown below:

Sector	Weight (%)	Effective duration	Spread duration
Treasury	38.00	4.60	—
Agencies	7.00	4.10	3.90
Mortgages	31.00	3.20	6.10
Corporates	20.00	5.10	5.40
ABS	4.00	2.70	5.80

a. What is the (effective) duration for the bond market index?
b. What is the spread duration for the bond market index?

13. Suppose that a portfolio manager uses as his benchmark the bond market index whose characteristics were described in the previous question. Assume further that the characteristics of the portfolio are as follows:

Sector	Weight (%)	Effective duration	Spread duration
Treasury	15.00	4.60	—
Agencies	7.00	4.10	3.90
Mortgages	35.00	3.20	6.10
Corporates	38.00	5.10	5.40
ABS	5.00	2.70	5.80

a. What is the portfolio's (effective) duration?
b. What is the portfolio's spread duration?
c. Compare the portfolio's risk exposure to changes in the level of Treasury rates and to changes in spread relative to the exposure of the bond market index.
d. Suppose that the manager alters the portfolio as follows:

Sector	Weight (%)	Effective duration	Spread duration
Treasury	16.00	4.60	—
Agencies	7.00	4.10	3.90
Mortgages	35.00	3.20	6.10
Corporates	20.00	5.10	5.40
ABS	22.00	2.70	5.80
	100.00%	3.76	4.75

How does this portfolio's risk exposure compare to that of the bond market index?

14. Alfred Leone, an assistant portfolio manager at Alpha Performers Asset Management, is preparing a memo for a corporate pension sponsor, Code Breakers Inc. The senior portfolio manager for the account is James Ingram. On January 4, 2002, Mr. Leone drafts the following memo on behalf of Mr. Ingram:

To: Trustees of Code Breakers Inc.
From: James Ingram, Alpha Performers Asset Management
Re: Risk Profile of Pension Portfolio

The trustees have asked that I provide a description of the risk profile of your fund's portfolio relative to the benchmark. The benchmark you have designated is the Merrill Lynch U.S. Broad Market Index. At this time, the index is comprised of four sectors: (1) governments, (2) corporates, (3) mortgages, and (4) fixed-rate asset-backed securities.

The risk profile of the portfolio relative to the benchmark can be described in terms of, first, the deviation between the holdings of the portfolio and the composition of the index, and, second, the deviation between the duration of the portfolio and the duration of the index. This information is provided below:

| | Benchmark | | Portfolio | | Difference in portfolio vs. benchmark |
	% of Bench.	Effective duration	% of Port.	Effective duration	% of holdings
Governments	41.50	5.36	41.50	4.04	0.00
Corporates	22.70	5.60	15.70	7.64	−7.00
Mortgages	33.90	3.24	41.20	3.01	7.30
Total Fixed Rate ABS	1.90	2.68	1.60	2.54	0.30
U.S. Broad Market Index	100.00	4.64	100.00	4.16	0.00

As shown in the table, we have decided to maintain a lower exposure to interest rate risk than the benchmark and, at the same time, to underweight the corporate sector and overweight the mortgage sector. The portfolio is basically neutral with respect to the governments sector and the fixed-rate ABS sector.

Mr. Ingram reviewed the memo and sent the following comment to Mr. Leone: "The problem with the description of the risk profile is that it does not quantify the impact on interest rate exposure resulting from deviations between the holdings and the benchmark. Please correct the memo accordingly."

a. What does Mr. Ingram's memo mean and how can Mr. Leone quantify the impact on interest rate risk of holdings that deviate from the benchmark?

b. Mr. Leone consulted with Joan Zhu, CFA, a senior portfolio manager, who suggested to him that the appropriate information for the memo might be the following:

| | Benchmark | | | Portfolio | | | Difference in portfolio vs. benchmark | |
	% of Bench.	Effective duration	Contr. to eff. duration	% of port.	Effective duration	Contr. to eff. duration	% of Holdings	Contr. to eff. duration
Governmentss	41.50	5.36		41.50	4.04		0.00	
Corporates	22.70	5.60		15.70	7.64		−7.00	
Mortgages	33.90	3.24		41.20	3.01		7.30	
Total Fixed Rate ABS	1.90	2.68		1.60	2.54		−0.30	
U.S. Broad Market Index	100.00	4.64		100.00	4.16		0.00	

where "Contr. to eff. duration" means "Contribution to effective duration."

Complete this table by computing the values in the three columns labeled "Contr. to eff. duration."

c. Based on the completed table in part (b), prepare a memo (incorporating the table) for Mr. Leone to send to the trustees describing the risk profile of the portfolio relative to the benchmark.

d. The memo completed in part (c) was sent by Mr. Ingram to Lawrence Robbins, a trustee of Code Breakers Inc.'s pension fund. After reviewing the memo, Mr. Robbins decided to retain you as a consultant. He asks you to respond to the following questions:

   i. Are the risks described in the memo sufficiently descriptive of the risk profile of the portfolio relative to the benchmark?

   ii. If not, what other risks should Alpha Performers Asset Management identify to the trustees?

Prepare a memo to Mr. Robbins responding to these two questions.

e. In your analysis of the index, you find that a more detailed breakdown of the index as follows:

Governments
    U.S. Treasury
    U.S. Agency
    Foreign Governments/Supranational

Corporates
    Financial
    Industrial
    Utility

Mortgages
    Freddie Mac and Fannie Mae 30 Year Passthroughs (FH&FN 30 Yr)
    Ginnie Mae 30 Year Passthroughs (GN 30 Yr)
    All 15 Year Passthroughs

Fixed Rate Asset-Backed Securities

You request that Mr. Robbins contact Alpha Performers Asset Management to provide the trustees with more detail on the portfolio's composition based on this more detailed breakdown of the index. Mr. Ingram provides Mr. Robbins with information so that you can prepare the following table:

	Benchmark			Portfolio			Difference in portfolio vs. benchmark	
	% of Bench.	Effective duration	Contr. to eff. duration	% of Port.	Effective duration	Contr. to eff. duration	% of Holdings	Contr. to eff. duration
Governments								
U.S. Treasury	26.70	5.90		8.60	2.20		−18.10	
U.S. Agency	11.70	4.27		21.00	4.20		9.30	
Foreign Govt/Supra	3.10	4.76		11.90	5.10		8.80	
Total Governments	41.50	5.36		41.50	4.04		0.00	
Corporates								
Financial	8.40	4.60		5.20	5.10		−3.20	
Industrial	12.80	6.29		9.40	9.30		−3.40	
Utility	1.50	5.36		1.10	5.40		−0.40	
Total Corporates	22.70	5.60		15.70	7.64		−7.00	
Mortgages								
FH&FN 30 Yr	21.20	3.18		12.20	3.10		−9.00	
GN 30 Yr	7.20	3.73		3.00	3.80		−4.20	
All 15 Yr	5.50	2.82		26.00	2.88		20.50	
Total Mortgages	33.90	3.24		41.20	3.01		7.30	
Total Fixed Rate ABS	1.90	2.68		1.60	2.54		−0.30	
U.S. Broad Market Index	100.00	4.64		100.00	4.16		0.00	

Complete the table on page 126.

f. Prepare a memo commenting on the risk profile of the portfolio relative to the benchmark in terms of the exposure to the government, corporate, and mortgage sectors.

g. Because of the greater exposure of the portfolio relative to the benchmark in the mortgage sector, you decide to do a further investigation. You request that Mr. Robbins obtain from Alpha Performers Asset Management the effective convexity of both the portfolio and the benchmark. Mr. Robbins asks why you require that information. Explain.

h. Alpha Performers Asset Management provides Mr. Robbins with the following information about the effective convexity:

	Benchmark	Fund
Freddie Mac and Fannie Mae 30 Year Passthroughs	−1.57	−0.65
Ginnie Mae 30 Year Passthroughs	−1.60	−1.00
All 15 Year Passthroughs	−0.99	−0.20

In addition, the following information was provided:

Effective convexity for benchmark = −0.13

Effective convexity for portfolio = −0.02

(Note that the magnitude of the convexity varies depending on how the measures are scaled.

What should you report to the trustees regarding the mortgage sector?

i. Several of the trustees are concerned that interest rates will rise over the next year. How does the exposure of the portfolio compare to that of the benchmark?

15. What is optionality risk?

16. Tom Swensen reviewed information about his portfolio and a benchmark index provided in a report. The information was provided by a new analytical system that Mr. Swensen's firm has purchased to assist the firm's portfolio managers. Unfortunately, some of the reports produced by the analytical system fail to explain the meaning of the values shown. Mr. Swensen has asked you to provide some insight as to the meaning of these numbers. Specifically, help Mr. Swensen with the following:

a. The report shows a measure called delta for the portfolio and for the benchmark index. Mr. Swensen is familiar with the term delta from his work in the options area. However, there are no options in the portfolio and therefore he cannot understand why the report provides delta values.

b. Mr. Swensen wants to know the significance of the fact that the reported delta for the portfolio is greater than the reported delta for the benchmark index.

c. A value reported for the portfolio is prepayment sensitivity. Specifically, the following appears in the report for the MBS sector:

"Prepayment sensitivity for a 1% increase in prepayments:

Portfolio = −1.15

Benchmark = −0.80

Difference = −0.35"

Mr. Swensen wants to know what the prepayment sensitivity measures.

d. Mr. Swensen notices that, while most of the values for the prepayment sensitivity for the individual securities are negative, there are two that are positive. He wants to know what positive and negative values mean for the prepayment sensitivity measure.

17. When assessing the risk exposure of a portfolio relative to a benchmark index why is it important to analyze the allocation within the MBS subsectors in terms of coupon?

18. In a multi-factor risk model, the predicted tracking error is classified into two general risks. What are these two general risks?

19. What is residual risk in a multi-factor risk model?

20. Luke Zavin, a pension fund trustee, reviewed a multi-factor risk report of the fund's portfolio provided by a pension consultant. The report states:

> "Our analysis of your fund, managed by ABC Asset Managers, indicates that the predicted (forward looking) tracking error is 94.87 basis points, consisting of predicted tracking error due to systematic risk of 90 basis points and predicted tracking error due to non-systematic of 30 basis points."

Mr. Zavin believes there is an error in the calculation because the sum of the predicted tracking error due to systematic risk and due to non-systematic risk is equal to 120 basis points, not 94.87 basis points.
How should the consultant respond?

21. In a multi-factor risk model, what is term structure risk?

22. Suppose that the predicted tracking error for a portfolio due to non-term structure risk is as follows:

Tracking error due to	Predicted tracking error
sector risk	40 basis points
quality risk	15 basis points
optionality risk	3 basis points
coupon risk	2 basis points
MBS sector risk	12 basis points
MBS volatility risk	9 basis points
MBS prepayment risk	14 basis points

a. Assuming that the correlation is zero between any pair of components of non-term structure risk, what is the tracking error due to non-term structure risk?

b. Assuming that the correlation between any pair of components of MBS risk is zero, what is the predicted tracking error due to MBS risk?

c. Suppose that the tracking error due to term structure risk is 100 basis points. Assuming that the correlation between the tracking error due to term structure risk and due to non-term structure risk is zero, what is the predicted tracking error due to systematic risk?

23. a. What are the components of non-systematic risk in a multi-factor risk model?
    b. Why does non-systematic risk occur?

CHAPTER 18

MANAGING FUNDS AGAINST A BOND MARKET INDEX

LEARNING OUTCOMES

After reading Chapter 18 you should be able to:

- describe the general principles for each of the following strategies: pure bond index matching, enhanced indexing/matching risk factors, enhanced indexing/minor risk factor mismatches, active management/larger risk factor mismatches, and unrestricted active management.
- explain the reasons for indexing.
- discuss the logistical problems with indexing.
- describe the methodologies used to replicate a benchmark index.
- describe interest rate expectations strategies, yield curve strategies, and inter- and intra-sector allocation strategies.
- compute the total return for a bond over a specified investment horizon.
- describe scenario analysis.
- explain how interest rate risk is controlled in a trade.
- explain why total return analysis and scenario analysis should be used to assess the potential performance of a trade before the trade is implemented.
- show how to use scenario analysis to evaluate the potential performance of a portfolio versus a benchmark index.
- explain how multi-factor risk models can be used to construct a portfolio that is managed against a benchmark index.
- explain the objectives of performance attribution analysis.
- explain the limitations of single-index performance evaluation measures.
- explain leverage.
- identify the advantages and disadvantages of leverage.
- explain a repurchase agreement.
- compute the dollar interest of a repurchase agreement.
- discuss the credit risks associated with a repurchase agreement.
- explain the factors that affect the repo rate.
- distinguish between special (or hot) collateral and general collateral.
- calculate the duration of a leveraged portfolio.

SUMMARY OVERVIEW

- Bond portfolio strategies are classified in terms of the degree to which a manager constructs a portfolio with a risk profile that differs from the risk profile of a benchmark index.
- Strategies can be classified as follows: (1) pure bond index matching, (2) enhanced indexing/matching risk factors, (3) enhanced indexing/minor risk factor mismatches, (4) active management/larger risk factor mismatches, and (5) unrestricted active management.
- The difference between indexing and active management is defined by the extent to which the portfolio can deviate from the risk factors associated with the benchmark index.
- A manager pursuing a pure index matching strategy encounters several logistical problems in constructing an indexed portfolio.
- An enhanced indexing strategy can be pursued so as to construct a portfolio to match the risk factors of the benchmark index without acquiring each issue in the benchmark index.
- A pure bond index matching strategy has the least risk of underperforming the benchmark index (that is, it has minimal predicted tracking error).
- The motivation for indexing includes (1) empirical evidence suggesting that historically the overall performance of active bond managers has been poor; (2) lower management advisory fees for an indexed portfolio compared to active management advisory fees, and (3) lower nonadvisory fees, such as custodial fees.
- Active managers might index a portion of a portfolio or, at times, index the entire portfolio.
- Two methodologies used to construct a portfolio to replicate a benchmark index are cell matching (stratified sampling) and tracking error minimization using a multi-factor risk model.
- Enhanced indexing/minor risk factor mismatches is an enhanced indexing strategy where the portfolio is constructed so as to have minor deviations from the risk factors that affect the performance of the benchmark index but the duration of the portfolio is matched to the duration of the benchmark index.
- Active bond strategies attempt to outperform the benchmark index by constructing a portfolio that has a greater index mismatch than is the case for enhanced indexing.
- In an active bond strategy the manager creates larger mismatches in terms of risk factors relative to the benchmark index, including minor mismatches in duration.
- In unrestricted active management, the manager is permitted to make a significant duration bet without any constraint and can make significant allocations to sectors not included in the benchmark index.
- Value added strategies seek to enhance return relative to a benchmark index and can be strategic or tactical.
- Strategic strategies include interest rate expectations strategies, yield curve strategies, and inter- and intra-sector allocation strategies.
- Tactical strategies are short-term trading strategies that include strategies based on rich/cheap analysis, yield curve trading strategies, and return enhancing strategies employing futures and options.
- Interest rate expectations strategies involve adjusting the duration of the portfolio relative to the benchmark index based on expected movements in interest rates.
- Top down yield curve strategies involve positioning a portfolio in a manner so as to capitalize on expected changes in the shape of the Treasury yield curve, following either a bullet strategy, barbell strategy, or ladder strategy.
- An inter-sector allocation strategy involves allocation of funds among the major bond sectors.

- In making inter- and intra-sector allocations, a manager is anticipating how spreads will change due to differences in credit risk, call risk (or prepayment risk), and liquidity risk.
- In evaluating potential swaps to enhance returns via intra-sector allocation, it is important that trades be constructed so as to maintain the same dollar duration as the initial position in order to avoid an unintentional interest rate bet.
- An active manager can use scenario analysis to assess the potential performance of (1) a trading strategy, (2) a portfolio, and (3) a portfolio relative to a benchmark index.
- The three sources of potential return from investing in a bond are: (1) the coupon interest payments, (2) capital gain (or capital loss), and (3) income from reinvestment of the coupon interest payments.
- Calculation of the total return to an investment horizon that is earlier than the maturity date requires specification of the reinvestment rate and the horizon yield.
- The horizon yield is required in order to calculate the price of the bond at the investment horizon.
- A semiannual return can be annualized either on a bond-equivalent basis or on an effective rate basis; the relevant basis depends on the manager's investment objective.
- For a mortgage-backed security, the calculation of total return requires an assumption about prepayment rates.
- Option-adjusted spread analysis can be incorporated into a total return analysis by specifying the OAS at the investment horizon.
- When the OAS is assumed to remain equal to its initial value, the total return is said to be calculated on a constant OAS basis.
- Scenario analysis involves calculating total return under different assumptions about the reinvestment rate and the horizon yield.
- A multifactor risk model is better than scenario analysis for assessing the potential performance of a portfolio relative to a a benchmark index.
- In addition to providing the opportunity to quantify the risk exposure of a portfolio relative to a benchmark index, a multi-factor risk model is an invaluable tool for constructing and rebalancing a portfolio in order to change the risk exposure of the portfolio.
- A multi-factor model is often used in conjunction with an optimizer to construct or rebalance a portfolio.
- Three single-index measures have been used to evaluate managers' relative performance: Treynor measure, Sharpe measure, and Jensen measure.
- The single-index measures of performance evaluation do not specify how or why a manager outperformed or underperformed a benchmark index.
- Performance attribution analysis seeks to identify the active management decisions that contributed to the performance of a portfolio and to provide a quantitative assessment of the contribution of each of these decisions.
- Leveraging is the investment approach of borrowing funds with the expectation of earning a return in excess of the cost of the borrowed funds.
- Leveraging magnifies the potential gain from investing in a security for a given change in the price of that security but also magnifies the potential loss.
- A repurchase agreement is the sale of a security with a commitment by the seller to buy the security back from the purchaser at the repurchase price on the repurchase date.
- The difference between the repurchase price and the sale price is the dollar interest cost of the loan.
- An overnight repurchase agreement has a maturity of one day; a term repurchase agreement has a maturity of more than one day.

- Investment guidelines should be clear as to the manager's prerogatives with respect to repo transactions.
- To reduce credit risk in a repurchase agreement, since the lender is exposed to the risk that the borrower will default, there is over collateralization of the loan (i.e., there is a repo margin) and the collateral is marked to market on a regular basis.
- When the borrower is required to deliver the collateral to the lender or to the lender's clearing agent, the collateral is said to be "delivered out," and at the repurchase date the lender returns the collateral to the borrower in exchange for the principal and interest payment.
- If the lender agrees to allow the borrower to hold the security in a segregated customer account, then the transaction is called a hold-in-custody repo and exposes the lender to greater credit risk than delivering out the securities.
- An alternative to delivering out the collateral is a tri-party repo, which requires that the borrower deliver the collateral to the lender's custodial account at the borrower's clearing bank.
- The repo rate for a given transaction depends on the quality of the collateral, term of the repo, delivery requirement, availability of collateral, and the prevailing federal funds rate.
- Collateral that is highly sought after by dealers is called hot or special collateral and can be used as a lower cost source of repo financing.

PROBLEMS*

1. What are the characteristics that distinguish bond index management (pure and enhanced) from active bond management?
2. Why is the minor risk factor mismatches approach to portfolio management considered an enhanced indexing strategy?
3. The Car Washer National Labor Union has assets of $300 million. Currently, $200 million is allocated to bonds and $100 million to equities. The funds allocated to equities are indexed to the S&P 500 but the funds allocated to bonds are actively managed. You have been retained as a consultant to the fund. A trustee of the fund has discussed with you the possibility of indexing $100 million of the bond allocation. The trustee has asked you to respond to the following questions:

   a. "Our equity managers index by buying all 500 stocks in the S&P 500. If we decide to index, shouldn't we require the managers we retain to index a part of our bond portfolio to follow the same strategy of buying all the bonds in the index?"
   b. "Our active managers are given the Lehman Aggregate Bond Index as their benchmark. If we decide to index, shouldn't we use the same index to be consistent?"
   c. "Some managers who do bond indexing have suggested an enhanced indexing strategy. Isn't enhanced indexing nothing more than another form of active management? If not, why is enhanced indexing necessary?"

4. What are the logistical problems associated with implementing a pure bond indexing strategy?
5. a. What is an inter-sector allocation strategy?
   b. What is an intra-sector allocation strategy?
   c. Why would a manager employ an inter-sector or an intra-sector allocation strategy?
6. Comment on the following statement: "Interest rate forecasting is important only for helping a manager decide on the duration of a portfolio relative to that of a benchmark index."

---

*All questions assume semiannual coupon payments unless otherwise noted.

7. An investor is considering the purchase of an option-free corporate bond with a coupon rate of 7.25% and 15 years remaining to maturity. The price of the bond is 106.1301 and the yield to maturity is 6.6%. Assume that the Treasury yield curve is flat at 6% and that the credit spread for this issuer is 60 basis points for all maturities. Compute (a) the 1-year total return on a bond-equivalent basis and (b) the 1-year total return on an effective rate basis. Assume

   i. the reinvestment rate is 4%
   ii. at the horizon date, the Treasury yield curve is flat at 5.65%
   iii. at the horizon date, the credit spread for this issuer is 50 basis points for all maturities

8. An investor is considering the purchase of an option-free high-yield corporate bond with a coupon rate of 10% and 9 years remaining to maturity. The price of the bond is 95.7420 and the yield to maturity is 10.75%. Assume that the Treasury yield curve is flat at 7.5% and that the credit spread for this issuer is 325 basis points for all maturities. Compute (a) the 1-year total return on a bond-equivalent basis and (b) the 1-year total return on an effective rate basis. Assume

   i. the reinvestment rate is 5%
   ii. at the horizon date, the Treasury yield curve does not change and therefore remains flat at 7.5%
   iii. at the horizon date, the credit spread for this issuer declines to 200 basis points for all maturities

9. Explain why a good valuation model is essential in order to perform total return analysis?

10. "The problem with total return analysis is (1) that it assumes the option-adjusted spread does not change and (2) that the yield curve is flat." Explain why you agree or disagree with this statement.

11. Typically, in the collateralized mortgage obligation market, the option-adjusted spread (OAS) on planned amortization class tranches (PACs) increases with the average life of the tranche. That is, the OAS for short average life PACs trades tighter (i.e., with a lower spread) to the collateral than intermediate average life PACs, and intermediate average life PACs trade tighter than long average life PACs. The collateral is the passthrough securities used to create the CMO.

    In December 1998, the shape of the OAS for PACs became U-shaped, that short average life PACs offered a higher OAS than intermediate PACs. To benefit from this anomaly, a portfolio manager could create a "barbell PAC" as a substitute for collateral. A barbell PAC is a combination of a short and a long average life PAC. The PaineWebber (now UBS) Mortgage Group assessed this strategy using scenario analysis. Table A shows the analysis. The PAC barbell was invested as follows: 71% FHR 2105 PA and 29% FHR 2105 PE. The comparison in the table is to a 6% coupon FNMA passthrough. The bottom panel of Table A shows the total return in different scenarios.

Table A: Analysis of PAC Barbell versus 6.0% Collateral

	Face	Proceeds	%	Price	Dur	Cnvx	OAS
FHR 2105 PA	23,082	23,446	71	101:03	1.83	−1.46	70
FHR 2105 PE	10,000	9,762	29	97:04+	9.55	0.66	70
Barbell	—	33,208	100	—	4.10	−0.84	70
30 yr FNMA 6.0%	10,000	9,892	100	98:22+	4.53	−1.72	59

Total Rate-of-Return Analysis

	−200	−150	−100	−50	Unch	50	100	150	200	Steep	Flat
FHR 2105 PA	3.74	4.08	5.24	6.67	6.19	5.36	4.40	3.40	2.38	6.62	5.72
FHR 2105 PE	24.31	20.51	15.70	10.95	6.49	1.99	−2.47	−6.87	−11.13	6.21	6.71
Barbell	10.00	9.04	8.37	7.94	6.28	4.37	2.41	0.44	−1.50	6.50	6.01
30 yr FNMA 6.0%	7.34	7.34	7.68	7.75	6.29	4.19	1.77	−0.68	−3.13	6.57	5.99
Difference	2.66	1.70	0.69	0.18	−0.02	0.18	0.64	1.12	1.63	−0.07	0.03

Source: Table 3 in "PAC Barbells: The Way to Go," *PaineWebber Mortgage Strategist* (December 15, 1998), p. 11.

     a. How do the duration of the PAC barbell and the collateral suggest that each will perform if interest rates change?

     b. What do the convexity measures of the collateral and the PAC barbell suggest about the performance of the two positions if interest rates change?

     c. Suppose that a portfolio manager owns the collateral. What do the results of the scenario analysis in Table A suggest as a trade that will enhance return?

     d. What are some important assumptions to consider when reviewing the results of the scenario analysis in Table A?

     e. Explain why the results in Table A would not have been predicted if only duration was taken into account.

12. Suppose that, in June 1998, a portfolio manager was considering the purchase of either a 3-year average life nonagency mortgage-backed security or a home equity loan (HEL) issue. The nonagency MBS was a RAST 1998-A5 and the HEL issue was an Amresco 1998-2. Summary information about these two issues is given below:

	3-Year nonagency MBS	3-Year home equity
Issue	RAST 1998-A5	Amresco 1998-2
Class	A2	A3
Speed	100 PPC (16% CPR in 12 Months)	24% PPC
Price	100:06+	100:08+
Yield	6.610	6.136
Avg. Life	3.19 yrs	2.96 yrs
Spread/AL	112 bps	65 bps

The table below shows the PPC (i.e., prospectus prepayment curve) and average life comparison for the two issues at the end of a 12-month investment horizon under different interest rate scenarios assuming a parallel shift in interest rates:

Spread and Average Life Comparison

	Basis point shifts						
	+150	+100	+50	0	−50	−100	−150
Nonagency MBS: RAST 1998-A5 A2							
PPC	63	75	87	100	125	187	218
Avg. Life	5.20	4.25	3.65	3.19	2.57	1.72	1.48
Home Equity: AMRESCO 1998-2 A3							
PPC	75	83	92	100	108	121	133
Avg. Life	4.25	3.76	3.34	2.96	2.64	2.35	2.12

The following table provides a total return comparison for different interest rate scenarios, based on a 12-month investment horizon, assuming that the spread to the average life is unchanged in each scenario:

Total Return Comparison

	Basis point shifts							Wt.
	+150	+100	+50	0	−50	−100	−150	avg.
Prob of Rate Chg. (%)	1.8	7.4	21.9	35.1	26.1	7.2	0.6	total
Total Return								return
Nonagency MBS	2.01	4.13	5.55	6.56	7.18	7.00	6.91	6.27
Home Equity	2.34	3.95	5.17	6.09	6.79	7.24	7.51	5.94
Advantage of								
Nonagency MBS	−0.33	0.18	0.38	0.47	0.39	−0.24	−0.60	0.33

Source: Adapted from Tables 2, 3, and 4 of "Short Alt-As: Alternative vs. Short Home Equities," *PaineWebber Mortgage Strategist* (June 23, 1998), pp. 10 and 11.

a. Based on the latest prepayment information at the time (June 1998) and the prevailing pricing levels, the Paine-Webber (now UBS) Mortgage Group concluded that the 3-year average life nonagency MBS provides relative value compared to the 3-year average life HEL, especially for investors expecting a modest increase in rates ("Short Alt-As: Alternative vs. Short Home Equities," Paine-Webber *Mortgage Strategist* (June 23, 1998), pp. 8-9.) Explain why.

b. PaineWebber assigned probabilities to the different scenarios. These probabilities are shown in the row below the interest rate scenarios. Based on the weighted average total return, which is the better issue to purchase? (Note: The weighted average total return is the weighted average of the total returns in the different scenarios. The weight for the total return in a given scenario is the probability of occurrence for that scenario.)

c. What are the critical assumptions in the relative analysis performed by PaineWebber?

13. In order to neutralize two positions against a small parallel shift in interest rates, the effective dollar durations of the two positions in a trade must be matched. It is not sufficient to match the effective durations of the two positions. Explain.

14. Mr. Lenox is a portfolio manager who owns $15 million par value of bond ABC. The market value of the bond is $13 million and the effective dollar duration for a 100 basis point change in rates is $1.2 million. Mr. Lenox is considering a swap out of bond ABC and into bond XYZ. The market price of bond XYZ is $75 per $100 of par value and the effective duration is 7. How much par value of bond XYZ would Mr. Lenox have to purchase in order to maintain the same exposure to a small parallel shift in interest rates as he has with bond ABC?

15. George Owens is responsible for marketing for an asset management company. In a meeting with a potential pension client, Linda Regan of the Marshall Furniture Company, Mr. Owens distributed a brochure describing the philosophy of the firm's fixed-income portfolio management team and the various tools the team uses. Ms. Regan asked Mr. Owens why a multi-factor risk model was not one of the tools described in the brochure. Mr. Owens responded as follows:

> Our team believes that the cost of acquiring and supporting such models is unwarranted given the information they provide. The only purpose of a multi-factor risk model is to describe the risk profile of the portfolios we manage relative

to the risk profile of the bond market index that our client specifies. Our team feels this can be done just as well by comparing the effective duration, spread duration, and key rate durations of the portfolio and the benchmark index.

Comment on Mr. Owens' response.

16. Kathy Radner, a portfolio manager at Asset Protector Management, made a presentation to a client. The purpose of the presentation was to provide an overview of the firm's approach to managing fixed income portfolios against a client designated bond market index. In the presentation she states:

> In evaluating a potential bond swap—that is, the exchange of one or more current holdings in the portfolio for one or more bonds not in our current holdings—we begin by using scenario analysis to get a rough idea of the potential affect of the swap on total return. However, this approach is limited. We follow up the analysis by using our multi-factor risk model which provides more information about the impact of potential bond swaps than the scenario analysis based on total return.

After making the presentation, the client asked Ms. Radner to explain the shortcomings of the scenario analysis based on total return and why the multi-factor risk model is more insightful. How should Ms. Radner reply?

17. Jason Lang is a portfolio manager for Asset Optimizers, a firm specializing in the management of fixed income portfolios. The firm uses a multi-factor risk model in constructing and rebalancing portfolios under its management. The firm has received a $400 million fixed income portfolio from a pension plan that is to be managed using the Salomon Broad Investment Grade Index as the benchmark. The portfolio was previously managed by another firm that was terminated following several years of poor performance.

   Upon receipt of information about the holdings of the portfolio, Mr. Lang analyzed the portfolio using his firm's multi-factor risk model. The analysis indicated that the predicted tracking error for the portfolio was 125 basis points. Mr. Lang discussed this finding with the client, and stated that it would take about a month to restructure the portfolio based on his firm's philosophy. In the interim, Mr. Lang suggested that he immediately rebalance the portfolio to reduce the predicted tracking error to the 20–25 basis point range. He indicated that he could do so on a cost effective basis. The client asked Mr. Lang to explain how he can accomplish this. Explain how Mr. Lang will attempt to accomplish his objective of reducing predicted tracking error on a cost efficient basis.

18. A bond portfolio manager whose benchmark is a broad-based bond market index believes that he can enhance return by using credit analysis to identify corporate bond issues that will be upgraded. How can this portfolio manager use a multi-factor risk model in conjunction with credit analysis to implement a return enhancement strategy?

19. A trustee of a pension fund discussed with the fund's consultant various ways to evaluate the performance of the fund's external managers. The trustee indicated that he knew of various measures such as the Sharpe measure, Jensen measure, and Treynor measure. The trustee asked the consultant which of these measures would be best to use in order to identify why a manager achieved inferior (or superior) performance relative to a benchmark index. How should the consultant respond?

20. The trustees of the Order.com pension fund are reviewing with a consultant the annual performance of the fund's three external bond managers (Rollins Group, M&M Company,

and Beta Associates). The benchmark for the external managers is the Lehman U.S. Aggregate Bond Index. The consultant provided a two-page summary of the performance of the managers. On the first page, the summary reported the following 1-year returns:

External manager			
Rollins Group	M&M Company	Beta Associates	Index
8.025%	7.806%	7.661%	7.000%

The second page was a performance attribution analysis for each external manager relative to the index for the 1-year evaluation period. The following values reported are as percents:

	Rollins Group	M&M Company	Beta Associates
I. Interest rate effect			
1. Expected	0.033	0.036	0.034
2. Unexpected	0.061	0.066	0.059
Subtotal	0.094	0.102	0.093
II. Interest rate management effect			
3. Duration	0.954	0.124	0
4. Convexity	−0.045	0.022	0
5. Yield curve shape change	0.148	0.101	0
Subtotal	1.057	0.247	0
III. Other management effects			
6. Sector/quality	−0.225	0.518	0.125
7. Bond selectivity	−0.286	−0.113	0.443
Subtotal	−0.511	0.405	0.568
IV. Trading activity return	0.385	0.052	0
V. Total return over index (sum I, II, III, and IV)	1.025	0.806	0.661

The third page of the report describes the sources of return. The framework for the model was developed by Gifford Fong Associates and is described in Gifford Fong, Charles Pearson, and Aldrich Vasicek, "Bond Performance: Analyzing Sources of Return," *Journal of Portfolio Management* (Spring 1983). The report summarized the analysis as follows:

> The analysis is divided into four sections. Section I shows the "Interest Rate Effect." This return is not controllable by the manager; it is the result of the external internal rate environment. Effectively, it is the cost of being in the bond market. There are two components of the interest rate effect: expected and unexpected. The expected interest rate effect results from rolling down the spot rate curve. The unexpected interest rate effect is the return attributable to the actual change in rates.
>
> Sections II and III show the factors controllable by the manager in generating the total return. The "Interest Rate Management Effect" (Section II), shows

the default-free return due to the duration, convexity, and yield curve shape exposure of the portfolio.

The trustee also reviewed the promotional material provided by each management firm, describing each firm's investment strategies. The consultant summarized the investment strategies, and the management fee, as follows:

Rollins Group: This management firm states that it can identify undervalued issues and bond sectors that will enhance returns relative to the benchmark index. The firm seeks a position that is close to neutral with respect to interest rate exposure relative to the benchmark index. (Management fee: 50 basis points)

M&M Company: This management firm states that it can enhance return through active management of the interest rate exposure of the portfolio relative to the benchmark index. Management seeks a position that is neutral with respect to bond sectors and quality. However, it believes that it can use analytical models to identify individual issues that are mispriced. (Management fee: 45 basis points)

Beta Associates: This management firm's strategy is to be neutral with respect to interest rate risk exposure relative to the benchmark index. Management believes it can add value relative to the benchmark index through credit analysis and by selecting issues that are likely to be upgraded. (Management fee: 30 basis points)

a. After evaluating the documents provided by the consultant, Trustee A stated his belief that the Rollins Group clearly outperformed the benchmark index as well as the other two managers. His belief is based on his observation that the Rollins Group had the largest return over the benchmark index, even after adjusting for its higher management fees. Moreover, he did not understand the need to review the reasons for the outperformance. How should the consultant respond to Trustee A?

b. How would the consultant assess the performance of the three external managers? What should the consultant suggest that the trustees discuss with each manager?

21. Suppose that an investor has $477,300 to invest and is considering the purchase of a 7% coupon 15.5-year Treasury security. The price is 95.46, there is no accrued interest, and the yield to maturity is 7.5%.

a. How much in par value can this investor purchase?

b. If the investor purchases this bond, what is the annual return (bond-equivalent yield) assuming the following horizon yields and corresponding horizon prices for a 6-month time horizon:

Horizon yield	Horizon price
9.00%	83.71
8.50%	87.42
8.00%	91.35
7.50%	95.54
7.00%	100.00
6.50%	104.75
6.00%	109.80

    c. Suppose the investor borrows $477,300 in order to purchase an additional amount of the bond. The annual borrowing rate is 10.8%. What is the annual return for each of the scenarios in part (b)?

    d. Suppose the investor borrows $1,909,200 in order to purchase an additional amount of the bond. The annual borrowing rate is 10.8%. What is the annual return for each of the scenarios in part (b)?

    e. Compare the annual returns computed in part (b) with those computed in parts (c) and (d). Comment on the results.

22. What is the difference between a repo transaction and a reverse repo transaction?

23. The investment guidelines for a pension fund specify that

> "The manager of the fund is permitted to enter into repurchase agreements."

    Why is this provision confusing?

24. The following statement appeared in an article in a popular daily publication. "Repurchase agreements are extremely risky vehicles." Explain why this statement is ambiguous.

25. Suppose that an investor purchases $3 million market value of a bond. The investor decides to borrow the funds via a repurchase agreement and the dealer is willing to lend 97% of the market value of the bond. The overnight repo rate is 7% and the 30-day term repo rate is 7.3%.

    a. What is the dollar interest cost of this borrowing arrangement if the investor borrows for one day?

    b. What is the dollar interest cost of this borrowing arrangement if the investor borrows for thirty days?

26. An assistant portfolio manager is reviewing a daily printout of Treasury security yields published by a government broker/dealer. He notices that the on-the-run 10-year Treasury note is trading at a yield considerably less than the yield for Treasury securities with similar maturity or similar duration. He believes that the issue is expensive (i.e., the price is too high). He asks you whether this Treasury issue is rich. What is your response?

27. Suppose that an investor owns a security that is on special in the repo market. If this investor wants to use this security to obtain financing, how will the repo rate compare to generic collateral for the same term?

28. a. Why is the lender of funds in a repo transaction exposed to credit risk?

    b. What is the credit risk for a hold-in-custody repo?

    c. How do lenders in a repo transaction reduce credit risk?

29. Tom Reed is a portfolio manager for the MMM Investment Management Company. Recently he received $200 million from a new client to invest. The investment guidelines established by the client allow the manager to leverage the portfolio up to 25% of the $200 million, or $50 million. The investment guidelines impose a restriction that the portfolio's duration not exceed 5.

    Mr. Reed invested the $200 million in bonds with a duration of 4. He then used the maximum permissible leverage and purchased $50 million of bonds with a duration of 5 via a 1-month repo transaction.

    a. What is the duration of the client's portfolio?

    b. Has Mr. Reed violated the duration restriction?

CHAPTER 19

PORTFOLIO IMMUNIZATION AND CASH FLOW MATCHING

LEARNING OUTCOMES

After reading Chapter 19 you should be able to:

- describe what an immunization strategy is and why it is used.
- identify the interest rate risk exposure for a portfolio whose duration is not equal to the duration of a liability.
- explain why the key to immunization is constructing a portfolio with a duration equal to a target investment horizon.
- identify the risks associated with immunizing a portfolio.
- explain the ways classical immunization has been extended.
- identify the factors to consider in creating an immunized portfolio.
- describe what a contingent immunization strategy is.
- identify the key considerations in implementing a contingent immunization strategy.
- describe for a contingent immunization strategy the following concepts: safety net level return, excess achievable return, return achievable with an immunization strategy, and trigger point.
- discuss the three conditions for creating an immunized portfolio to satisfy multiple liabilities.
- explain the different approaches suggested for valuing defined benefit plan liabilities.
- illustrate how a cash flow matching strategy can be used to construct a portfolio to satisfy multiple liabilities.
- explain the advantages and disadvantages of a cash flow matching strategy relative to multiple liability immunization.
- explain a combination matching strategy.

SUMMARY OVERVIEW

- Classical immunization is defined as the process of creating a bond portfolio to provide a target return for a specific time horizon irrespective of interest rate changes.

- The fundamental mechanism for immunization theory is to create a portfolio structure that balances the change in the portfolio value at the end of the investment horizon with the return from the reinvestment of portfolio cash flows.
- To immunize a portfolio's target accumulated value (target yield) against a change in the market yield, a manager must construct a bond portfolio such that the portfolio's duration is equal to the liability's duration, and the portfolio's initial present value of its cash flows equals the present value of the future liability.
- Immunization risk is effectively reinvestment risk.
- A natural extension of classical immunization theory is a technique for modifying the assumption of parallel shifts in the yield curve.
- One strategy to handle an arbitrary yield curve shift is to construct an immunization risk measure which is related to the relative dispersion of the portfolio's cash flows around the investment horizon. This measure can then be minimized over a range of yield curve changes using optimization techniques.
- In contingent immunization, the manager pursues an active strategy until an adverse investment drives the then available potential return to a prespecified safety net return, at which time, the manager must then immunize the portfolio.
- A contingent immunization strategy involves the identification of both the available immunization target rate and a lower safety net return with which the investor would be satisfied.
- The three key considerations in implementing a contingent immunization strategy are establishing accurate immunized initial and ongoing available target returns, identifying a suitable and immunizable safety net return, and implementing an effective monitoring procedure to ensure the safety net return is not violated.
- An immunization strategy can also be used to construct a portfolio to satisfy multiple liabilities.
- The three conditions for immunization in the case of multiple liabilities are the present value of the assets must be at least equal to the present value of the liabilities, the duration of the assets must be equal to the duration of the liabilities, and the distribution of durations of portfolio assets must be wider than the distribution of the liabilities.
- When valuing liabilities, a single interest rate should not be used.
- Two approaches have been suggested for selecting interest rates to be used for valuing liabilities for defined benefit pension plans: (1) Treasury spot rate curve and (2) Treasury yield curve plus a spread (e.g., a corporate bond index yield curve).
- Cash flow matching is an alternative to immunization when there are multiple liabilities.
- In cash flow matching, bonds are selected so the portfolio's cash flow matches the liabilities as close as possible in terms of dollar amount and timing (to minimize reinvestment risk) at each liability date.
- In constructing a cash flow matched portfolio, the objective is to do so at minimum cost subject to constraints such as the credit quality permitted in the portfolio.
- There is a trade-off between immunization and cash flow matching to construct a portfolio to satisfy multiple liabilities.
- An immunization strategy exposes the manager to immunization risk which is not present in a cash flow matching strategy, but the initial cost of a cash flow matched portfolio is typically higher than for an immunization portfolio.
- The basic cash flow matching strategy, in which only asset cash flows occurring prior to a liability date can be used to satisfy a liability, can be extended to handle situations in which cash flows occurring before and after the liability date can be used to meet a liability.
- Combination matching or horizon matching uses a portfolio that is duration matched with the added constraint that it be cash matched in the first few years.

PROBLEMS

1. Why will the matching of the maturity of a coupon bond to an investment horizon date not lock in a return?
2. What is the objective of a bond immunization strategy?
3. a. Why is a portfolio that has a duration of 5 not immunized against a parallel shift in the level of interest rates if the investment horizon is 3 years?
   b. How is a portfolio that has a duration of 5 impacted by a rise in interest rates over a 3-year investment horizon?
   c. Why is a portfolio that has a duration of 3 not immunized against a parallel shift in the level of interest rates if the investment horizon is 7 years?
   d. How is a portfolio that has a duration of 3 impacted by a rise in interest rates over a 7-year investment horizon?
4. What is the basic underlying principle in an immunization strategy?
5. A portfolio manager is contemplating the implication of an immunization strategy. He believes that one advantage of the strategy is that it requires no management of the portfolio once the initial portfolio is constructed. That is, it is simply a "buy-and-hold strategy." Explain whether or not you agree with the portfolio manager's assessment of the immunization strategy as a "buy-and-hold strategy."
6. A portfolio manager is considering an immunization strategy for a client. The portfolio manager is concerned that the portfolio must be rebalanced very frequently in order to match the duration of the portfolio each day to the time remaining in the investment horizon. Comment on this portfolio manager's concern.
7. A portfolio manager made the following statement: "To immunize a portfolio in order to satisfy a single liability, all that is necessary is that (1) the market value of the assets be equal to the present value of the liability and (2) the duration of the portfolio be equal to the duration of the liability. There are absolutely no risks except for the risk that any of the bonds in the portfolio will default or decline in value due to credit downgrades." Explain whether or not you agree with this statement.
8. "I can immunize a portfolio by simply investing in zero-coupon bonds." Comment on this statement.
9. Several trustees of a pension fund are discussing with the fund's consultant the fund's bond portfolio to meet future liabilities. The trustees understand there are two possibilities for structuring the portfolio: multiperiod immunization and cash flow matching. Which strategy has less risk of not satisfying the future liabilities and why?
10. A portfolio manager considering the use of multiperiod immunization is concerned about using the strategy for its pension fund clients. The manager's concern is that its clients have projected liabilities that are beyond 30 years and therefore it would not be possible to immunize a portfolio for 30 years since bond durations do not extend that long. Is this portfolio manager's concern regarding the lack of longer duration bonds justified?
11. a. What is the problem with using an actuarially assumed interest rate for valuing the liabilities of a defined benefit pension plan?
    b. What is the argument in favor of valuing the liabilities of a defined benefit pension plan using Treasury spot rates?
    c. What concerns would you have with using a corporate bond index yield curve to value the liabilities of a defined benefit pension plan?
12. A client has granted permission for one of its external managers, ABC Financial Management, to employ a contingent immunization strategy. The amount invested by

the client is $50 million and the client is willing to accept a 10% rate of return over a 4-year planning horizon. At the same time the client has determined that an immunized rate of return of 12% is possible.

a. What is the safety net return for this contingent immunization strategy?
b. What is the cushion spread?
c. What is the minimum target value for the portfolio assuming semiannual compounding?
d. What are the required assets at the inception of the strategy to achieve the minimum target value at the end of 4 years?
e. What is the initial dollar safety margin?
f. Suppose that the minimum target return that the client had set was 11% instead of 10%. What would be the cushion spread and the initial dollar safety margin?
g. What is the relationship between the minimum target return and the initial dollar safety margin?
h. Suppose that the manager invests the entire $50 million in a 12% coupon 20-year bond selling at par to yield 12%. The next coupon payment for this bond is six months from now. Suppose that six months later, market interest rates for this bond decline to 9%. What is the market value of the bonds plus coupon interest six months from now?
i. Assuming that the client had specified a minimum return of 10% at inception 6 months ago, how much would be necessary to achieve the minimum target return found in part (c) if the portfolio in part (h) can be immunized at the prevailing interest rate of 9%?
j. Given the portfolio value found in part (h) and the required assets in part (i), would ABC Financial Management be required to pursue an immunized strategy or allowed to continue with an active strategy? If an active strategy may be continued, what is the dollar safety margin?
k. Suppose that instead of declining to 9% in six months, interest rates rose to 14.26%. What is the market value of the bonds in part (h) plus coupon interest six months from inception?
l. Assuming that the client specifies a minimum target return of 10%, how much would be necessary to achieve the minimum target value found in part (c) if the portfolio in part (h) can be immunized at the prevailing interest rate of 14.26%?
m. Given the portfolio value found in part (k) and the required assets in part (l), would ABC Financial Management be required to pursue an immunized strategy or continue with an active strategy? If an active strategy may be continued, what is the dollar safety margin?

CHAPTER 20

RELATIVE-VALUE METHODOLOGIES FOR GLOBAL CREDIT BOND PORTFOLIO MANAGEMENT

LEARNING OUTCOMES

After reading Chapter 20 you should be able to:

- identify the types of securities that fall into the "credit asset class."
- explain what is meant by relative value.
- describe primary market analysis.
- describe the credit structures that dominate the bond market.
- explain the strategic portfolio implications of specific security structures that have come to dominate the credit markets.
- explain how short-term and long-term liquidity for a bond influences portfolio management decisions.
- explain the popular reasons for executing trades in the secondary market (yield/spread pickup trades, credit-upside trades, credit-defense trades, new issue swaps, sector-rotation trades, yield curve-adjustment trades, structure trades, and cash flow reinvestment).
- identify the main rationales for not trading.
- explain the reason for accepting swap spread as a relative-value measure.
- explain the commonly used spread tools for making decisions (mean-reversion analysis, quality-spread analysis, and percent yield analysis) and their limitations.
- explain structure analysis.
- describe the typical shape of a credit spread curve and the difference in the slope of the curve for different quality issuers.
- understand the dominant role of fundamental credit analysis, the most important determinant of successful credit portfolio management.
- explain sector-rotation strategies.

SUMMARY OVERVIEW

- Superior credit analysis has been and will remain the most important determinant of the relative performance of credit bond portfolios, allowing managers to identify potential credit upgrades and to avoid potential downgrades.

- The "corporate asset class" includes more than pure corporate entities; this segment of the global bond market is more properly called the "credit asset class," including sovereigns, supranationals, agencies of local government authorities, nonagency mortgage-backed securities, commercial mortgage-backed securities, and asset-backed securities.
- Relative value refers to the ranking of fixed-income investments by sectors, structures, issuers, and issues in terms of their expected performance during some future interval.
- Relative-value analysis refers to the methodologies used to generate expected return rankings.
- Within the global credit market, classic relative-value analysis combines top-down and bottom-up approaches, blending the macro input of chief investment officers, strategists, economists, and portfolio managers with the micro input of credit analysts, quantitative analysts, and portfolio managers.
- The objective of relative value analysis is to identify the sectors with the most potential upside, populate these favored sectors with the best representative issuers, and select the structures of the designated issuers at the yield curve points that match the investor's outlook for the benchmark yield curve.
- The main methodologies for credit relative-value maximization are total return analysis, primary market analysis, liquidity and trading analysis, secondary trading rationales and constraints analysis, spread analysis, structure analysis, credit curve analysis, credit analysis, and asset allocation/sector analysis.
- Credit relative-value analysis starts with a detailed decomposition of past returns and a projection of expected returns.
- Primary market analysis refers to analyzing the supply and demand for new issues.
- The global credit market has become structurally more homogeneous, with intermediate maturity (5 to 10 years) bullet structure (noncallable issues) coming to dominate the investment-grade market.
- The trend toward bullet securities does not pertain to the high-yield market, where callable structures dominate the market.
- Short-term and long-term liquidity influence portfolio management decisions.
- Credit market liquidity changes over time, varying with the economic cycle, credit cycle, shape of the yield curve, supply, and the season.
- Despite the limitations of yield measures, yield/spread pickup trades account for the most common secondary market trades across all sectors of the global credit market.
- Credit-upside trades seek to capitalize on expectations of issues that will be upgraded in credit quality with such *trades particularly popular in the crossover sector (securities with ratings between Ba2/BB and Baa3/BBB—by a major rating agency)*.
- Credit-defense trades involve trading up in credit quality as economic or geopolitical uncertainty increases.
- Sector-rotation trades involve altering allocations among sectors based on relative-value analysis; such strategies can be used within the credit bond market (intra-asset class sector rotation) and among fixed-income asset classes.
- Sector-rotation trades are not as popular in the bond market as in the equity market because of less liquidity and higher costs of trading; however, with the expected development of enhanced liquidity and lower trading transaction costs in the future, sector-rotation trades should become more prevalent in the credit asset class.
- Trades undertaken to reposition a portfolio's duration are called yield curve-adjustment trades, or simply, curve-adjustment trades.

- Structure trades involve swaps into structures (e.g., callable structures, bullet structures, and put structures) that are expected to have better performance given anticipated movements in volatility and the shape of the yield curve.
- Portfolio managers should review their main rationales for not trading.
- Portfolio constraints are the single biggest contributor to the persistence of market inefficiency across the global credit bond market.
- Many U.S. practitioners prefer to cast the valuations of investment-grade credit securities in terms of option-adjusted spreads (OAS), but given the rapid reduction of credit structures with embedded options since 1990, the use of OAS in primary and secondary pricing has diminished within the investment-grade credit asset class.
- Swap spreads have become a popular valuation yardstick for European credit, Asian credit, and U.S. MBS, CMBS, agency, and ABS sectors.
- In the global credit bond market, nominal spread (the yield difference between credit and government bonds of similar maturities) has been the basic unit of relative-value analysis.
- Mean-reversion analysis is the most common technique for analyzing spreads among individual securities and across industry sectors.
- Mean-reversion analysis can be misleading because the mean or average value is highly dependent on the time period analyzed.
- In quality-spread analysis, a manager examines the spread differentials between low- and high-quality credits.
- Structural analysis involves analyzing different structures' performance on a relative-value basis.
- Put structures provide investors with a partial defense against sharp increases in interest rates; this structure should be favored as an outperformance vehicle only by those investors with a decidedly bearish outlook for interest rates.
- Credit curves, both term structure and credit structure, are almost always positively sloped.
- In credit barbell strategies, many portfolio managers choose to take credit risk in short and intermediate maturities and to substitute less risky government securities in long-duration portfolio buckets.
- Like the underlying Treasury benchmark curve, credit spread curves change shape over the course of economic cycles; typically, spread curves steepen when the bond market becomes more wary of interest rate and general credit risk.

PROBLEMS

1. What is meant by relative value in the credit market?
2. a. What is the dominant type of structure in the investment-grade credit market?
   b. What are the strategic portfolio implications of the dominant structure answer in part (a)?
   c. What is the dominant structure in the high-yield corporate bond market and why is it not the same structure as discussed in part (a)?
3. The following quote is from Lev Dynkin, Peter Ferket, Jay Hyman, Erik van Leeuwen, and Wei Wu, "Value of Security Selection versus Asset Allocation in Credit Markets," Fixed Income Research, Lehman Brothers, March 1999, p. 3:

> Most fixed income investors in the United States have historically remained in a single-currency world. Their efforts to outperform their benchmarks have focused on yield curve placement, sector and quality allocations, and security

selection. The style of market participants is expressed in the amount of risk assumed along each of these dimensions (as measured by the deviation from their benchmarks), and their research efforts are directed accordingly.

   a. What is meant by "yield curve placement, sector and quality allocations, and security selection"?
   b. What is meant by the statement: "The style of market participants is expressed in the amount of risk assumed along each of these dimensions (as measured by the deviation from their benchmarks)"?

4. The following two passages are from Peter J. Carril, "Relative Value Concepts within the Eurobond Market," Chapter 29 in Frank J. Fabozzi (ed.), *The Handbook of Corporate Debt Instruments* (New Hope, PA: Frank J. Fabozzi Associates, 1998), p. 552.

   a. In discussing Eurobond issuers, Carril wrote: "Many first time issuers produce tighter spreads than one may anticipate because of their so called scarcity value." What is meant by scarcity value?
   b. In describing putable bonds Carril wrote: "Much analytical work has been devoted to the valuation of the put's option value, especially in the more mature U.S. investment-grade market." However, he states that in the high-yield market the overriding concern for a putable issue is one of credit concern. Specifically, he wrote: "traditional analysis used to quantify the option value which the issuer has granted the investor is overridden by the investor's specific view of the creditworthiness of the issuer at the time of first put." Explain why.

5. In describing the approaches to investing in emerging markets credits, Christopher Taylor wrote the following in "Challenges in the Credit Analysis of Emerging Market Corporate Bonds," Chapter 16 in Frank J. Fabozzi (ed.), *The Handbook of Corporate Debt Instruments* (New Hope, PA: Frank J. Fabozzi Associates, 1998), p. 311:

   > There traditionally have been two approaches to investing in emerging market corporate bonds: top-down and bottom-up. . . . The *top-down approach* essentially treats investing in corporates as "sovereign-plus." The *bottom-up approach* sometimes has a tendency to treat emerging market corporates as "U.S. credits-plus."

   What do you think Mr. Taylor means by "sovereign-plus" and "U.S. credits-plus"?

6. Chris Dialynas in "The Active Decisions in the Selection of Passive Management and Performance Bogeys," (in Frank J. Fabozzi (ed.), *Perspectives on Fixed Income Portfolio Management*, Volume 2) wrote:

   > Active bond managers each employ their own methods for relative value analysis. Common elements among most managers are historical relations, liquidity considerations, and market segmentation. Market segmentation allegedly creates opportunities, and historical analysis provides the timing cure.

   a. What is meant by "historical relations, liquidity considerations, and market segmentation" that Chris Dialynas refers to in this passage?
   b. What is meant by: "Market segmentation allegedly creates opportunities, and historical analysis provides the timing cure"?

7. The following passages are from Leland Crabbe "Corporate Spread Curve Strategies," Chapter 28 in Frank J. Fabozzi (ed.), *The Handbook of Corporate Debt Instruments* (New Hope, PA: Frank J. Fabozzi Associates, 1998).

> In the corporate bond market, spread curves often differ considerably across issuers . . .

> Most fixed income investors understand the relation between the term structure of interest rates and implied forward rates. But some investors overlook the fact that a similar relation holds between the term structure of corporate spreads and forward corporate spreads. Specifically, when the spread curve is steep, the forward spreads imply that spreads will widen over time. By contrast, a flat spread curve gives rise to forwards that imply stability in corporate spreads. Essentially the forward spread can be viewed as a breakeven spread . . .

> Sometimes, investors may disagree with the expectations implied by forward rates, and consequently they may want to implement trading strategies to profit from reshapings of the spread curve.

   a. What is meant by "spread curves" and in what ways do they differ across issuers?
   b. Previously the relationship between the term structure of interest rates and implied forward rates (or simply forward rates) was explained. What is a "forward spread" that Mr. Crabbe refers to and why can it be viewed as a breakeven spread?
   c. How can implied forward spreads be used in relative-value analysis?

8. What is the limitation of a yield-pickup trade?

9. Increases in investment-grade credit securities new issuance have been observed with contracting yield spreads and strong relative bond returns. In contrast, spread expansion and a major decline in both relative and absolute returns usually accompanies a sharp decline in the supply of new credit issues. These outcomes are in stark contrast to the conventional wisdom held by many portfolio managers that supply hurts credit spreads. What reason can be offered for the observed relationship between new supply and changes in credit spreads?

10. a. What is meant by the "crossover sector of the bond market"?
    b. How do portfolio managers take advantage of potential credit upgrades in the crossover sector?

11. When would a portfolio manager consider implementing a credit-defense trade?

12. What is the motivation for portfolio managers to trade into more current and larger sized "on-the-run" issues?

13. a. Why has the swap spread framework become a popular valuation yardstick in Europe for credit securities?
    b. Why might U.S. managers embrace the swap spread framework for the credit asset class?
    c. Compare the advantages/disadvantage of the nominal spread framework to the swap spread framework.

14. An ABC Corporate issue trades at a bid price of 120 bp over the 5-year U.S. Treasury yield of 6.00% at a time when LIBOR is 5.70%. At the same time, 5-year LIBOR-based swap spreads equal 100 bp (to the 5-year U.S. Treasury).

   a. If a manager purchased the ABC Corporate issue and entered into a swap to pay fixed and receive floating, what spread over LIBOR is realized until the first swap reset date?

b. Why would a total return manager buy the issue and then enter into a swap to pay fixed and receive floating?

15. The following was reported in the "Strategies" section of the January 3, 2000 issue of *BondWeek* ("Chicago Trust to Move Up in Credit Quality," p. 10):

    > The Chicago Trust Co. plans to buy single-A corporate bonds with intermediate maturities starting this quarter, as the firm swaps out of lower-rated, triple B rated paper to take advantage of attractive spreads from an anticipated flood of single-A supply. . . .

    The portfolio manager gave the following reasoning for the trade:

    > . . . he says a lack of single-A corporate offerings during the fourth quarter has made the paper rich, and he expects it will result in a surge of issuance by single-A rated companies this quarter, blowing out spreads and creating buying opportunities. Once the issuance subsides by the end of the quarter, he expects spreads on the single-A paper will tighten.

    a. What type of relative value analysis is the portfolio manager relying on in making this swap decision and what are the underlying assumptions? (Note: When answering this question, keep the following in mind. The manager made the statement at either the last few days of December 1999 or the first two days in January 2000. So, reference to the fourth quarter means the last quarter in 1999. When the statement refers to the end of the quarter or to "this quarter" it is meant the first quarter of 2000.)
    b. Further in the article, it was stated that the portfolio manager felt that on an historical basis the corporate market as a whole was cheap. The portfolio manager used new cash to purchase healthcare credits, doubling the portfolio's allocation to the healthcare sector. The portfolio manager felt that the issuers in the healthcare sector he purchased for the portfolio had fallen out of favor with investors as a result of concerns with healthcare reform. He thought that the cash flows for the issuers purchased were strong and the concerns regarding reform were "overblown." Discuss the key elements to this strategy.

16. The following was reported in the "Strategies" section of the January 3, 2000 issue of *BondWeek* (". . . Even as Wright Moves Down." p. 10):

    > Wright Investors Services plans to buy triple B-rated corporate paper in the industrial sector and sell higher rated corporate paper on the view that stronger-than-anticipated economic growth will allay corporate bond investor fears.

    In the article, the following was noted about the portfolio manager's view:

    > spreads on higher rated investment grade paper already have come in some from last summer's wides, but he believes concerns over year-end and rising rates have kept investors from buying lower rated rated corporate paper, keeping spreads relatively wide.

    Discuss the motivation for this strategy and the underlying assumptions.
17. The following appeared in the "Strategies" section of the September 27, 1999 issue of *BondWeek* ("Firm Sticks to Corps, Agencies," p. 6):

The firm, which is already overweight in corporates, expects to invest cash in single A corporate paper in non-cyclical consumer non-durable sectors, which should outperform lower-quality, cyclicals as the economy begins to slow.

Discuss this strategy and its assumptions.

18. a. Suppose that a manager believes that credit spreads are mean reverting. Below are three issues along with the current spread, the mean (average) spread over the past six months, and the standard deviation of the spread. Assuming that the spreads are normally distributed, which issue is the most likely to be purchased based on mean-reversion analysis.

Issue	Current spread	Mean spread for past 6 months	Standard deviation of spread
A	110 bp	85 bp	25 bp
B	124	100	10
C	130	110	15

b. What are the underlying assumptions in using mean-reversion analysis?

19. Ms. Xu is the senior portfolio manager for the Solid Income Mutual Fund. The fund invests primarily in investment-grade credit and agency mortgage-backed securities. For each quarterly meeting of the board of directors of the mutual fund, Ms. Xu provides information on the characteristics of the portfolio and changes in the composition of the portfolio since the previous board meeting. One of the board members notices two changes in the composition of the portfolio. First, he notices that while the percentage of the portfolio invested in credit was unchanged, there was a sizeable reduction in callable credit relative to noncallable credit bonds. Second, while the portfolio had the same percentage of mortgage passthrough securities, there was a greater percentage of low-coupon securities relative to high-coupon securities.

When Ms. Xu was asked why she changed the structural characteristics of the securities in the portfolio, she responded that it was because the management team expects a significant drop in interest rates in the next quarter and the new structures would benefit more from declining interest rates than the structures held in the previous quarter. One of the directors asked why. How should Ms. Xu respond?

20. Ms. Smith is the portfolio manager of the Good Corporate Bond Fund, which invests primarily in investment-grade corporate bonds. The fund currently has an overweight within the retail industrial sector bonds of retailers. Ms. Smith is concerned that increased competition from internet retailers will negatively affect the earnings and cash flow of the traditional retailers. The fund is also currently underweighted in the U.S. dollar-denominated bonds of European issuers placed in the United States, which she believes should benefit from increased opportunities afforded by European Union. She believes that many of these companies may come to market with new U.S. dollar issues to fund some of their expansion throughout Europe.

Formulate and support a strategy for Ms. Smith that will capitalize on her views about the retail and European corporate sectors of her portfolio. What factors might negatively impact this strategy?

CHAPTER 21

INTERNATIONAL BOND PORTFOLIO MANAGEMENT

LEARNING OUTCOMES

After reading Chapter 21 you should be able to:

- explain how the investor's investment objectives are related to international bond portfolio management.
- explain how international bond portfolio investment guidelines should incorporate the investor's investment objectives.
- identify the benchmarks available to international bond investors.
- explain the difference between the active approach to currency management and a fully hedged or unhedged approach.
- identify the key trading blocs for international bonds.
- discuss the styles of international bond portfolio management (the experienced trader, the fundamentalist, the black box, and the chartist).
- explain the broad strategies (currency selection, duration management/yield curve plays, bond market selection, sector/credit/security selection, and off benchmark investing) that can potentially generate excess returns relative to an international bond index.
- identify the fundamental economic factors used by a portfolio manager to create an economic outlook for a country.
- explain objective measures of value and technical indicators used by international bond portfolio managers (real yields, technical analysis, and market sentiment surveys).
- explain the three excess return components (excess returns on bonds, excess returns on currencies, and short-term interest rate risk) that can be generated from international bond portfolio management.
- explain what a currency forward contract is.
- compute the fair value of a currency forward contract.
- explain what interest rate parity is.
- explain what covered interest arbitrage is.
- explain the following strategies for managing currency risk exposure: hedge, cross currency hedge, and proxy hedge.
- compute the components of excess returns for an unhedged strategy, a hedged strategy, a cross currency hedged strategy, and a proxy hedged strategy.
- determine whether a manager should employ an unhedged or some hedged strategy to manage currency risk exposure.

- adjust bond yields for coupon payment frequency.
- explain what bond and currency breakeven rates are.
- explain the role of forward interest rates and forward currency rates in identifying investment opportunities.

SUMMARY OVERVIEW

- Most investors are attracted to international bonds because of their historically higher returns than U.S. bonds; others are attracted by the diversification value of international bonds in reducing overall portfolio risk.
- The investor's investment objectives (total return, diversification or risk reduction, current income, or asset/liability matching) have implications for the management of an international bond portfolio.
- The investor's investment objectives should be reflected in the investment guidelines, including return objectives, risk tolerances, benchmark selection, and appropriate time horizon for evaluating performance.
- For an investor interested in the diversification benefits of international bond investing, the investment performance time horizon is important.
- In selecting a benchmark for an international bond portfolio, the choice of a pure capitalization (market value) weighted index may create a benchmark that exposes the investor to a disproportionate share in some countries' markets relative to the investor's liabilities or diversification preferences.
- International bond benchmarks may be hedged, unhedged, or partially hedged depending on an investor's objectives.
- Studies of U.S. dollar-based currency hedging suggest that a partially hedged benchmark offers superior risk-adjusted returns as compared to either a fully hedged or unhedged benchmark.
- Historically, the returns from different currency exposures (unhedged, partially hedged, and fully hedged) are highly variable depending on the time period chosen.
- Because international investing entails currency risk, a portfolio manager can actively manage currency exposure, be fully hedged to currency exposure, or be unhedged to currency exposure.
- Bond markets can be divided into four trading blocs: dollar bloc (the U.S., Canada, Australia, and New Zealand); European bloc; Japan; and, emerging markets.
- The European bloc can be further divided into the euro zone market bloc (which has a common currency) and the non-euro zone market bloc.
- The U.K. market often trades on its own economic fundamentals, as well as being influenced by both the euro zone market bloc and the U.S. market.
- It is useful to think in terms of trading blocs because each bloc has a benchmark market that greatly influences price movements in the other markets within the bloc.
- Investment guidelines should specify limits on investments in countries outside the benchmark.
- Risk limits on duration are usually specified in investment policy statements despite the shortcomings of duration as an aggregate measure of interest rate risk when applied across countries.
- There are a number of means portfolio managers can enhance returns relative to a benchmark with major excess return sources coming from broad bond market and currency allocation decisions.

- International bond managers often employ one or more different management styles and these styles can be divided into four general categories: experienced trader; fundamentalist; black box; and chartist.
- The seasoned trader uses experience and intuition to identify market opportunities.
- The fundamental style assumes bonds and currencies trade according to the economic cycle, and that the cycle can be forecasted; managers using this approach rely mostly upon economic analysis and forecasts in selecting bond markets and currencies.
- The black box style is used by quantitative managers who believe computer models can identify market relationships that people cannot.
- The chartist style involves looking at daily, weekly, and monthly charts to ascertain the strength of market trends, or to identify potential turning points in markets.
- Excess returns for an international bond portfolio relative to its benchmark can be generated through a combination of five broad strategies: bond market selection; currency selection; duration management/yield curve plays; sector/credit/security selection, and; if permitted, investing in markets outside the benchmark.
- Because most benchmarks include only government bonds, investing in non-government bonds can also enhance returns.
- In a fundamental-based approach to global bond investing, the strategic decision of which bond markets and currencies to overweight typically starts with an outlook for the economic cycle and forecasts for the bond and currency markets considered for investment.
- The long-run economic cycle is closely correlated with changes in bond yields, and trends in both the economic cycle and bond yields tend to persist for a year or longer.
- Forecasting interest rates is extremely difficult and the academic literature generally holds that interest rate forecasts are unable to generate consistent risk-adjusted excess returns.
- The manager's economic outlook forms the foundation for bond and currency strategic allocation.
- The economic outlook must be compared with either consensus economic forecasts, or some market value measure to identify attractive investment opportunities.
- The volatilities and correlations of the various bond and currency markets should be used to assess the incremental impact of any position on overall portfolio risk compared with its expected return.
- The strategic allocation decision (markets to overweight or underweight relative to the benchmark) is a complex interaction of expected returns derived from assessments of economic trends, technical and value factors, and risk factors, estimated from historical volatilities and cross-market correlations.
- The key economic fundamental categories that need to be evaluated against market expectations to determine their likely affect on bond and currency prices are: cyclical economic indicators, inflation, monetary policy, fiscal policy, debt, balance of payments, and politics.
- Identifying economic fundamental trends can help identify attractive market investment opportunities.
- While determining relative value is highly subjective, the three more objective measures of value are: real yields, technical analysis, and market sentiment surveys.
- Sources of return for an international bond portfolio can be separated into three components: excess returns on bonds, excess returns on currencies, and the risk-free rate.
- Partitioning return sources into three components can assist a portfolio manager in identifying where market prices are most out of line with the strategic outlook and whether bond market exposures should be hedged or unhedged.

- The most common vehicle used to alter exposure to exchange rates is a currency forward contract.
- Based on covered interest arbitrage, the spot exchange rate and the short-term interest rates in two countries will determine the forward exchange rate.
- The relationship among the spot exchange rate, the short-term interest rates in two countries, and the forward rate is called interest rate parity.
- Whether or not a manager will hedge the exposure to a given country's exchange rate using a forward exchange rate depends on (1) the manager's expectation as to the percentage return from exposure to a currency and (2) the forward discount or premium.
- If the manager expects the percentage return from exposure to a currency is greater than the forward discount or premium, the manager will not use a forward contract to hedge the exposure to that currency.
- If the manager expects the currency return to be less than the forward discount or premium, the manager will use a forward contract to hedge the exposure to that currency.
- Cross forward hedging replaces the currency exposure of country i with currency exposure of country j; rather than hedging with a forward contract between country i and the home currency, the manager elects to hold country j's currency instead of country i's currency using a forward contract between country j and country i.
- Proxy hedging involves shorting a second currency, currency j; that is, proxy hedging keeps the currency exposure in country i, but creates a hedge by establishing a short position in country j's currency.
- A proxy hedge would normally be considered only where the currencies of country i and j are highly correlated, and the hedge costs in country j are lower than in country i.
- The expected return for country i using proxy hedging depends on the short-term interest rate in the home country plus (1) the excess bond return (or the differential between the bond return for country i and the short-term interest rate for country i), and (2) the excess currency return (the difference between the long currency position in country i relative to the home country and the short currency position in country j relative to the home country, minus the forward premium between countries i and j comprised of the short-term interest rate differential between the two countries).
- An unhedged expected return is equal to the short-term interest rate in the home country plus (1) the excess bond return (or the differential between the bond return for country i and the short-term interest rate for country i), and (2) the excess currency return (the long currency position in country i relative to the home country minus the forward premium between the home country and country i comprised of the short-term interest rate differential between the two countries).
- The short-term interest rate differential is integral to the currency hedge decision.
- The return for a strategy can be divided into three distinct components of return: the short-term interest rate for the home currency; the excess bond return of country i over the short-term interest rate of country i, and; the excess currency return (either unhedged, hedged, cross-hedged, or proxy hedged).
- The excess currency return is the currency return in excess of the forward premium (or discount) and becomes the basis for the decision of currency hedging.
- In evaluating relative value in international bond markets, it is necessary to either convert the economic outlook into point forecasts for bond and currency levels, or look at the forward rates implied by current market conditions and compare them with the economic outlook.

- When making conventional yield comparisons between countries it is necessary to make an adjustment if there is a difference in the frequency of coupon payments between the two countries.
- Bond and currency breakeven rates are rates that make two investments produce identical total returns.
- Comparisons of forward interest rates can be instrumental in identifying where differences between the strategic outlook and market prices may present investment opportunities.

PROBLEMS

1. Mr. Johnson is a trustee for the Wilford Corporate pension fund. At the present time the pension fund's investment guidelines do not permit investment in non-U.S. bonds. A pension fund consultant suggested the trustees invest 30% of its fixed income portfolio in non-U.S. bonds. The benefit, according to the consultant, is that international diversification will allow the pension fund to realize a higher expected return for a given level of risk. Moreover, the consultant noted that there are benefits from "currency plays."

    Mr. Johnson asked the consultant to provide empirical support identifying the benefits from international bond investing from 1985 to 1996. More specifically, he asked for a monthly return analysis over several time periods based on an allocation of 70% to domestic bonds and 30% to international bonds. Mr. Johnson also asked for the performance if foreign currency exposure were unhedged or hedged. The consultant provided the analysis shown below:

Lehman Aggregate Portfolio vs. a Portfolio with 30% International Bond Exposure

	1985–96	1985–88	1989–92	1993–96	1989–96
Annualized Total Return					
Unhedged Portfolio	11.40%	15.78%	10.54%	8.16%	9.33%
Hedged Portfolio	9.69	11.30	10.14	7.70	8.90
U.S. Aggregate Index	10.10	11.76	11.66	6.94	9.28
Standard Deviation of Returns					
Unhedged Portfolio	4.79	5.82	4.51	3.63	4.12
Hedged Portfolio	3.64	4.38	3.10	3.20	3.18
U.S. Aggregate Index	4.86	5.90	4.12	4.24	4.22
Sharpe Ratio					
Unhedged Portfolio	1.13	1.54	0.87	0.99	0.91
Hedged Portfolio	1.02	1.02	1.14	0.98	1.04
U.S. Aggregate Index	0.84	0.84	1.23	0.56	0.87

   a. For the period 1985–1996, how did the performance of a portfolio of 30% international bonds compare to that of the U.S. Aggregate Index (i.e., U.S. bonds only) if the portfolio is unhedged?
   b. Is the performance of an unhedged bond portfolio with 30% international bonds dependent on the time period selected?
   c. If the currency risk is hedged, what does the evidence suggest about the performance of a bond portfolio with 30% international bonds compared to an all U.S. bond portfolio?

2. Why might an absolute total-return investor be less concerned about how a portfolio's composition differs from a benchmark?

3. For a client that is interested in the diversification benefits of international bond investing, why might the selection of a longer-term time horizon (such as two to three years) be preferred to a short-term time horizon (for example, one quarter) to evaluate the performance of a manager?

4. Why is international bond investing more complex than investing in the U.S. bond market?

5. a. Coupon payments on U.K. government bonds are semiannual. What is the yield on an annual-pay basis for a U.K. government bond for which the conventional yield is 5%?

   b. Coupon payments on German government bonds are annual. What is the bond-equivalent yield on a semiannual-pay basis for a German government bond for which the conventional yield is 5.6%?

6. A portfolio manager is reviewing a report that shows the conventional yield on a 10-year U.S. Treasury bond (6%) and the conventional yield on a 10-year of Spanish government bond (5%). Coupon interest is paid annually on Spanish government bonds. The yield spread between the Spanish government bond and the U.S. government bond shown in the report was *not* −100 basis points. The manager does not understand why. Explain to this manager why the yield spread would not be −100 basis points. (No computation is required.)

7. Suppose the spot exchange rate between U.S. dollars and the local currency for Country A is US $2 for one unit of the local currency (LC). Assume the following interest rates in both countries:

Maturity	United States	Country A
1 month	3.0%	8.5%
3 months	3.5%	9.0%
1 year	4.0%	10.00%
5 years	4.9%	11.00%

Assume that within each country, the borrowing and lending rate is the same. A 1-year forward exchange rate contract is available between U.S. dollars and the local currency.

   a. What should the 1-year forward exchange rate be?
   b. If the 1-year forward exchange rate between U.S. dollars and the local currency of Country A is US $2.1 for one unit of the local currency, demonstrate how a U.S. portfolio manager can exploit this pricing for the forward contract?
   c. If the 1-year forward exchange rate between U.S. dollars and the local currency of Country A is US $1.7 for one unit of the local currency, demonstrate how a portfolio manager in Country A can exploit this pricing for the forward contract?

8. a. How can a portfolio manager hedge a long position exposure to a currency?
   b. How does a cross hedge differ from a proxy hedge?

9. A U.S. portfolio manager is considering whether or not to hedge his exposure to Country X's currency. The following is the relevant information available to the manager, as well as the manager's expectations:

   Expected bond return in Country X = 4.0%

   Short-term interest rate in Country X = 3.2%

   Expected currency appreciation of currency X relative to U.S. $ = 5.1%

   Short-term U.S. interest rate = 4.6%

a. What is the unhedged expected *excess currency* return?
b. What is the unhedged expected total return?
c. What is the hedged expected total return?
d. Should the manager hedge the position?
e. Suppose that the manager is considering cross hedging with Country Y's currency and the following information is available along with an additional assumption:

> Short-term interest rate in Country Y = 4.0%
>
> Expected currency appreciation of currency Y relative to U.S. $ = 4.6%

> What is the expected *excess currency* return from cross hedging using Country Y's currency?

f. What is the hedged expected total return from the cross hedge?
g. Based on your answer to part f, is a cross hedge attractive relative to hedging currency X directly and an unhedged strategy?
h. Suppose that the manager wants to use Country Y's currency for proxy hedging. What is the expected *excess currency* return for this proxy hedge strategy?
i. What is the expected total return from this proxy hedge strategy?
j. Should a proxy hedge strategy be employed?

10. A British portfolio manager is considering whether or not to hedge the portfolio's exposure to Country A's currency. The following is the relevant information available to the manager, as well as the manager's expectations:

> Expected bond return in Country A = 3.3%
>
> Short-term interest rate in Country A = 2.9%
>
> Expected currency appreciation of currency A relative to British £ = −1.2%
>
> > (Note a negative sign means depreciation of the currency.)
>
> Short-term British interest rate = 4.6%

a. What is the unhedged expected *excess currency* return?
b. What is the unhedged expected total return?
c. What is the hedged expected total return?
d. Should the manager hedge the position?
e. Suppose that the British portfolio manager is considering cross hedging with the currency of Country B and the following information is available to the manager, along with the manager's assumptions:

> Short-term interest rate in Country B = 4.2%
>
> Expected currency appreciation of currency B relative to British £ = −3.5%

> What is the expected *excess currency* return from cross hedging using Country B's currency?

f. What is the hedged expected total return from the cross hedge?
g. Based on your answer to part f, is a cross hedge attractive relative to hedging currency A and an unhedged strategy?

h. Suppose that the manager wants to use Country B's currency for proxy hedging. What is the expected *excess currency* return for this proxy hedge strategy?
i. What is the expected return from this proxy hedge strategy?
j. Should a proxy hedge strategy be employed?

11. Before making country and currency allocation decisions based on market outlook, an international bond portfolio manager should examine the expectations priced into the market.

a. Where can a manager obtain information about the expectations priced into the market?
b. Why does information priced into the market provide a benchmark for comparing a manager's interest rate and currency outlook for the countries in which the manager plans to invest?
c. Why might a portfolio manager who expects Country Y's currency will depreciate in the next year still want to increase currency exposure to that country's currency?

12. Suppose that on some date the following information is available for the 10-year government benchmark of Country M and the United States:

Country	Yield to maturity	Duration
M	3.2%	6
U.S.	7.0%	4

From the perspective of a portfolio manager in country M, there is a 3.8% annual yield advantage to invest in the United States. Suppose that the manager is interested in investing in either the benchmark government bond of his own country or the U.S. government benchmark bond and the investment horizon is three months.

a. Explain how the 380 basis point annual yield advantage from investing in the U.S. can be eliminated over the next three months?
b. What is the breakeven spread movement for the yield in Country M?
c. What is the breakeven spread movement for the yield in the United States?
d. Suppose that the 3-month rates were 2.5% in Country M and 6.5% in the U.S. What is the expected hedged return to a portfolio manager in Country M over a 3-month period assuming no change in interest rates?
e. On a hedged basis, what is the breakeven spread movement in terms of a tightening of the spread in Country M?
f. On an unhedged investment even if yields do not change in the U.S. or Country M, currency movements can eliminate the yield advantage from investing in the U.S. government bond. What is the view that the portfolio manager in Country M must have in order to benefit from the additional yield from investing in the U.S. government bond?

CHAPTER 22

CONTROLLING INTEREST RATE RISK WITH DERIVATIVES

LEARNING OUTCOMES

After reading Chapter 22 you should be able to:

- identify the advantages of using interest rate futures rather than Treasury securities to control the interest rate risk of a portfolio.
- explain the basic principles of controlling interest rate risk.
- determine the position in a futures contract that adjusts the current dollar duration of a portfolio to that of the target dollar duration.
- calculate the number of futures contracts that must be bought or sold in order to achieve a portfolio's target duration.
- compute the dollar duration of a futures contract.
- explain why hedging is a special case of controlling interest rate risk.
- describe a short hedge and a long hedge and explain when each hedge is used.
- explain what a cross hedge is.
- identify the steps in the hedging process.
- identify the factors that are important for determining the appropriate hedging instrument.
- describe basis risk and explain why hedging with futures substitutes basis risk for price risk.
- describe which price or rate is locked in when hedging with a futures contract.
- describe convergence for a futures contract.
- calculate the number of futures contracts that must be sold to hedge a position against a rise in interest rates.
- explain how the position in a Treasury bond futures contract is adjusted for the cheapest-to-deliver issue.
- explain why an assumption must be made about the yield spread between a bond to be hedged and the hedging instrument.
- describe yield beta and explain how it is used to adjust the number of futures contracts in a hedge.
- identify the major sources of hedging error.
- show how the cash flows of an entity can be altered using an interest rate swap.
- calculate the cash flows of an entity that has taken a position in an interest rate swap.

- compute the dollar duration of an interest rate swap.
- explain how positions in an interest rate swap change the dollar duration of an entity.
- describe the basic hedging strategies that use options.
- explain how the outcome of a protective put buying strategy differs from that of a hedge using futures contracts.
- explain the limitations of a covered call writing strategy for hedging.
- describe a collar strategy.
- compute the appropriate strike price when using futures options to hedge a nondeliverable bond.
- compute the number of futures options required to hedge a position.
- explain how interest rate caps and floors can be used in asset/liability management.

SUMMARY OVERVIEW

- Buying an interest rate futures contract increases a portfolio's duration; selling an interest rate futures contract decreases a portfolio's duration.
- The advantages of adjusting a portfolio's duration using futures rather than cash market instruments are that transaction costs are lower, margin requirements are lower, selling short in the futures market is easier, and a portfolio with a longer duration than is available using cash market securities can be constructed.
- The general principle in controlling interest rate risk with futures is to combine the dollar exposure of the current portfolio and that of a futures position so that it equals the target dollar exposure.
- The number of futures contracts needed to achieve the target dollar duration depends on the current dollar duration of the portfolio without futures and the dollar duration per futures contract.
- Hedging with futures calls for taking a futures position as a temporary substitute for transactions to be made in the cash market at a later date, with the expectation that any loss realized in one position (whether cash or futures) will be offset by a profit on the other position.
- Hedging is a special case of controlling interest rate risk in which the target duration or target dollar duration is zero.
- Cross hedging occurs when the bond to be hedged is not identical to the bond underlying the futures contract.
- A short or sell hedge is used to protect against a decline in the cash price of a bond; a long or buy hedge is employed to protect against an increase in the cash price of a bond.
- The steps in hedging include: (1) determining the appropriate hedging instrument; (2) determining the target for the hedge; (3) determining the position to be taken in the hedging instrument; and, (4) monitoring and evaluating the hedge.
- The key factor in identifying which futures contract will provide the best hedge is the correlation between the price on the futures contract and the interest rate that creates the underlying risk that the manager seeks to eliminate.
- The manager should determine the target rate or target price for the hedge.
- The hedge ratio is the number of futures contracts needed for the hedge.
- The basis is the difference between the spot price (or rate) and the futures price (or rate).
- In general, when hedging to the delivery date of the futures contract, a manager locks in the futures rate or price.

- Hedging with Treasury bond futures and Treasury note futures is complicated by the delivery options embedded in these contracts.
- For a hedge lifted prior to the delivery date, the shorter the term of the hedge, the more closely the effective rate (or price) approximates the current spot rate rather than the futures rate.
- The target for a hedge that is to be lifted prior to the delivery date depends on the basis.
- Basis risk is the uncertainty associated with the target rate basis or target price basis.
- Hedging substitutes basis risk for price risk.
- Hedging non-Treasury securities with Treasury bond futures requires that the hedge ratio consider two relationships: (1) that between the cash price of the non-Treasury security and the cheapest-to-deliver issue and (2) that between the price of the cheapest-to-deliver issue and the futures price.
- The yield beta is important in computing the hedge ratio for nondeliverable securities; regression analysis is used to estimate the yield beta and captures the relationship between yield levels and yield spreads.
- After a target is determined and a hedge is set, the hedge must be monitored during its life and evaluated after it is over.
- It is important to ascertain the sources of error in a hedge in order to gain insights that can be advantageous in subsequent hedges.
- An interest rate swap can be used to hedge interest rate risk by altering the cash flow characteristics of a portfolio of assets so as to match liability cash flows.
- The dollar duration of a swap follows from its economic interpretation as a leveraged position.
- For the fixed-rate receiver, the dollar duration of a swap is approximately equal to the duration of a fixed-rate bond.
- For the fixed-rate payer, the dollar duration of a swap is approximately equal to the negative of the duration of a fixed-rate bond.
- A swap in which a manager pays floating and receives fixed increases the duration of a portfolio; a swap in which a manager pays fixed and receives floating decreases the duration of a portfolio.
- Three popular hedge strategies are the protective put buying strategy, the covered call writing strategy, and the collar strategy.
- A manager can use a protective put buying strategy to hedge against rising interest rates.
- A protective put buying strategy is a simple combination of a long put option with a long position in a cash bond.
- A covered call writing strategy involves selling call options against the bond portfolio.
- A covered call writing strategy entails much more downside risk than buying a put to protect the value of the portfolio and many managers do not consider covered call writing a hedge.
- It is not possible to say that the protective put buying strategy or the covered call writing strategy is necessarily the better or more correct options hedge; the best strategy (and the best strike prices) depends upon the manager's view of the market and risk tolerance.
- A collar strategy is a combination of a protective put buying strategy and a covered call writing strategy.
- A manager who implements a collar strategy eliminates part of the portfolio's downside risk by giving up part of its upside potential.

- The steps in options hedging include determining the option contract that is the best hedging vehicle, finding the appropriate strike price, and determining the number of options contracts.
- At initiation of an options hedge, a minimum effective sale price can be calculated for a protective put buying strategy and a maximum effective sale price can be computed for a covered call writing strategy.
- The best options contract to use in a hedging strategy depends upon the option price, liquidity, and correlation with the bond(s) to be hedged.
- For a cross hedge, the manager converts the strike price for the options that are bought or sold into an equivalent strike price for the actual bonds being hedged.
- When using Treasury bond futures options, the hedge ratio is based on the relative dollar duration of the current portfolio, the cheapest-to-deliver issue, the futures contract at the option expiration date, and the conversion factor for the cheapest-to-deliver issue.
- While there are some mechanical differences in the way options on physicals and options on futures are traded and there may be substantial differences in their liquidity, the basic economics of the hedging strategies are virtually identical for both contracts.
- Using options on physicals frequently eliminates much of the basis risk associated with an options hedge.
- An interest rate floor can be used to establish a minimum rate for a floating-rate security.
- An interest rate cap can be used to set a maximum funding cost.

PROBLEMS

1. Mr. Dawson is a portfolio manager who is responsible for the account of the Pizza Delivery Personnel Union (PDPU). At this time, the trustees have not authorized Mr. Dawson to take positions in Treasury bond futures contracts. At his quarterly meeting with PDPU's board of trustees, Mr. Dawson requested that the board grant him authorization to use Treasury bond futures to control interest rate risk. One of the trustees asked whether it was necessary to use Treasury bond futures contracts to control risk. The trustee noted that Mr. Dawson already had authorization by the investment guidelines to short Treasury securities and that should be sufficient to control interest rate risk when combined with the opportunity to buy Treasury securities. What advantages could Mr. Dawson present to the trustee for using Treasury futures contracts to control risk rather than using Treasury securities?

2. The trustees of the Egg Craters pension fund are discussing with their consultant, Mr. William, about establishing a new benchmark for the fund's external bond managers. The benchmark would be based on the projected duration of the fund's liabilities. Currently, the investment guidelines of the fund do not permit its managers to leverage the portfolio or utilize futures.

   At the time of the meeting, the duration of the universe of Treasury coupon bonds with more than 25 years to maturity was 6. Mr. William reported that the duration of the liabilities is approximately 11. He explained that, under the current investment guidelines, if a bond portfolio must be created to have a duration of 11, the managers will have to invest a good portion of their portfolio in longer-term zero-coupon bonds. To avoid this and still allow the managers to create a portfolio with a duration of 11, it will be necessary for the trustees to change the fund's investment guidelines to (1) permit the managers to employ leverage and/or (2) permit the managers to use futures contracts.

The trustees asked Mr. William why it was necessary to revise the investment guidelines as he suggested. Explain this reasoning to the trustees.

3. Ms. Marcus is a portfolio manager who is responsible for a $200 million portion of the bond portfolio of UltraChip.com's pension fund. The current investment guidelines specify that the duration for the portfolio can be in a range of minus one and plus one of the benchmark. Currently, the duration for the benchmark is 4 and the duration for the portfolio is 5. Ms. Marcus expects that rates will rise. She wants to reduce the duration of the portfolio to the lower end of the duration range, 3, by using Treasury bond futures contracts, which she is authorized to use by the pension fund's investment guidelines.

   a. What position (long or short) should Ms. Marcus take in Treasury bond futures to reduce the duration from 5 to 3?

   b. Suppose that the dollar duration per Treasury bond futures contract (based on the cheapest-to-deliver issue) for a 50 basis point change in rates is $5,000. How many Treasury bond futures contracts must be bought or sold?

4. Suppose that the dollar duration for the cheapest-to-deliver issue for the Treasury bond futures contract is $6,000 per 50 basis point change in rates and the conversion factor for that issue is 0.90. What is the dollar duration for the futures contract per 50 basis point change in rates?

5. Why is hedging a special case of interest rate risk management?

6. What factors should a portfolio manager consider when selecting which futures contract will best control a portfolio's interest rate risk?

7. a. What is meant by the "target price" for a hedge?

   b. How does a manager use information about the target price for a hedge when deciding whether or not to hedge?

8. Mr. Ulston is a bond portfolio manager who, although familiar with interest rate futures, has not previously used them in managing a portfolio. Recently, Mr. Ulston received authorization from several clients to use interest rate futures and so contacted one of his brokers to obtain information on using futures to control interest rate risk. The broker suggested that Mr. Ulston contact the risk manager of the brokerage firm, Ms. Alvarez, so that she could explain how she uses interest rate futures to control the firm's interest rate risk. In his conversation with Ms. Alvarez, Mr. Ulston asked her about what he would be able to lock in by using interest rate futures. Was it the current price of the bond to be hedged or was it the futures price? Ms. Alvarez responded that when she used interest rate futures to hedge her firm's bond position overnight, she was basically locking in the current price.

   Mr. Ulston also contacted a former associate, James Granger, who manages a bond portfolio and has experience using interest rate futures. When Mr. Ulston asked Mr. Granger the same question he had asked Ms. Alvarez, he received a different answer. Mr. Granger said that typically he puts on hedges that are removed near the delivery date of the futures contract and that he locks in the futures price.

   Mr. Ulston is confused as to why Ms. Alvarez and Mr. Granger indicated that they were locking in different prices by using interest rate futures. He asks you to explain which price is being locked in by using interest rate futures to hedge and who was correct, Ms. Alvarez or Mr. Granger. What is your response?

9. a. In a hedging strategy, what is meant by basis risk?

   b. Explain why hedging substitutes basis risk for price risk?

   c. Explain why a manager would be willing to substitute basis risk for price risk?

10. Explain what is meant by a cross hedge?
11. What are the two important relationships in cross hedging mortgage passthrough securities using Treasury note futures contracts?
12. Mr. Denton has a $20 million par value position in an investment-grade corporate bond. He has decided to hedge the position for one month using Treasury bond futures contracts that settle in one month. Mr. Denton's research assistant provided the following information:

Information about the corporate bond:	*Information about the Treasury bond futures contract*:
coupon rate (semiannual pay) = 8%	settlement date = 1 month
years to maturity = 30	futures price = 106
par value = $20 million	cheapest-to-deliver issue:
market price = 100	coupon rate (semiannual pay) = 10%
yield to maturity = 8%	years to maturity = 22
structure = bullet bond	price = 133.42
duration *at the settlement date* = 11.3	yield to maturity = 7%
	duration *at the settlement date* = 10.4
	conversion factor = 1.16

Assumptions:

1. The yield spread between the corporate bond and the CTD issue remains unchanged at 100 basis points.
2. The CTD issue will not change at the time the hedge is removed in one month.
3. Delivery will be made on the last business day of the Treasury bond futures contract settlement month.

a. What is the target price for the cheapest-to-deliver issue?
b. Based on the target price for the CTD issue found in part (a), what is the target yield for the CTD issue?
c. What is the target yield for the corporate bond?
d. Given the target yield found in part (c), what is the target price for the corporate bond given the target yield found in part (c)?
e. What is the dollar duration per $100,000 par value of the CTD issue per 50 basis point change in rates based on the price for the CTD issue one month from now? (Remember that dollar duration calculations are based on prices at the delivery date. Assume no change in yield.)
f. What is the dollar duration per $20 million of par value of the corporate bond to be hedged per 50 basis point change in rates based on the price for the corporate bond one month from now? (Remember that dollar duration calculations are based on prices at the delivery date. Assume no change in yield.)
g. How many futures contracts should Mr. Denton short?

13. In cross hedging, what is meant by a "yield beta" and how is it used in constructing a hedge (i.e., computing the number of contracts to buy or sell when hedging)?
14. A portfolio manager estimated that the duration for his $1 billion portfolio is 5.2. Suppose that the manager wants to hedge this portfolio with a Treasury bond futures contract and that the dollar duration of the Treasury bond futures contract for a 50 basis point change in rates is $4,000. How many Treasury bond futures contracts should the manager sell?

15. Mr. Elmo is a portfolio manager who has recently begun to use interest rate futures for risk control. In his first attempt to hedge a long position in a particular bond, he did partially offset the loss associated with a decline in the value of that bond. However, the hedge did not perform as expected. Specifically, he incurred a loss on the hedged position that was considerably greater than he had anticipated. When discussing the outcome with a colleague, Ms. Rosetta, she suggested that there were three things that might have gone wrong when Mr. Elmo constructed the hedge. First, Mr. Elmo might have miscalculated the dollar duration (price sensitivity) of both the futures contract and the bond being hedged. Second, the basis could have changed adversely. Finally, the relationship between the yield movement of the bond to be hedged and the yield on the underlying for the futures contract may have changed.

    Mr. Elmo was not quite sure what Ms. Rosetta meant and has asked you to explain the reasons Ms. Rosetta offered as to why the hedge did not work out as expected. Explain Ms. Rosetta's comments.

16. Mr. Eddy is a portfolio manager for a finance company. The company has a portfolio of consumer loans with a par value of $500 million. Unlike typical auto loans, the borrowers for the loans in the portfolio make no periodic principal payments. Instead, the borrowers make quarterly interest payments and repay the principal at the maturity date of the loan. (That is, the loans are not amortizing loans.) All of the loans have two years to maturity and have a fixed interest rate of 12%.

    Mr. Eddy was able to fund the $500 million for the consumer loans by borrowing at a cost of 3-month LIBOR plus 56 basis points. He recognizes that there is a mismatch between the liabilities to repay the borrowed funds and the cash flow from the consumer loans. He is considering using an interest rate swap to control this risk. The following terms are available for a 2-year interest rate swap: pay fixed of 7.2% and receive LIBOR.

    a. Suppose that Mr. Eddy enters into this swap transaction with a notional amount of $500 million. What is the expected outcome of this swap for each quarter?
    b. What assumption is made about defaults and prepayments in your answer to part (a)?

17. Explain, in terms of equivalent cash market positions, the effect on the dollar duration of a bond portfolio of adding an interest rate swap in which the portfolio manager agrees to pay floating and receive fixed.

18. Why would a bond portfolio manager employ a protective put buying strategy?

19. The investment guidelines of the Wycoff Pension Fund prohibit the fund's external bond managers from using options in any capacity. At a meeting between the trustees of the Wycoff Pension Fund, its consultant, and one of its external portfolio managers, the issue of relaxing this restriction was discussed.

    One trustee agreed that its external managers should be permitted to use options. However, the trustee was adamant that the manager only be allowed to write options on bonds in the portfolio. The trustee felt that in contrast to buying options a strategy of writing call options would not result in a loss to the fund if options expired unexercised nor would the fund have wasted the option premium. In the case of writing call options, the trustee argued that even if the option is exercised, there is no loss to the fund because it collected the option premium and, besides, it is just taking out of its portfolio a bond that it already owns.

    The portfolio manager responded that he was uncomfortable with such a restrictive policy because it is not a true hedging strategy. Moreover, he believes that there are costs associated with the strategy.

The consultant was asked to comment on the statements made by the trustee and the portfolio manager. How should the consultant respond?

20. Why does the payoff of a collar strategy using options have the elements of a protective put buying strategy, a covered call writing strategy, and an unhedged position?

21. Mr. Zhao is a corporate bond portfolio manager. He is interested in hedging a bond with a 20-year maturity and an 8% coupon rate, paid semiannually. The corporate issue is option free (i.e., it is a bullet bond). Mr. Zhao owns $10 million par value of this issue. The bond is trading at par value.

    Mr. Zhao would like to purchase a put option on the issue with a strike price of 90.80. However, because an exchange-traded option with the corporate issue as the underlying does not exist, Mr. Zhao has decided to purchase an exchange-traded put option on a Treasury bond futures contract.

    The yield on the corporate issue is 8% and the yield on the cheapest-to-deliver issue for the futures contract is 6.75%. The cheapest-to-deliver issue has a 20-year maturity and a 7.75% coupon rate, paid semiannually. Mr. Zhao expects that the spread between the corporate issue and the CTD issue will be constant at 125 basis points. The conversion factor for the CTD issue is 0.95.

    What is the strike price for the put option on the Treasury bond futures contract that will be equivalent to a strike price on the corporate issue of 90.80?

22. Suppose that a manager owns a portfolio of bonds with a current market value of $100 million. There are no options in the current portfolio. The manager wants to purchase put options on the Treasury bond futures contract to protect against a decline in the value of the portfolio. Suppose that, based on the strike price, the manager selects for the puts, the dollar duration for a 50 basis point change in rates of the cheapest-to-deliver issue is $4,500 at the expiration date of the put option. Also assume that (1) the duration of the current portfolio is 7 at the expiration date of the put option and (2) the conversion factor for the cheapest-to-deliver issue is 0.90. How many put options should be purchased?

23. A commercial bank owns a portfolio of floating-rate notes. All of the notes have as their reference rate 3-month LIBOR and they all have a cap of 9%.

    a. Suppose the portfolio manager is concerned that interest rates will rise so that the cap on the floating-rate notes will be realized. Explain how the portfolio manager can use an interest rate cap agreement to hedge this risk.
    b. Suppose the portfolio manager is concerned that interest rates will fall below the bank's funding cost of acquiring the floating-rate notes. Explain how an interest rate floor agreement can be used by a portfolio to hedge this risk.

CHAPTER 23

HEDGING MORTGAGE SECURITIES TO CAPTURE RELATIVE VALUE

LEARNING OUTCOMES

After reading Chapter 23 you should be able to:

- identify the risks associated with investing in mortgage securities.
- explain why a mortgage security can exhibit both positive and negative convexity.
- demonstrate how a mortgage security's negative convexity will affect the performance of a hedge.
- explain why a portfolio manager avoids hedging spread risk when hedging a mortgage security.
- distinguish between an individual mortgage security and a Treasury security with respect to the importance of hedging yield curve risk.
- appraise hedging a mortgage security using only a duration-based framework.
- contrast a hedge using two hedging instruments from two maturity sectors of the yield curve to a hedge using one hedging instrument from one maturity sector of the yield curve.
- define "cuspy-coupon" mortgage securities.
- discuss the modification of a two-bond hedge when hedging cuspy-coupon mortgage securities.

SUMMARY OVERVIEW

- The price-yield relationship for a mortgage security exhibits both positive and negative convexity.
- For a security that exhibits negative convexity, the price increase when interest rates decline is less than the price decrease when interest rates rise.
- For a security that exhibits negative convexity, there is an adverse change in duration when interest rates change.
- Because of the negative convexity characteristics of a mortgage security, investors consider mortgages to be market-directional investments that should be avoided when one expects interest rates to decline.
- When properly managed, mortgage securities are not market-directional investments.

- At the portfolio level, without proper hedging to offset the changes in the duration of mortgage securities caused by interest rate movements, the portfolio's duration would drift adversely from its target duration.
- An agency mortgage security position is equivalent to a position in a comparable-duration Treasury security and selling a call option.
- The yield of a mortgage security is the sum of the yield on an equal interest-rate risk Treasury security and a spread.
- For a mortgage security, the spread is the sum of the option cost (i.e., the expected cost of bearing prepayment risk) and the option-adjusted spread (i.e., the risk premium for bearing the remaining risks).
- There are five principal risks in mortgage securities: spread, interest-rate, prepayment, volatility, and model risk.
- Because a portfolio manager wants to capture an attractive option-adjusted spread, the manager does not seek to hedge spread risk but only interest rate risk.
- After hedging the interest rate risk of a mortgage security, the portfolio manager has the potential to earn the Treasury bill rate plus the OAS.
- For a mortgage security, yield curve risk is considerably greater than for a Treasury security.
- A portfolio manager can manage volatility risk by buying options or hedging dynamically.
- A portfolio manager will hedge dynamically when the volatility implied in the option price is high and the portfolio manager believes that future realized volatility will be lower than implied volatility.
- A portfolio manager will hedge by purchasing options when the implied volatility in option prices is low and the portfolio manager believes that actual future volatility will be higher than implied.
- Implied volatility is computed using the Monte Carlo simulation valuation framework.
- In hedging a mortgage security, it is difficult to use key rate duration to manage yield curve risk.
- An alternative approach is to investigate how yield curves have changed historically and incorporate typical yield curve change scenarios into the hedging process.
- Studies have found that yield curve changes are not parallel and that when the level of interest rates changes, 2-year yields move about twice as much as long-term yields.
- Studies suggest that the two most important factors in explaining changes in the yield curve are changes in the level and twist (i.e., steepening and flattening).
- To properly hedge the interest rate risk associated with a mortgage security, the portfolio manager needs to estimate how mortgage security prices will change taking into account (1) how the yield curve can change over time and (2) the effect of changes in the yield curve on the prepayment option granted to homeowners.
- The interest rate sensitivity measure is superior to effective duration for assessing the impact of a change in the yield curve on the price of a mortgage security.
- The interest rate sensitivity measure quantifies a security's percentage price change in response to a shift in the yield curve.
- Since two factors (the "level" and "twist" factors) have accounted for most of the changes in the yield curve, in hedging a mortgage security two Treasury notes (typically the 2-year and 10-year) are used.
- A hedge in which two hedging instruments representing different maturity sectors of the yield curve are used is referred to as a two-bond hedge.
- The basic principle in constructing a two-bond hedge is to express a particular mortgage security's exposure to a change in the level and twist of the yield curve in terms of

an equivalent position in U.S. Treasuries or an equivalent position in Treasury futures contracts.

- By mathematically expressing a mortgage security's exposure to a change in the level of interest rates and a twist in the yield curve, a portfolio manager can compute the unique quantities of the two hedging instruments that will simultaneously hedge the mortgage security's price response to both level and twist scenarios.

- Determining the amount of the two hedging instruments requires several steps that involve estimating the price changes of the mortgage security to be hedged and the two hedging instruments for an assumed change in the level of interest rates and an assumed change in the twist of the yield curve.

- One of the important assumptions in constructing the two-bond hedge is that the average price change is a good approximation of how a mortgage security's price will change for a small movement in interest rates

- The average price change less accurately approximates price changes for a cuspy-coupon mortgage security than for a current-coupon mortgage security.

- A cuspy-coupon mortgage security is a mortgage security for which changes in interest rates have large effects on prepayments and hence on price. For such securities, using the average price change will not provide the correct information for hedging.

- Hedging cuspy-coupon mortgage securities only with Treasury notes or futures contracts exposes a portfolio manager to more negative convexity than is desired.

- The addition to a two-bond hedge of an appropriate number of interest rate options enables a portfolio manager to offset some or all of the negative convexity of a cuspy-coupon mortgage security.

PROBLEMS

1. Roger McFee is a fixed income portfolio manager for Wells Asset Management Partners. In a meeting with his firm's client, Mr. McFee discussed his current strategy. He explained that it is his firm's view that there are a number of opportunities available in the mortgage sector of the fixed-income market for enhancing return. The strategy involved purchasing what were viewed to be undervalued mortgage products and hedging the interest rate risk. After Mr. McFee's presentation, the client questioned him as to the prudence of the strategy. The client stated: "If you are going to hedge the interest rate risk then why bother buying mortgage products? After hedging, won't you be earning simply a short-term risk-free rate?"

   How should Mr. McFee respond to this question?

2. Laura Sze is the fixed-income strategist for a brokerage firm. She is responsible for setting the allocation of funds among the major sectors of the investment-grade fixed-income market. Her economic forecast is that interest rates will decline dramatically and that prepayments on mortgages will accelerate. Because of this she recommended in a report distributed to her firm's clients who manage funds versus a U.S. broad-based market index that they consider underweighting high-coupon mortgage passthroughs and overweighting Treasuries. After receiving the report, she received the following e-mail message from the junior portfolio manager of an account customer: "Read your report. I am confused. If you expect interest rates to decline, why would I prefer Treasuries to mortgage passthroughs. Won't both Treasuries and passthroughs appreciate if interest rates decline? Please explain the rationale for your recommendation."

   How should Ms. Sze respond to this customer?

3. James Neutron is a trustee for a pension fund. In a recent report he received from one of the fund's asset managers, he noticed the overweighting of mortgage passthrough securities relative to the manager's benchmark. Mr. Neutron was concerned by the overweighting for the reason described in the following e-mail he sent to the asset manager, Ron Prain:

> Dear Mr. Prain:
>
> Just received your report on the portfolio composition. I am troubled by your overweighting of mortgage passthroughs. While I recognize that the investment guidelines grant you the authority to overweight as you have done, my concern is with the prudence of doing so. It is well known that mortgage passthrough securities are market-directional securities.
>
> Sincerely,
>
> James Neutron

    What should Mr. Prain's response be?

4. You are the portfolio manager of a mortgage portfolio. A new junior portfolio manager, Alexander Coffee, wants you to explain risk management strategies for the mortgage portfolio. Mr. Coffee understands that there are several risk exposures associated with the portfolio but is especially interested in knowing how volatility risk can be hedged. Explain to Mr. Coffee how this can be done.

5. What is the problem of using duration only to hedge a mortgage security?

6. Carol Ryan manages an MBS portfolio. She is considering the purchase of $10 million par value of a Freddie Mac passthrough selling at 99.895 because of its attractive option-adjusted spread. She would like to hedge against an adverse movement in interest rates in order to lock in the benefit from the attractive OAS and wants to do so using a two-bond hedge. The hedging instruments she will use are the 2-year and 10-year Treasury note futures. At the time of the purchase/hedge, the prices for the 2-year Treasury note futures and 10-year Treasury note futures are 106.650 and 111.190, respectively.

    Using her firm's proprietary MBS valuation model which computes the value of an MBS based on her firm's typical shift in the level and twist in the yield curve, the following prices are computed for the Freddie Mac passthrough to be hedged, per $100 of par value:

Price for increase in yield:	97.955
Price for decrease in yield:	101.100
Flattening of the yield curve:	99.450
Steepening of the yield curve:	100.350

    Ms. Ryan's firm uses a standard model for pricing futures. Based on typical yield curve shifts used to obtain the price of the Freddie Mac passthrough above, the following prices for the futures are computed:

	Treasury note futures	
	2-year	10-year
Price for increase in yield:	106.122	109.250
Price for decrease in yield:	107.300	113.600
Flattening of the yield curve:	106.104	110.850
Steepening of the yield curve:	107.268	111.790

    a. What type of convexity (positive or negative) does this passthrough exhibit based on the proprietary valuation model? Explain your answer.

    b. Determine the appropriate hedge position in the two hedging instruments.

7. What are the critical assumptions underlying the hedging of a mortgage security?

8. a. What is meant by a "cuspy-coupon mortgage security"?

    b. What modification to the two-bond hedge is recommended for hedging a cuspy-coupon mortgage security?

CHAPTER 24

CREDIT DERIVATIVES IN BOND PORTFOLIO MANAGEMENT

LEARNING OUTCOMES

After reading Chapter 24 you should be able to:

- identify the different types of credit derivatives: total return swaps, credit default products, and credit spread products.
- explain the three ways credit risk can affect a portfolio (default risk, credit spread risk, and downgrade risk).
- illustrate what a total return swap is and how it can be used by a portfolio manager to hedge or acquire credit exposure.
- explain what a credit default swap is and how it can be used to acquire credit protection.
- explain the types of credit events that can be included in a credit default swap to trigger a payout.
- compare the use of a credit default swap and a total return swap.
- explain the two types of credit default options written on an underlying asset (binary credit option on a credit risk asset and binary credit option on a credit spread).
- reproduce the payoff function for a credit spread option where the underlying is a credit risky asset.
- reproduce the payoff function for a credit spread option where the underlying is a credit spread.
- explain a synthetic collateralized debt obligation and how a credit default swap is used in this structured credit product.
- explain the different types of basket default swaps.
- compare the different types of basket default swaps in terms of credit protection provided.

SUMMARY OVERVIEW

- Credit derivatives are financial instruments that are designed to transfer the credit exposure of an underlying asset or issuer between two parties.
- Credit derivatives may take the form of total return swaps, credit default products, or credit spread swaps.

- A portfolio manager can either acquire or hedge credit risk using credit derivatives.
- Market participants in the credit derivatives market include protection buyers, protection sellers, and intermediaries.
- Credit risk may adversely affect a portfolio in three ways: default risk, credit spread risk, and downgrade risk.
- Default risk is the risk that the issuer will default on its obligations.
- Credit spread risk is the risk that the interest rate spread for a credit-risky bond over a riskless bond will increase after the credit risky bond has been purchased.
- Spread duration can be used to approximate credit spread risk.
- Downgrade risk occurs when a nationally recognized statistical rating organization reduces its credit rating for an issuer.
- In the fixed-income market, in a total return swap one party (the total return receiver) makes periodic floating payments to a counterparty (the total return payer) in exchange for the total return realized on an individual reference obligation or a basket of reference obligations.
- A total return swap transfers all of the economic exposure of a reference obligation or a reference basket of obligations to the total return receiver.
- A total return credit swap is different from a credit default swap in that the credit default swap is primarily used to hedge a credit exposure while the total return credit swap can be used to increase credit exposure; in a total return swap, the total return receiver is exposed to both credit risk and interest rate risk.
- Credit default products include credit default swaps and default options on credit-risky assets.
- The most popular type of credit derivative is the credit default swap.
- In a credit default swap, the protection buyer pays a fee (called the swap premium) to the protection seller in return for the right to receive a payment conditional upon the occurrence of a credit event by the reference obligation or the reference entity.
- In a credit default swap, there can be cash or physical settlement.
- The International Swap and Derivatives Association provides a list of potential credit events and a definition for each.
- In a credit default swap, if restructuring is included as a credit event the parties may select from among three ISDA definitions for restructuring.
- In a default option on a credit risky asset, there is a binary credit option with a predetermined payout based on default or based on a credit rating downgrade.
- Credit spread products include credit spread options and credit spread forwards.
- Credit spread options include credit spread options where the underlying is a reference obligation with a fixed credit spread and credit spread options where the underlying is a credit spread on a reference obligation.
- A problem with a credit spread option where the underlying is a reference obligation with a fixed credit spread is that the payoff is affected by both changes in the level of interest rates and the credit spread.
- The payoff for a credit spread option where the underlying is a credit spread is computed as the difference in the credit spreads multiplied by a specified notional amount and by a risk factor, where the risk factor is based on the interest rate price sensitivity of the financial obligation (the dollar value of a 1 basis point change in the credit spread).
- Credit spread forward contracts may be contracted to have an underlying that is either a credit-risky asset or a credit spread.
- Unlike a credit option, with a credit spread forward a portfolio manager shares in both the upside and the downside resulting from a change in the credit spread.

- A synthetic collateralized debt obligation is a structured credit product.
- The bondholders in a synthetic CDO are paid from (1) the cash flow from the collateral which consists of low risk assets and (2) a swap payment from a basket credit default swap.
- The bondholders in a synthetic CDO have sold credit protection on the reference obligations and the return to the bondholders is adversely affected by payments that must be made to the credit protection buyer.
- In a basket default swap, there is more than one reference entity (typically, three to five).
- Basket default swaps are classified as Nth-to-default swaps, subordinate basket default swaps, and senior basket default swaps.

PROBLEMS

1. Why would a portfolio manager be willing to assume the credit risk of a bond or an issuer?
2. Explain the relationship between credit spread risk and downgrade risk.
3. If a portfolio manager wants to estimate a portfolio's credit spread risk exposure what analytical measure can be used?
4. Explain the risk exposures the total return receiver accepts in a total return swap.
5. Why is a total return swap more transactionally efficient than cash market transactions to obtain exposure to a diversified portfolio of corporate bonds?
6. How can a total return swap be used to short a corporate bond?
7. Raul Martinez is a fixed-income portfolio manager. His firm's credit research group has just released a credit report on M&L Global Comm-Tech Corporation. The credit research group feels strongly that within one year the firm's credit fundamentals will strengthen such that the market will demand a lower credit spread. Mr. Martinez believes that the conclusion of the credit research group is correct.

   Next week, M&L Global Comm-Tech Corporation will be coming to market with a 12-year senior bond issue at par with a coupon rate of 11%, offering a spread of 500 basis points over the 12-year Treasury issue.

   Rather than purchase the bonds, Mr. Martinez prefers to express his view on the company's credit risk by entering into a total return swap that matures in one year with the reference obligation being the senior bonds that will be issued by M&L Global Comm-Tech Corporation. The total return swap calls for an exchange of payments semiannually with the total return receiver paying the 6-month Treasury rate plus 250 basis points. The notional amount for the contract is $15 million.

   Suppose that over the one year, the following occurs:

   - the 6-month Treasury rate is 5% initially
   - the 6-month Treasury rate for computing the second semiannual payment is 6%
   - at the end of one year the 11-year Treasury rate is 6.5%
   - at the end of one year the credit spread for the reference obligation is 350 basis points

   a. Would Mr. Martinez enter the total return swap as the total return receiver or total return payer? Explain why.
   b. What is the 12-year Treasury rate at the time the bonds are issued?
   c. If at the end of one year the 11-year Treasury rate is 6.5% and the credit spread declines to 350 basis points, what will be the price of the reference obligation?

d. What is the cash flow paid for the year to the total return receiver assuming that the issuer makes the coupon payments?

e. What are the payments that will be made by the total return receiver?

f. What is the net payment made by the total return receiver?

8. Gary Lawrence manages a corporate bond portfolio. He is interested in seeking credit protection for one bond issue in his portfolio, XYX Senior Bonds that mature in 7 years. The par value of XYX Senior Bonds in the portfolio is $25 million and the market value of the bonds is 60.

   Mr. Lawrence is considering the purchase of a credit default swap with a scheduled term of five years and with XYX Senior Bonds the reference obligations. The swap premium is 600 basis points and the payments are made quarterly. This is the first time he is using a credit default swap and he has asked you the following questions:

   a. What is meant by the credit default swap having a "scheduled term of five years"?

   b. How much should the notional value of the credit default swap be if he wants to protect the entire market value of XYX Senior Bonds in his portfolio?

   c. If the first quarter in which the swap premium must be paid has 90 days, how much will the payment be?

   d. If a credit event occurs, what happens to the credit default swap after payment is received from the protection seller?

   e. If there is a restructuring of the XYX Senior Bonds, will that trigger a payment from the protection seller?

   f. If there is an obligation acceleration of the XYX Senior Bonds, will that trigger a payment from the protection seller?

9. a. What is meant by a restructuring in a credit derivative?

   b. How can restructuring be treated in a credit default swap?

10. All other factors constant, for a given reference obligation and a given scheduled term, explain whether a credit default swap using full (old) restructuring or modified restructuring would be more expensive.

11. A portfolio manager purchases a binary credit put option on a bond of Company X. The option pays out only if the credit rating of Company X declines below investment grade. At the maturity of the option at time T, the payout to the option buyer per $1,000 par value is expressed as:

$$\text{Payout} = \begin{cases} \$1,000 - \text{Value of the bond at time } T; \text{ if the credit rating is below BBB} \\ \$0; \text{ if the credit rating is BBB or higher} \end{cases}$$

   a. Suppose that at the maturity of the option, the credit rating of Company X is BBB and its bonds are worth $950 per bond. What is the payout on this binary credit put option?

   b. Suppose that at the maturity of the option, the credit rating of Company X is BB and its bonds are worth $920 per bond. What is the payout on this binary credit put option?

   c. Suppose that at the maturity of the option, the credit rating of Company X is BB+ and its bonds are worth $1,010 per bond. What is the payout on this binary credit put option?

12. Jonathan Rivers of We Have You Covered Insurance Inc. (WHYCI) manages the insurance company's asset portfolio. He is concerned about a large position in one credit—bond MMM, a high-yield corporate bond issue. For certain reasons, this position cannot be disposed of for another six months. More specifically, he was not concerned with the bankruptcy of the credit but with a rating downgrade that could lead to a widening of the credit spread.

    After reading an article on credit derivatives, Mr. Rivers decides to meet with credit derivative specialists of three dealer firms. Here were their recommendations.

    • Mr. Barnes of Dealer A recommended a 6-month total return swap in which the reference obligation is the bond issue of MMM held by WHYCI and the notional amount is the market value of the bond. WHYCI would be the total return receiver and Dealer A would be the total return payer.
    • Ms. Hepburn of Dealer B recommended the purchase of a 6-month credit spread put option.
    • Mr. Tracy of Dealer C recommended the purchase of a 6-month credit spread call option.

    a. Evaluate the recommendation of Mr. Barnes from Dealer A and make a recommendation to Mr. Rivers about the proposed trade.
    b. Mr. Rivers is confused by the recommendations of Ms. Hepburn and Mr. Tracy. Both are recommending a trade involving credit spread options. However, one is recommending the purchase of a put and the other a call. Explain to Mr. Rivers the source of the confusion.
    c. Of the three proposals which would you recommend to Mr. Rivers?

13. What is the purpose of the "risk factor" in credit derivatives where the payout is based on a change in the credit spread?

14. Suppose the 10-year bond of Izzobaf.com was trading to yield 8.2%. The 10-year Treasury bond was yielding 6.2% at the time for a credit spread of 200 basis points.

    a. Suppose that a portfolio manager felt that the issue was overvalued and that the credit spread would be at least 300 basis points one year from now and could purchase a credit spread option where the underlying is a credit spread struck at 200 basis points. What type of credit spread option would the portfolio manager purchase, a put or a call?
    b. Suppose the risk factor for the Izzobaf.com bond was 6. Assuming that the manager purchased the option in part (a) with a strike credit spread of 200 basis points, ignoring the cost of the option what is the payoff for this option assuming a notional amount of $10 million?
    c. Suppose that the premium paid for the credit spread option in part (a) is $120,000 and that the manager's expectations are realized and the credit spread in one year is 300 basis points. What is the profit from the purchase of this credit spread option?

15. On January 1, a portfolio manager purchases a 5-year bond from Company Y with a par value of $1,000. The bonds are issued at par on January 1 at a credit spread of 200 basis points over a comparable 5-year U.S. Treasury note rate of 6.5%. The first semiannual coupon payment is due on July 1.

On January 31, the portfolio manager purchases a credit spread put option on the bond at a strike credit spread of 250 basis points over the 5-year U.S. Treasury note rate. The option matures on July 1 and costs the portfolio manager $10. On July 1, the credit quality of Company Y has deteriorated and its bonds now trade at a credit spread of 300 basis points over the 5-year U.S. Treasury note rate. On July 1, the yield on a 5-year U.S. Treasury note remains unchanged at 6.5%.

a. What is the strike price for this credit spread put option?
b. What is the payoff for the option by exercising on July 1?
c. What is the profit from the purchase of this option?

16. A high-yield portfolio manager wants to protect her portfolio from macroeconomic shocks that might increase credit spreads. Her portfolio market value is $500 million, and has an average credit spread to the 5-year U.S. Treasury note of 250 basis points. The risk factor of her portfolio is 3.25.

On July 1, she purchases a credit spread forward contract to protect against declines in the value of her total portfolio. The credit forward contract has a contracted credit spread of 300 basis points relative to the 5-year Treasury rate and matures on December 31.

In November, a large U.S. company defaults on its outstanding bonds, and credit spreads increase across the credit spectrum. On December 31, the average credit spread on the manager's portfolio is 350 basis points.

What is the payoff to the credit spread forward contract?

17. In 1999, Standard & Poor's developed two credit spread indices—one for the investment-grade corporates and one for the high-yield corporates. The index for the high-yield market is called the *S&P U.S. Industrial Speculative Grade Credit Index*. Beginning in April 2000, S&P published the average credit spreads daily for both indices. Option-adjusted spread (OAS) analysis is used to determine the credit spreads. Specifically, the two indices will measure the difference between the option-adjusted yield on a selected basket of corporate bonds and comparable U.S. Treasury securities.

Credit derivatives could be structured using these two indexes. A high-yield bond portfolio manager could use a forward or option contract to gain exposure to the S&P U.S. Industrial Speculative Grade Credit Index.

Consider first a forward credit spread involving the Credit Index. This credit derivative is a special case of a credit swap where there is only one period where there is a payoff. For a forward credit spread, the payoff at the maturity date would be:

[credit spread at maturity for
    Credit Index − forward credit spread] × risk factor × notional amount

A positive value for the payoff means that the buyer of a forward credit spread contract would receive the dollar amount computed above; a negative value means that the buyer of the contract would pay the amount computed above.

Next consider a credit spread option based on the index. The payoff for a credit spread call option before deducting the cost of the option is:

[credit spread at maturity for
    Credit Index − strike Credit Index spread] × risk factor × notional amount

For a credit spread put option, the payoff before deducting the cost of the option is

[strike Credit Index spread − credit spread
at maturity for Credit Index] × risk factor × notional amount

In answering the questions below, assume that the S&P U.S. Industrial Speculative Grade Credit Index existed in 1998.

a. The default by the Russian government on $40 billion in August 1998 resulted in credit spreads increasing dramatically and affected the domestic U.S. credit markets. Explain how a high-yield portfolio manager could have used a forward credit spread based on the S&P U.S. Industrial Speculative Grade Credit Index to hedge credit spread risk. Be sure to explain whether the portfolio manager would buy or sell a forward credit spread.

b. Suppose that the dollar value of the portfolio that a manager wished to protect was $500 million and the risk factor for both the bond portfolio and the S&P Industrial Speculative Grade Credit Index was 2.5. Assume that on August 1, 1998 the manager purchased a 3-month forward credit spread on the Credit Index struck at a fair forward credit spread of 350 basis points. At maturity of the forward credit spread on November 1, 1998, the credit spread for high-yield bonds was (according to the Credit Index) about 600 basis points above comparable U.S. Treasury bonds. What would be the payoff of this forward credit spread?

c. Suppose that over the same time frame, credit spreads in the S&P index had improved by 50 basis points rather than widening as they actually did. That is, suppose that the credit spread had declined from 350 basis points to 300 basis points. What would have been the manager's obligation under the credit forward contract?

d. Suppose that instead of a forward credit spread, the manager wanted to purchase an option to protect against a widening of spreads. What type of credit spread option on the index would the manager buy, a put or call?

e. Suppose that the manager on August 1, 1998 had purchased a 3-month credit spread option of the type in the answer to part (d) and with a strike index spread of 350 basis points. Also assume that the cost of the option would have been $10 million. At maturity of the credit spread option on November 1, 1998, as noted in part (b) the credit spread for high-yield bonds was according to the Credit Index about 600 basis points above comparable U.S. Treasury bonds. What would have been the payoff after deducting the cost of the option?

f. What is the advantage and disadvantage of the credit spread option versus a forward credit spread in hedging credit risk?

g. Why did S&P use the option-adjusted spread in constructing its Credit Index rather than the nominal spread?

18. a. In a synthetic collateralized debt obligation, what type of credit derivative is used?
    b. In a synthetic collateralized debt obligation is the collateral manager the protection buyer or protection seller?
    c. In what types of securities will the collateral manager invest?
    d. Assuming that the reference obligations do not trigger a payout, what is the return earned by the collateral manager?

19. a. Why is a basket default swap rather than a single-name credit default swap used in a synthetic CDO?

b. If a credit event occurs requiring a payout, what is the impact on investors in a synthetic CDO?

20. Suppose that a basket default swap covers four reference entities and the losses realized over the tenor of the swap on the four reference entities are as follows:

> Loss resulting from default of first reference entity = $7 million
>
> Loss result from default of second reference entity = $14 million
>
> Loss result from default of third reference entity = $16 million
>
> Loss result from default of fourth reference entity = $18 million

a. Suppose that the basket default swap is a *subordinate* basket default swap that specifies that the payout is $10 million for a reference entity and a maximum aggregate payout of $25 million. What is the payout to the credit protection buyer and when does the swap terminate?

b. Suppose that the basket default swap is a *senior* basket default swap with a maximum payout for each reference entity of $10 million and a default loss threshold of $25 million. What is the payout to the credit protection buyer and when does the swap terminate?

PART II

SOLUTIONS

CHAPTER 1

FEATURES OF DEBT SECURITIES

SOLUTIONS

1. All other factors constant, the longer the maturity, the greater the price change when interest rates change. So, Bond B is the answer.

2.

Quoted price	Price per $1 par value (rounded)	Par value	Dollar price
96¼	0.9625	$1,000	962.50
102⅞	1.0288	$5,000	5,143.75
109⁹⁄₁₆	1.0956	$10,000	10,956.25
68¹¹⁄₃₂	0.6834	$100,000	68,343.75

3.

	1-year Treasury rate	Coupon rate
First reset date	6.1%	6.4%
Second reset date	6.5%	6.8%
Third reset date	6.9%	7.0%
Fourth reset date	6.8%	7.0%
Fifth reset date	5.7%	6.0%
Sixth reset date	5.0%	5.3%
Seventh reset date	4.1%	4.5%
Eighth reset date	3.9%	4.5%
Ninth reset date	3.2%	4.5%
Tenth reset date	4.4%	4.7%

4. a. This provision is a make-whole redemption provision (also called a yield maintenance premium provision).

   b. A make-whole premium provision provides a formula for determining the redemption price, called the make-whole redemption price. The purpose of the provision is to protect the yield of those investors who purchased the issue at its original offering.

5. For this bond the excerpt tells us that the issue may be redeemed prior to May 1, 1995 but they may not be refunded—that is, they cannot be called using a lower cost of funds than the issue itself. After May 1, 1995, the issue may be redeemed via a refunding. The issue can be called using any source of funds such as a new bond issue with a lower coupon rate than the issue itself.

6. a. While it may be true that the Company can call the issue if rates decline, there is a nonrefunding restriction prior to January 1, 2006. The Company may not refund the issue with a source of funds that costs less than 7.75% until after that date.

   b. This is only true if the issuer redeems the issue as permitted by the call schedule. In that case the premium is paid. However, there is a sinking fund provision. If the issuer calls in the particular certificates of the issue held by the investor in order to satisfy the sinking fund provision, the issue is called at par value. So, there is no guarantee that the issue will be paid off at a premium at any time if the issue is called to satisfy the sinking fund provision.

   c. It is commonly thought that the presence of a sinking fund provision reduces the risk that the issuer will not have sufficient funds to pay off the amount due at the maturity date. But this must be balanced against the fact that a bondholder might have his or her bonds taken away at par value when the issuer calls a part of the issue to satisfy the sinking fund provision. If the issue is trading above par value, the bondholder only receives par. So, for example, if the issue is trading at 115 and it is called by the Company to satisfy the sinking fund provision, the investor receives par value (100), realizing a loss of 15.

   d. As in part c, while it may seem that the right of the issuer to make additional payments beyond the required amount of the sinking fund will reduce the likelihood that the issuer will have insufficient funds to pay off the issue at the maturity date, there is still the potential loss if the issue is called at par. Moreover, the issuer is likely to make additional payments permitted to retire the issue via the sinking fund special call price of 100 when the bond is trading at a premium, because that is when interest rates in the market are less than the coupon rate on the issue.

   e. The assistant portfolio manager cannot know for certain how long the bond issue will be outstanding because it can be called per the call schedule. Moreover, because of the sinking fund provision, a portion of their particular bonds might be called to satisfy the sinking fund requirement. (One of the major topics in fixed income analysis is that because of the uncertainty about the cash flow of a bond due to the right to call an issue, sophisticated analytical techniques and valuation models are needed.)

7. The borrowers whose loans are included in the pool can at lower interest rates refinance their loans if interest rates decline below the rate on their loans. Consequently, the security holder cannot rely on the schedule of principal and interest payments of the pool of loans to determine with certainty future cash flow.

8. a. An accelerated sinking fund provision grants the issuer the right to redeem more than the minimum amount necessary to satisfy the sinking fund requirement.

   b. An accelerated sinking fund provision is an embedded option granted to an issuer because it allows the issuer to retire the issue at par value when interest rates have declined. The issuer can do this even if the issue is nonrefundable or noncallable at that time.

9. When an investor is considering the purchase of a bond, he or she should evaluate any provision granted to the issuer that may affect their expected return over their desired

time horizon. Moreover, when a bond is purchased in the secondary market at a price above par value, the concern is that the issue may be paid off prior to the maturity date. The result would be the loss of the premium. So, for example, if an investor believes that a bond is noncallable but the issue has a sinking fund requirement, it is possible that the issue held by an investor can be called at the special redemption price of 100 when the issue is trading at a premium.

10. An investor can purchase a stand alone option on an exchange or in the over-the-counter market. When an investor purchases a bond, there are choices or "options" provided for in the indenture that grants either the bondholder or the issuer the right or option to do something. These choices are commonly referred to as embedded options.

11. a. Institutional investors typically use a repurchase agreement to finance the purchase of a bond.

   b. A term repo is a repurchase agreement where the borrowing is for more than one day; an overnight repo involves borrowing for only one day.

CHAPTER 2

RISKS ASSOCIATED WITH INVESTING IN BONDS

SOLUTIONS

1. a. Below par value since the coupon rate is less than the yield required by the market.
   b. Below par value since the coupon rate is less than the yield required by the market.
   c. Below par value since the coupon rate is less than the yield required by the market.
   d. Above par value since the coupon rate is greater than the yield required by the market.
   e. Par value since the coupon rate is equal to the yield required by the market.

	Issue	Coupon rate	Required yield by the market	Price
a.	A	5 1/4%	7.25%	Below par
b.	B	6 5/8%	7.15%	Below par
c.	C	0%	6.20%	Below par
d.	D	5 7/8%	5.00%	Above par
e.	E	4 1/2%	4.50%	Par

2. The price of a callable bond can be expressed as follows:

   price of callable bond = price of option-free bond − price of embedded call option

   An increase in interest rates will reduce the price of the option-free bond. However, to partially offset that price decline of the option-free bond, the price of the embedded call option will decrease. This is because as interest rates rise the value of the embedded call option to the issuer is worth less. Since a lower price for the embedded call option is subtracted from the lower price of the option-free bond, the price of the callable bond does not fall as much as that of an option-free bond.

3. a. A floating-rate security's exposure to interest rate risk is affected by the time to the next reset date. The shorter the time, the less likely the issue will offer a below-market interest rate until the next reset date. So, a daily reset will not expose the investor of this floater to interest rate risk due to this factor. However, there is interest rate risk which we will see in part b.
   b. The reason there is still interest rate risk with a daily reset floating-rate security is that the margin required by the market may change. And, if there is a cap on the floater, there is cap risk.

4. a. While both assistant portfolio managers are correct in that they have identified two features of an issue that will impact interest rate risk, it is the interaction of the two that will affect an issue's interest rate risk. From the information provided in the question, it cannot be determined which has the greater interest rate risk.

   b. You, as the senior portfolio manager, might want to suggest that the two assistant portfolio managers compute the duration of the two issues.

5. The information for computing duration:

$$\text{price if yields decline by 30 basis points} = 83.50$$

$$\text{price if yields rise by 30 basis points} = 80.75$$

$$\text{initial price} = 82.00$$

$$\text{change in yield in decimal} = 0.0030$$

Then,

$$\text{duration} = \frac{83.50 - 80.75}{2(82.00)(0.0030)} = 5.59$$

6. Since the duration is the approximate percentage price change for a 100 basis point change in interest rates, a bond with a duration of 5 will change by approximately 5% for a 100 basis point change in interest rates. Since the market value of the bond is $8 million, the change in the market value for a 100 basis point change in interest rates is found by multiplying 5% by $8 million. Therefore, the change in market value per 100 basis point change in interest rates is $400,000. To get an estimate of the change in the market value for any other change in interest rates, it is only necessary to scale the change in market value accordingly.

   a. for 100 basis points = $400,000
   b. for 50 basis points = $200,000 (= $400,000/2)
   c. for 25 basis points = $100,000 ($400,000/4)
   d. for 10 basis points = $40,000 ($400,000/10)

7. To calculate duration, the price must be estimated for an increase and decrease (i.e., a rate shock) of the same number of basis points. A valuation model must be employed to obtain the two prices. With an extremely complex bond issue, the valuation models by different analysts can produce substantially different prices when rates are shocked. This will result in differences in estimates of duration.

8. For an individual bond, duration is an estimate of the price sensitivity of a bond to changes in interest rates. A portfolio duration can be estimated from the duration of the individual bond holdings in the portfolio. To use the portfolio's duration as an estimate of interest rate risk it is assumed that when interest rates change, the interest rate for all maturities change by the same number of basis points. That is, it does not consider non-parallel changes of the yield curve.

9. The approach briefly discussed in this chapter for doing so is *rate duration*. Specifically, the 5-year rate duration indicates the approximate percentage change in the value of the portfolio if the yield on all maturities are unchanged but the yield for the 5-year maturity changes by 100 basis points.

10. The first form of reinvestment risk is due to the likelihood the proceeds from the called issue will be reinvested at a lower interest rate. The second form of reinvestment risk is the typical risk faced by an investor when purchasing a bond with a coupon. It is necessary to reinvest all the coupon payments at the computed yield in order to realize the yield at the time the bond is purchased.

11. Credit risk includes default risk, credit spread risk, and downgrade risk. While an investor holds a bond in his or her portfolio, if the issuer does not default there is still (1) the risk that credit spreads in the market will increase (credit spread risk) causing the price of the bond to decline and (2) the risk that the issue will be downgraded by the rating agencies causing the price to decline or not perform as well as other issues (downgrade risk).

12. a. The probability that a bond rated BBB will be downgraded is equal to the sum of the probabilities of a downgrade to BB, B, CCC or D. From the corresponding cells in the exhibit: 5.70% + 0.70% + 0.16% + 0.20% = 6.76%. Therefore, the probability of a downgrade is 6.76%.

   b. The probability that a bond rated BBB will go into default is the probability that it will fall into the D rating. From the exhibit we see that the probability is 0.20%.

   c. The probability that a bond rated BBB will be upgraded is equal to the sum of the probabilities of an upgrade to AAA, AA, or A. From the corresponding cells in the exhibit: 0.04% + 0.30% + 5.20% = 5.54%. Therefore, the probability of an upgrade is 5.54%.

   d. The probability that a bond rated B will be upgraded to investment grade is the sum of the probabilities that the bond will be rated AAA, AA, A or BBB at the end of the year. (Remember that the first four rating categories are investment grade.) From the exhibit: 0.01% + 0.09% + 0.55% + 0.88% = 1.53%. Therefore, the probability that a bond rated B will be upgraded to investment grade is 1.53%.

   e. The probability that a bond rated A will be downgraded to noninvestment grade is the sum of the probabilities that the bond will be downgraded to below BBB. From the exhibit: 0.37% + 0.02% + 0.02% + 0.05% = 0.46%, therefore, the probability that a bond rated A will be downgraded to noninvestment grade is 0.46%.

   f. The probability that a bond rated AAA will not be downgraded is 93.2%.

13. The market bid-ask spread is the difference between the highest bid price and the lowest ask price. Dealers 3 and 4 have the best bid price ($96^{15}/_{32}$). Dealer 2 has the lowest ask price ($96^{17}/_{32}$). The market bid-ask spread is therefore $^2/_{32}$.

14. If this manager's portfolio is marked-to-market, the manager must be concerned with the bid prices provided to mark the position to market. With only one dealer, there is concern that if this dealer decides to discontinue making a market in this issue, bids must be obtained from a different source. Finally, this manager intends to finance the purchase. The lender of the funds (the dealer financing the purchase) will mark the position to market based on the price it determines and this price will reflect the liquidity risk. Consequently, this manager should be concerned with the liquidity risk even if the manager intends to hold the security to the maturity date.

15. a. The purchase of a 30-year Treasury exposes the investor to interest rate risk since at the end of one year, the security is a 29-year instrument. Its price at the end of one year depends on what happens to interest rates one year later.

   b. The major difference in risk is with respect to credit risk. Specifically, the AAA issue exposes the investor to credit risk.

c. There is reinvestment risk for the 1-year zero-coupon Treasury issue because the principal must be reinvested at the end of one year.

d. The major difference is the quantity of credit risk exposure of both issues. The U.S. corporate bond issue has greater credit risk. (Note that the sovereign issue is dollar denominated so that there is no exchange rate risk.)

e. The less actively traded issue will have greater liquidity risk.

f. There are two differences in risk. First, there is the greater credit risk of investing in Italian government bonds relative to U.S. Treasury bonds. Second investing in the Italian government bonds denominated in lira exposes a U.S. investor to exchange rate risk.

16. Probably the first thing that Ms. Peters should ask is what the investment objectives are of HPLU. Addressing directly the two statements Mr. Steven made, consider the first. Mr. Stevens believes that by buying investment grade bonds the portfolio will not be exposed to a loss of principal. However, all bonds—investment grade and non-investment grade—are exposed to the potential loss of principal if interest rates rise (i.e., interest rate risk) if an issue must be sold prior to its maturity date. If a callable bond is purchased, there can be a loss of principal if the call price is less than the purchase price (i.e., call risk). The issue can also be downgraded (i.e., downgrade risk) or the market can require a higher spread (i.e., credit spread risk), both resulting in a decline in the price of an issue. This will result in a loss of principal if the issue must be sold prior to the maturity date.

The request that the bond portfolio have 40% in issues that mature within three years will reduce the interest rate risk of the portfolio. However, it will expose the HPLU to reinvestment risk (assuming the investment horizon for HPLU is greater than three years) since when the bonds mature there is the risk that the proceeds received may have to be reinvested at a lower interest rate than the coupon rate of the maturing issues.

17. a. It is reasonable to assume that the municipality will not need to redeem proceeds from the pension fund to make current payments to beneficiaries. Instead, the investment objective is to have the fund grow in order to meet future payments that must be made to retiring employees. Investing in just high investment grade securities that mature in one month or less exposes the pension fund to substantial reinvestment risk. So, while the fund reduces its interest rate risk by investing in such securities, it increases exposure to reinvestment risk. In the case of a pension fund, it would be expected that it can absorb some level of interest rate risk but would not want to be exposed to substantial reinvestment risk. So, this investment strategy may not make sense for the municipality's pension fund.

b. The opposite is true for the operating fund. The municipality can be expected to need proceeds on a shorter term basis. It should be less willing to expose the operating fund to interest rate risk but willing to sacrifice investment income (i.e., willing to accept reinvestment risk).

18. When the proposed redemption was announced, the securities were treated as short-term investments with a maturity of about six weeks—from the announcement date of January 26th to the redemption date of March 15th. When GECC canceled the proposed redemption issue and set the coupon rate as allowed by the indenture, the price of the issue declined because the new coupon rate was not competitive with market rates for issues with GECC's rating with the same time to the next reset date in three years.

19. A major risk is foreign exchange risk. This is the risk that the Japanese yen will depreciate relative to the British pound when a coupon payment or principal repayment is received. There is still the interest rate risk associated with the Japanese government bond that results from a rise in Japanese interest rates. There is reinvestment risk. There is also credit risk, although this risk is minimal. Sovereign risk is also a minimal concern.

20. Certain events can impair the ability of an issue or issuer to repay its debt obligations. For example, a corporate takeover that increases the issuer's debt can result in a downgrade. Regulatory changes that reduce revenues or increase expenses of a regulated company or a company serving a market that is adversely affected by the regulation will be downgraded if it is viewed by the rating agency that the ability to satisfy obligations has been impaired.

21. This statement about sovereign risk is incomplete. There are actions that can be taken by a foreign government other than a default that can have an adverse impact on a bond's price. These actions can result in an increase in the credit spread risk or an increase in downgrade risk.

CHAPTER 3

OVERVIEW OF BOND SECTORS AND INSTRUMENTS

SOLUTIONS

1. None of the statements is correct and therefore one must disagree with each statement for the following reasons.

   a. The foreign bond market sector of the Japanese bond market consists of non-Japanese entities that issue bonds in Japan.
   b. All but U.S. government bonds are rated.
   c. The guarantee of semi-government bonds varies from country to country. Some may carry the full faith and credit of the central government while others may have an implied or indirect guarantee.
   d. In the United States, federally related agency securities (with some exceptions) carry the full faith and credit of the U.S. government. Government sponsored enterprises (with some exceptions) have an implied guarantee.

2. The reason for assigning two types of ratings is that historically the default frequency for government issues denominated in a foreign currency is different from that of government issues denominated in the local currency.

3. a. In a single-price auction, all winning bidders are awarded securities at the highest yield bid. In a multiple-price auction, all winning bidders are awarded securities at the yield they bid.
   b. In a tap system, a government issues additional bonds of a previously outstanding bond issue via an auction.

4. a. Since the inflation rate (as measured by the CPI-U) is 3.6%, the semiannual inflation rate for adjusting the principal is 1.8%.

   (i) The inflation adjustment to the principal is

   $$\$1,000,000 \times 0.018\% = \$18,000$$

(ii) The inflation-adjusted principal is

$1,000,000 + the inflation adjustment to the principal

$$= \$1,000,000 + \$18,000 = \$1,018,000$$

(iii) The coupon payment is equal to

inflation-adjusted principal × (real rate/2)

$$= \$1,018,000 \times (0.032/2) = \$16,288.00$$

b. Since the inflation rate is 4.0%, the semiannual inflation rate for adjusting the principal is 2.0%.

(i) The inflation adjustment to the principal is

$$\$1,018,000 \times 0.02\% = \$20,360$$

(ii) The inflation-adjusted principal is

$1,018,000 + the inflation adjustment to the principal

$$= \$1,018,000 + \$20,360 = \$1,038,360$$

(iii) The coupon payment is equal to

inflation-adjusted principal × (real rate/2)

$$= \$1,038,360 \times (0.032/2) = \$16,613.76$$

5. a. The inflation rate selected is the non-seasonally adjusted U.S. City Average All Items Consumer Price Index for All Urban Consumers (denoted CPI-U).
   b. The Treasury has agreed that if the inflation-adjusted principal is less than the initial par value, the par value will be paid at maturity.
   c. When a TIPS issue is purchased between coupon payments, the price paid by the buyer has to be adjusted for the inflation up to the settlement date. That is why the Treasury reports a daily index ratio for an issue.
6. Agency debentures are securities issued by government sponsored enterprises that do not have any specific collateral securing the bond. The ability to pay bondholders depends on the ability of the issuing GSE to generate sufficient cash flow to satisfy the obligation.
7. a. Monthly mortgage payment = $1,797.66
   Monthly mortgage rate = 0.00583333 (0.07/12)

Month	Beginning of month mortgage balance	Mortgage payment	Interest	Scheduled principal repayment	End of month mortgage balance
1	200,000.00	1,797.66	1,166.67	630.99	199,369.01
2	199,369.01	1,797.66	1,162.99	634.67	198,734.34
3	198,734.34	1,797.66	1,159.28	638.37	198,095.97
4	198,095.97	1,797.66	1,155.56	642.10	197,453.87
5	197,453.87	1,797.66	1,151.81	645.84	196,808.03
6	196,808.03	1,797.66	1,148.05	649.61	196,158.42

b. In the last month (month 180), after the final monthly mortgage payment is made, the ending mortgage balance will be zero. That is, the mortgage will be fully paid.

    c. The cash flow is unknown even if the borrower does not default. This is because the borrower has the right to prepay in whole or in part the mortgage balance at any time.

8. a. A prepayment is additional principal paid by the borrower in excess of the monthly mortgage payment.

    b. The monthly cash flow of a mortgage-backed security is made up of three elements: (1) net interest (i.e., interest less servicing and other fees), (2) scheduled principal repayments (amortization), and (3) prepayments.

    c. A curtailment is a form of prepayment. Rather than prepaying the entire outstanding mortgage balance, a curtailment is a pay off of only part of the outstanding balance—it shortens (or "curtails") the life of the loan.

9. Prepayment risk is the uncertainty regarding the receipt of cash flows due to prepayments. Because of prepayments the investor does not know when principal payments will be received even if borrowers do not default on their mortgage loan.

10. a. In a mortgage passthrough security, the monthly cash flow from the underlying pool of mortgages is distributed on a pro rata basis to all the certificate holders. In contrast, for a collateralized mortgage obligation, there are rules for the distribution of the interest (net interest) and the principal (scheduled and prepaid) to different tranches.

    b. The rules for the distribution of interest and rules for the distribution of principal to the different tranches in a CMO structure effectively redistributes prepayment risk among the tranches.

11. Two government-sponsored enterprises that issue mortgage-backed securities are Fannie Mae and Freddie Mac.

12. An unlimited tax general obligation bond is a stronger form of a general obligation bond than a limited tax general obligation bond. The former is secured by the issuer's unlimited taxing power. The latter is a limited tax pledge because for such debt there is a statutory limit on tax rates that the issuer may levy to service the debt.

13. A moral obligation bond is a municipal bond that in the case of default of an issuer allows the state where the issuer is located to appropriate funds that are scheduled to be paid to the defaulted issuer and use those funds to meet the defaulted issuer's obligation. This is a nonbinding obligation that depends on the best efforts of the state to appropriate the funds to satisfy the defaulted issuer's obligation.

14. An insured municipal bond is an issue that is backed by an insurance policy written by a commercial insurance company such that the insurer agrees to pay bondholders any principal and/or coupon interest that the municipal issuer fails to pay.

15. a. A prerefunded bond is a municipal bond that may have originally been a general obligation bond or a revenue bond that is effectively refunded by creating a portfolio of Treasury securities that generates a cash flow equal to the debt service payments on the issue.

    b. Regardless of the credit rating of the issue prior to prerefunding, after prerefunding the issue is effectively collateralized by a portfolio of Treasury obligations such that the cash flow of the Treasury portfolio matches the payments on the issue when they are due. Hence, a prerefunded issue has no credit risk if properly structured.

16. a. In a liquidation, all the assets of a corporation will be distributed to the holders of claims and no corporate entity will survive. In a reorganization, a new corporate entity will be created and some security holders will receive in exchange for their claims cash and/or new securities in the new corporation.

    b. The absolute priority principle is that senior creditors are paid in full before junior creditors are paid anything.

    c. The statement is true in a liquidation; however, this is not necessarily the case in a reorganization. In fact, studies suggest that the principle of absolute priority is the exception rather than the rule in a reorganization.

17. a. An unsecured bond is called a debenture. Subordinated debenture bonds are issues that rank after secured debt, after debenture bonds, and often after some general creditors in their claim on assets and earnings.

    b. A negative pledge clause prohibits a corporation from creating or assuming any lien to secure a debt issue at the expense of existing creditors. This is an important provision for unsecured creditors.

18. a. The performance of corporate bonds will depend not only on the default rate, but the recovery rate as well as the spread over Treasury securities.

    b. The reason for the discrepancy is that these studies are measuring defaults over different periods. Studies that find that one-third default look at cumulative default rates over a period of time. The 2.15% to 2.4% figure is an annual default rate.

    c. The comment is wrong for two reasons. First, studies have found that the recovery rate is about 38% of the trading price at the time of default. Second studies have found that the higher the level of seniority, the greater the recovery rate.

19. a. A medium-term note and corporate bond differ as to how they are distributed to investors when they are initially sold. For a MTN, an issuer offers securities on a continuous basis via an investment banking firm or a broker/dealer acting as an agent by posting rates daily as to the rate it is willing to pay for specific maturities. In contrast, a corporate bond is issued on a discrete basis—it is issued at a given point in time by an investment banker.

    b. An issuer can couple a medium-term note offering with one or more positions in derivative instruments to create an instrument that has a coupon rate customized with respect to risk-return characteristics for an institutional investor. Such medium-term notes are called structured notes.

    c. With an index amortizing note (IAN), the coupon rate is fixed and the principal payments are made prior to the stated maturity date based on the prevailing value for some reference interest rate. Specifically, the principal payments decrease when the reference interest rate increases (hence the maturity increases) and increases when the reference interest rate decreases (hence the maturity decreases). The risk faced by the investor is that an IAN will be outstanding for a longer period when interest rates rise, just when the investor would like proceeds to reinvest at a higher interest rate; there is reinvestment risk when interest rates fall because more principal is paid as rates decline, just when the investor would not want to receive principal.

20. a. Since negotiable certificates of deposit issued by U.S. banks typically exceed the federally insured amount of $100,000, there is credit risk for the amount invested in excess of $100,000.

    b. LIBOR refers to the London interbank offered rate and it is the interest rate paid on Eurodollar certificates of deposit. "1-month LIBOR" is the interest rate that major international banks are offering to pay to other on a Eurodollar CD that matures in one month.

21. Investing in bankers acceptances exposes the investor to the risk that neither the borrower nor the accepting bank will be able to pay the principal due at the maturity date; that is, the investor faces credit risk. On the surface, there is liquidity risk because

there are few dealers who make a market in bankers acceptances. However, investors typically purchase bankers acceptances with the intent of holding them to maturity. Consequently, in practice, liquidity risk is not a concern to such investors.

22. The advantage is that depending on the quality of the consumer loan portfolio, this BBB rated issuer may be able to issue an asset-backed security with a higher rating than BBB and thereby reduce its borrowing costs, net of the cost of credit enhancement.

23. A special purpose vehicle allows a corporation seeking funds to issue a security backed by collateral such that the security will be rated based on the credit quality of the collateral rather than the entity seeking funds. Effectively, the special purpose vehicle is the owner of the collateral so that the creditors of the entity seeking funds cannot claim the collateral should the entity default.

24. a. External credit enhancement includes corporate guarantees, a letter of credit, and bond insurance.

    b. A disadvantage of an external credit enhancement is that it exposes the asset-backed security structure to a credit downgrading should the third-party guarantor be downgraded.

25. a. A collateralized debt obligation is a structure backed by a portfolio of one or more fixed income products—corporate bonds, asset-backed securities, mortgage-backed securities, bank loans, and other CDOs. Funds are raised to purchase the assets by the sale of the CDO. An asset manager manages the assets.

    b. The statement is incorrect. When a CDO is issued, the notes are rated. Restrictions are imposed on the asset manager in order to avoid a downgrading of the tranches or the possibility that the trustee must begin paying off the principal to the senior tranches.

    c. The distinction between an arbitrage transaction from a balance sheet transaction is based on the motivation of the sponsor of the CDO. Arbitrage transactions are motivated by the objective to capture the spread between the yield offered on the pool of assets underlying the CDO and the cost of borrowing which is the yield offered to sell the CDO. In balance sheet transactions, typically undertaken by financial institutions such as banks and insurance companies, the motivation is to remove assets from the balance sheet thereby obtaining capital relief in the form of lower risk-based capital requirements.

26. A bought deal is a form of a bond underwriting. The underwriting firm or group of underwriting firms offers an issuer a firm bid to purchase a specified amount of the bonds with a certain coupon rate and maturity. The issuer is given a short time period to accept or reject the bid. If the bid is accepted, the underwriting firm has bought the deal.

27. In the United States, SEC Rule 144A eliminates the two-year holding period requirement for privately placed securities by permitting large institutions to trade securities acquired in a private placement among themselves without having to register these securities with the SEC. As a result, private placements are classified in two types. The first type are Rule 144A offerings which are underwritten securities. The second type are the traditional private placements which are referred to as non-Rule 144A offerings.

28. The two major types of electronic bond trading systems are the dealer-to-customer systems and exchange systems. The former are further divided into single-dealer systems and multiple-dealer systems. Single-dealer systems are based on a customer dealing with a single, identified dealer over the computer. In multi-dealer systems a customer

can select from any of several identified dealers whose bids and offers are provided on a computer screen.

The second type of electronic system for bonds is the exchange system. In this system, dealer and customer bids and offers are entered into the system on an anonymous basis, and the clearing of the executed trades is done through a common process. Exchange systems can be further divided into continuous trading and call auction systems. Continuous trading permits trading at continuously changing market determined prices throughout the day. Call auctions provide for fixed price auctions at specific times during the day.

CHAPTER 4

UNDERSTANDING YIELD SPREADS

SOLUTIONS

1. Market participants look at the key indicators watched by the Fed in order to try to predict how the Fed will react to the movement in those indicators.

2. Ms. Peters should inform her client that under one theory of the term structure of interest rates, the pure expectations theory, a downward sloping yield curve does suggest that short-term interest rates in the future will decline. According to the liquidity preference theory a downward sloping yield curve suggests that rates are expected to decline. But it should be noted that the liquidity preference theory does not view a positive yield curve as one where rates may be expected to rise. This is because the yield premium for liquidity can be large enough so that even if expected future rates are expected to decline, the yield curve would be upward sloping. A downward sloping yield curve according to the market segmentation theory cannot be interpreted in terms of the market's expectations regarding future rates.

3. The pure expectations theory asserts that the only factor affecting the shape of the yield curve is expectations about future interest rates. The liquidity preference theory asserts that there are two factors that affect the shape of the yield curve: expectations about future interest rate and a yield premium to compensate for interest rate risk.

4. According to the pure expectations theory, a humped yield curve means that short-term interest rates are expected to rise for a time and then begin to fall.

5. a. The data clearly indicate that yield spreads are at their 12-month highs.

   b. A callable agency issue offers a higher yield spread than a noncallable agency issue because of the call risk faced by investors in the former.

   c. For a given maturity, the longer the deferred call period the lower the call risk. Hence, the yield spread for a callable issue is less the longer the deferred call period.

   d. Because yield spreads are not adjusted for call risk, they are referred to as nominal spreads.

   e. The compensation for credit risk, liquidity risk, and call risk are lumped together in the nominal spreads (i.e., yield spreads shown in the second panel). The OAS is an estimate of the yield spread after adjusting for the call (or option) risk. So, the OAS is less than the nominal yield spread.

6. While it is true that a Ginnie Mae mortgage-backed security has no credit risk and that part of the yield spread between a Ginnie Mae mortgage-backed security and a U.S. Treasury security is due to differences in liquidity, the major reason for the yield

spread is the prepayment risk of a mortgage-backed security. This risk is ignored in the statement made by the representative of the investment management firm.

7. a. Part of the yield spread between a non-Treasury bond with an embedded option and a Treasury security (which is an option-free security) is due to the value of the embedded option. For example, for a callable non-Treasury bond, the yield spread relative to a Treasury security represents compensation for the following: (1) credit risk, (2) liquidity risk, and (3) call risk. When a spread measure includes all three forms of compensation, it is called a "nominal spread." However, investors want to know the yield spread after adjusting for the value of the embedded options (the call option in our illustration).

   b. The option-adjusted spread seeks to measure the part of the yield spread between a non-Treasury security and a Treasury security once the portion attributed to the call risk is removed. So, the option-adjusted spread is less than the nominal spread. The option-adjusted spread allows an investor to better compare the yield spread on bonds with and without embedded options.

8. a. absolute yield spread $= 7.25\% - 6.02\% = 1.23\% = 123$ basis points

   b. relative yield spread $= \dfrac{7.25\% - 6.02\%}{6.02\%} = 0.204 = 20.4\%$

   c. yield ratio $= \dfrac{7.25\%}{6.02\%} = 1.204$

9. a. The percent yield spread is the relative yield spread.

   b. Analysts recognize that historical comparisons of the absolute yield spread for assessing how yield spreads are changing do not take into account the level of yields. For example, a 40 basis point absolute yield spread in a 5% interest rate environment is quite different from a 40 basis point absolute yield spread in a 10% yield environment.

10. Tax-exempt municipal securities offer a lower yield than Treasury securities because of the value of the tax-exempt feature. This feature is more attractive to high tax bracket investors than to low tax bracket investors. A reduction in marginal tax rates makes the tax-exempt feature less attractive to investors. This would require that tax-exempt municipals to offer higher yields compared to yields prior to the reduction.

   Anticipating a reduction in tax rates would affect municipal yields. The extent of this effect would depend on the market's assessment of the probability the proposal would be enacted.

11. a. Because municipals are tax-exempt, their return or yield spread depends on each investor's marginal tax rate. Treasuries are subject to federal income tax so comparing the two yields to calculate a yield spread would be different for various investors.

   b. The AAA rated municipal general obligation yield curve is used because it offers a similar tax-exempt status to compare its yield against when considering other tax-exempt municipal bonds.

12. a. The after-tax yield is

$$0.05 \times (1 - 0.40) = 0.03 = 3\%$$

   b. The taxable-equivalent yield is

$$\frac{0.031}{(1 - 0.39)} = 0.0508 = 5.08\%$$

13. A funded investor who borrows short term is interested in the spread above the borrowing cost. Since LIBOR is the global cost of borrowing, a LIBOR yield curve is a more appropriate measure for assessing the potential return than the Treasury yield curve.

14. The swap rate is the sum of the 5-year Treasury yield of 4.4% and the swap spread of 120 basis points. The swap rate is therefore 5.6%.

15. The swap spread is an important spread measure because it is related to credit spreads and therefore can be used in relative value analysis.

16. a. From the Treasury yield curve, the relevant rate is the 2-year rate because the swap has a two year term. The swap rate is 6.8%, computing by adding the 2-year rate of 5.8% and the swap spread of 100 basis points.

    b. The annual payment made by the fixed-rate payer of a $10 million notional amount interest rate swap with a swap rate of 6.8% is: $10,000,000 × 0.068 = $680,000. Since the swap specifies quarterly payments, the quarterly payment is $170,000 (=$680,000/4).

    c.

If 3-month LIBOR is	Annual dollar amount	Amount of payment
5.00%	$500,000	$125,000
5.50%	550,000	137,500
6.00%	600,000	150,000
6.50%	650,000	162,500
7.00%	700,000	175,000
7.50%	750,000	187,500
8.00%	800,000	200,000
8.50%	850,000	212,500

    d. The net payment is equal to the floating-rate payment received by the fixed-rate payer less the fixed-rate payment made by the fixed-rate payer. The quarterly fixed-rate payment is $170,000. In the table below, a negative sign means that the fixed-rate payer must make a payment.

If 3-month LIBOR is	Floating-rate received	Net payment by fixed-rate payer
5.00%	$125,000	−$45,000
5.50%	137,500	−32,500
6.00%	150,000	−20,000
6.50%	162,500	−7,500
7.00%	175,000	5,000
7.50%	187,500	17,500
8.00%	200,000	30,000
8.50%	212,500	42,500

17. a. The risk that the investor faces is that, if 6-month LIBOR falls below 5%, then the return from the floater for the 6-month period (on an annual basis) would be less than the 7% borrowing cost (the fixed coupon rate of 7%). Thus, the investor is exposed to the risk of a decline in 6-month LIBOR. In general terms, the investor is mismatched with respect to assets (which are floating) and liabilities (which are fixed).

b. When there is a mismatch of the assets and liabilities as this investor faces, an interest rate swap can be used to convert a floating-rate asset into a fixed-rate asset or a fixed-rate liability into a floating-rate liability.

c. Note that the payments for the floater, the fixed-rate liability, and the swap are semiannual. Here are the cash flows from the asset, the liability, and the swap:

Cash inflow from the floater = 6-month LIBOR + 200 basis points
Cash inflow from the swap   = 7.3%
_____

Total cash inflow   = 9.3% + 6-month LIBOR

Cash outflow for the note issued = 7%
Cash outflow for the swap   = 6-month LIBOR
_____

Total cash outflow   = 7% + 6-month LIBOR
Net cash flow = annual income spread = 2.3% = 230 basis points

CHAPTER 5

INTRODUCTION TO THE VALUATION OF DEBT SECURITIES

SOLUTIONS

1. The value is 107.6655 as shown below:

Year	Cash flow	PV at 5.6%
1	7	7.0076
2	7	6.6360
3	7	6.2841
4	7	5.9508
5	107.4	81.7871
	Total	107.6655

2. The value is $96,326.46 as shown below

Year	Cash flow	PV at 7.8%
1	$23,998.55	$22,262.11
2	23,998.55	20,651.30
3	23,998.55	19,157.05
4	23,998.55	17,770.92
5	23,998.55	16,485.09
	Total	96,326.47

3. a. The present value of the cash flows for the three discount rates is provided below:

Year	Cash flow	PV at 4.5%	Cash flow	PV at 6.2%	Cash flow	PV at 7.3%
1	$6.2	$5.9330	$6.2	$5.8380	$6.2	$5.7782
2	6.2	5.6775	6.2	5.4972	6.2	5.3851
3	6.2	5.4330	6.2	5.1763	6.2	5.0187
4	6.2	5.1991	6.2	4.8741	6.2	4.6773
5	106.2	85.2203	106.2	78.6144	106.2	74.6665
	Total	107.4630	Total	100.0000	Total	95.5258

b. The following relationship holds:

- When the coupon rate (6.2%) is greater than the discount rate (4.5%), the bond's value is a premium to par value ($107.4630).
- When the coupon rate is equal to the discount rate, the bond's value is par value.
- When the coupon rate (6.2%) is less than the discount rate (7.3%), the bond's value is a discount to par value ($95.5258).

4. A basic property of a discount bond is that its price increases as it moves toward maturity assuming that interest rates do not change. Over the one year that the portfolio is being reviewed, while market yields have increased slightly, the bonds selling at a discount at the beginning of the year can increase despite a slight increase in the market yield since the beginning of the year.

5. a. The price is $95.9353 as shown below:

Year	Cash flow	PV at 7%
1	5.8	5.4206
2	5.8	5.0659
3	5.8	4.7345
4	105.8	80.7143
	Total	$95.9353

b. The price of the 3-year 5.8% coupon bond assuming the yield is unchanged at 7% is $96.8508, as shown below.

Year	Cash flow	PV at 7%
1	5.8	5.4206
2	5.8	5.0659
3	105.8	86.3643
	Total	$96.8508

c. The price is $98.9347 as shown below:

Year	Cash flow	PV at 6.2%
1	5.8	5.4614
2	5.8	5.1426
3	105.8	88.3308
	Total	$98.9347

d.

Price change attributable to moving to maturity (no change in discount rate)	$0.9155 (96.8508 − 95.9353)
Price change attribute to an increase in the discount rate from 7% to 6.2%	$2.0839 (98.9347 − 96.8508)
Total price change	$2.9994

6. The value is $94.2148 as shown below:

Year	Discount rate	Cash flow	PV
1	5.90%	5.8	5.4769
2	6.40%	5.8	5.1232
3	6.60%	5.8	4.7880
4	6.90%	5.8	4.4414
5	7.30%	105.8	74.3853
		Total	$94.2148

7. The value is $107.7561 as shown below:

Period	Discount rate	Cash flow	PV at 2.8%
1	0.028	3.7	3.5992
2	0.028	3.7	3.5012
3	0.028	3.7	3.4058
4	0.028	3.7	3.3131
5	0.028	3.7	3.2228
6	0.028	3.7	3.1350
7	0.028	3.7	3.0496
8	0.028	3.7	2.9666
9	0.028	3.7	2.8858
10	0.028	103.7	78.6770
		Total	107.7561

Alternatively, the short-cut formula can be used.

$$\text{semiannual coupon payment} = \$3.70$$
$$\text{semiannual discount rate} = 2.8\%$$
$$\text{number of years} = 5$$

then

$$\$3.70 \times \left[\frac{1 - \dfrac{1}{(1.028)^{5 \times 2}}}{0.028} \right] = \$31.8864$$

To determine the price, the present value of the maturity value must be added to the present value of the coupon payments. The present value of the maturity value is

$$\text{present value of maturity value} = \frac{\$100}{(1.028)^{5 \times 2}} = \$75.8698$$

The price is then $107.7561 ($31.8864 + $75.8698). This agrees with our previous calculation for the price of this bond.

8. $\dfrac{\$1,000,000}{(1.038)^{40}} = \$224,960.29$

9. a. First, w must be calculated. We know that

Days between settlement date and next coupon payment	115
Days in the coupon period	183

Therefore,

$$w \text{ periods} = \frac{115}{183} = 0.6284$$

Since the discount rate is 5.6%, the semiannual rate is 2.8%. The present value of the cash flows is $108.8676 and is therefore the full price.

Period	Cash flow	PV at 2.8%
1	3.7	3.6363
2	3.7	3.5373
3	3.7	3.4410
4	3.7	3.3472
5	3.7	3.2561
6	3.7	3.1674
7	3.7	3.0811
8	3.7	2.9972
9	3.7	2.9155
10	103.7	79.4885
	Total	108.8676

b. The accrued interest is

$$AI = \text{semiannual coupon payment} \times (1 - w)$$

$$AI = \$3.7 \times (1 - 0.6284) = 1.3749$$

c. The clean price is

$$\text{clean price} = \text{full price} - \text{accrued interest}$$

$$\$108.8676 - \$1.3749 = \$107.4927$$

10. a. The arbitrage-free value was found to be $111.3324.
     b. The price based on single discount rate of 5.65% is $111.1395 as shown below:

Period	Years	Cash flow	PV at 2.825%
1	0.5	3.7	3.5983
2	1.0	3.7	3.4995
3	1.5	3.7	3.4033
4	2.0	3.7	3.3098
5	2.5	3.7	3.2189
6	3.0	3.7	3.1305
7	3.5	3.7	3.0445
8	4.0	3.7	2.9608
9	4.5	3.7	2.8795
10	5.0	3.7	2.8004
11	5.5	3.7	2.7234
12	6.0	3.7	2.6486
13	6.5	3.7	2.5758
14	7.0	3.7	2.5051
15	7.5	3.7	2.4362
16	8.0	103.7	66.4048
		Total	111.1395

c. Dealers would buy the 7.4% 8-year issue for $111.1395, strip it, and sell the Treasury strips for $111.3324. The arbitrage profit is $0.1929 ($111.3324 − $111.1395). The table below shows how that arbitrage profit is realized.

Period	Years	Sell for	Buy for	Arbitrage profit
1	0.5	3.6453	3.5983	0.0470
2	1.0	3.5809	3.4995	0.0814
3	1.5	3.5121	3.4033	0.1087
4	2.0	3.4238	3.3098	0.1140
5	2.5	3.3155	3.2189	0.0966
6	3.0	3.2138	3.1305	0.0833
7	3.5	3.1167	3.0445	0.0722
8	4.0	3.0291	2.9608	0.0683
9	4.5	2.9407	2.8795	0.0612
10	5.0	2.8516	2.8004	0.0513
11	5.5	2.7621	2.7234	0.0387
12	6.0	2.6723	2.6486	0.0237
13	6.5	2.5822	2.5758	0.0064
14	7.0	2.5026	2.5051	−0.0024
15	7.5	2.4240	2.4362	−0.0123
16	8.0	65.7597	66.4048	−0.6451
Total		111.3324	111.1395	0.1929

d. The process of bidding up the price of the 7.4% 8-year Treasury issue by dealers in order to strip it will increase the price until no material arbitrage profit is available—the arbitrage-free value of $111.3324.

11. a. The arbitrage-free value was found to be $89.3155.
    b. The price based on a single discount rate of 5.65% is as shown below to be $89.4971.

Period	Years	Cash flow	Present value 2.825%
1	0.5	2	1.9451
2	1.0	2	1.8916
3	1.5	2	1.8396
4	2.0	2	1.7891
5	2.5	2	1.7399
6	3.0	2	1.6921
7	3.5	2	1.6457
8	4.0	2	1.6004
9	4.5	2	1.5565
10	5.0	2	1.5137
11	5.5	2	1.4721
12	6.0	2	1.4317
13	6.5	2	1.3923
14	7.0	2	1.3541
15	7.5	2	1.3169
16	8.0	102	65.3162
		Total	89.4971

c. The dealer will buy a package of Treasury strips such that the cash flow from the package will replicate the cash flow of a 4% 8-year Treasury issue and sell the overvalued Treasury issue. The cost of buying the package of Treasury strips is $89.3155. The value of selling the Treasury issue or, if reconstituted, the value of the synthetic coupon Treasury created is $89.4971. The arbitrage profit is therefore $0.1816 ($89.4971 − $89.3155).

d. The process of dealers selling the Treasury issue will drive down its prices until the market price is close to the arbitrage-free value of $89.3154.

CHAPTER 6

YIELD MEASURES, SPOT RATES, AND FORWARD RATES

SOLUTIONS

1. The three sources are (1) coupon interest, (2) any capital gain (or loss, a reduction in return), and (3) reinvestment income.

2. a. The current yield for the bond is

$$\text{annual coupon payment} = 0.09 \times \$100 = \$9$$

$$\text{current yield} = \frac{\$9}{\$112} = 0.0804 = 8.04\%$$

   b. The current yield measure only considers coupon interest and ignores any capital gain or loss (a capital loss of $12 for the bond in our example), and reinvestment income.

3. The present value of the cash flows of a 6.5% 20-year semiannual-pay bond using the three discount rates is shown below:

Discount rate (annual BEY)	Semiannual rate (half annual rate)	Present value of cash flows
7.2%	3.6%	92.64
7.4	3.7	90.68
7.8	3.9	86.94

Since 3.7% equates the present value of the cash flows to the price of 90.68, 3.7% is the semiannual yield to maturity. Doubling that rates gives a 7.4% yield to maturity on a bond-equivalent basis.

4. This question requires no calculations. (Note that the maturity of each bond is intentionally omitted.) The question tests for an understanding of the relationship between coupon rate, current yield, and yield to maturity for a bond trading at par, a discount, and a premium.

   - Bond A's current yield is incorrect. The current yield should be equal to the coupon rate.
   - Bond B is fine. That is, it has the expected relationship between coupon rate, current yield, and yield to maturity for a bond trading at a premium.

- Bond C's yield to maturity is incorrect. Since the bond is a premium bond, the yield to maturity should be less than the coupon rate.
- Bond D is fine. That is, it has the expected relationship between coupon rate, current yield, and yield to maturity for a bond trading at a discount.
- Bond E is incorrect. Both the current yield and the yield to maturity should be greater than the coupon rate since the bond is trading at a discount.

5. The statement is misleading in that while it is true that the yield to maturity computed on a bond-equivalent basis is flawed, it is not the reason why the yield to maturity is limited. The major reason is that it assumes that the bond is held to maturity and the coupon payments are assumed to be reinvested at the computed yield to maturity.

6. a. The total future dollars are found as follows:

$$\$108.32(1.035)^{10} = \$152.80$$

b. Since the total future dollars are $152.80 and the investment is $108.32, the total interest from the CD is $44.48.

c. The answer is the same as for parts a and b. The total future dollars are $152.80. The total dollar return is the same as the total interest, $44.48.

d. The answer is the same as for part c:

$$\text{total future dollars} = \$152.80$$

$$\text{total dollar return} = \$44.48$$

e.

$$\text{coupon interest} = \$45.00$$

$$\text{capital gain/loss} = -\$8.32$$

$$\text{reinvestment income} = \$7.80$$

$$\overline{}$$

$$\text{total dollar return} = \$44.48$$

f. The percentage of the total dollar return that must be generated from reinvestment income is 17.5% ($7.80/$44.48).

g. The $7.80 reinvestment income must be generated by reinvesting the semiannual coupon payments from the time of receipt to the maturity date at the semiannual yield to maturity, 3.5% in this example. The reinvestment income earned on a given coupon payment of $4.50 if it is invested from the time of receipt in period t to the maturity date (10 periods in our example) at a 3.5% semiannual rate is:

$$\$4.50(1.035)^{10-t} - \$4.50$$

The reinvestment income for each coupon payment is shown below:

Period	Periods reinvested	Coupon payment	Reinvestment income at 3.5%
1	9	$4.5	$1.63
2	8	4.5	1.43
3	7	4.5	1.23
4	6	4.5	1.03

Period	Periods reinvested	Coupon payment	Reinvestment income at 3.5%
5	5	4.5	0.84
6	4	4.5	0.66
7	3	4.5	0.49
8	2	4.5	0.32
9	1	4.5	0.16
10	0	4.5	0.00
		Total	7.79

The reinvestment income totals $7.79 which differs from $7.80 due to rounding.

7. a. Bond X has no dependence on reinvestment income since it is a zero-coupon bond. So it is either Bond Y or Bond Z. The two bonds have the same maturity. Since they are both selling at the same yield, Bond Z, the one with the higher coupon rate, is more dependent on reinvestment income.

b. As explained in part a, since Bond X is a zero-coupon bond, it has the least dependence (in fact, no dependence) on reinvestment income.

8. The reinvestment risk is that to realize the computed yield, it is necessary to reinvest the interim cash flows (i.e., coupon payments in the case of a nonamortizing security and principal plus coupon payments in the case of an amortizing security) at the computed yield. The interest rate risk comes into play because it is assumed the security will be held to the maturity date. If it is not, the yield no longer applies because there is the risk of having to sell the security below its purchase price.

9. a. The bond-equivalent yield is

$$2[(1.056)^{0.5} - 1] = 0.0552 = 5.52\%$$

b. The annual yield is

$$[(1.028)^2 - 1] = 0.0568 = 5.68\%$$

10. a. The cash flows for this bond to the maturity date are (1) 30 coupon payments of $5 and (2) $100 at the maturity date. The table below shows the present values of the coupon payments and maturity value for the three interest rates in the question:

Annual interest rate (%)	Semiannual interest rate (%)	Present value of 30 payments of $5	Present value of $100 30 periods from now	Present value of cash flows
7.0	3.5	91.9602	35.6278	127.5880
7.4	3.7	89.6986	33.6231	123.3217
7.8	3.9	87.5197	31.7346	119.2543

Since a semiannual interest rate of 3.5% produces a present value equal to the price of the bond ($127.5880), the yield to maturity is 7% on a bond-equivalent basis.

b. The cash flows for this bond up to the first call date are (1) 10 coupon payments of $5 and (2) $105 ten 6-month periods from now. The table below shows the present values of the coupon payments and maturity value for the three interest rates in the question:

Annual interest rate (%)	Semiannual interest rate (%)	Present value of 10 payments of $5	Present value of $105 10 periods from now	Present value of cash flows
4.55	2.275	44.2735	83.8483	128.1218
4.65	2.325	44.1587	83.4395	127.5982
4.85	2.425	43.9304	82.6284	126.5588

Since of the three interest rates in the question, a semiannual interest rate of 2.325% makes the present value of the cash flows closest to the price of $127.5880, the yield to the first call date is 4.65% on a bond-equivalent basis.

   c. The cash flows for this bond up to the first par call date are (1) 20 coupon payments of $5 and (2) $100 twenty 6-month periods from now. The table below shows the present values of the coupon payments and maturity value for the three interest rates in the question:

Annual interest rate (%)	Semiannual interest rate (%)	Present value of 20 payments of $5	Present value of $100 20 periods from now	Present value of cash flows
6.25	3.125	73.5349	54.0407	127.5756
6.55	3.275	72.5308	52.4923	125.0231
6.75	3.375	71.8725	51.4860	123.3585

Since of the three interest rates in the question, a semiannual interest rate of 3.125% makes the present value of the cash flows closest to the price of $127.5880, the yield to the first par call date is 6.25% on a bond-equivalent basis.

11. The cash flows to the put date are (1) 8 coupon payments of $2.50 and (2) $100 (the put price) eight 6-month periods from now. The table below shows the present values of the coupon payments and maturity value for the three interest rates in the question:

Annual interest rate (%)	Semiannual interest rate (%)	Present value of 8 payments of $2.5	Present value of $100 8 periods from now	Present value of cash flows
3.38	1.690	18.5609	87.4529	106.0136
3.44	1.720	18.5367	87.2467	105.7834
3.57	1.785	18.4846	86.8020	105.2866

Since of the three interest rates in the question, a semiannual interest rate of 1.785% makes the present value of the cash flows closest to the price of $105.2877, the yield to the put date is 3.57% on a bond-equivalent basis.

12. First, the semiannual effective yield is computed from the monthly yield by compounding it for six months as follows:

$$\text{effective semiannual yield} = (1.0041)^6 - 1 = 0.024854 = 2.4854\%$$

Next, the effective semiannual yield is doubled to get the annual cash flow yield on a bond-equivalent basis. Thus, the cash flow yield on a bond-equivalent basis is 4.97% (2 times 2.4854%).

13. You should agree with Manager B. The cash flow yield, as with any other yield measure such as the yield to maturity or any yield to call date, requires that the investor be able to reinvest any interim cash flows in order to realize the computed yield. A

cash flow yield is even more dependent on reinvestment income because the interim cash flows are monthly coupon and principal, rather than simply semiannual coupon for a standard coupon bond. Consequently, the reinvestment risk is greater with an amortizing security.

14. The table below shows the present value using the three discount margins:

5-year floater
current LIBOR 5.00%
quoted margin   30 basis points

				Present value ($) at assumed margin of		
	LIBOR	Coupon	Cash flow	40	50	55
Period	(annual rate) (%)	(%)	($)	5.400%	5.500%	5.550%
1	5.00	5.300	2.65	2.5803	2.5791	2.5784
2	5.00	5.300	2.65	2.5125	2.5100	2.5088
3	5.00	5.300	2.65	2.4464	2.4429	2.4411
4	5.00	5.300	2.65	2.3821	2.3775	2.3752
5	5.00	5.300	2.65	2.3195	2.3139	2.3110
6	5.00	5.300	2.65	2.2585	2.2519	2.2486
7	5.00	5.300	2.65	2.1991	2.1917	2.1879
8	5.00	5.300	2.65	2.1413	2.1330	2.1289
9	5.00	5.300	2.65	2.0850	2.0759	2.0714
10	5.00	5.300	102.65	78.6420	78.2601	78.0700
			Total	99.5669	99.1360	98.9214

When a margin of 50 basis points is used, the present value of the cash flows is equal to the price ($99.1360).

15. The discount margin ignores both and hence is a limitation of this measure. The cap is not considered because the reference rate is assumed to be unchanged at the current value for the reference rate. The only way in which the cap is considered is in the special case where the current value for the reference rate is capped and in this case it assumes that the reference rate will not fall below the cap for the life of the floater.

16. a. The yield on a discount basis, d, is

$$(1 - 0.989)\left(\frac{360}{105}\right) = 0.0377 = 3.77\%$$

b. The price of this Treasury bill, p, per $1 dollar of maturity value is:

$$1 - 0.0368(275/360) = 0.971889$$

c. The yield on a discount basis has two major shortcomings. First, it relates the interest return to the maturity or face value rather than the amount invested. Second, it is based on a 360-day year rather than 365-day year as used for Treasury coupon securities.

17. Beyond the 1-year maturity, there are only a few on-the-run Treasury issues available: 2 year, 5 year, and 10 year. For the 30-year maturity, market participants estimate the yield based on the last 30-year Treasury bond that was issued by the U.S. Department of the Treasury. The yield for interim maturities is calculated using an interpolation methodology. The simplest is linear interpolation; however, more elaborate statistical methods can be used.

18. We will use the same notation as in the chapter. One-half the annualized spot rate for a 6-month period will be denoted by z_{t_i}. We know that the 6-month Treasury bill yield is 4.6% and the 1-year Treasury yield is 5.0%, so

$$z_1 = 4.6\%/2 = 2.3\% \quad \text{and} \quad z_2 = 5.0\%/2 = 2.5\%$$

Now we use the bootstrapping methodology. The 1.5-year Treasury yield from the Treasury yield curve is selling to yield 5.4%. Since the price of the issue is its par value, the coupon rate is 5.4%. So, the cash flow for this issue is:

$$0.5 \text{ year } 0.054 \times \$100 \times 0.5 = \$2.70$$

$$1.0 \text{ year } 0.054 \times \$100 \times 0.5 = \$2.70$$

$$1.5 \text{ years } 0.054 \times \$100 \times 0.5 + \$100 = \$102.70$$

The present value of the cash flows is then:

$$\frac{2.7}{(1+z_1)^1} + \frac{2.7}{(1+z_2)^2} + \frac{102.7}{(1+z_3)^3}$$

Substituting the first two spot rates we have:

$$\frac{2.7}{(1.023)^1} + \frac{2.7}{(1.025)^2} + \frac{102.7}{(1+z_3)^3}$$

The goal is to find z_3. Since the value of this cash flow must be equal to the price of the 1.5-year issue which is par value, we can set the previous equation equal to 100:

$$\frac{2.7}{(1.023)^1} + \frac{2.7}{(1.025)^2} + \frac{102.7}{(1+z_3)^3} = 100$$

We then solve for z_3 as follows:

$$2.639296 + 2.569899 + \frac{102.7}{(1+z_3)^3} = 100$$

$$\frac{102.7}{(1+z_3)^3} = 94.7908$$

$$z_3 = 0.027073 = 2.7073\%$$

Doubling this yield we obtain the bond-equivalent yield of 5.4146%.

The equation for obtaining the 2-year, 2.5-year, and 3-year spot rates are given below.

For the 2-year spot rate, the coupon rate from the Treasury yield curve is 5.8%. So, the present value of the cash flow is:

$$\frac{2.9}{(1+z_1)^1} + \frac{2.9}{(1+z_2)^2} + \frac{2.9}{(1+z_3)^3} + \frac{102.9}{(1+z_4)^4}$$

Substituting: $z_1 = 2.3\%$ $z_2 = 2.5\%$ $z_3 = 2.7073\%$

and setting the present value equal to the price of the 2-year issue (100), we obtain:

$$\frac{2.9}{(1.023)^1} + \frac{2.9}{(1.025)^2} + \frac{2.9}{(1.027073)^3} + \frac{102.9}{(1+z_4)^4} = 100$$

Solving the above equation we would find that z_4 is 2.9148%. Therefore, the 2-year spot rate on a bond-equivalent basis is 5.8297%.

For the 2.5-year spot rate, we use the 2.5-year issue from the par yield curve. The yield is 6.4% and therefore the coupon rate is 6.4%. The present value of the cash flow for this issue is then:

$$\frac{3.2}{(1+z_1)^1} + \frac{3.2}{(1+z_2)^2} + \frac{3.2}{(1+z_3)^3} + \frac{3.2}{(1+z_4)^4} + \frac{103.2}{(1+z_5)^5}$$

Substituting: $z_1 = 2.3\%$ $z_2 = 2.5\%$ $z_3 = 2.7073\%$ $z_4 = 2.9148\%$
and setting the present value equal to the price of the 2.5-year issue (100), we obtain:

$$\frac{3.2}{(1.023)^1} + \frac{3.2}{(1.025)^2} + \frac{3.2}{(1.027073)^3} + \frac{3.2}{(1.029148)^4} + \frac{103.2}{(1+z_5)^5} = 100$$

Solving the above equation we would find that z_5 is 3.2333%. Therefore, the 2.5-year spot rate on a bond-equivalent basis is 6.4665%.

For the 3-year spot rate, we use the 3-year issue from the par yield curve. The yield is 7.0% and therefore the coupon rate is 7.0%. The present value of the cash flow for this issue is then:

$$\frac{3.5}{(1+z_1)^1} + \frac{3.5}{(1+z_2)^2} + \frac{3.5}{(1+z_3)^3} + \frac{3.5}{(1+z_4)^4} + \frac{3.5}{(1+z_5)^5} + \frac{103.5}{(1+z_6)^6}$$

Substituting: $z_1 = 2.3\%$ $z_2 = 2.5\%$ $z_3 = 2.7073\%$ $z_4 = 2.9148\%$ $z_5 = 3.2333\%$
and setting the present value equal to the price of the 3-year issue (100), we obtain:

$$\frac{3.5}{(1.023)^1} + \frac{3.5}{(1.025)^2} + \frac{3.5}{(1.027073)^3} + \frac{3.5}{(1.029148)^4} + \frac{3.5}{(1.032333)^5} + \frac{103.5}{(1+z_6)^6}$$
$$= 100$$

Solving the above equation we would find that z_6 is 3.5586%. Therefore, the 3-year spot rate on a bond-equivalent basis is 7.1173%.

To summarize the findings for the spot rates:

Period	Year	Annualized spot rate (BEY)	z_t
1	0.5	4.6000%	2.3000%
2	1.0	5.0000	2.5000
3	1.5	5.4146	2.7073
4	2.0	5.8297	2.9148
5	2.5	6.4665	3.2333
6	3.0	7.1173	3.5586

19. To obtain the arbitrage-free value of an 8% coupon 3-year Treasury bond, the cash flows for the bond are discounted at the spot rates in the previous question as shown below:

Period	Annual spot rate (%)	Semiannual spot rate (%)	Cash flow	PV of CF
1	4.6000	2.3000	$4.0	$3.9101
2	5.0000	2.5000	4.0	3.8073
3	5.4146	2.7073	4.0	3.6919
4	5.8297	2.9148	4.0	3.5657
5	6.4665	3.2333	4.0	3.4116
6	7.1173	3.5586	104.0	84.3171
			Total	$102.7037

The arbitrage-free value of this bond is $102.7037.

20. The nominal spread fails to take into consideration (1) the shape of the yield curve (and therefore spot rates) and (2) any option embedded in a bond.

21. The Z-spread relative to the Treasury spot rate curve is the spread that when added to all the Treasury spot rates will produce a present value for the cash flows equal to the market price. The present value using each of the three spreads in the question—80, 90, and 100 basis points—is shown below:

Period	Years to maturity	Spot rate (BEY) (%)	Semiannual spot rate (%)	Cash flow	PV at assumed spread (bp) 80	90	100
1	0.5	5.0	2.50	$3	$2.9155	$2.9140	$2.9126
2	1.0	5.4	2.70	3	2.8223	2.8196	2.8168
3	1.5	5.8	2.90	3	2.7216	2.7176	2.7137
4	2.0	6.4	3.20	3	2.6042	2.5992	2.5942
5	2.5	7.0	3.50	3	2.4777	2.4717	2.4658
6	3.0	7.2	3.60	3	2.3709	2.3641	2.3573
7	3.5	7.4	3.70	3	2.2645	2.2569	2.2493
8	4.0	7.8	3.90	103	73.5466	73.2652	72.9849
				Total	91.7233	91.4083	91.0947

The last three columns in the table show the assumed spread. One-half of the spread is added to the column showing the semiannual spot rate. Then the cash flow is discounted used the semiannual spot rate plus one-half the assumed spread.

As can be seen, when a 90 basis point spread is used, the present value of the cash flow is equal to the price of the non-Treasury issue, $91.4083. Therefore, the Z-spread is 90 basis points.

22. When the yield curve is flat, all the cash flows are discounted at the same rate. Therefore, if Treasury securities are the benchmark, the nominal spread will be equal to the Z-spread. So, in the case of the corporate bond issues where there is no embedded option, using either measure is acceptable. In contrast, for corporate bonds issues in the portfolio with embedded options, the option-adjusted spread is more appropriate than either the nominal spread or the Z-spread regardless of the shape of the yield curve. Consequently, Joan Thomas would have to agree that the option-adjusted spread should be used for the corporate issues with embedded options.

23. a. There are several assumptions that are made in valuing bonds with embedded options. One important assumption is interest rate volatility. Because these assumptions differ from dealer to dealer, the OAS values may differ substantially.

b. The relationship between the OAS, Z-spread, and option cost is as follows:

$$\text{option cost} = \text{Z-spread} - \text{OAS}$$

If a bond has no embedded option, then there is no option cost. That is, the option cost is zero. Substituting zero into the above equation, we have

$$\text{Z-spread} = \text{OAS}$$

That is, the Z-spread is equal to the OAS. This is the reason why Mr. Tinker observed that for the issues with no embedded options the OAS is the same as the Z-spread.

c. A negative value for the option cost means that the investor has purchased an option from the issuer. A putable bond is an example of where the investor purchases an option. This explains why Mr. Tinker finds that a negative value for the option cost was reported for the putable bond issues. When there is no embedded option, the option cost is zero and that is why Mr. Tinker finds this value for issues with this characteristic. A positive value for the option cost means that the investor has sold an option to the issuer. This occurs for callable bond issues, as Mr. Tinker observes.

24. a. Because the Treasury securities are the benchmark, the OAS reflects a spread to compensate for credit risk and liquidity risk. (Remember that option risk has already been removed.)

b. Since the benchmark is the issuer's on-the-run yield curve, the spread already reflects credit risk. So, basically the OAS reflects compensation for liquidity risk. (Remember that option risk has already been removed.)

c. The answer depends on the benchmark interest rates used by the dealer firm. If the benchmark interest rates are Treasury rates, then the OAS is better for the issue that Mr. Dumas is considering. If the benchmark is the issuer's on-the-run yield curve, then the issue that the dealer is offering to Mr. Dumas is more attractive. However, the qualifier is that the answer also depends on the interest rate volatility assumed by the dealer and the interest rate volatility assumed by Mr. Dumas when analyzing the issue using System A and System B. Without knowing the assumed interest rate volatilities, no statement can be made about the relative value of these two issues.

25. We will use the notation in the chapter:

f will denote the forward rate

t will be the subscript before f and will indicate the length of time that the rate applies

m will be the subscript after f and will indicate when the forward rate begins

All periods are equal to six months.
The forward rate is then found as follows:

$$_tf_m = \left[\frac{(1 + z_{m+t})^{m+t}}{(1 + z_m)^m} \right]^{1/t} - 1$$

a. For the 6-month forward rate six months from now, $t = 1$ and $m = 1$. Therefore,

$$_1f_1 = \left[\frac{(1 + z_{1+1})^{1+1}}{(1 + z_1)^1} \right]^{1/1} - 1$$

or

$$_1f_1 = \left[\frac{(1+z_2)^2}{(1+z_1)^1}\right]^1 - 1$$

Since

$$z_1 = 5.0\%/2 = 2.5\% \quad \text{and} \quad z_2 = 5.4\%/2 = 2.7\%$$

then

$$_1f_1 = \left[\frac{(1.027)^2}{(1.025)^1}\right]^1 - 1 = 0.029004 = 2.9004\%$$

Then the annualized 6-month forward rate six months from now on a bond-equivalent basis is 5.8008%.

b. For the 6-month forward rate one year from now, $t = 1$ and $m = 2$. Therefore,

$$_1f_2 = \left[\frac{(1+z_{2+1})^{2+1}}{(1+z_2)^2}\right]^{1/1} - 1$$

or

$$_1f_2 = \left[\frac{(1+z_3)^3}{(1+z_2)^2}\right]^1 - 1$$

Since

$$z_2 = 5.4\%/2 = 2.7\% \quad \text{and} \quad z_3 = 5.8\%/2 = 2.9\%$$

then

$$_1f_2 = \left[\frac{(1.029)^3}{(1.027)^2}\right]^1 - 1 = 0.033012 = 3.3012\%$$

Then the annualized 6-month forward rate one year from now on a bond-equivalent basis is 6.6023%.

c. For the 6-month forward rate three years from now, $t = 1$ and $m = 6$. Therefore,

$$_1f_6 = \left[\frac{(1+z_{6+1})^{6+1}}{(1+z_6)^6}\right]^{1/1} - 1$$

or

$$_1f_6 = \left[\frac{(1+z_7)^7}{(1+z_6)^6}\right]^{1/1} - 1$$

Since

$$z_6 = 7.2\%/2 = 3.6\% \quad \text{and} \quad z_7 = 7.4\%/2 = 3.7\%$$

then

$$_1f_6 = \left[\frac{(1.037)^7}{(1.036)^6} \right]^{1/1} - 1 = 0.04302 = 4.302\%$$

Then the annualized 6-month forward rate three years from now on a bond-equivalent basis is 8.6041%.

d. For the 2-year forward rate one year from now, $t = 4$ and $m = 2$. Therefore,

$$_4f_2 = \left[\frac{(1 + z_{4+2})^{4+2}}{(1 + z_2)^2} \right]^{1/4} - 1$$

or

$$_4f_2 = \left[\frac{(1 + z_6)^6}{(1 + z_2)^2} \right]^{1/4} - 1$$

Since

$$z_2 = 5.4\%/2 = 2.7\% \quad \text{and} \quad z_6 = 7.2\%/2 = 3.6\%$$

then

$$_4f_2 = \left[\frac{(1.036)^6}{(1.027)^2} \right]^{1/4} - 1 = 0.04053 = 4.053\%$$

Then the annualized 2-year forward rate one year from now on a bond-equivalent basis is 8.1059%.

e. For the 1-year forward rate two years from now, $t = 2$ and $m = 4$. Therefore,

$$_2f_4 = \left[\frac{(1 + z_{2+4})^{2+4}}{(1 + z_4)^4} \right]^{1/2} - 1$$

or

$$_2f_4 = \left[\frac{(1 + z_6)^6}{(1 + z_4)^4} \right]^{1/2} - 1$$

Since

$$z_4 = 6.4\%/2 = 3.2\% \quad \text{and} \quad z_6 = 7.2\%/2 = 3.6\%$$

then

$$_2f_4 = \left[\frac{(1.036)^6}{(1.032)^4} \right]^{1/2} - 1 = 0.04405 = 4.405\%$$

Then the annualized 1-year forward rate two years from now on a bond-equivalent basis is 8.810%.

26. The 6-month forward rate six months from now as found in the previous question is 5.8008%. The two alternatives are:

> Alternative 1: Invest $X at the 1-year spot rate of 5.4% for one year
>
> Alternative 2: Invest $X today at the 6-month spot rate of 5.0% and reinvest at the end of six months the proceeds at the 6-month forward rate of 5.8008%

For Alternative 1, the amount at the end of one year will be:

$$\$X \ (1 + 0.054/2)^2 = 1.054729 \ (\$X)$$

For Alternative 2, the amount at the end of one year will be:

$$\$X \ (1 + 0.05/2)(1 + 0.058008/2) = 1.054729 \ (\$X)$$

Thus, the two alternatives produce the same future value if the 6-month forward rate six months from now is 5.8008%.

27. Discounting at spot rates and forward rates will produce the same value for a bond. This is because spot rates are nothing more than packages of short-term forward rates. So, the second sales person's comment is wrong about the superiority of forward rates for valuation compared to spot rates.

28. a. The forward discount factor for period T is computed as follows.

$$\frac{1}{(1 + z_1)(1 +_1 f_1)(1 +_1 f_2)\ldots(1 +_1 f_{T-1})}$$

Therefore,

Period	Annual forward rate (BEY)	Semiannual rate	Forward discount factor
1	4.00%	2.00%	0.980392
2	4.40	2.20	0.959288
3	5.00	2.50	0.935891
4	5.60	2.80	0.910399
5	6.00	3.00	0.883883
6	6.40	3.20	0.856476

b. The value is found by multiplying each cash flow by the forward discount factor for the period as shown below:

Period	Forward discount factor	Cash flow	PV of cash flow
1	0.980392	$4	$3.921569
2	0.959288	4	3.837151
3	0.935891	4	3.743562
4	0.910399	4	3.641598
5	0.883883	4	3.535532
6	0.856476	104	89.073470
		Total	$107.752881

The value of this bond is $107.752881.

CHAPTER 7

INTRODUCTION TO THE MEASUREMENT OF INTEREST RATE RISK

SOLUTIONS

1. While it is true that a disadvantage of the full valuation approach is that it requires revaluing the bonds in the portfolio, it is not true that the duration/convexity approach does not require a valuation model. A valuation model is required in order to obtain the prices when rates are shocked that are used in the duration and convexity adjustment formulas.

2. The duration/convexity approach does not take into consideration how the yield curve can shift. However, this is not correct for the full valuation approach since yield curve scenarios are part of the full valuation method. In addition, the two bonds may have different prices and coupons thus leading to different percentage price change for the two bonds.

3. The statement is not correct. While two bonds may have the same duration, they can have different convexities.

4. The problem here is in the definition of price volatility. It can be measured in terms of dollar price change or percentage price change. Smith is correct that there is greater price volatility for bond B because of its higher modified duration—that is, a higher percentage price change. Robertson is correct that bond A has greater price volatility but in terms of dollar price change. Specifically, for a 100 basis point change in rates, bond A will change by $3.60 (4% times 90); for bond B the dollar price change will be $3 (6% times 50) for a 100 basis point rate change.

5. a. Mr. Renfro's definition is a temporal definition and it is best not to use such an interpretation. Duration is related to the percentage price change of a bond when interest rates change.

   b. Mr. Renfro's response is correct.

   c. Mr. Renfro's response is correct.

   d. The computation of effective duration requires a valuation model to determine what the new prices will be when interest rates change. These models are based on assumptions. When duration is taken from different sources, there is no consistency of assumptions. While it is true that there is a formula for computing duration once the new prices for the bond are determined from a valuation model when rates are shocked, there is no simple valuation formula for bonds with embedded options.

Mr. Renfro incorrectly overrode duration measures. It is possible—and it does occur in practice—to have a duration for a bond that is greater than the maturity of the bond. A negative duration does occur for some securities as well. For example, certain mortgage-backed securities have a negative duration. A negative duration of -3, for example, would mean that if interest rates increased by 100 basis points, the price of the bond will increase by approximately 3%. That is, the price of the bond moves in the same direction as the change in rates. In fact, for the types of bonds that have a duration longer than maturity and a negative duration, modified duration is not what the manager would want to use.

e. The first part of the statement is correct. However, the second part is not true. Two portfolios can have the same duration but perform differently when rates change because they have different convexities. Also, the portfolios may have different yield and coupon characteristics.

6. A negative convexity adjustment simply means that a bond's price appreciation will be less than its price decline for a large change in interest rates (200 basis points in the question). Whether or not a bond with negative convexity is attractive depends on its price and expectations about future interest rate changes.

7. If one interprets duration as some measure of time, it is difficult to understand why a bond will have a duration greater than its maturity. Duration is the approximate percentage price change of a bond for a 100 basis point change in interest rates. It is possible to have a security with a maturity of 10 years and a duration of 13.

8. Bond ABC exhibits negative convexity—for a 100 basis point change in rates, the gain is less than the loss; Bond XYZ exhibits positive convexity. A high coupon bond will exhibit negative convexity. A low coupon bond will exhibit positive convexity. Therefore, bond ABC is probably the high coupon bond while bond XYZ is probably the low coupon bond.

9. a. Modified duration is an inappropriate duration measure for a high coupon callable bond because it fails to recognize that as interest rates change, the expected cash flows will change.

   b. A better measure for a high-coupon callable bond is effective or option-adjusted duration.

10. Because the issue's coupon rate is substantially below the prevailing rate at which the issue can be refunded (500 basis points below), this issue is not likely to be called. Basically, if rates are shocked up and down, the expected cash flows are not likely to change because the coupon rate is so far below the market rate. Thus, modified duration—which assumes that the expected cash flow will not change when rates are changed—will be a good approximation for effective duration.

11. a. For a 25 basis point rate shock, the duration formula is:

$$\text{duration} = \frac{V_- - V_+}{2V_0(0.0025)}$$

		5%, 4 year	5%, 25 year	8%, 4 year	8%, 25 year
Initial value	V_0	100.0000	100.0000	110.7552	142.5435
Value at 4.75%	V_-	100.9011	103.6355	111.7138	147.2621
Value at 5.25%	V_+	99.1085	96.5416	109.8066	138.0421
Duration		3.59	14.19	3.44	12.94

b. For a 50 basis point rate shock, the duration formula is:

$$\text{duration} = \frac{V_- - V_+}{2V_0(0.0050)}$$

		5%, 4 year	5%, 25 year	8%, 4 year	8%, 25 year
Initial value	V_0	100.0000	100.0000	110.7552	142.5435
Value at 4.50%	V_-	101.8118	107.4586	112.6826	152.2102
Value at 5.50%	V_+	98.2264	93.2507	108.8679	133.7465
Duration		3.59	14.21	3.44	12.95

12. For a 25 basis point rate shock, the value for C is:

$$C = \frac{V_+ + V_- - 2V_0}{2V_0(0.0025)^2}$$

		5%, 4 year	5%, 25 year	8%, 4 year	8%, 25 year
Initial value	V_0	100.0000	100.0000	110.7552	142.5435
Value at 4.75%	V_-	100.9011	103.6355	111.7138	147.2621
Value at 5.25%	V_+	99.1085	96.5416	109.8066	138.0421
C		7.68	141.68	7.23	121.89

13. a. For a 10 basis point change:

duration for 8% 4-year bond $= 3.44$
duration for 8% 25-year bond $= 12.94$

$$\Delta y_* = 0.0010$$

For the 8% 4-year bond: approximate percentage price change for 10 basis point change in yield ($\Delta y_* = 0.0010$):

10 basis point increase:

   approximate percentage price change $= -3.44 \times (0.0010) \times 100 = -0.34\%$

10 basis point decrease:

   approximate percentage price change $= -3.44 \times (-0.0010) \times 100 = +0.34\%$

For the 8% 25-year bond: approximate percentage price change for 10 basis point change in yield (0.0010):

10 basis point increase:

   approximate percentage price change $= -12.94 \times (0.0010) \times 100 = -1.29\%$

10 basis point decrease:

   approximate percentage price change $= -12.94 \times (-0.0010) \times 100 = +1.29\%$

b. For the 4-year bond, the estimated percentage price change using duration is excellent for a 10 basis point change, as shown below:

	Duration estimate	Actual change
10 bp increase	−0.34%	−0.34%
10 bp decrease	+0.34%	+0.35%

For the 25-year bond, the estimated percentage price change using duration is excellent for a 10 basis point change, as shown below:

	Duration estimate	Actual change
10 bp increase	−1.29%	−1.28%
10 bp decrease	+1.29%	+1.31%

14. a. For a 200 basis point change:

$$\text{duration for 8\% 4-year bond} = 3.44$$
$$\text{duration for 8\% 25-year bond} = 12.94$$
$$\Delta y_* = 0.02$$

For the 8% 4-year bond: approximate percentage price change for 200 basis point change in yield ($\Delta y_* = 0.02$):

200 basis point increase:

approximate percentage price change $= -3.44 \times (0.02) \times 100 = -6.89\%$

200 basis point decrease:

approximate percentage price change $= -3.44 \times (-0.02) \times 100 = +6.89\%$

For the 8% 25-year bond: approximate percentage price change for 200 basis point shock:

200 basis point increase:

approximate percentage price change $= -12.94 \times (0.02) \times 100 = -25.88\%$

200 basis point decrease:

approximate percentage price change $= -12.94 \times (-0.02) \times 100 = +25.88\%$

b. For the 4-year bond, the estimated percentage price change using duration is very good despite a 200 basis point change, as shown below:

	Duration estimate	Actual change
200 bp increase	−6.88%	−6.61%
200 bp decrease	+6.88%	+7.19%

For the 25-year bond, the estimated percentage price change using duration is poor for a 200 basis point change, as shown below:

	Duration estimate	Actual change
200 bp increase	−25.88%	−21.62%
200 bp decrease	+25.88%	+31.54%

15. a. The convexity adjustment for the two 25-year bonds is:
For the 5% 25-year bond:

$$C = 141.68$$
$$\Delta y_* = 0.02$$

convexity adjustment to percentage price change $= 141.68 \times (0.02)^2 \times 100 = 5.67\%$

For the 8% 25-year bond:

$C = 121.89$

convexity adjustment to percentage price change $= 121.89 \times (0.02)^2 \times 100 = 4.88\%$

b. Estimated price change using duration and convexity adjustment.
For the 5% 25 year bond:

duration $= 14.19$

$\Delta y_* = 0.02$

approximate percentage price change based on duration $= -14.19 \times 0.02 \times 100 = -28.38\%$

convexity adjustment $= 5.67\%$

Therefore,

Yield change (Δy_*)	+200 bps
Estimated change using duration	−28.38%
Convexity adjustment	5.67%
Total estimated percentage price change	−22.71%

Yield change (Δy_*)	−200 bps
Estimated change using duration	28.38%
Convexity adjustment	5.67%
Total estimated percentage price change	34.05%

For the 8% 25-year bond:

duration $= 12.94$

$\Delta y_* = 0.02$

approximate percentage price change based on duration $= -12.94 \times 0.02 \times 100 = -25.88\%$

convexity adjustment $= 4.88\%$

Yield change (Δy_*)	+200 bps
Estimated change using duration	−25.88%
Convexity adjustment	4.88%
Total estimated percentage price change	−21.00%

Yield change (Δy_*)	−200 bps
Estimated change using duration	25.88%
Convexity adjustment	4.88%
Total estimated percentage price change	30.76%

c. For a large change in rates of 200 basis points, duration with the convexity adjustment does a pretty good job of estimating the actual percentage price change, as shown below.

	Duration/convexity estimate	Actual change
For 5% 25-year bond		
200 bp increase	−22.71%	−23.46%
200 bp decrease	+34.05%	+35.00%
For 8% 25-year bond		
200 bp increase	−21.00%	−21.62%
200 bp decrease	+30.76%	+31.54%

16. a. The price value of a basis point is

$$\$114.1338 - \$114.0051 = \$0.1287$$

   b. Using equation (2), the approximate percentage price change for a 1 basis point increase in interest rates (i.e., $\Delta y = 0.0001$), ignoring the negative sign in equation (2), is:

$$11.28 \times (0.0001) \times 100 = 0.1128\%$$

   Given the initial price of 114.1338, the dollar price change estimated using duration is

$$0.1128\% \times 114.1338 = \$0.1287$$

17. Duration even after adjusting for convexity indicates what the exposure of a bond or bond portfolio will be if interest rates change. However, to capture fully the interest rate exposure, it is necessary to know how volatile interest rates are. For example, in comparing duration of government bonds in different countries, the duration only indicates the sensitivity of the price to changes in interest rates by a given number of basis points. It does not consider the volatility of rates. In a country with little volatility in rates but where the government bonds have a high duration, just looking at duration misleads the investor as to the interest rate risk exposure.

TERM STRUCTURE AND VOLATILITY OF INTEREST RATES

SOLUTIONS

1. Historically, four shapes have been observed for the yield curve. A positively sloping or normal yield curve is where the longer the maturity, the higher the yield. A flat yield curve is where the yield for all maturities is approximately the same. A negatively sloped or inverted yield curve is where yield decreases as maturity increases. A humped yield curve is where yield increases for a range of maturities and then decreases.

2. The slope of the yield curve is measured by the difference between long-term Treasury yields and short-term Treasury yields. While there is no industrywide accepted definition of the maturity used for the long-end and the maturity for the short-end of the yield curve, some market participants define the slope of the yield curve as the difference between the 30-year yield and the 3-month yield while other market participants define the slope of the yield curve as the difference between the 30-year yield and the 2-year yield. The more accepted measure is the latter. However, for some sectors of the bond market such as the mortgage sector, the slope of the yield curve is measured by the spread between the 10-year yield and 2-year yield.

3. Historically, the slope of the long end of the yield curve has been flatter than the slope of the short end of the yield curve.

4. a. Studies have shown that there have been three factors that affect Treasury returns: (1) changes in the level of yields, (2) changes in the slope of the yield curve, and (3) changes in the curvature of the yield curve.

   b. The most important factor is the change in the level of interest rates.

   c. The implication is that the manager of a Treasury portfolio should control for its exposure to changes in the level of interest rates. For this reason it is important to have a measure such as duration to quantify exposure to a parallel shift in the yield curve.

   d. The second most important factor is changes in the yield curve slope.

   e. The implication is that a measure such as duration must be supplemented with information about a portfolio's exposure to changes in the slope of the yield curve—a measure such as key rate duration.

5. a. One limitation is that there is a large gap between maturities for the on-the-run issues and a linear extrapolation is used to get the yield for maturities between the

on-the-runs. A second limitation is that information is lost about the yield on other Treasury securities. Finally, one or more of the on-the-run issues may be on special in the repo market and thereby distort the true yield for these issues.

b. Since there may be more than one Treasury issue for a given maturity and since there are callable securities and securities trading at a price different from par (leading to tax issues), a methodology for handling these problems must be used. The bootstrapping methodology does not deal with such problems.

6. a. There are three problems with using the observed rates on Treasury strips (1) there is a liquidity premium for the observed yields in the strips market because strips are not as liquid as Treasury coupon securities; (2) the tax treatment of strips is different from that of Treasury coupon securities—the accrued interest on strips is taxed even though no cash is received by the investor—resulting in the yield on strips reflecting this tax disadvantage; and, (3) there are maturity sectors where non-U.S. investors find it advantageous to trade off yield for tax advantages in their country that are associated with a strip.

b. A practitioner may restrict the use of Treasury strips to construct the theoretical spot rate curve to coupon strips because of the tax aspect mentioned in part a. Specifically, certain foreign tax authorities allow their citizens to treat the difference between the maturity value and the purchase price as a capital gain and tax this gain at a favorable tax rate. Some will grant this favorable treatment only when the strip is created from the principal rather than the coupon. Any such bias can be avoided by just using coupon strips.

7. The advantages are that (1) there are typically more points available to construct a swap curve than a government bond yield curve; (2) there are no distortions in yields caused by bonds being on special in the repo market; and (3) comparisons across countries are easier because there is almost no government regulation and no distortions caused by tax benefits.

8. If the country has a liquid swap market with a wide spectrum of maturities, a swap curve can be developed. By the bootstrapping methodology, the spot rate curve for that country can be derived.

9. a. The convention in the swap market is to quote the fixed rate (i.e., the swap rate) as a spread over an estimated government yield for a bond with the same maturity as the swap. That spread is called the swap spread.

b. Since the credit risk in a swap is that the counterparty will fail to make the contractual payments and typically the counterparty is a high credit quality bank, the swap spread is a gauge of the credit risk associated with the banking sector.

10. a. The pure expectations theory postulates that no systematic factors other than expected future short-term rates affect forward rates. According to the pure expectations theory, forward rates exclusively represent expected future rates. Thus, the entire term structure at a given time reflects the market's current expectations of the family of future short-term rates.

b. The pure expectations theory neglects the risks inherent in investing in bonds. If forward rates were perfect predictors of future interest rates, then the future prices of bonds would be known with certainty. The return over any investment period would be certain and independent of the maturity of the instrument acquired. However, with the uncertainty about future interest rates and, therefore, about future prices of bonds, these instruments become risky investments in the sense that the return over some investment horizon is unknown.

11. The broadest interpretation of the pure expectations theory asserts that there is no difference in the 4-year total return if an investor purchased a 7-year zero-coupon bond or a 15-year zero-coupon bond.

12. The local expectations form of the pure expectations theory asserts that the total return over a 6-month horizon for a 5-year zero-coupon bond would be the same as for a 2-year zero-coupon bond.

13. The first sentence of the statement is correct. Moreover, it is correct that studies have shown that forward rates are poor predictors of future interest rates. However, the last sentence of the statement is incorrect. Forward rates should not be ignored because they indicate break-even rates and rates that can be locked in. So, they play an important role in investment decisions.

14. The two interpretations of forward rates are that they are break-even rates and they are rates that can be locked in.

    a. For the 1-year forward rate seven years from now of 6.4% the two interpretations are as follows:

       (i) 6.4% is the rate that will make an investor indifferent between buying an 8-year zero-coupon bond or investing in a 7-year zero-coupon bond and when it matures reinvesting in a zero-coupon bond that matures in one year, and

       (ii) 6.4% is the rate that can be locked in today by buying an 8-year zero-coupon bond rather than investing in a 7-year zero-coupon bond and when it matures reinvesting in a zero-coupon bond that matures in one year.

    b. For the 2-year forward rate one year from now of 6.2% the two interpretations are as follows:

       (i) 6.2% is the rate that will make an investor indifferent between buying a 3-year zero-coupon bond or investing in a 1-year zero-coupon bond and when it matures reinvesting in a zero-coupon bond that matures in two years, and

       (ii) 6.2% is the rate that can be locked in today by buying a 3-year zero-coupon bond rather than investing in a 1-year zero-coupon bond and when it matures reinvesting in a zero-coupon bond that matures in two years.

    c. For the 8-year forward rate three years from now of 7.1% the two interpretations are as follows:

       (i) 7.1% is the rate that will make an investor indifferent between buying an 11-year zero-coupon bond or investing in a 3-year zero-coupon bond and when it matures reinvesting in a zero-coupon bond that matures in eight years, and

       (ii) 7.1% is the rate that can be locked in today by buying an 11-year zero-coupon bond rather than investing in a 3-year zero-coupon bond and when it matures reinvesting in a zero-coupon bond that matures in eight years.

15. All expectations theories—the pure expectations theory, the liquidity preference theory, and the preferred habitat theory—share a hypothesis about the behavior of short-term forward rates and also assume that the forward rates in current long-term bonds are closely related to the market's expectations about future short-term rates. While the

pure expectations theory postulates that no systematic factors other than expected future short-term rates affect forward rates, the liquidity preference theory and the preferred habitat theory postulate that there are other factors and therefore are referred to as biased expectations theories. The liquidity preference theory asserts that investors demand a liquidity premium for extending maturity so that the forward rates are biased by this premium. The preferred habitat theory asserts that investors must be induced by a yield premium in order to accept the risks associated with shifting funds out of their preferred sector and forward rates embody the premium for this inducement.

16. a. Proponents of the pure expectations theory would assert that an upward sloping yield curve is a market's forecast of a rise in interest rates. If that is correct, an expected rise in interest rates would mean that the manager should shorten or reduce the duration (i.e., interest rate risk) of the portfolio. However, the pure expectations has serious pitfalls and the forward rates are not good predictors of future interest rates.

   b. The preferred habitat form of the biased expectations theory is consistent with the shape of the spot rate curve observed. The preferred habitat theory asserts that if there is an imbalance between the supply and demand for funds within a given maturity sector, market participants (i.e., borrowers and investors) will agree to shift their financing and investing activities out of their preferred maturity sector to take advantage of any such imbalance. However, participants will demand compensation for shifting out of their preferred maturity sector in the form of a yield premium. Consequently, any shape for the spot rate curve (and yield curve) can result, such as the one observed in the question. Therefore, the trustee's statement is incorrect.

   (*Note*: The question only asked about *expectations* theories of the term structure of interest rates. Another theory, the market segmentation theory described in Level 1 (Chapter 4), asserts that when there are supply and demand imbalances within a maturity sector, market participants will not shift out of their preferred maturity sector. Consequently, different maturity sectors reflect supply and demand imbalances within each sector and the type of yield curve observed in the question is possible.)

17. a. Portfolio A is the bullet portfolio because its 10-year key rate duration dominates by far the key rate duration for the other maturities. Portfolio B is the laddered portfolio because the key rate durations after year 2 are roughly equal. Portfolio C is the barbell portfolio with the short end of the barbell at 5 years and the long end of the barbell at 20 years.

   b. The bullet portfolio has the highest 10-year key rate duration and will therefore increase the most if the 10-year spot rate decreases while the key rates for the other maturities do not change much.

   c. Adding up the key rate durations for each portfolio gives 6.2. This is the duration of all three portfolios if the spot rate for all key maturities changes by the same number of basis points—that is, a parallel shift in the spot rate for the key maturities.

18. The information for computing the daily standard deviation for yield volatility is shown below:

t	y_t	$X_t = 100[Ln(y_t/y_{t-1})]$	$(X_t - \overline{X})^2$
0	5.854		
1	5.843	−0.18808	0.00060
2	5.774	−1.18793	1.04922
3	5.719	−0.95711	0.62964

t	y_t	$X_t = 100[\mathrm{Ln}(y_t/y_{t-1})]$	$(X_t - \overline{X})^2$
4	5.726	0.12232	0.08176
5	5.761	0.60939	0.59753
6	5.797	0.62295	0.61868
7	5.720	−1.33717	1.37724
8	5.755	0.61002	0.59851
9	5.787	0.55450	0.51568
10	5.759	−0.48502	0.10330
	Total	−1.63613	5.57216825

$$\text{sample mean} = \overline{X} = \frac{-1.63613}{10} = -0.163613\%$$

$$\text{variance} = \frac{5.57216825}{10 - 1} = 0.6191298$$

$$\text{std dev} = \sqrt{0.6191298} = 0.786848\%$$

19. a. Using 250 days: $\sqrt{250}\,(0.786848\%) = 12.44\%$
    b. Using 260 days: $\sqrt{260}\,(0.786848\%) = 12.69\%$
    c. Using 365 days: $\sqrt{365}\,(0.786848\%) = 15.03\%$

20. This is not necessarily the case because with the same data there are still choices that the managers must make that may result in quite different estimates of historical volatility. These choices include the number of days to use and the annualization of the daily standard deviation.

21. Since the current level of the 2-year Treasury yield is 5%, then the annual standard deviation of 7% translates into a 35 basis point (5% times 7%) standard deviation. Assuming that yield volatility is approximately normally distributed, we can use the normal distribution to construct an interval or range for what the future yield will be. There is a 68.3% probability that the yield will be between one standard deviation below and above the expected value. The expected value is the prevailing yield. If the annual standard deviation is 35 basis points and the prevailing yield is 5%, then there is a 68.3% probability that the yield next year will be between 4.65% (5% minus 35 basis points) and 5.35% (5% plus 35 basis points). There is a 99.7% probability that the yield next year will be within three standard deviations. In our case, three standard deviations is 105 basis points. Therefore there is a 99.7% probability that the yield will be between 3.95% (5% minus 105 basis points) and 6.05% (5% plus 105 basis points).

22. a. Yield volatility can be estimated from the observed prices of interest rate options and caps. A yield volatility estimated in this way is called implied volatility and is based on some option pricing model. An input to any option pricing model in which the underlying is a Treasury security or Treasury futures contract is expected yield volatility. If the observed price of an option is assumed to be the fair price and the option pricing model is assumed to be the model that would generate that fair price, then the implied yield volatility is the yield volatility that when used as an input into the option pricing model would produce the observed option price.

    b. The problems with using implied volatility are that (1) it is assumed the option pricing model is correct, and (2) since option pricing models typically assume that volatility is constant over the life of the option interpreting an implied volatility becomes difficult.

23. a. There are reasons to believe that market participants give greater weight to recent movements in yield when determining volatility. To incorporate this belief into the estimation of historical volatility, different weights can be assigned to the observed changes in daily yields. More specifically, observations further in the past should be given less weight.

    b. Some market practitioners argue that in forecasting volatility the expected value or mean that should be used in the formula for the variance is zero.

CHAPTER 9

VALUING BONDS WITH EMBEDDED OPTIONS

SOLUTIONS

1. This statement is incorrect. While there are different models such as the binomial and trinomial models, the basic features of all these models are the same. They all involve assessing the cash flow at each node in the interest rate tree and determining whether or not to adjust the cash flow based on the embedded options. All these models require a rule for calling the issue and all require an assumption about the volatility of interest rates. The backward induction method is used for all these models.

2. The procedure for determining the value of a bond with an embedded option starts at the maturity date on the interest rate tree (i.e., the end of the tree) and values the bond moving backward to the root of the tree—which is today's value. Hence the procedure is called backward induction.

3. The reason is that in constructing the interest rate tree the on-the-run issues are used and interest rates on the tree must be such that if the on-the-run issue is valued using the tree, the model will produce the market value of the on-the-run issue. When a model produces the market value of the on-the-run issues it is said to be "calibrated to the market" or "arbitrage free."

4. a. In the interest rate tree, the forward rates for a given period are shown at each node. (In the illustrations in the chapter, each period is one year.) Since there is more than one node for each period (after the root of the tree), there is not one forward rate for a given period but several forward rates.

   b. The binomial interest rate tree is constructed based on an assumption about interest rate volatility. If a different volatility assumption is made, a new interest rate tree is constructed and therefore there are different interest rates at the nodes for a given period and therefore a different set of forward rates.

5. a.

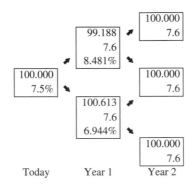

b.

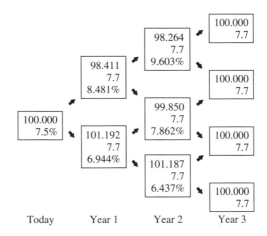

c. The value of an 8.5% coupon 3-year bond using the spot rates is as follows:

$$\frac{8.5}{(1.07500)} + \frac{8.5}{(1.07604)^2} + \frac{108.5}{(1.07710)^3} = \$102.076$$

d.

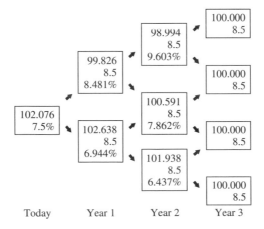

e. The value of this callable bond is 100.722.

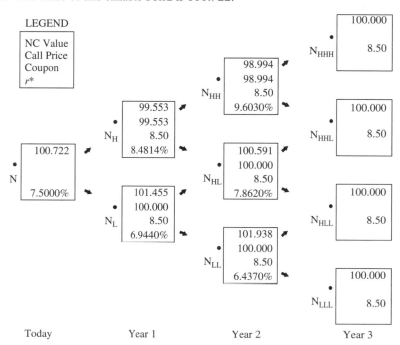

f. The value of the embedded call option is $1.354 which is equal to the value of the option-free bond ($102.076) minus the value of the callable bond ($100.722).

6. The statement is wrong. The option-adjusted spread is a byproduct (i.e., is obtained from) of a valuation model. Any assumptions that must be made in a valuation model to obtain the arbitrage-value of a bond also apply to the option-adjusted spread. For example, if a valuation model assumes that interest rate volatility is x%, then the OAS is based on a volatility of x%.

7. Despite the fact that both the dealer and the pricing service used the same model and same benchmark, there are other inputs to the model that could cause a 1 point difference. The major reason is probably that the two may have used a different volatility assumption. A second reason is that the call rule used by the two may be quite different.

8. One of the first questions should be what is the benchmark that the spread is relative to. The other key question is what is the assumed interest rate volatility.

9. This statement is not necessarily correct. An OAS can be computed based on any benchmark interest rates. For example, the on-the-run rates for the issuer or the on-the-run rates for issuers in the same bond sector and having the same credit rating can be used.

10. a. The value of a callable bond is equal to the value of an otherwise option-free bond minus the value of the embedded call option. The value of the embedded call option is higher the greater the assumed interest rate volatility. Therefore, a higher value for the embedded call option is subtracted from the value of the option-free bond, resulting in a lower value for the callable bond.

   b. The value of a putable bond is equal to the value of an otherwise option-free bond plus the value of the embedded put option. The value of the embedded put option is higher the greater the assumed interest rate volatility. Therefore, a higher value for the embedded put option is added to the value of the option-free bond, resulting in a higher value of the putable bond.

11. While it is true that the value of a bond that is callable and putable is conceptually equal to the value of the option-free bond adjusted for the value of the put option and the value of the call option, this is not the procedure used in a model such as the binomial model that uses the backward induction method. The reason is that these embedded options exist simultaneously so that the exercise of one option would extinguish the value of the other option. What is done in the backward induction method is to value the callable/putable bond by simultaneously considering the two embedded options. The way this works is at each node it will be determined whether or not the call option will be exercised based on the call rule and then whether or not the put option will be exercised. If either option is exercised, the corresponding exercise value for the bond is used in subsequent calculations in the backward induction process.

12. There are two types of duration and convexity—modified and effective. Modified forms of duration and convexity assume that when interest rates change the cash flows do not change. In contrast, the effective forms assume that when interest rates change the cash flows may change. When the binomial model is used to determine the values when rates are increased and decreased, the new values reflect how the cash flows may change. That is, the cash flow at each node of the binomial interest tree when rates are shifted up and down are allowed to change depending on the rules for when an option will be exercised. Thus, the resulting duration and convexity are effective duration and convexity.

13. It is true that there is a standard formula for computing duration by shocking (i.e., changing) interest rates and substituting the values computed in the duration formula. However, for a bond with an embedded option, such as a callable bond, it is necessary to have a valuation model (such as the binomial model) to determine the value of the bond when interest rates are changed. Valuation models can give different values for the same bond depending on the assumptions used. For example, suppose that the vendor and the dealer use the same valuation model but employ (1) a different volatility assumption, (2) different benchmark interest rates, and (3) a different call rule. The values produced by the two models that are substituted into the (effective) duration formula can result in the difference of 5.4 versus 4.5.

14. It is assumed that the option-adjusted spread is constant when interest rates change.

15. The starting point is defining what the benchmark interest rates are that the spread is being measured relative to. It is based on the benchmark that one interprets what the option-adjusted spread is compensation for.

Manager 1 is wrong. The option-adjusted spread is adjusting any spread for the option risk. That is, it is netting out from the spread the option risk.

Manager 2 is partially correct. If the benchmark interest rates are the on-the-run Treasury issues, then the option-adjusted spread is indicating compensation for credit risk. But it also captures liquidity risk. Moreover, it is not necessarily true that the benchmark interest rates are the on-the-run Treasury rates.

Manager 3 is correct if the benchmark interest rates are the on-the-run Treasury issues. However, other benchmark interest rates have been used and in such cases Manager 3's interpretation would be incorrect.

Manager 4 is incorrect. Even if the benchmark interest rates are the rates for the issuer's on-the-run issues, the spread would not reflect compensation for credit risk.

16. It is incorrect to state that the 20 basis point OAS is a spread over the issuer's 10-year on-the-run issue. That is, it is not a spread over one point on the yield curve. Rather, from the issuer's on-the-run yield curve, the rates at each node on the interest rate tree are determined. These rates are the one-period forward rates. The OAS is the spread that when added to all these forward rates will produce a value for the callable bond equal to the market price of the bond. So, it is a spread over the forward rates in the interest rate tree which are in turn generated from the benchmark interest rates.

17. Without knowing the benchmark interest rate used to compute the OAS, no statement can be made. If the benchmark is the Treasury sector or a corporate sector with a higher credit quality than the issue being analyzed, then the statement is correct. However, if the benchmark is the issuer's yield curve, then an OAS of zero means that the issue is fairly priced.

18. a. The coupon rate on a floater is paid in arrears. This means that for a floater the rate determined in the current period is not paid until the end of the period (or beginning of the next period). This requires that an adjustment be made to the backward induction method.

    b. The adjustment is made to the backward induction method by discounting the coupon payment to be made in the next period for a floater based on the beginning of the period reference rate.

    c. A cap on a floater is handled by determining at each node if the cap is reached. At a node where the coupon rate exceeds the cap, the coupon rate is replaced by the capped rate.

19. a. A convertible bond grants the investor the option to call the common stock of the issuer. Thus, a convertible bond has an embedded call option on the common stock. However, most convertible bonds are callable. That is, there is a second embedded call option granting the issuer the right to retire the bond.

    b. The complication that arises is that one of the options, the call on the common stock granted to the investor, depends on the future price of the common stock. However, the call on the bond granted to the issuer depends on future interest rates. Thus, valuing a callable convertible bond requires including in one valuation model both future stock price movements and future interest rate movements.

20. The conversion ratio is found by dividing the par value of $1,000 by the conversion price stated in the prospectus of $45 per share. The conversion ratio is then 22.22 ($1,000/$45).

21. a. conversion value = market price of common stock × conversion ratio
$$= \$25 \times 30 = \$750$$

    b. market conversion price $= \dfrac{\text{market price of convertible bond}}{\text{conversion ratio}} = \dfrac{\$900}{30} = \$30$

    c. conversion premium per share
$$= \text{market conversion price} - \text{market price of common stock}$$
$$= \$30 - \$25 = \$5$$

    d. conversion premium ratio $= \dfrac{\text{conversion premium per share}}{\text{market price of common stok}} = \dfrac{\$5}{\$25} = 20\%$

    e. premium over straight value $= \dfrac{\text{market price of convertible good}}{\text{straight value}} - 1 = \dfrac{\$900}{\$700} - 1$
$$= 28.6\%$$

f. favorable income differential per share

$$= \frac{\text{coupon interest from bond} - \text{conversion ratio} \times \text{dividend per share}}{\text{conversion ratio}}$$

$$= \frac{\$85(30 \times \$1)}{30} = \$1.833$$

g. premium payback period $= \dfrac{\text{market conversion premium per share}}{\text{favorable income differential per share}} = \dfrac{\$5}{\$1.833}$

$$= 2.73 \text{ years}$$

22. a. If the price increases to $54, the conversion value will be

$$\text{conversion value} = \$54 \times 30 = \$1{,}620$$

Assuming that the convertible bond's price does not exceed the conversion value (that is why the question asked for an approximate return), then the return on the $900 investment in the convertible bond is:

$$\frac{\$1{,}620}{\$900} - 1 = 0.8 = 80\%$$

b. The return realized if $25 had been invested in the common stock is equal to:

$$\frac{\$54 - \$25}{\$25} = 1.16 = 116\%$$

c. The reason for the lower return by buying the convertible bond rather than the stock directly is that the investor has effectively paid $5 more for the stock.

23. a. If the price decreases to $10, the conversion value will be

$$\text{conversion value} = \$10 \times 30 = \$300$$

However, it is assumed in the question that the straight value is unchanged at $700. The convertible bond will trade at the greater of the straight value or the conversion value. In this case, it is $700. The return is then:

$$\frac{\$700}{\$900} - 1 = -0.22 = -22\%$$

b. The return realized if $25 had been invested in the common stock is equal to:

$$\frac{\$10 - \$25}{\$25} = -0.6 = -60\%$$

c. The return is greater for convertible bond because of the assumption made that the straight value did not change. If the straight value did decline, the loss would be greater than −22% but it would still be probably less than the loss on the direct purchase of the stock. The key here is that the floor (straight value) is what cushion's the decline—but it is moving floor.

24. a. If the stock price is low so that the straight value is considerably higher than the conversion value, the bond will trade much like a straight bond. The convertible in such instances is referred to as a "busted convertible."
    b. Since the market value of a busted convertible is very close to that of a straight bond, the premium over straight value would be very small.
    c. By restricting the convertible bonds in which Mr. Caywood would invest to higher investment grade ratings, he is reducing credit risk.
    d. By seeking bonds not likely to be called, Mr. Caywood is reducing call risk that would result in a forced conversion to the common stock.
25. The measure assumes that the straight value does not decline.
26. a. A "factor" is the stochastic (or random) variable that is assumed to affect the value of a security. The two factors in valuing a convertible bond are the price movement of the underlying common stock (which affects the value of the embedded call option on the common stock) and the movement of interest rates (which affects the value of the embedded call option on the bond).
    b. In practice, models used to value convertible bonds have been one-factor models with the factor included being the price movement of the underlying common stock.

CHAPTER 10

MORTGAGE-BACKED SECTOR OF THE BOND MARKET

SOLUTIONS

1. a.

Month	Beginning mortgage	Mortgage payment	Interest	Sch. Prin repayment	End of month balance
1	150,000.00	1,023.26	906.25	117.01	149,882.99
2	149,882.99	1,023.26	905.54	117.72	149,765.26
3	149,765.26	1,023.26	904.83	118.43	149,646.83
4	149,646.83	1,023.26	904.12	119.15	149,527.68
5	149,527.68	1,023.26	903.40	119.87	149,407.82
6	149,407.82	1,023.26	902.67	120.59	149,287.22
7	149,287.22	1,023.26	901.94	121.32	149,165.90
8	149,165.90	1,023.26	901.21	122.05	149,043.85
9	149,043.85	1,023.26	900.47	122.79	148,921.06
10	148,921.06	1,023.26	899.73	123.53	148,797.52
11	148,797.52	1,023.26	898.99	124.28	148,673.25
12	148,673.25	1,023.26	898.23	125.03	148,548.21
13	148,548.21	1,023.26	897.48	125.79	148,422.43
14	148,422.43	1,023.26	896.72	126.55	148,295.88

b.

Month	Beginning mortgage	Mortgage payment	Interest	Sch. Prin repayment	End of month balance
357	4,031.97	1,023.26	24.36	998.90	3,033.07
358	3,033.07	1,023.26	18.32	1,004.94	2,028.13
359	2,028.13	1,023.26	12.25	1,011.01	1,017.12
360	1,017.12	1,023.26	6.15	1,017.12	0.00

2. a. The monthly servicing fee is found by dividing the servicing fee of 0.005 (50 basis points) by 12. The monthly servicing fee is therefore 0.0004167. Multiplying the monthly servicing fee by the beginning mortgage balance gives the servicing fee for the month.

Month	Beginning mortgage	Mortgage payment	Servicing fee	Net interest	Sch. Prin repayment	End of month balance
1	150,000.00	1,023.26	62.50	843.75	117.01	149,882.99
2	149,882.99	1,023.26	62.45	843.09	117.72	149,765.26
3	149,765.26	1,023.26	62.40	842.43	118.43	149,646.83
4	149,646.83	1,023.26	62.35	841.76	119.15	149,527.68
5	149,527.68	1,023.26	62.30	841.09	119.87	149,407.82
6	149,407.82	1,023.26	62.25	840.42	120.59	149,287.22

b. The investor's cash flow is the sum of the net interest and the scheduled principal repayment.

Month	Net interest	Sch. Prin repayment	Investor cash flow
1	843.75	117.01	960.76
2	843.09	117.72	960.81
3	842.43	118.43	960.86
4	841.76	119.15	960.91
5	841.09	119.87	960.96
6	840.42	120.59	961.01

3. The statement is incorrect. While the guarantee by the U.S. government means that there will not be a loss of principal and that interest payments will be made in full, there is uncertainty about the timing of the principal repayments because the borrower may prepay at any time, in whole or in part.

4. a and b. The weighted average coupon (WAC) and weighted average maturity (WAM) for the mortgage pool are computed below:

Loan	Outstanding mortgage balance	Weight in pool	Mortgage rate	Months remaining	WAC	WAM
1	$215,000	26.06%	6.75%	200	1.7591%	52.12
2	$185,000	22.42%	7.75%	185	1.7379%	41.48
3	$125,000	15.15%	7.25%	192	1.0985%	29.09
4	$100,000	12.12%	7.00%	210	0.8485%	25.45
5	$200,000	24.24%	6.50%	180	1.5758%	43.64
Total	$825,000	100.00%			7.02%	191.79

WAC = 7.02%   WAM = 192 (rounded)

5. a. The SMM is equal to

$$\frac{\$2,450,000}{\$260,000,000 - \$1,000,000} = 0.009459 = 0.9459\%$$

b. Mr. Jamison should interpret the SMM as follows: 0.9459% of the mortgage pool available to prepay in month 42 prepaid in the month.

c. Given the SMM, the CPR is computed using equation (2) in the chapter:

$$CPR = 1 - (1 - SMM)^{12}$$

Therefore,

$$CPR = 1 - (1 - 0.009459)^{12} = 0.107790 = 10.78\%$$

d. Mr. Jamison should interpret the CPR as follows: ignoring scheduled principal payments, approximately 10.79% of the outstanding mortgage balance at the beginning of the year will be prepaid by the end of the year.

6. The CPR and SMM for each month are shown below:

Month	PSA	CPR	SMM
5	100	0.010	0.000837
15	80	0.024	0.002022
20	175	0.070	0.006029
27	50	0.027	0.002278
88	200	0.120	0.010596
136	75	0.045	0.003829
220	225	0.135	0.012012

7. According to the PSA prepayment benchmark, after month 30 the CPR is constant over the life of the security. Specifically, it is equal to

$$CPR = 6\% \times (PSA/100)$$

So, for example, if the assumed PSA is 225, the CPR for the life of the security is

$$CPR = 6\% \times (225/100) = 13.5\%$$

Thus, the statement is correct that one CPR can be used to describe the PSA 30 months after the origination of the mortgages.

8. The amount of the prepayment for the month is determined as follows:

(Beginning mortgage balance − scheduled principal payment) × SMM

We know that
$$(\$537,000,000 - \$440,000) \times SMM$$

The CPR for month 140 assuming 175 PSA is

$$CPR = 6\% \times (175/100) = 10.5\%$$

The SMM is then

$$SMM = 1 - (1 - 0.105)^{0.08333} = 0.009201$$

Therefore, the prepayment in month 140 is

$$(\$537,000,000 - \$440,000) \times 0.009201 = \$4,936,889 \text{ (rounded)}$$

(Note: You will get a slightly different answer if you carried the SMM to more decimal places.)

9. The PSA model, or PSA prepayment benchmark, is not a prepayment model in that it does not predict prepayments for a mortgage-backed security. It is a generic benchmark that hypothesizes about what the pattern of prepayments will be over the life of a mortgage-backed security—that there is a prepayment ramp (that increases linearly) for 30 months, after which when the CPR is assumed to be constant for the life of the security.

10. a. GNMA refers to passthrough securities issued by the Government National Mortgage Association. "30-YEAR" indicates that the mortgage loans were originated with 30-year terms.

    b. This means GNMA 30-year passthrough securities with a coupon rate of 8.5% that were originated in 1994.

    c. These are the prepayment rates that are projected for various periods. The prepayment rates are expressed in term of the PSA prepayment benchmark. There is a prepayment rate projection for each of the subsequent three months, a prepayment rate projection for one year, and a long-term prepayment rate.

    d. First, the prepayments is only for 7.5% coupon GNMA issues originated in 1993. But there are many 7.5% coupon GNMA issues that were issued in 1993. The prepayments are for a generic issue. This means that when a specific Ginnie Mae 7.5% coupon originated in 1993 is delivered to the buyer, it can realize a prepayment rate quite different from the generic prepayment rate in the report, but on average, 1993 GNMA 7.5%'s are projected to have this prepayment rate.

    e. One factor that affects prepayments is the prevailing mortgage rate relative to the rate that borrowers are paying on the underlying mortgages. As noted in the question, the mortgage rate at the time was 8.13%. The higher the coupon rate, the higher the rate that the borrowers in the underlying mortgage pool are paying and the greater the incentive to prepay. So, as the coupon rate increases, prepayments are expected to be greater because of the incentive to prepay.

11. Since the mortgage passthrough being analyzed has been outstanding for more than 15 years, there have been probably several opportunities for borrowers in the underlying mortgage pool to refinance at a lower rate than they are paying. Consequently, the low mortgage rate of 8% relative to 13% may not result in an increase in prepayments and the same is true for a further decline over the year to 7%. This characteristic of prepayments is referred to as "prepayment burnout."

12. An investor in a short-term security is concerned with extension risk. This is the risk that the security's average life will increase.

13. a. For tranche A:

Month	Sch. Principal repayment + prepayments	Beginning principal	Tranche A principal repayment	Interest at 6%	Cash flow
1	520,000	3,000,000	520,000	15,000	535,000
2	510,000	2,480,000	510,000	12,400	522,400
3	490,000	1,970,000	490,000	9,850	499,850
4	450,000	1,480,000	450,000	7,400	457,400
5	448,000	1,030,000	448,000	5,150	453,150
6	442,000	582,000	442,000	2,910	444,910
7	410,000	140,000	140,000	700	140,700
		Total	3,000,000		

From months 8 through 48, the principal repayment, interest, and cash flow are zero.

b. For tranche B:

Month	Sch. Principal repayment + prepayments	Beginning principal	Tranche B principal repayment	Interest at 7%	Cash flow
1	520,000	8,000,000	0	46,667	46,667
2	510,000	8,000,000	0	46,667	46,667
3	490,000	8,000,000	0	46,667	46,667
4	450,000	8,000,000	0	46,667	46,667
5	448,000	8,000,000	0	46,667	46,667
6	442,000	8,000,000	0	46,667	46,667
7	410,000	8,000,000	270,000	46,667	316,667
8	405,000	7,730,000	405,000	45,092	450,092
9	400,000	7,325,000	400,000	42,729	442,729
10	396,000	6,925,000	396,000	40,396	436,396
11	395,000	6,529,000	395,000	38,086	433,086
12	390,000	6,134,000	390,000	35,782	425,782
13	388,000	5,744,000	388,000	33,507	421,507
14	385,000	5,356,000	385,000	31,243	416,243
15	380,000	4,971,000	380,000	28,998	408,998
16	377,000	4,591,000	377,000	26,781	403,781
17	375,000	4,214,000	375,000	24,582	399,582
18	370,000	3,839,000	370,000	22,394	392,394
19	369,000	3,469,000	369,000	20,236	389,236
20	366,000	3,100,000	366,000	18,083	384,083
21	300,000	2,734,000	300,000	15,948	315,948
22	298,000	2,434,000	298,000	14,198	312,198
23	292,000	2,136,000	292,000	12,460	304,460
24	290,000	1,844,000	290,000	10,757	300,757
25	287,000	1,554,000	287,000	9,065	296,065
26	285,000	1,267,000	285,000	7,391	292,391
27	283,000	982,000	283,000	5,728	288,728
28	280,000	699,000	280,000	4,078	284,078
29	278,000	419,000	278,000	2,444	280,444
30	275,000	141,000	141,000	823	141,823
		Total	8,000,000		

For months 31 through 48 the principal payment, interest, and cash flow are zero.

c. For tranche C:

Month	Sch. Principal repayment + prepayments	Beginning principal	Tranche C principal repayment	Interest at 8%	Cash flow
1	520,000	30,000,000	0	200,000	200,000
2	510,000	30,000,000	0	200,000	200,000
3	490,000	30,000,000	0	200,000	200,000
4	450,000	30,000,000	0	200,000	200,000

Month	Sch. Principal repayment + prepayments	Beginning principal	Tranche C principal repayment	Interest at 8%	Cash flow
5	448,000	30,000,000	0	200,000	200,000
6	442,000	30,000,000	0	200,000	200,000
7	410,000	30,000,000	0	200,000	200,000
8	405,000	30,000,000	0	200,000	200,000
9	400,000	30,000,000	0	200,000	200,000
10	396,000	30,000,000	0	200,000	200,000
11	395,000	30,000,000	0	200,000	200,000
12	390,000	30,000,000	0	200,000	200,000
13	388,000	30,000,000	0	200,000	200,000
14	385,000	30,000,000	0	200,000	200,000
15	380,000	30,000,000	0	200,000	200,000
16	377,000	30,000,000	0	200,000	200,000
17	375,000	30,000,000	0	200,000	200,000
18	370,000	30,000,000	0	200,000	200,000
19	369,000	30,000,000	0	200,000	200,000
20	366,000	30,000,000	0	200,000	200,000
21	300,000	30,000,000	0	200,000	200,000
22	298,000	30,000,000	0	200,000	200,000
23	292,000	30,000,000	0	200,000	200,000
24	290,000	30,000,000	0	200,000	200,000
25	287,000	30,000,000	0	200,000	200,000
26	285,000	30,000,000	0	200,000	200,000
27	283,000	30,000,000	0	200,000	200,000
28	280,000	30,000,000	0	200,000	200,000
29	278,000	30,000,000	0	200,000	200,000
30	275,000	30,000,000	134,000	200,000	334,000
31	271,000	29,866,000	271,000	199,107	470,107
32	270,000	29,595,000	270,000	197,300	467,300
33	265,000	29,325,000	265,000	195,500	460,500
34	260,000	29,060,000	260,000	193,733	453,733
35	255,000	28,800,000	255,000	192,000	447,000
36	252,000	28,545,000	252,000	190,300	442,300
37	250,000	28,293,000	250,000	188,620	438,620
38	245,000	28,043,000	245,000	186,953	431,953
39	240,000	27,798,000	240,000	185,320	425,320
40	210,000	27,558,000	210,000	183,720	393,720
41	200,000	27,348,000	200,000	182,320	382,320
42	195,000	27,148,000	195,000	180,987	375,987
43	190,000	26,953,000	190,000	179,687	369,687
44	185,000	26,763,000	185,000	178,420	363,420
45	175,000	26,578,000	175,000	177,187	352,187
46	170,000	26,403,000	170,000	176,020	346,020
47	166,000	26,233,000	166,000	174,887	340,887
48	164,000	26,067,000	164,000	173,780	337,780

d. The average life for tranche A is computed as follows:

Month	Tranche A principal repayment	Month × principal repayment
1	520,000	520,000
2	510,000	1,020,000
3	490,000	1,470,000
4	450,000	1,800,000
5	448,000	2,240,000
6	442,000	2,652,000
7	140,000	980,000
Total	3,000,000	10,682,000

$$\text{Average life} = \frac{\$10,682,000}{12(\$3,000,000)} = 0.30$$

14. a. The coupon interest that would be paid to tranche C is diverted as principal repayment to tranche A. In the table below, the total principal paid to tranche A is tranche A's principal repayment as in KMF-01 plus the interest diverted from tranche C.

Month	Beginning principal for tranche A	Principal repayment before C int*	Interest at 6%	Principal for tranche C	Tranche C diverted to tranche A	Principal repayment for tranche A	Cash flow
1	3,000,000	520,000	15,000	30,000,000	200,000	720,000	735,000
2	2,280,000	510,000	11,400	30,200,000	201,333	711,333	722,733
3	1,568,667	490,000	7,843	30,401,333	202,676	692,676	700,519
4	875,991	450,000	4,380	30,604,009	204,027	654,027	658,407
5	221,964	448,000	1,110	30,808,036	205,387	221,964	223,074
					Total	3,000,000	

* This is the amount before the accrued interest from Tranche C is allocated to Tranche A.

b. The principal balance for tranche C is increased each month by the amount of interest diverted from tranche C to tranche A. The principal balance for the first five months is shown in the fifth column of the schedule for part a.

c.

Month	Principal repayment for tranche A	Month × principal
1	720,000	720,000
2	711,333	1,422,667
3	692,676	2,078,027
4	654,027	2,616,107
5	221,964	1,109,822
	3,000,000	7,946,622

$$\text{Average life} = \frac{\$7,946,622}{12(\$3,000,000)} = 0.22$$

The average life is shorter for tranche A in KMF-02 relative to KMF-01 due to the presence of the accrual tranche.

15. There is typically a floor placed on an inverse floater to prevent the coupon rate from being negative. In order to fund this floor, the floater must be capped.

16. The principal payments that would have gone to the tranche used to create the floater and inverse floater are distributed proportionately to the floater and inverse floater based on their percentage of the par value. That is, if the floater's par value is 80% of the tranche from which it is created and the inverse floater 20%, then if $100 is received in principal payment $80 is distributed to the floater and $20 to the inverse floater. The effect is that the average life for the floater and the inverse floater will be the same as the tranche from which they are created, six years in this example.

17. A CMO redistributes prepayment risk by using rules for the distribution of principal payments and interest payments from the collateral. The collateral for a CMO has prepayment risk and its cash flow consists of interest payments and principal payments (both scheduled principal and prepayments). Prepayment risk consists of contraction risk and extension risk. In a CMO there are different bond classes (tranches) which are exposed to different degrees of prepayment risk. The exposure to different degrees of prepayment risk relative to the prepayment risk for the collateral underlying a CMO is due to rules as to how the principal and the interest are to be redistributed to the CMO tranches—hence, redistributing prepayment risk amongst the tranches in the structure. In the simplest type of CMO structure—a sequential-pay structure—the rules for the distribution of the cash flow are such that some tranches receive some protection against extension risk while other tranches in the CMO have some protection against contraction risk. In a CMO with PAC tranches, the rules for the distribution of the cash flow result in the PAC tranches having protection against both contraction risk and extension risk while the support tranches (non-PAC tranches) have greater prepayment risk than the underlying collateral for the CMO.

18. By creating any mortgage-backed security, prepayment risk cannot never be eliminated. Rather, the character of prepayment risk can be altered. Specifically, prepayment risk consists of contraction risk and extension risk. A CMO alters but does not eliminate the prepayment risk of the underlying mortgage loans. Therefore, the statement is incorrect.

19. Ms. Morgan should inform the trustee that the statement about the riskiness of the different sectors of the mortgage-backed securities market in terms of prepayment risk is incorrect. There are CMO tranches that expose an investor to less prepayment risk—in terms of extension or contraction risk—than the mortgage passthrough securities from which the CMO was created. There are CMO tranche types such as planned amortization classes that have considerably less prepayment risk than the mortgage passthrough securities from which the CMO was created. However, in order to create CMO tranches such as PACs, it is necessary to create tranches where there is considerable prepayment risk—prepayment risk that is greater than the underlying mortgage passthrough securities. These tranches are called support tranches.

20. A support tranche is included in a structure in which there are PAC tranches. The sole purpose of the support tranche is to provide prepayment protection for the

PAC tranches. Consequently, support tranches are exposed to substantial prepayment risk.

21. The manager of an S&L portfolio is concerned with prepayment risk but more specifically extension risk. Moreover, to better match the average life of the investment to that of the S&L's funding cost, the manager will seek a shorter term investment. With the Fannie Mae PAC issue with an average life of 2 years the manager is buying a shorter term security and one with some protection against extension risk. In contrast, the Fannie Mae passthrough is probably a longer term average life security because of its WAM of 310 months and it will expose the S&L to substantial extension risk. Therefore, the Fannie Mae PAC tranche is probably a better investment from an asset/liability perspective.

22. Since the prepayments are assumed to be at a constant prepayment rate over the PAC tranche's life at 140 PSA which is within the PSA collar in which the PAC was created, the average life will be equal to five years.

23. a. The PAC tranche will have the least average life variability. This is because the PAC tranche is created to provide protection against extension risk and contraction risk—the support tranches providing the protection.

   b. The support tranche will have the greatest average life variability. This is because it is designed to absorb the prepayment risk to provide protection for the PAC tranche.

24. The PAC structure in KMF-06 will have less prepayment protection than in KMF-05 because the support tranche is smaller ($200 million in KMF-06 versus $350 for KMF-05).

25. a. The PAC II is a support tranche and as a result will have more average life variability than the PAC I tranche. Consequently, PAC I has the less average life variability.

   b. The support tranche without a schedule must provide prepayment protection for both the PAC I and the PAC II. Therefore, the support tranche without a schedule will have greater average life variability than the PAC II.

26. In a PAC tranche structure in which the PAC tranches are paid off in sequence, the support tranches absorb any excess prepayments above the scheduled amount. Once the support tranches are paid off, any prepayments must go to the PAC tranche that is currently receiving principal payments. Thus, the structure effectively becomes a typical (plain vanilla) sequential-pay structure.

27. If the prepayments are well below the initial upper PAC collar this means that there will be more support tranches available four years after the deal is structured than if prepayments were actually at the initial upper PAC collar. This means that there will be more support tranches to absorb prepayments. Hence, the effective upper collar will increase.

28. The notional amount of an 8% IO tranche is computed below:

Tranche	Par amount	Coupon rate	Excess interest	Excess dollar interest	Notional amount for 8% coupon rate IO
A	$400,000,000	6.25%	1.75%	$7,000,000	$87,500,000
B	$200,000,000	6.75%	1.25%	$2,500,000	$31,250,000
C	$225,000,000	7.50%	0.50%	$1,125,000	$14,062,500
D	$175,000,000	7.75%	0.25%	$437,500	$5,468,750
			Notional amount for 8% IO		$138,281,250

29. a. The coupon rate for tranche G is found as follows:

$$\text{coupon interest for tranche F in Structure I} = \$500,000,000 \times 0.085$$

$$= \$42,500,000$$

$$\text{coupon interest for tranche F in Structure II} = \$200,000,000 \times 0.0825$$

$$= \$16,500,000$$

coupon interest available to tranche G in Structure II

$$= \$42,500,000 - \$16,500,000 = \$26,000,000$$

$$\text{coupon rate for tranche G} = \frac{\$26,000,000}{\$300,000,000} = 0.0867 = 8.67\%$$

   b. There is no effect on the average life of the PAC tranches because the inclusion of the PAC II only impacts the support tranche in Structure I compared to Structure II.

   c. There is greater average life variability for tranche G in Structure II than tranche F in Structure I because tranche G must provide prepayment protection in Structure II for not only the PACs but also tranche F.

30. A broken or busted PAC is a structure where all of the support tranches (the tranches that provide prepayment support for the PAC tranches in a structure) are completely paid off.

31. a. The formula for the cap rate on the inverse floater

$$\frac{\text{inverse floater interest when reference rate for floater is zero}}{\text{principal for inverse floater}}$$

The total interest to be paid to tranche C if it was not split into the floater and the inverse floater is the principal of \$96,500,000 times 7.5%, or \$7,237,500. The maximum interest for the inverse floater occurs if 1-month LIBOR is zero. In that case, the coupon rate for the floater is

$$\text{1-month LIBOR} + 1\% = 1\%$$

Since the floater receives 1% on its principal of \$80,416,667, the floater's interest is \$804,167. The remainder of the interest of \$7,237,500 from tranche C goes to the inverse floater. That is, the inverse floater's interest is \$6,433,333 (=\$7,237,500 − \$804,167). Since the inverse floater's principal is \$16,083,333.33, the cap rate for the inverse floater is

$$\frac{\$6,433,333}{\$16,083,333} = 40.0\%$$

   b. Assuming a floor of zero for inverse floater, the cap rate is determined as follows:

$$\text{cap rate for floater} = \frac{\text{collateral tranche interest}}{\text{principal for floater}}$$

The collateral tranche interest is $7,237,500. The floater principal is $80,416,667. Therefore,

$$\text{cap rate for floater} = \frac{\$7,237,500}{\$80,416,667} = 9\%$$

32. a. The PAC collar indicates the prepayment protection afforded the investor in a PAC tranche. Prepayment protection means the ability of the collateral to satisfy the PAC tranche's schedule of principal payments. The initial PAC collar only indicates the protection at issuance. As prepayments occur over time, the amount of the support tranches decline and, as a result, the PAC collars change. In fact, in the extreme case, if the support tranches pay off completely, there is no longer a PAC collar since there is no longer prepayment protection for the PAC tranche.

   b. To assess the prepayment protection at any given time for the PAC tranche, the effective PAC collar is computed. This measure is computed by determining the PSA prepayment rate range that given the current amount of the support tranche would be able to meet the remaining PAC schedule.

33. a. For a mortgage loan, the higher the loan-to-value ratio, the greater the credit risk faced by a lender. The reason is that if the property is repossessed and sold, the greater the ratio, the greater the required sale price necessary to recover the loan amount.

   b. Studies of residential mortgage loans have found that the loan-to-value ratio is a key determinant of whether a borrower will default and that the higher the ratio, the greater the likelihood of default.

34. a. Mortgage strips are created when the principal (both scheduled principal repayments plus prepayments) and the coupon interest are allocated to different bond classes. The tranche that is allocated the principal payments is called the principal-only mortgage strip and the tranche that is allocated the coupon interest is called the interest-only mortgage strip.

   b. With an interest-only mortgage strip, there is no specific amount that will be received over time since the coupon interest payments depend on how prepayments occur over the security's life. In contrast, for a Treasury strip created from the coupon interest, the amount and the timing of the single cash flow is known with certainty.

   c. Because prepayments increase when interest rates decrease and prepayments decrease when interest rates increase, the expected cash flow changes in the same direction as the change in interest rates. Thus, when interest rates increase, prepayments are expected to decrease and there will be an increase in the expected coupon interest payments since more of the underlying mortgages are expected to be outstanding. This will typically increase the value of an interest-only mortgage strip because the increase in the expected cash flow more than offsets the higher discount rates used to discount the cash flow. When interest rates decrease, the opposite occurs. So, an interest-only mortgage strip's value is expected to change in the same direction as the change in interest rates.

35. a. The purchase price per $100 par value is 1.02. Therefore

$$1.02 \times \$10,000,000 \times 0.72 = \$7,344,000$$

The investor pays $7,344,000 plus accrued interest.

b. Because the value and characteristics of a principal-only mortgage strip are highly sensitive to the underlying mortgage pool, an investor would not want the seller to have the option of which specific trust to deliver. If the trade is done on a TBA basis, the seller has the choice of the trust to deliver. To avoid this, a trade is done by the buyer specifying the trust that he or she is purchasing.

36. Ginnie Mae, Fannie Mae, and Freddie Mac have underwriting standards that must be met in order for a mortgage loan to qualify for inclusion in a mortgage pool underlying an agency mortgage-backed security. Mortgage loans that do qualify are called conforming loans. A loan may fail to be conforming because the loan balance exceeds the maximum permitted by the underwriting standard or the loan-to-value ratio is too high, or the payment-to-income ratio is too high. Loans that do not qualify are called nonconforming loans.

37. Since there is no implicit or explicit government guarantee for a nonagency mortgage-backed security, a mechanism is needed to reduce credit risk for bondholders when there are defaults. That is, there is a need to "enhance" the credit of the securities issued. These mechanisms are called credit enhancements of which there are two types, internal and external.

38. With a residential mortgage loans the lender relies on the ability of the borrower to repay and has recourse to the borrower if the payment terms are not satisfied. In contrast, commercial mortgage loans are nonrecourse loans which means that the lender can only look to the income-producing property backing the loan for interest and principal repayment. Should a default occur, the lender looks to the proceeds from the sale of the property for repayment and has no recourse to the borrower for any unpaid balance.

39. The figure used for "value" in the loan-to-value ratio is either market value or appraised value. In valuing commercial property, there can be considerable variance in the estimates of the property's market value. Thus, investors tend to be skeptical about estimates of market value and the resulting LTVs reported for properties in a pool of commercial loans. Therefore, the debt-to-service ratio is more objective, and a more reliable measure of risk.

40. a. Call protection at the loan level is provided in one or more of the following forms: (1) prepayment lockout, (2) defeasance, (3) prepayment penalty points, and (4) yield maintenance charges. A prepayment lockout is a contractual agreement that prohibits any prepayments during the lockout period (from 2 to 5 years). After the lockout period, call protection comes in the form of either prepayment penalty points or yield maintenance charges. With defeasance, rather than prepaying a loan, the borrower provides sufficient funds for the servicer to invest in a portfolio of Treasury securities that replicates the cash flows that would exist in the absence of prepayments. Prepayment penalty points are predetermined penalties that must be paid by the borrower if the borrower wishes to refinance. Yield maintenance charge provisions are designed to make the lender whole if prepayments are made.

b. A CMBS deal can be structured as a sequential-pay structure, thereby providing tranches some form of protection against prepayment risk at the structure level.

41. Typically commercial loans are balloon loans that require substantial principal payment at the end of the term of the loan. Balloon risk is the risk that a borrower will not be able to make the balloon payment because either the borrower cannot arrange for refinancing at the balloon payment date or cannot sell the property to generate sufficient funds to pay off the balloon balance. Since the term of the loan will be extended by the lender during the workout period, balloon risk is also referred to as extension risk.

CHAPTER 11

ASSET-BACKED SECTOR OF THE BOND MARKET

SOLUTIONS

1. a. Since Caterpillar Financial Funding Corporation sold the retail installment sales contracts to Caterpillar Financial Asset Trust 1997-A, Caterpillar Financial Funding Corporation would be referred to in the prospectus as the "Seller."

   b. The special purpose vehicle in a securitization issues the securities and therefore is referred to as the "Issuer." In this transaction, Caterpillar Asset Financial Trust 1997-A is the "Issuer."

   c. Without having a full description of the waterfall for this structure, it appears that Bond Classes A-1, A-2, and A-3 are the senior classes.

   d. Without having a full description of the waterfall for this structure, it appears that Bond Class B is the subordinate class.

   e. Credit tranching in this structure was done by creating the senior and subordinate tranches. Prepayment tranching appears to have been done by offering three classes of the senior tranche.

2. a. In the securitization process, the attorneys prepare the legal documentation which includes (i) the purchase agreement between the seller of the assets and the special purpose vehicle, (ii) how the cash flows are divided among the bond classes, and (iii) the servicing agreement between the entity engaged to service the assets and the special purpose vehicle.

   b. The independent accountant verifies the accuracy of all numerical information (e.g. yield and average life) placed in either the prospectus or private placement memorandum and then issues a comfort letter.

3. How the principal repayments from the collateral are used by the trustee in a securitization transaction depends on the waterfall which, in turn, is affected by the character of the collateral (amortizing versus non-amortizing). In a typical structure backed by amortizing assets, the principal repayments are distributed to the bond classes. In a typical structure backed by non-amortizing assets, the principal repayments for a specified period of time (the lockout period) are used to purchase new assets and after that period (assuming no early amortization provision is triggered), the principal repayments are distributed to the bond classes. This structure is referred to as a revolving structure.

4. The excess servicing spread is determined as follows:

	Gross weighted average coupon	= 8.60%
−	Servicing fee	= 0.50%
	Spread available to pay tranches	= 8.10%
−	Net weighted average coupon	= 7.10%
	Excess servicing spread	= 1.00% = 100 basis points

5. a. The amount of overcollateralization is the difference between the value of the collateral, $320 million, and the par value for all the tranches, $300 million. In this structure it is $20 million.
   b. If the losses total $15 million, then the loss is entirely absorbed by the overcollateralization. No tranche will realize a loss.
   c. through e.

	Total loss	Senior tranche	Subordinate tranche 1	Subordinate tranche 2
c.	$35 million	zero	zero	$15 million
d.	$85 million	zero	$35 million	$30 million
e.	$110 million	$10 million	$50 million	$30 million

6. a. For a non-amortizing loan, there is no schedule for repayment of principal. Consequently, for individual loans of this type there can be no prepayments.
   b. While there may be no prepayments for individual loans that are non-amortizing, the securities that are backed by these loans may be prepayable. For example, credit card receivable-backed securities can be prepaid under certain conditions. Such conditions are referred to as "early amortization" or "rapid amortization" events or triggers.
7. The rating agencies take the weak-link approach to credit enhancement. Typically a structure cannot receive a rating higher than the rating on any third-party providing an external guarantee. Since the question specifies that the only form of credit enhancement is the letter of credit, then the rating will not exceed the single A rating of the bank providing the letter credit. Thus, a triple A rating is not likely.
8. Since credit agencies take the weak-link approach to credit enhancement, if an insurance company wants to offer bond insurance for an asset-backed security transaction where a triple A credit rating is sought, the insurance company must have a triple A credit rating.
9. Both a cash reserve fund and an excess servicing spread account are forms of internal credit enhancement. A cash reserve fund is provided by a deposit of cash at issuance. Excess servicing spread account is the cash available to absorb losses from the collateral after payment of interest to all the tranches and to the servicer.
10. The excess servicing spread account builds up over time in order to offset future losses. However, if losses occur early in the life of the collateral, there may not be enough time to accumulate the excess servicing spread to adequately cover future losses.
11. a. A senior-subordinate structure is a form of internal credit enhancement because it does not rely on the guarantee of a third party. Instead, the enhancement comes from within the structure by creating senior and subordinate tranches. The subordinate tranches provide credit protection for the senior tranche.

b. Once a deal is closed, the percentage of the senior tranche and the percentage of the subordinate tranche change when the underlying assets are subject to prepayments. If the subordinate interest in a structure decreases after the deal is closed, the credit protection for the senior tranche decreases. The shifting interest mechanism seeks to prevent the senior tranche's credit protection provided by the subordinate tranche (or tranches) from declining by establishing a schedule that provides for a higher allocation of the prepayments to the senior tranche in the earlier years.

12. a. The senior prepayment percentage is the percentage of prepayments that are allocated to the senior tranche. The senior prepayment percentage is specified in the prospectus.

b. Because the shifting interest mechanism results in a greater amount of the prepayments be paid to the senior tranche in the earlier years than in the absence of such a mechanism, the senior tranches are exposed to greater contraction risk.

13. The outstanding bonds in a structure can be called if either (1) the collateral outstanding reaches a predetermined level before the specified call date or (2) the call date has been reached even if the collateral outstanding is above the predetermined level.

14. a. The cash flow for a closed-end home equity loan is the same as for a standard mortgage loan: interest, regularly scheduled principal repayments (i.e., regular amortization), and prepayments.

b. The statement is incorrect. Typically, a closed-end home equity loan borrower is a credit impaired borrower.

15. For month 1, the CPR for 100% PPC is 5%, so the CPR for 200% PPC is 10% (= 2 × 5%). For month 2, the CPR for 100% PPC is 5% plus 1.8% which is 6.8%. Therefore, the CPR for 200% PPC for month 2 is 13.6% (2 × 6.8%).

In month 12, the CPR for 100% PPC is

$$5\% + 1.8\% \times 11 = 24.8\%$$

Therefore, the CPR for 200% PPC is 49.6% (2 × 24.8%). For all months after month 12, the CPR for 200% CPR is 49.6%.

Month	CPR	Month	CPR	Month	CPR
1	10.0%	11	46.0%	30	49.6%
2	13.6%	12	49.6%	125	49.6%
3	17.2%	13	49.6%	150	49.6%
4	20.8%	14	49.6%	200	49.6%
5	24.4%	15	49.6%	250	49.6%
6	28.0%	16	49.6%	275	49.6%
7	31.6%	17	49.6%	300	49.6%
8	35.2%	18	49.6%	325	49.6%
9	38.8%	19	49.6%	350	49.6%
10	42.4%	20	49.6%	360	49.6%

16. The base case prepayment specified in the prospectus is called the prospectus prepayment curve (PPC). It is unique to each issuer and should be used instead of the generic PSA prepayment benchmark. However, it is not a generic prepayment benchmark for all closed-end home equity loan-securities as Mr. Tellmen assumes.

17. For adjustable-rate HELs, the reference rate is typically 6-month LIBOR. However, the floating-rate securities that these loans back typically are referenced to 1-month

LIBOR in order to make them attractive to investors who fund themselves based on 1-month LIBOR. As a result, there will be a mismatch between the reference rate on the floating-rate HELs used as collateral and the securities backed by that collateral that will prevent the cap from being fixed over the life of the securities. In addition, there are periodic caps and a lifetime cap.

18. a. Since month 36 is in the first five years after issuance, the schedule specifies that all prepayments are allocated to the senior tranche and none to the subordinate tranches. Thus, the prepayments of $100,000 are allocated only to the senior tranche.

    b. According to the schedule, if prepayments occur 8 years after issuance, 20% is allocated to the senior tranche and the balance is paid to the subordinate tranches. Since the prepayments are assumed to be $100,000, the senior tranche receives $20,000 and the subordinate tranches $80,000.

    c. All prepayments that occur 10 years after issuance are paid to the subordinate tranches. Thus, the $100,000 of prepayments some time in year 10 are paid to the subordinate tranches.

19. The schedule in the prospectus is the base schedule. The schedule can change so as to allocate less to the subordinate tranches if the collateral's performance deteriorates after the deal is closed. Determination of whether or not the base schedule should be overridden is made by the trustee based on tests that are specified in the prospectus.

20. The protection is provided by establishing a schedule for the allocation of principal payments (both regularly scheduled principal payments and prepayments) between the NAS tranche and the non-NAS tranches such that contraction risk and extension risk are reduced. For example, a schedule would specify a lockout period for the principal payments to the NAS tranche. This means that the NAS tranche would not receive any payments until the lockout period ends and therefore contraction risk is mitigated. Extension risk is provided by allocating a large percentage to the NAS tranche in later years.

21. a. The cash flow is the same as for mortgage-backed securities backed by standard mortgage loans: (1) interest, (2) regularly scheduled principal repayments (amortization), and (3) prepayments.

    b. The reasons why the securities backed by manufactured housing loans tend not to be sensitive to refinancing are:

       1. the loan balances are typically small so that there is no significant dollar savings from refinancing.
       2. the rate of depreciation of manufactured homes may be such that in the earlier years depreciation is greater than the amount of the loan paid off, making it difficult to refinance the loan.
       3. typically borrowers are of lower credit quality and therefore find it difficult to obtain funds to refinance.

22. The deals are more akin to the nonagency market since there is no guarantee by a federally related agency or a government sponsored enterprise as in the United States. As such, the deals must be rated and therefore require credit enhancement.

23. a. The cash flow for auto-loan backed securities consists of: (1) interest, (2) regularly scheduled principal repayments (amortization), and (3) prepayments.

    b. Prepayments due to refinancing on auto loans tend to be of minor importance.

24. A conditional prepayment rate measures prepayments relative to the amount outstanding in the previous year that could prepay. For a monthly CPR, called the single monthly mortality rate, SMM, prepayments are measured relative to the amount available in the previous month that was available to prepay.

    The absolute prepayment speed, denoted ABS, is the monthly prepayment expressed as a percentage of the *original* collateral amount.

25. a. $\text{SMM} = \dfrac{0.015}{1 - [0.015 \times (21 - 1)]} = 0.0214 = 2.14\%$

    b. $\text{ABS} = \dfrac{0.019}{1 + [0.019 \times (11 - 1)]} = 0.016 = 1.60\%$

26. The trustee is wrong. For certain student loans the government will guarantee up to 98% of the principal plus accrued interest (assuming the loans have been properly serviced). Moreover, there are securities backed by alternative student loans that carry no government guarantee.

27. While a student is in school, no payments are made by the student on the loan. This period is the deferment period. Upon leaving school, the student is extended a period of time (typically six month) when no payments on the loan must be made. This is called the grace period.

28. a. The cash flow for an SBA-backed security consists of (1) interest for the period, (2) the scheduled principal repayment, and (3) prepayments.

    b. The interest is based on a coupon formula where the prime rate is the reference rate. The rate on the loan is reset monthly on the first of the month or quarterly on the first of January, April, July, and October.

29. a. During the lockout period, only finance charges and fees collected are distributed to the bondholders.

    b. During the lockout period, principal paid by borrowers is reinvested in new receivables and not distributed to the bondholders.

    c. The statement is incorrect because principal repayment can be made by either (1) a bullet payment structure (as stated in the question), (2) a controlled amortization structure, or (3) a passthrough structure.

30. While there is no schedule of principal repayments for credit card borrowers, there is the potential risk of contraction for the securities. This is because there is a provision for early or rapid amortization if certain triggers are reached.

    There is also the potential for extension risk because principal repayment from the credit card borrowers and defaults and delinquencies may be such that the schedule specified for principal repayment of the security during the amortization period may not be adequate to completely pay off bondholders by the stated maturity.

    While these are nontrivial risks, neither of these occurs frequently.

31. a. The monthly payment rate (MPR) expresses the monthly payment of a credit card receivable portfolio as a percentage of debt outstanding in the previous month. The monthly payment includes finance charges, fees, and any principal repayment collected.

    b. There are two reasons why the MPR is important. First, if the MPR reaches an extremely low level, there is a chance that there will be extension risk with respect to the repayment of principal. The length of time until the return of principal is largely a function of the monthly payment rate. Second, if the MPR is very low, then there is a chance that there will not be sufficient cash flow to pay off principal. This is one of the events that could trigger early amortization of the principal.

c. The net portfolio yield for a credit card receivable portfolio is equal to the gross portfolio yield minus charge-offs. The gross portfolio yield includes finance charges collected and fees. From the gross portfolio yield charge offs are deducted. Charge-offs represent the accounts charged off as uncollectible.

32. The typical structure of a CDO is as follows. There is (1) a senior tranche (between 70% and 80% of the deal) with a floating rate, (2) different layers of subordinate or junior debt tranches with a fixed rate, and (3) an equity tranche.

33. The statement is incorrect. The asset manager responsible for purchasing the debt obligations for the portfolio will have restrictions that are imposed by the rating agencies that rate the securities in the deal (coverage and quality tests). There will be certain tests that must be satisfied for the tranches in the CBO to maintain its credit rating at the time of issuance.

34. The statement is not correct. In fact, it is because of interest rate swaps that the risk is reduced for the senior tranche. This is because the collateral is typically fixed-rate bonds and the senior tranche must be paid a floating rate. An interest rate swap is used to convert the fixed-rate payments from the collateral into floating-rate payments that can be made to the senior tranche.

35. The key determinant is whether or not the CDO can be issued such that the subordinate/equity tranche can be offered a competitive return.

36. a. Given that the senior tranche is $150 million and the junior tranche is $30 million, the equity tranche is $20 million ($200 million minus $180 million).

   b. The collateral will pay interest each year (assuming no defaults) equal to the 8-year Treasury rate of 6% plus 600 basis points. So the interest will be:

   Interest from collateral: $12\% \times \$200,000,000 = \$24,000,000$

   The interest that must be paid to the senior tranche is:

   Interest to senior tranche: $\$150,000,000 \times (\text{LIBOR} + 90 \text{ bp})$

   The coupon rate for the junior tranche is 6% plus 300 basis points. So, the coupon rate is 9% and the interest is:

   Interest to junior tranche: $9\% \times \$30,000,000 = \$2,700,000$

   For the interest rate swap, the asset manager is agreeing to pay the swap counterparty each year 6% (the 8-year Treasury rate) plus 120 basis points, or 7.2%. Since the swap payments are based on a notional amount of $150 million, the asset manager pays to the swap counterparty:

   Interest to swap counterparty: $7.2\% \times \$150,000,000 = \$10,800,000$

   The interest payment received from the swap counterparty is LIBOR based on a notional amount of $150 million. That is,

   Interest from swap counterparty: $\$150,000,000 \times \text{LIBOR}$

The interest for the CBO is:

Interest from collateral $24,000,000
Interest from swap counterparty ..... $150,000,000 × LIBOR
—————————————————————————————————
Total interest received .... $24,000,000 + $150,000,000 × LIBOR

The interest to be paid out to the senior and junior tranches and to the swap counterparty include:

Interest to senior tranche .... $150,000,000 × (LIBOR + 90 bp)
Interest to junior tranche $2,700,000
Interest to swap counterparty $10,800,000
—————————————————————————————————
Total interest paid ..... $13,500,000 + $150,000,000 × (LIBOR + 90 bp)

Netting the interest payments paid and received:

Total interest received ..... $24,000,000 + $150,000,000 × LIBOR
− Total interest paid ...... $13,500,000 + $150,000,000 × (LIBOR + 90 bp)
—————————————————————————————————
Net interest .... $10,500,000 − $150,000,000 × (90 bp)

Since 90 bp times $150 million is $1,350,000, the net interest remaining is $9,150,000. This is the cash flow ignoring the asset management fee.

c. The amount available for the equity tranche is $9,150,000. This is the cash flow computed in part (b).

37. The return includes:

the return on a portfolio of high-quality debt instruments
plus
the payment from the asset manager as part of the credit default swap
minus
the payment that must be made by a junior tranche due to a credit event

38. By issuing a synthetic CDO, a bank can remove the economic risk of bank loans without having to notify any borrowers that they are selling the loans to another party. Thus, no consent would be needed from borrowers to transfer loans, a requirement in some countries.

CHAPTER 12

VALUING MORTGAGE-BACKED AND ASSET-BACKED SECURITIES

SOLUTIONS

1. a. The convention is to determine the nominal spread relative to the spread on a Treasury security with the same maturity as the average life of the mortgage-backed security. Since the average life is 8 years, the benchmark Treasury issue is the 8-year issue. The nominal spread is then 7.5% minus the 6.3% of the 8-year Treasury issue. So, the nominal spread is 120 basis points.

   b. For the 7.5% cash flow yield to be realized the following must occur:

   - actual prepayments must be 200 PSA over the life of the security
   - the monthly cash flow (interest plus principal repayment) must be reinvested at a rate of 7.5%
   - the security must be held until the last mortgage pays off

2. The monthly cash flow yield, i_M, is 0.0074. Therefore,

$$\text{bond-equivalent yield} = 2[(1.0074)^6 - 1] = 0.0905 = 9.05\%$$

3. The binomial model used to value a corporate bond with an embedded option can handle securities in which the decision to exercise a call option is not dependent on how interest rates evolved over time. That is, the decision of a corporate issuer to call a bond will depend on the level of the rate at which the issue can be refunded relative to the issue's coupon rate. The decision to call does not depend on the path interest rates took to get to that rate. Ms. Howard must understand that this is not a characteristic of mortgage-backed securities. These securities are "interest rate path-dependent," meaning that the cash flow received in one period is determined not only by the interest rate level at that period, but also by the path that interest rates took to get to that rate.

   For example, in the case of passthrough securities, prepayments are interest rate path-dependent because this month's prepayment rate depends on whether there have been prior opportunities to refinance since the underlying mortgages were originated. For CMOs there are typically two sources of path dependency in a CMO tranche's cash flows. First, the collateral prepayments are path-dependent as just described. Second, the cash flows to be received in the current month by a CMO tranche depend on the outstanding balances of the other tranches in the deal. Thus, we need the history of prepayments to calculate these balances.

4. a. To generate the path of short-term interest rates, an assumption about the volatility of short-term interest rates must be made.

   b. If the short-term interest rates on each path are used without an adjustment, there is no assurance that the Monte Carlo simulation model will correctly value the on-the-run Treasury issues. An adjustment to the short-term interest rates is required in order to have the model properly price on-the-run Treasury issues so that the model will provide arbitrage-free values.

   c. In moving from the short-term interest rates to the refinancing rates, it is necessary to make an assumption about the spread between these rates.

5. In the Monte Carlo simulation model, a prepayment *model* is used. The prepayment model provides a prepayment rate for each month on each interest rate path. Thus, no specific PSA prepayment assumption is made. Consequently, the statement by Mr. Ruthledge that a 175 PSA was made is inconsistent with the Monte Carlo simulation model. Therefore, Mr. Hawthorne should have been confused by Mr. Ruthledge's response.

6. On an interest rate path, the short-term interest rates are the forward rates. It is the forward rates plus an appropriate spread that is used to value a mortgage-backed security on an interest rate path.

7. The investor in a passthrough security has effectively sold a call option to borrowers (homeowners). The higher the assumed interest rate volatility the greater the value of this embedded call option and therefore the lower the price of a passthrough security. Securities 1 and 2 have the correct relationship between price and assumed interest rate volatility. Security 3 has the opposite relationship. Therefore, the error that Mr. Rodriquez discovered is with the relationship between assumed interest rate volatility and price for Security 3.

8. a. Since the collateral is trading at a premium, a slowdown in prepayments will allow the investor to receive the higher coupon for a longer period of time. This will increase the value of the collateral.

   b. Because Tranche Y is selling at a premium, its value will increase with a slowdown in prepayments. In contrast, because Tranche X is selling at a discount, a slowdown in prepayments will decrease its value. This is because for Tranche X, there will be less principal returned to be reinvested at the new, higher rates. Also, assuming that X was purchased when it was trading at a discount, there will be less of a capital gain realized (since principal is returned at par).

9. The theoretical value based on the ten interest rate paths is the average of the present value of the interest rate paths. The average value is 89.1.

10. a. Rather than sampling a large number of interest rate paths, some vendors of mortgage analytical systems have developed computational procedures that reduce the number of paths required. The procedure involves using statistical techniques to reduce the number of interest rate paths to sets of similar paths. These paths are called representative paths. The security is then valued on each of the representative interest rate paths—16 in the question.

    b. The theoretical value of a security when the representative interest rate paths are used is the weighted average of the 16 representative paths. The weight for a path is the percentage of that representative path relative to the total paths in a full Monte Carlo analysis.

c. The trade-off between the full Monte Carlo analysis and the 16 representative paths is one of speed versus accuracy. The full Monte Carlo analysis provides the true value of the security—*true only based on all the assumptions of the model.* Using 16 representative sample is less accurate but requires less computational time.

11. The theoretical value is the weighted average of the present value of the representative interest rate paths. The weighted average of the present value of the representative interest rate paths is 77.94 as shown below:

Weight	PV	Weight × PV
0.20	70	14.00
0.18	82	14.76
0.16	79	12.64
0.12	68	8.16
0.12	74	8.88
0.12	86	10.32
0.06	91	5.46
0.04	93	3.72
Theoretical value		77.94

12. a. While there is no credit risk for a Ginnie Mae mortgage product, there is liquidity risk (relative to on-the-run Treasury issues) and modeling risk. The latter risk is due to the assumptions that must be made in valuing a mortgage-backed security. If those assumptions prove incorrect or if the parameters used as inputs are wrong, the valuation model will not calculate the true level of risk. A major portion of the compensation for a Ginnie Mae mortgage product reflects payment for this model uncertainty.

b. The OAS should differ by the type of Ginnie Mae mortgage product. The more complex the security to model and value, the greater the OAS should be to reflect the associated modeling risk. Moreover, the more complex the security, the less liquid the security tends to be. Consequently, the OAS will also differ because of liquidity risk.

13. Using the representative interest rate paths, the theoretical value of a mortgage-backed security is the weighted average of the present value of the paths. Since it is assumed in the question that each path has the same weight, the theoretical value is the simple average of the present values of the interest rate paths. For the four spreads, the average PV is given below:

Representative path	Present value if the spread used is			
	70 bps	75 bps	80 bps	85 bps
Average PV	82.6	79.5	76.3	73.8

a. The option-adjusted spread is the spread that will make the theoretical value equal to the market price. Since the question assumes that Tranche L has a market price of 79.5, then a spread of 75 basis points will produce a theoretical value equal to the market price of 79.5. Therefore, the OAS is 75 basis points.

b. If the price is 73.8 instead of 79.5, then the OAS is the spread that will make the theoretical value equal to 73.8. From the table above it can be seen that a spread of

85 basis points will produce a theoretical value equal to 73.8. Therefore, the OAS is 85 basis points.

14. Tranche M has a substantial variation in the present value for the paths. This is a characteristic of a support tranche since a support tranche is exposed to substantial prepayment risk. Tranche N has little variation in the present value for the paths and this is a characteristic of a PAC tranche. Therefore, Tranche M is probably the support tranche and Tranche N is probably the PAC tranche.

15. a. The option cost is the difference between the Z-spread and the OAS. Therefore,

$$\text{PAC I A: } 60 - 50 = 10 \text{ basis points}$$

$$\text{PAC II A: } 150 - 80 = 70 \text{ basis points}$$

$$\text{Support S1: } 165 - 35 = 130 \text{ basis points}$$

  b. Typically, the OAS increases with effective duration. The two longer PAC tranches, PAC I C and PAC I D, have lower OAS than the two shorter duration PACs. Therefore, the two longer duration PACs appear to be expensive.

  c. On a relative value basis, all but PAC II A appear to be expensive. PAC II B has a lower OAS than PAC II A even though it has a higher effective duration. The other two support tranches without a schedule have a low OAS relative to their effective durations.

  d. Investors who do not appreciate the significance of the option risk associated with a tranche can be induced to buy PAC II B because they look exclusively at the nominal spread. While the nominal spread is not provided as part of the information in the question, it can be estimated from the Z-spread. A Z-spread of 280 basis point is extremely appealing to investors for a security with no credit risk (since the deal is an agency CMO deal). Also, investors who do not realize that a PAC II is a support bond will believe that they have purchased a PAC tranche with a high "spread" to Treasuries.

16. The effective duration and effective convexity require the calculation of V_- and V_+. To calculate V_-, each path of short-term interest rates is decreased by a small number of basis points, say 25 basis points. Then, the cash flows are generated for each interest rate path. When the new cash flows are valued using the short-term interest rates plus a spread, the spread used is the original OAS. That is, it is assumed that the OAS does not change when interest rates are decreased. The same procedure is followed to compute V_+, but each path of short-term rates is increased by the same small number of basis points as was used to compute V_-. Again, it is assumed that the OAS does not change, so the new short-term interest rates plus the original OAS are used to discount the new cash flows on the interest rate paths.

17. First it is important to note that the CMO tranche is a support tranche and therefore has considerable prepayment risk. Despite Mr. Winters having been told that all the dealer firms used the Monte Carlo simulation model to compute the effective duration, there are assumptions in the model that can vary from dealer to dealer. This is the reason for the variation in the effective duration. These different assumptions in computing the value of a mortgage-backed security include:

  1. differences in the amount of the rate shock used

2. differences in prepayment models
3. differences in option-adjusted spread (recall that the OAS is held constant when rates are shocked)
4. differences in the relationship between short-term interest rates and refinancing rates

18. This statement is incorrect. From a collateral with negative convexity, tranches with both positive and negative convexity can be created. For example, a PAC bond that is well protected will have little prepayment risk and therefore positive convexity—effectively the convexity of an option-free bond. However, one or more of the other tranches in the deal would have to have more negative convexity than the collateral itself, since the tranching of the collateral can only reallocate prepayment risk; it cannot eliminate it entirely.

19. a. Cash flow duration is computed assuming that if interest rates are changed the prepayment rate will change when computing the new value.

   b. The problem is that this duration measure is based on one initial prepayment speed and when rates are changed it is assumed the prepayment speed will change to another prepayment speed. It is a static approach because it considers only one prepayment speed if rates change. It does not consider the dynamics that interest rates can change in the future and therefore there is not just one potential cash flow or prepayment rate that must be considered in valuing a mortgage-backed security.

20. To compute the coupon curve duration the assumption is that if the yield declines by 100 basis points, the price of the 9% coupon passthrough will increase to the price of the current 10% coupon passthrough. Thus, the price will increase from 99.50 to 102.60. Similarly, if the yield increases by 100 basis points, the assumption is that the price of the 9% coupon passthrough will decline to the price of the 8% coupon passthrough (97.06). Using the duration formula, the corresponding values are:

$$V_0 = 99.50$$

$$V_+ = 97.06$$

$$V_- = 102.60$$

$$\Delta y = 0.01$$

The estimated duration based on the coupon curve is then:

$$\frac{102.60 - 97.06}{2(99.50)(0.01)} = 2.78$$

21. Empirical duration is computed using statistical analysis. It requires good price data for the tranche whose empirical duration is to be computed. A major problem with applying empirical duration to complex CMO tranches is that a reliable series of price data is often not available for a thinly traded mortgage product or the prices may be matrix priced or model priced rather than actual transaction prices. The second problem is that an empirical relationship does not impose a structure for the options embedded in a mortgage-backed security and this can distort the empirical duration. Finally, the volatility of the spread to Treasury yields can distort how the price of a mortgage-backed security reacts to yield changes.

22. The nominal spread of an asset-backed security hides the associated option or prepayment risk. For auto loan-backed securities, refinancing is not an important factor and therefore prepayment risk is not significant. For credit card receivables, there is prepayment risk only at the security level—that is, a credit card borrower cannot prepay because there is no schedule of payments but a security can be prepaid if certain rapid or early amortization triggers are realized. However, prepayment risk is not significant. In contrast, for home equity loan-backed securities prepayment risk is significant and the nominal spread reflects that risk. Consequently, assessing relative value for these three types of asset-backed securities based on the nominal spread is incorrect because the spread is not adjusted for the prepayment risk. Home equity loan-backed securities offer a higher nominal spread because of the prepayment risk.

23. The appropriate valuation approach depends on whether or not the borrower has an option to prepay. Furthermore, even if the borrower has the right to prepay, it depends on whether or not the borrower will take advantage of this option to prepay when interest rates decline. Since the security involves future royalties, there is no prepayment option. Consequently, there is no option value and the appropriate valuation approach is the zero-volatility spread.

24. While there is an option to prepay, if the empirical evidence is correct that borrowers do not prepay when rates decline, then the option value is zero. Consequently, the zero-volatility spread approach is the appropriate approach since the OAS is equal to the zero-volatility spread.

25. a. Since high quality borrowers are observed to take advantage of refinancing opportunities, there is a value to the prepayment option. Consequently, the option-adjusted spread approach is appropriate when the underlying pool of home equity loans are those of high quality borrowers.

    b. Since low quality borrowers may prepay but have been observed not to take advantage of refinancing opportunities, there is very little value to the prepayment option. Since the option cost has a value of zero, the zero-volatility spread is equal to the option-adjusted spread. Consequently, the zero-volatility spread approach can be used to value securities backed by a pool of home equity loans of low quality borrowers.

    However, there is a caveat here regarding the behavior of low quality borrowers. The answer ignores the adverse selection impact of borrowers who upgrade their credit profile and refinance out, leaving a potentially longer average life, and worse credit, pool.

CHAPTER 13

INTEREST RATE DERIVATIVE INSTRUMENTS

SOLUTIONS

1. A derivative instrument involves two parties. Counterparty risk is the risk that a counterparty to a derivative instrument will fail to meet its obligation. This will occur if market movements are unfavorable to the counterparty.

2. This statement is not correct. A forward contract is a privately negotiated contract between two parties. One or both parties may require that the positions be marked to market.

3. This statement is not correct. The counterparty in a futures contract is a futures exchange or the clearinghouse associated with a futures exchange. The counterparty risk is viewed as minimal. In contrast, the counterparty risk in a forward contract depends on the credit risk of the counterparty.

4. When a position is taken in a futures contract, initial margin is required. However, the margin obligation does not stop at that point. At the close of each trading day a position is marked to market. If the position falls below the maintenance margin, additional margin in the form of cash must be provided. Failure to provide the cash will result in a liquidation of the position. Any additional margin payments, called variation margin, are the contingency payments that Ms. Gomez is advising Ms. Morris to have sufficient cash available to satisfy.

5. The broker should respond that while there may not be a deliverable, delivery of some Treasury bond issue is required. That is, the contract is not a cash settlement contract. There is a list of issues that are acceptable for delivery and the futures price is adjusted based on which issue is delivered.

6. a. A conversion factor for each deliverable issue is necessary because the value of each issue differs due to the different maturity and coupon rate of each issue. In the case of a Treasury bond futures contract, the buyer expects delivery of the equivalent of $100,000 par value of a 6% coupon 20-year issue. The conversion factor makes delivery equitable to both the long and the short by adjusting the invoice price so that the equivalent of $100,000 par value of a 6% coupon 20-year issue is delivered.

   b. The converted price for a deliverable issue is found by multiplying the futures price by the conversion factor for that issue.

7. The invoice price is equal to

   contract size × futures settlement price × conversion factor + accrued interest

The futures settlement price is 105–08 or $105.25 (= 105 + $^8/_{32}$). The futures settlement price per $1 of par value is therefore 1.0525. The invoice price is then:

$$\$100,000 \times 1.0525 \times 1.21 + \$5,300 = \$132,652.50$$

8. The proceeds received are:

$$\text{converted price} = \text{futures price} \times \text{conversion factor}$$
$$= \$102 \times 0.9305 = \$94.9110$$

The interest from reinvesting the interim coupon based on a term repo rate of 5% is:

$$\text{interest from reinvesting the interim coupon payment} = \$4 \times 0.05 \times \frac{35}{360}$$
$$= \$0.0194$$

Summary:

converted price	=	$94.9110
accrued interest received	=	1.7315
interim coupon payment	=	4.0000
interest from reinvesting the interim coupon payment	=	0.0194
proceeds received	=	$100.6619

The cost of the investment is the purchase price for the issue plus the accrued interest paid, as shown below:

$$\text{cost of the investment} = \$96 + \$3.2219 = \$99.2219$$

The implied repo rate is then:

$$\text{implied repo rate} = \frac{\$100.6619 - \$99.2219}{\$99.2219} \times \frac{360}{114} = 0.0458 = 4.58\%$$

9. a. The implied repo rate for a deliverable Treasury issue is the rate of return that can be earned by buying the issue in the market, simultaneously selling a Treasury futures contract, and delivering the purchased issue to satisfy delivery at the futures settlement date.

   b. The cheapest-to-deliver issue is the one deliverable Treasury issue that offers the highest implied repo rate.

10. Determination of the cheapest-to-deliver requires computing the implied repo rate (i.e., the rate of return on a cash and carry trade over the next six months). Note that there is no accrued interest paid, nor is there any interim coupon payment that can be reinvested. This is because it is assumed that the next coupon payment is six months from now when the futures contract settles.

   To show how the implied repo rate is computed, let's use the first of the four issues. The cost of the investment for this issue is $79.48. (Remember there is no accrued interest paid to purchase this issue.)

   The proceeds received in six months when the contract settles is the converted price plus accrued interest from delivering the issue. The converted price per $100 of par value is:

$$= \$99.50 \times 0.8215 = \$81.7393$$

Since the assumption is that there is no accrued interest and the next coupon payment is six months from now, the accrued interest at the settlement date when the bond is delivered for our four issues is the semiannual dollar coupon. For issue 1, it is $2 per $100 of par value since the coupon rate is 4%. Thus, the proceeds at the settlement date of the contract will be equal to $83.7393 ($81.7393 + 2). The semiannual return is then:

$$\frac{\$83.7393 - \$79.48}{\$79.48} = 0.0536 = 5.36\%$$

The returns can be annualized but the relative return will not change. Ignoring annualizing, the semiannual rate of return can be computed for the other three issues as shown in the table below:

Issue	Market price	Coupon rate	Conversion factor	Dollar coupon	Proceeds at settlement	Dollar return	Semiannual rate of return
1	$79.48	4.0%	0.8215	$2.00	$81.7393	83.7393	5.36%
2	86.54	5.7	0.8942	2.85	88.9729	91.8229	6.10
3	104.77	9.0	1.0544	4.50	104.9128	109.4128	4.43
4	109.22	9.6	1.1123	4.80	110.6739	115.4739	5.73

The cheapest-to-deliver issue is the one that offers the highest rate of return. For the four issues it is Issue 2.

11. a. There are several acceptable Treasury bonds that may be delivered to satisfy a Treasury bond futures contract. The quality or swap option allows the seller to select the issue to deliver.

    b. Unlike a typical futures contract, there is not a settlement date for a Treasury bond futures contract but a delivery month. The timing option allows the seller to select when in the delivery month to deliver.

    c. The wild card option allows the seller to deliver after the futures price has been determined by the CBOT at the end of the trading day up to 8 pm.

12. The maximum that can be lost by the buyer of an option is the option price paid.

13. a. The investor will exercise the call option because the price of the futures contract exceeds the strike price. By exercising the investor receives a long position in the Treasury bond futures contract and the call option writer receives the corresponding short position. The futures price for both parties is the strike price of $91. The positions are then marked to market using the futures price of $96 and the option writer must pay the option buyer $5 (the difference between the futures price of $96 and the strike price of $91).

    After this, the positions look as follows:

    • the investor (the buyer of the call option) has a long position in the Treasury bond futures contract at $96 and cash of $5

    • the writer of the call option has a short position in the Treasury bond futures contract at $96 and has paid cash of $5

    b. If the futures price at the option expiration date is $89, the investor will not exercise the call option because it is less than the strike price. Thus, the option will expire worthless.

14. a. If the futures price at the option expiration date is $99, the put option will not be exercised because this price exceeds the strike price.

   b. The investor will exercise the put option because the price of the futures contract is less than the strike price. By exercising the investor receives a short position in the Treasury bond futures contract and the put option writer receives the corresponding long position. The futures price for both parties is the strike price of $97. The positions are then marked to market using the futures price of $91 and the option writer must pay the option buyer 6 (the difference between the strike price of $97 and the futures price of $91).

   After this, the positions look as follows:

   - the investor (the buyer of the put option) has a short position in the Treasury bond futures contract at $91 and cash of $6
   - the writer of the put option has a long position in the Treasury bond futures contract at $91 and has paid cash of $6

15. a. Institutional investors will purchase an OTC option to obtain a customized option. For example, the option can be customized with respect to the underlying instrument—it could be a particular corporate bond rather than a Treasury bond. It could be customized for the settlement date and/or the strike price. The customization permits an institutional investor to create an option that better satisfies its investment objective.

   b. An investor who wants to speculate on interest rate movements using options is better off using exchange-traded options. OTC options are less liquid and there is no need for customization. Moreover, the counterparty risk may be greater for an OTC option compared to an exchange-traded option.

16. The swap rate is the fixed rate that the fixed-rate payer agrees to pay over the life of the swap. The swap spread is the spread that is added to a benchmark Treasury security (from the Treasury yield curve) to obtain the swap rate.

17. a. The fixed-rate payer agrees to pay the swap rate (i.e., the fixed rate). Since Mr. Munson has agreed to pay the swap rate, he is the fixed-rate payer. The commercial bank is the fixed-rate receiver.

   b. Since the swap rate is 5.6%, the fixed-rate payment each quarter will be:

$$\$40,000,000 \times (0.056/4) = \$560,000$$

   (In the next chapter, this number will be fine tuned to allow for the fact that not every quarter has the same number of days.)

   c. Since 3-month LIBOR is 3.6%, the first quarterly payment will be:

$$\$40,000,000 \times (0.036/4) = \$360,000$$

18. A swap can be interpreted in the following two ways: (i) as a package of forward contracts and (ii) as a package of cash market instruments. It is a package of forward contracts because basically the fixed-rate payer is agreeing to pay a fixed amount for "something." That something is the reference rate and therefore the value of what the fixed-rate receiver is receiving in exchange for the fixed-rate payment at an exchange date will vary. This is equivalent to a forward contract where the underlying is the reference rate. There is not just one forward contract but one for each date at which

an exchange of payments will be made over the life of the swap. Thus, it is a package of forward contracts.

The second interpretation is that an interest rate swap is a package of cash market instruments. Specifically, from the perspective of the fixed-rate payer—the party paying fixed and receiving floating—it is equivalent to buying a floating-rate note (with the reference rate for the note being the reference rate for the swap) and funding (i.e., obtaining the funds to buy the floating-rate note) by issuing a fixed-rate bond (with the coupon rate for the bond being the swap rate). The par value of the floating-rate note and the fixed-rate bond is the notional amount of the swap. For the fixed-rate receiver, a swap is equivalent to purchasing a fixed-rate bond and funding it by issuing a floating-rate note.

19. a. If interest rates decrease, the fixed-rate payer will lose, as an appreciation in the value of the swap will cause an unrealized loss in value to the short position. This is because the swap rate (i.e., a fixed rate) is being paid but that rate is above the prevailing market rate necessary to receive the reference rate.

   b. If interest rates decrease, the fixed-rate receiver will realize an appreciation in the value of the swap. This is because the fixed-rate receiver is being paid a higher rate (i.e., the swap rate) than prevailing in the market in exchange for the reference rate.

20. A investor who is short the bond market benefits if interest rates increase. The party to an interest rate swap that benefits if interest rates increase is the fixed-rate payer. Thus, a fixed-rate payer is said to be short the bond market.

21. There is no payoff to the cap if the cap rate exceeds 3-month LIBOR. For Periods 2 and 3, there is no payoff because 3-month LIBOR is below the cap rate. For Periods 1 and 4, there is a payoff and the payoff is determined by:

$$\$10 \text{ million} \times (3\text{-month LIBOR} - \text{cap rate})/4$$

The payoffs are summarized below:

Period	3-month LIBOR (%)	Payoff ($)
1	8.7%	17,500
2	8.0	0
3	7.8	0
4	8.2	5,000

22. There is a payoff to the floor if 3-month LIBOR is less than the floor rate. For Periods 1 and 2, there is no payoff because 3-month LIBOR is greater than the floor rate. For Periods 3 and 4, there is a payoff and the payoff is determined by:

$$\$20 \text{ million} \times (\text{floor rate} - 3\text{-month LIBOR})/4$$

The payoffs are summarized below:

Period	3-month LIBOR (%)	Payoff ($)
1	4.7%	0
2	4.4	0
3	3.8	10,000
4	3.4	30,000

23. Once the fee for the interest rate floor is paid, the seller of an interest rate floor is not exposed to counterparty risk. Only the seller, not the buyer, must perform.

24. a. An interest rate cap or floor is equivalent to a package of interest rate options. So, for example, if an interest rate cap is for three years and payments are made quarterly, this is equivalent to 12 interest rate options.

    b. Since a cap is equivalent to a package of interest rate options, each option in the package is called a caplet. So, if an interest rate cap, for example, is for three years and makes quarterly payments, then there are 12 interest rate options and there are then 12 caplets. Similarly, since a floor is equivalent to a package of interest rate options, each interest rate option in the package is called a floorlet.

CHAPTER 14

VALUATION OF INTEREST RATE DERIVATIVE INSTRUMENTS

SOLUTIONS

1. a. The cash and carry trade involves the following:

   Sell the futures contract that settles in four months at $101.

   Borrow $98 for four months at 7.2% per year.

   With the borrowed funds purchase the underlying bond for the futures contract.

   The borrowed funds are used to purchase the bond, so there is no cash outlay for this strategy (ignoring initial margin and other transaction costs). Four months from now, the following must be done:

   Deliver the purchased bond to settle the futures contract.

   Repay the loan.

   When the bond is delivered to settle the futures contract four months from now, the amount received is the futures price of $101 plus the accrued interest. Since the coupon rate is 9% for the bond delivered and the bond is held for four months, the accrued interest is $3 [(9% × $100)/3]. Thus, the amount received is $104 ($101 + $3). The amount that must be paid to repay the loan is the principal borrowed of $98 plus interest cost. Since the interest rate for the loan is 7.2% and the loan is for four months, the interest cost is $2.35. Thus, the amount paid is $100.35($98 + $2.35). Therefore,

Cash inflow from delivery of the bond	=	$104.00
Cash outflow from repayment of the loan	=	−$100.35
Profit	=	$3.65

   Therefore, the arbitrage profit is $3.65.

   b. The reverse cash and carry trade involves the following:

   Buy the futures contract that settles in four months at $96

Sell (short) the bond underlying the futures contract for $98.

Invest (lend) the proceeds from the short sale of $98 for four months at 7.2% per year.

Once again, there is no cash outlay if we ignore the initial margin for the futures contract and other transaction costs. Four months from now when the futures contract must be settled, the following must be done:

Purchase the underlying bond to settle the futures contract.

Receive proceeds from repayment of the funds lent.

When the bond is delivered to settle the futures contract four months from now, the amount that must be paid is $99 (the futures price of $96 plus the accrued interest of $3.00). The amount that will be received from the proceeds lent for four months is $100.35. Therefore, at the end of four months the following will be the cash flow:

$$
\begin{aligned}
\text{Cash inflow from the amount invested (lent)} &= \$100.35 \\
\text{Cash outflow to purchase the bond} &= -\$99.00 \\
\text{Profit} &= \quad \$1.35
\end{aligned}
$$

An arbitrage profit of $1.35 will be realized.

c. The inputs for computing the theoretical futures price, using the notation in the chapter, are:

$$
r = 0.072 \quad P - 98 \quad t = 4/12 = 1/3
$$

The current yield is found by dividing the annual coupon of $9 by the cash market price of the bond ($98). Thus,

$$
c = 9/98 = 0.0918 = 9.18\%
$$

$$
F = 98 + 98 \times (1/3) \times (0.072 - 0.0918) = 97.35
$$

The theoretical futures price is $97.35

d. To demonstrate using the cash and carry trade that the price of $97.35 does not allow an arbitrage profit, the following strategy is employed:

Sell the futures contract that settles in four months at 97.35.
Borrow $98 for four months at 7.2% per year.
With the borrowed funds purchase the underlying bond for the futures contract.

When the bond is delivered to settle the futures contract four months from now, the amount received is the futures price of $97.35 plus accrued interest of $3. Therefore the proceeds received will be $100.35. The amount to repay the loan is $100.35. Therefore, at the end of four months the cash flow will be:

$$
\begin{aligned}
\text{Cash inflow from delivery of the bond} &= \quad \$100.35 \\
\text{Cash outflow from repayment of the loan} &= -\$100.35 \\
\text{Profit} &= \qquad 0
\end{aligned}
$$

This demonstrates that if the futures price is $97.35, there is no arbitrage profit.

2. a. The inputs for computing the theoretical futures price, using the notation in the chapter, are:

$$r = 0.046 \quad P = 94 \quad t = 5/12 = 0.41667$$

The current yield is found by dividing the annual coupon of $6 by the cash market price of the bond ($94). Thus,

$$c = 6/94 = 0.06383 = 6.383\%$$

$$F = 94 + 94 \times (0.41667) \times (0.046 - 0.06383) = 93.30$$

The theoretical futures price is $93.30

b. If the futures price is $93.25 and the theoretical futures price is $93.30, then there is an opportunity to generate an arbitrage profit. The futures price is cheap. This means that to capture the arbitrage profit, the futures contract is purchased and the bond is sold. That is, a reverse cash and carry trade should be implemented.

c. If the borrowing rate is 4.7%, then the upper boundary for the theoretical futures price would be:

$$r_B = 0.047 \quad c = 0.06383 \quad P = 94 \quad t = 0.41667$$

$$F(\text{upper boundary}) = 94 + 94 \times (0.41667) \times (0.047 - 0.06383) = 93.34$$

The lower boundary for the theoretical futures price would be found using 4.3% for r_L:

$$F(\text{lower boundary}) = 94 + 94 \times (0.41667) \times (0.043 - 0.06383) = 93.18$$

The range for the theoretical futures price that prevents an arbitrage profit is then:

$$\$93.18 \text{ to } \$93.34$$

Since the futures price is $93.25, no arbitrage opportunity is available.

3. The delivery options are granted to the short. These options have a value to a short and are a disadvantage to the long. Consequently, the theoretical futures price is reduced by the estimated value of the delivery options.

4. The general formula for the theoretical price of a futures contract that considers only the cash market price and the cost of carry fails to take into consideration the nuances of a Treasury bond futures contract. These nuances include the delivery options granted to the short which reduce the theoretical futures price below that given by a general formula for any futures contract that considers only the cost of carry. If the general formula is used for Treasury bond futures contracts, the theoretical price derived will be greater than the theoretical futures price after correctly adjusting for the delivery options. Consequently, Mr. Thompson's observation that there is mispricing is incorrect and it is questionable whether he will be able to identify and exploit any opportunities to enhance portfolio return.

5. a. The fixed-rate payer will receive:

$$\text{notional amount} \times (\text{3-month LIBOR}) \times \frac{\text{no. of days in period}}{360}$$

The number of days from January 1 of year 1 to March 31 of year 1 is 90. If 3-month LIBOR is 5.7%, then the fixed-rate payer will receive a floating-rate payment on March 31 of year 1 equal to:

$$\$40,000,000 \times 0.057 \times \frac{90}{360} = \$570,000$$

b. The forward rate and the floating-rate payment for each quarter are shown below:

Quarter starts	Quarter ends	No. of days in quarter	3-month Eurodollar CD futures price	Forward rate (%)*	Floating-rate payment at end of quarter
April 1, 1999	June 30, 1999	91	94.10	5.90	596,556
July 1, 1999	Sept 30, 1999	92	94.00	6.00	613,333
Oct 1, 1999	Dec 31, 1999	92	93.70	6.30	644,000
Jan 1, 2000	Mar 31, 2000	90	93.60	6.40	640,000
April 1, 2000	June 30, 2000	91	93.50	6.50	657,222
July 1, 2000	Sept 30, 2000	92	93.20	6.80	695,111
Oct 1, 2000	Dec 31, 2000	92	93.00	7.00	715,556

*The forward rate is the 3-month Eurodollar futures rate.

c. The floating-rate swap payment at the end of each quarter is shown in the last column in the table in part b.

6. a. The fixed-rate payment for each quarter is computed as follows:

$$\text{notional amount} \times \text{swap rate} \times \frac{\text{no. of days in period}}{360}$$

Since the swap rate is 7% and the notional amount is $20 million:

$$\$20,000,000 \times 0.07 \times \frac{\text{no. of days in period}}{360}$$

For each of the eight quarters the fixed-rate payment is:

Period quarter	Days in quarter	Notional amount	Fixed-rate payment
1	92	20,000,000	357,778
2	92	20,000,000	357,778
3	90	20,000,000	350,000
4	91	20,000,000	353,889
5	92	20,000,000	357,778
6	92	20,000,000	357,778
7	90	20,000,000	350,000
8	91	20,000,000	353,889

b. When payments are made semiannually rather than quarterly, the number of days in the two quarters comprising the 6-month period is determined and the same formula is applied to determine the fixed-rate payment. The semiannual fixed-rate payments for the four 6-month periods are shown below:

Period quarter	Days in period	Notional amount	Fixed-rate payment
1			
2	184	20,000,000	715,556
3			
4	181	20,000,000	703,889
5			
6	184	20,000,000	715,556
7			
8	181	20,000,000	703,889

c. The semiannual fixed-rate payment is:

Period quarter	Days in period	Notional amount	Fixed-rate payment
1			
2	184	20,000,000	715,556
3			
4	181	20,000,000	703,889
5			
6	184	12,000,000	429,333
7			
8	181	12,000,000	422,333

7. The period forward rate is computed as follows:

$$\text{period forward rate} = \text{annual forward rate} \times \left(\frac{\text{days in period}}{360} \right)$$

The forward discount factor for period t is computed as follows:

$$\frac{\$1}{(1+\text{forward rate for period1})(1+\text{forward rate for period 2})\cdots (1+\text{forward rate for period } t)}$$

Applying the above formulas to current 3-month LIBOR and the forward rates obtained from the Eurodollar CD futures contract, we would find:

Period	Days in quarter	Current 3-month LIBOR (%)	3-month Eurodollar CD futures price	Forward rate (%)*	Period forward rate (%)	Forward discount factor
1	90	5.90		5.90	1.4750	0.98546440
2	91		93.90	6.10	1.5419	0.97049983
3	92		93.70	6.30	1.6100	0.95512236
4	92		93.45	6.55	1.6739	0.93939789
5	90		93.20	6.80	1.7000	0.92369507
6	91		93.15	6.85	1.7315	0.90797326

*The forward rate is the 3-month Eurodollar futures rate.

8. a. The swap rate is determined as follows:

$$SR = \frac{\text{PV of floating-rate payments}}{\displaystyle\sum_{t=1}^{10} \text{notional amount} \times \frac{\text{Days}_t}{360} \times \text{FDF}_t}$$

Since the present value of the floating-rate payments is equal to $16,555,000 and the denominator of the swap rate formula is $236,500,000, the swap rate is:

$$SR = \frac{\$16,555,000}{\$236,500,000} = 0.07 = 7\%$$

b. The swap spread is the difference between the swap rate of 7% and the yield for the maturity from the on-the-run Treasury yield curve with the same maturity as the swap, 6.4% (the 5-year yield). The swap spread is therefore 60 basis points.

9. a. The present value of the payments made by the fixed-rate payer over the remaining life of the swap is $910,000; however, the floating-rate payments that will be received have a present value of $710,000. Thus, the fixed-rate payer has a liability of $200,000. This means that the value of the swap from the perspective of the fixed-rate payer is −$200,000.

b. The present value of the payments the fixed-rate receiver will receive over the remaining life of the swap is $910,000; the present value of the floating-rate payments that will be paid is $710,000. Therefore, the fixed-rate receiver has an asset with a value of $200,000.

10. a. The answer is the same as for Question 7 for the first four periods.

Period	Days in quarter	Current 3-month LIBOR (%)	3-month Eurodollar CD futures price	Forward rate (%)*	Period forward rate (%)	Forward discount factor
1	90	5.90		5.90	1.4750	0.98546440
2	91		93.90	6.10	1.5419	0.97049983
3	92		93.70	6.30	1.6100	0.95512236
4	92		93.45	6.55	1.6739	0.93939789

*The forward rate is the 3-month Eurodollar futures rate.

   b.

Period	Days in quarter	Period forward rate (%)	Floating-rate payment
1	90	1.4750	737,500
2	91	1.5419	770,972
3	92	1.6100	805,000
4	92	1.6739	836,944

   c.

Period	Days in quarter	Fixed-rate payment based on swap rate
1	90	1,000,000
2	91	1,011,111
3	92	1,022,222
4	92	1,022,222

d. From part a the forward discount factor is determined. From parts b and c the floating-rate and fixed-rate payments, respectively, are determined. Therefore,

Period	Forward discount factor	Floating-rate payment	PV of floating-rate payment	Fixed-rate payment	PV of fixed-rate payment
1	0.98546440	737,500	726,780	1,000,000	985,464
2	0.97049983	770,972	748,228	1,011,111	981,283
3	0.95512236	805,000	768,874	1,022,222	976,347
4	0.93939789	836,944	786,224	1,022,222	960,273
		Total	3,030,106		3,903,367

For fixed rate payer	−873,262
For fixed rate receiver	873,262

For the fixed-rate payer the present value of the payments is $3,903,367. The present value of the payments to be received by the fixed-rate payer (i.e., the present value of the floating-rate payments) is $3,030,106. Therefore, for the fixed-rate payer, the value of the swap is −$873,262.

e Given the values for the fixed-rate and floating-rate payments in part d, the value of the swap from the perspective of the fixed-rate receiver is $873,262 because the fixed-rate payments to be received have a present value of $3,903,367 and the floating-rate payments to be paid have a present value of $3,030,106.

11.

Type of option	Strike price	Bond's price	Option price	In, at, or out of the money	Intrinsic value	Time value
call	94	90	7	out of the money	0	7
call	102	104	6	in the money	2	4
call	88	88	3	at the money	0	3
put	106	110	5	out of the money	0	5
put	92	92	9	at the money	0	9
put	95	89	11	in the money	6	5

12. While it is true that a rise in interest rates will decrease the price of a call option on bond futures because the price of the underlying bond decreases, there are other factors that affect the value of a call option. One such factor is interest rate volatility—an increase in interest rate volatility increases the value of a call option. The question specifies that the increase in interest rates was a result of extreme interest rate volatility. Consequently, the increase in interest rate volatility can increase the price of a call option more than a rise in interest rates decreases it.

13. While the Black-Scholes option pricing model is appropriate for valuing options on common stock, the assumptions underlying the model make it less suitable for valuing options on bonds and in some cases may give an option value that makes no economic sense. The three assumptions that do not reflect the realities of bonds are:

  i. The model places no restriction on the possible price of a bond when in fact the maximum price is the sum of the undiscounted cash flows.
  ii. The model assumes that short-term rates are constant when in fact changes in the short-term rate cause bond prices to change and therefore the value of the option to change.

iii. The model assumes that return volatility is constant when in fact return volatility declines as a bond moves toward maturity.

14. a. The value of the 3-year Treasury bond is 103.373, as shown below:

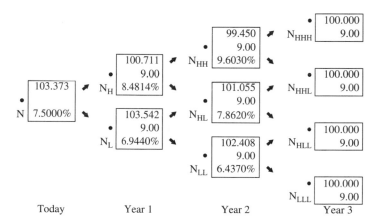

b. The current price of the bond is 103.373 as found in part a and the price assumed in the question. The value of the 2-year call option is $2.5886, as shown below:

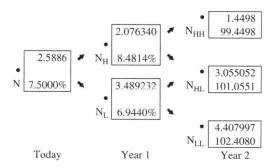

c. Again, it is assumed that the current price is the value found in part a. The value of the put option is $3.4570.

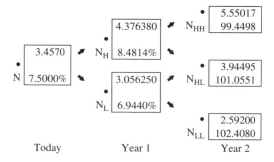

15. a. The most common model is the Black model that was developed for valuing European options on forward contracts.

    b. The Black model does not overcome the problems associated with the Black-Scholes option pricing model. Because it fails to incorporate the yield curve into the model, there will not be a consistency between the pricing of Treasury bond futures and options on Treasury bond futures. The second problem is that the model is for valuing European options, not American options.

16. This call option is deep out of the money—the price of the underlying bond is substantially below the strike price. If the price of the underlying bond increases by $1 to 71, the price of the call option would *not* be expected to change at all. Consequently, the delta is close to zero.

17. Delta measures the sensitivity of an option's price to a change in the price of the underlying bond. This parameter plays the same role as duration. Gamma is used to improve the estimate of the change in the option's price using delta. It plays the same role as the convexity measure for improving the price change estimated using duration.

18. a. Theta measures how quickly the time value of the option changes as the option moves towards expiration. Buyers prefer that the value not decline quickly. Thus, the buyer of an option prefers an option with a low theta rather than a high theta.

    b. The kappa of an option on a bond measures the price sensitivity to changes in expected interest rate volatility. An investor who anticipates an increase in interest rate volatility that is not already priced into the option will prefer an option with a high kappa rather than a low kappa.

19. a. The value of the Year 1 caplet is $226,291 as shown below:

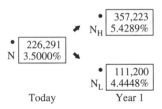

b. The value of the Year 2 caplet is $412,105 as shown below:

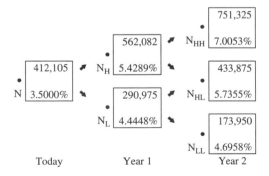

c. The value of the Year 3 caplet is $632,464 as shown below:

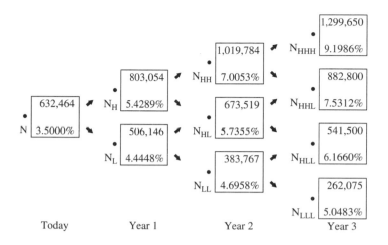

Today   Year 1   Year 2   Year 3

d. The value of the 3-year cap is equal to the value of the three caplets:

$$\$226,291 + \$412,105 + \$632,464 = \$1,270,860$$

20. a. The value of the Year 1 floorlet is $272,056 as shown below:

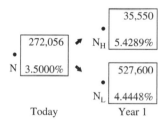

Today   Year 1

b. The value of the Year 2 floorlet is $92,992 as shown below:

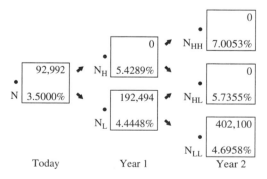

Today   Year 1   Year 2

c. The value of the Year 3 floorlet is $24,944 as shown below:

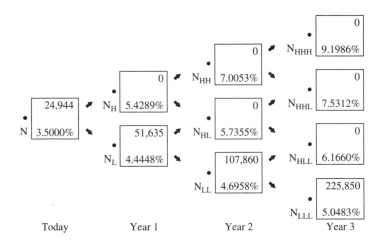

d. The value of the 3-year floor is the sum of the three floorlets:

$$\$272,056 + \$92,992 + \$24,944 = \$389,992$$

CHAPTER 15

GENERAL PRINCIPLES OF CREDIT ANALYSIS

SOLUTIONS

1. Credit risk is more general than the statement in the quote. Credit risk encompasses three types of risk: default risk, credit spread risk, and downgrade risk. The quote in the question refers to default risk only. (Credit spread risk is the risk that the credit spread will increase. Downgrade risk is the risk that the issue will be downgraded.) Thus, one should disagree with the statement in the question.

2. a. Information in addition to the credit rating that is provided by a rating agency includes rating watches (or credit watches), rating outlooks, and transition tables. The first two are useful in assessing default risk, while the last is useful for assessing downgrade risk.

   When an issue is put on rating watch (credit watch), this means that the rating agency is reviewing the issue with the potential for an upgrade or a downgrade. A rating outlook is a projection of whether an issue in the long term (from six months to two years) is likely to be upgraded (positive outlook), downgraded (negative outlook), or maintain its current rating (stable outlook).

   A rating transition table is published periodically by a rating agency. It shows the percentage of issues of each rating at the beginning of a period that was downgraded or upgraded by the end of the time period.

   b. A credit rating is a forward-looking assessment of credit risk. For long-term debt obligations, it is an assessment of (1) the probability of default and (2) the relative magnitude of the loss should a default occur. For short-term debt obligations, a credit rating is an assessment of only the probability of default.

3. The factors considered include strategic direction of management, financial philosophy, management's track record, succession planning, and control systems.

4. a. While there are various forms of back-up credit facilities, some forms are stronger than others. A back-up credit facility where the lender is contractually bound and contains no provisions that permit the lender to refuse to provide funds is the strongest form. There are non-contractual facilities such as lines of credit. For such facilities, the analyst should be concerned because the lender has the right to refuse to lend funds.

   b. A "material adverse change clause" in a back-up credit facility allows a bank to refuse funding if the bank feels that the borrower's financial condition or operating position has deteriorated significantly. Consequently, as explained in part a, this is a weaker form of back-up credit facility.

5. a. With high-yield issuers there tends to be more bank loans in the debt structure and the loans tend to be short term. Also, the loans tend to be floating rate rather than fixed. As a result, the analyst must look at the ability of the issuer to access short-term funding sources for liquidity to meet not only possible higher interest payments (when interest rates rise), but to pay off a maturing loan. High-yield issuers, however, have fewer alternatives for short-term funding sources than high-grade issuers.

   b. At any given point in time, the cushion (as measured by coverage ratios) may be high. However, the concern is with future cash flows to satisfy obligations. If the coverage ratio is adequate and is predicted to change little in the future and the degree of confidence in the prediction is high, that situation would give greater comfort to a bondholder than one where the coverage ratio is extremely high but can fluctuate substantially in the future. Because of this variability it is difficult to assign a high degree of confidence to coverage ratios that are projected and there must be recognition that the coverage ratio may fall well below acceptable levels.

   c. Financial flexibility means the ability to sustain operations should there be a down turn in business and to sustain current dividends without reliance on external funding.

   d. Unfunded pension liabilities may not be listed as debt but they are effectively a form of borrowing by the firm. Hence, Moody's is considering them as part of the debt obligation. Guarantees represent potential liabilities if the corporate entity whose debt is guaranteed does not meet its obligations. If Moody's views the obligation as one that the company may have to satisfy, the obligation of the corporate entity whose debt is guaranteed is a form of borrowing and should be included in total debt.

   e. Ratios represent a snapshot of a particular aspect of a firm's financial position at a given point in time. Ratings reflect an assessment of the future financial position and the assessment of future cash flows. This involves looking at a myriad of factors that impact future cash flows such as competition, potential earnings growth, and future capital requirements. This is a major limitation of ratio analysis as a sole indicator of an entity's financial strength—it is not forward looking in that it does not look at how factors in the future can alter cash flows.

6. By analyzing the statement of cash flows, creditors can examine such aspects of the business as (1) the source of financing for business operations, (2) the company's ability to meet its debt obligations, (3) the company's ability to finance expansion through operating cash flow, (4) the company's ability to pay dividends, and (5) the flexibility given to management in financing its operations.

7. a. Free operating cash flow, according to S&P, is obtained by reducing operating cash flow by capital expenditures.

      Discretionary cash flow is found by reducing free operating cash flow by cash dividends.

      Prefinancing financing cash flow is found by adjusting discretionary cash flow by (1) decreasing it by acquisitions and (2) increasing it by asset disposals, and then further adjusting by the net of other sources (uses) of cash.

   b. Free operating cash flow according to S&P is the cash flow that can be used to pay dividends and make acquisitions. Reducing free operating cash flow by cash dividends gives discretionary cash flow that management can use to make acquisitions. Adjusting discretionary cash flow for managerial discretionary decisions for acquisition of other companies, the disposal of assets (e.g., lines of business or subsidiaries), and others sources or uses of cash gives prefinancing cash flow, which represents the extent to which company cash flow from all internal sources have been sufficient to cover all internal needs.

8. a. Since covenants deal with limitations and restrictions on the borrower's activities, certain covenants provide protection for a bondholder and this protection must be factored into the credit analysis.

   b. A negative covenant is one that requires the borrower not to take certain actions. An example of a negative covenant is a restriction on the company's ability to incur additional debt.

   c. A review of the covenants in a high-yield corporate issue may help the analyst understand management strategy regarding future funding and operational strategies to determine if they are consistent with what management is stating to investors. Loopholes in covenants may provide further clues as to management's future plans.

9. Agency risk is the risk that management will make decisions in its own self interest, thereby reducing firm value.

10. a. The motivation for developing a corporate governance rating is the belief that in the long run firms that focus on corporate governance and transparency will generate superior returns and economic performance and lower their cost of capital.

    b. Every firm that has developed a corporate governance rating uses its own criteria. Typically what is considered (using the S&P criteria) is ownership structure and external influences, shareholder rights and stakeholder relations, transparency, disclosure and audit process, and board structure and effectiveness.

11. a. The typical structure for a high-yield corporate issuer includes bank debt. This debt is senior to all other debt claims. As a result, bonds that are labeled "senior bonds" are subordinated to bank debt despite their title.

    b. The interest for a zero-coupon bond increases over time due to the accrual of the unpaid interest. As a result, assuming no other changes in the firm's debt structure, the percentage of a zero-coupon bond in the firm's debt structure increases over time. If these bonds are senior bonds (senior relative to the subordinated bonds, not to bank debt as discussed in part a), then the zero-coupon bond's percentage increases relative to the subordinated bonds. This may increase the credit risk of the subordinated bonds over time and adversely impact subordinated bondholders in the event of bankruptcy. Hence, in the quote Mr. Bernstein is stating that it is preferred to have zero-coupon bonds (or any deferred coupon bonds) as subordinated bonds rather than senior bonds.

12. In a holding company structure, the parent company issues debt as well as the operating subsidiaries. Consequently, the analyst in projecting the cash flows available to pay the creditors of the holding company must understand any restrictions on payments that can be made to the parent company (dividends or loans) by the operating subsidiaries.

13. In the risk-return spectrum, high-yield bonds are between high-grade corporate bonds and common stocks. High-yield corporate bonds have an equity component as evidenced by the higher correlation between stock returns and high-yield bond returns compared to high-grade bond returns and high-yield bond returns. Consequently, some portfolio managers such as Mr. Esser firmly believe that high-yield bond analysis should be viewed from an equity analyst's perspective. It is believed that the equity

approach can provide more insight than traditional credit analysis. A manager using an equity approach, it is believed by Mr. Esser, will give that manager an edge in identifying attractive issues for purchase or avoiding or disposing of unattractive issues relative to other managers who rely solely on traditional credit analysis.

14. Given the projected cash flow for the collateral under various scenarios, the next step is to determine how the cash flow would be distributed among the different tranches in the structure. So, by itself projection of the cash flow is insufficient because it will not indicate if any, or all, of the tranches (i.e., bonds) will realize a loss. The allocation of the cash flow in a given scenario will permit the determination of which tranches may realize losses and the extent of those losses.

15. A servicer may be required to make advances to cover interest payments to bondholders when there are delinquencies. Consequently, the servicer must have the financial capacity to fulfill this obligation. This requires an assessment of the financial condition of the servicer.

16. a. In a "true securitization" the role of the servicer is basically routine. There are basic daily administrative tasks performed and the cash flow is not depend to any significant extent on the servicer to perform. Where the role of the servicer is more than administrative in order to generate the cash flow, the transaction is referred to as a "hybrid transaction."

    b. The analysis of a "hybrid transaction" uses both the standard methodology for evaluating an asset-backed security transaction and the analysis of a corporate entity—basically as a service business. The latter approach is referred to by S&P as a "quasi-corporate" approach. The final assessment of a rating agency is a subjective weighting of the credit quality using the two approaches. The more the transaction's cash flow is dependent on the performance of the servicer, the greater the weight given to the quasi-corporate approach.

17. The four basic categories are: (1) the issuer's debt structure; (2) the issuer's ability and political discipline to maintain sound budgetary policy; (3) the specific local taxes and intergovernmental revenues available to the issuer, as well as obtaining historical information on tax collection rates, and; (4) the issuer's overall socioeconomic environment.

18. a. The payment of the obligations of a revenue bond must come from the cash flow generated from the enterprise for which the bonds were issued. Thus, just as in the case of a corporate bond, the underlying principle in assessing an issuer's credit worthiness is whether or not sufficient cash flow will be generated to satisfy the obligations due bondholders.

    b. A rate covenant specifies how charges will be set on the product or service sold by the enterprise. A rate covenant is included so the enterprise will set charges so as to satisfy both expenses and debt servicing, or to create a certain amount of reserves.

19. Because the issuer is a sovereign entity, if the issuer refuses to pay there is little legal remedy for the debt holder. Thus, it becomes necessary to understand the factors other than legal recourse that will increase the likelihood that the issuer will repay.

20. a. The reason for assigning two ratings is that the currency denomination of the payments may be either the local currency or a foreign currency. (Historically, the default frequency had differed by the currency denomination of the debt. It has been observed by rating agencies that defaults have been greater on foreign currency denominated debt.)

b. To generate sufficient local currency to satisfy its debt obligations denominated in its local currency, a government must be willing to raise taxes and control its domestic financial system. In contrast, a national government must purchase foreign currency to meet a debt obligation in that foreign currency. Consequently, a government has less control with respect to its exchange rate and faces exchange rate risk (i.e., depreciation of its currency) when it issues a foreign currency denominated bond.

The implication of this is that the factors a rating agency will emphasize in assessing the credit worthiness of a national government's local currency debt and foreign currency debt will differ to some extent. S&P, for example, focuses on domestic government policies that affect the likelihood of the government's ability to repay local currency denominated debt. For foreign currency debt, the same rating agency focuses on the interaction of domestic and foreign government policies. Specifically, the areas of analysis that S&P assesses is a country's balance of payments and the structure of its external balance sheet (i.e., the net public debt, total net external debt, and net external liabilities).

21. When analyzing domestic corporate bonds an analyst does factor in intangible and non-quantitative elements, the most important of which is the quality of management. Moreover, a factor that is considered in assessing the credit quality of a tax-backed municipal bond issue is the willingness of the issuing entity to generate funds to repay the obligation by raising taxes. So, the statement that intangible and non-quantitative elements are not considered in analyzing domestic corporate and domestic municipal bonds but only with sovereign bonds is incorrect.

22. All the financial ratios—actual and projected for 2001—clearly indicate that the credit worthiness of Krane Products is improving. Using as benchmarks the S&P median ratios, the coverage ratios were already by fiscal year 2000 approaching that of the median BBB rated issuer. The capitalization ratios, while improving, were still well below that of the median BBB rated issuer. Consequently, by fiscal year 2000 an analyst would have been well advised to monitor this issuer's credit for a possible upgrade and to examine how it was trading in the market. That is, was it trading like a BB or BBB credit?

If Ms. Andrews' projections are correct for fiscal year 2001, the ratios shown in the table are at least as good as the median BBB rated company. Consequently, based on her projections she would recommend the purchase of Krane Products Inc. bonds if that issuer's bonds continue to trade like a BB credit since, based on her analysis, the bonds are likely to be upgraded to BBB.

23. Credit scoring models tend to classify firms as likely to default, not only most of the firms that do eventually default, but also many firms that do not default. Some of the firms that appear to be troubled credits by credit scoring models hire new management and are then revitalized without defaulting. Thus, a credit analyst must recognize the possibility of a turnaround for a firm that the model has classified as likely to default. Furthermore, there are reasons why a firm may default that have nothing to do with the financial variables used in a credit scoring model.

24. Structural models and reduced form models are the two types of credit risk models for valuing corporate bonds.

The foundation of structural models, also know as "firm-value models," is the Black-Scholes-Merton option pricing model. The basic idea of these models is that a company defaults on its debt if the value of the assets of the company falls below a certain default point. The default process of a corporation is driven by the value of its assets. Since the value of any option depends on the volatility of the asset value in structural models, the probability of default is explicitly linked to the expected volatility of a corporation's asset value. Thus, in structural models, both the default process and recovery rates should a bankruptcy occur depend on the corporation's structural characteristics.

Reduced form models do not look "inside the firm," but instead model directly the probability of default or downgrade. That is, the default process and the recovery process are (1) modeled independently of the corporation's structural features and (2) are independent of each other.

CHAPTER 16

INTRODUCTION TO BOND PORTFOLIO MANAGEMENT

SOLUTIONS

1. a. The two dimensions of a liability are the timing of the required cash outlay and the amount of the cash outlay required to satisfy the obligation.

   b. For some products sold by financial institutions or created by pension plans, the amount of the cash outlay and/or the timing of the cash outlay are not known with certainty. Many times the estimates of the liability depend on actuarial assumptions.

2. The economic surplus of an institution is the difference between the market value of the assets and the market value of the liabilities. The market value of the liabilities is the present value of the liabilities, using an appropriate interest rate to compute the present value.

3. a. A funded investor borrows funds and uses those funds to purchase securities.

   b. The investment objective of a funded investor is to earn a return greater than the cost of the borrowed funds.

4. The investment objective of a defined benefit pension plan is to generate sufficient cash flow from its portfolio of assets to satisfy its future liabilities. By selecting a broad-based bond market index, there is no assurance that the cash flow generated by the portfolio will be sufficient to satisfy the pension fund's future obligations.

5. The cash flow characteristics of broad-based bond market indexes may differ significantly from the cash outlays that are projected to be required for a pension plan. For example, the duration of a typical defined benefit pension plan's liabilities may exceed that of a broad-based bond market index. Thus, there would be a mismatch between the duration of the assets (as determined by the broad-based bond market index) and the duration of the pension fund's liabilities. Specialized indexes for defined benefit pension funds seek to correct this problem.

6. Ms. Florez should inform the client that Reliable did in fact outperform the benchmark specified in the investment objective. The failure of the client to meet the liabilities was probably due to the fact that the wrong benchmark was selected by the client. Assuming that Reliable had nothing to do with establishing the benchmark, the unfortunate failure to meet the liability was due to the client's benchmark selection, not the performance of Reliable's managers. The client should reconsider the benchmark to ensure that it more accurately reflects the characteristics of the liabilities it faces.

7. Tax considerations are important in selecting the asset classes in which a manager may invest. For example, a qualified tax-exempt pension fund would not find tax-exempt

securities (such as municipal bonds) acceptable because they offer a lower yield relative to taxable securities.

8. In an active strategy, the investment policy permits the manager to create a portfolio that deviates from the characteristics of the benchmark. The deviations are based on the manager's view as to where the performance will be better than that of the benchmark index. For example, if the manager believes that corporate bonds will outperform Treasury securities, then the manager will overweight the amount invested in corporate bonds relative to the benchmark index and underweight Treasury securities relative to the benchmark index.

   With a passive strategy, the manager creates a portfolio that has characteristics identical to (or very similar to) those of the benchmark. That is, a mini-version of the index is created.

9. a. Tracking error is a measure indicating the degree to which the future performance of a portfolio might depart from the future performance of a benchmark index.

   b. Tracking error occurs because the risk profile of a portfolio is different from the risk profile of the benchmark index.

10. With an indexing strategy, tracking error occurs when the performance deviates from the benchmark. It does not matter whether the tracking error is positive or negative. While the Conservative Management Company did outperform the benchmark (i.e., positive tracking error), this indicates a risk position significantly different from that of the index, and demonstrates a lack of ability to index a portfolio. The firm's claim of superior performance is incorrect given the investment objective. Thus, it is likely that you as a consultant would recommend not using Conservative Management Company as an indexer—however, you might recommend that the firm be retained as an active manager!

11. a. A holder of a liability may be able to terminate the liability prior to the stated maturity date. This occurs when interest rates rise and the holder of the liability wants to benefit by reinvesting proceeds at the then prevailing higher interest rate. The risk faced by the issuer of the liability is call risk.

    b. A funded investor typically borrows on a floating-rate basis and seeks to invest in a floating-rate asset. The latter typically has a cap (i.e., maximum interest rate). The liability does not have a cap. Thus, if rates rise, the rate paid on the floater will eventually reach the cap but the liability's rate will continue to increase. At some interest rate level, the rate on the floater will be less than the cost of the borrowed funds. This risk is cap risk.

12. a. The market value of the bond portfolio is £14 billion. (£14 billion assets minus £6 billion liabilities gives a surplus of £8 billion.)

    b. Since the duration of the assets is 6, then for a 100 basis point change in interest rates the change in the value of the asset portfolio will be approximately 6%. The dollar duration per £100 par value is then £6.

    c. A duration of 5 for the liabilities means that if interest rates change by 100 basis points, the present value of the liabilities will change by approximately 5%. Per £100 of present value, the liabilities will change by £6 and be equal to the dollar duration.

    d. If interest rates increase by 100 basis points, because the market value of the assets is £14 billion and the dollar duration per £100 market value is $3, the market value will decrease by approximately £840 million. For a 50 basis point increase in rates, the market value of the assets will decrease by half that amount, £420 million. The present value of the liabilities will decrease by approximately £150 million for a 50 basis point change. Thus, a 50 basis point increase in interest rates decreases the assets by £420 million and decreases the liabilities by £150 million. The net effect on the surplus is a decline of £270 million. Since the initial surplus is £8 billion, the surplus, after a 50 basis point rate increase would be £7.73 billion (£8 billion minus £270 million).

    e. If interest rates decrease by 50 basis points, the value of the assets will increase by £420 million and the value of the liabilities will increase by £150 million. Hence, the surplus will increase *to* £8.27 billion (£8 billion plus £270 million).

13. a. "By borrowing short" means that S&Ls were borrowing on a short-term basis. Thus, when interest rates increased, S&Ls had to retain depositors by offering a higher deposit rate or, if they borrowed funds in the market, they had to pay a higher interest rate. S&L's lent long by investing in long maturity assets (such as mortgages loans and mortgage-backed securities) with a fixed coupon rate.

    b. When any entity borrows short and lends long it is adversely affected by a rise in interest rates. This is because its cost of funds increases (since the cost of funds rises when interest rates increase) while the coupon income from the long term asset does not change.

    c. The duration of the assets exceeds the duration of the liabilities. That is, there is a mismatch between the duration of the assets and the duration of the liabilities.

14. A depository institutions seeks to generate spread income. If its assets and liabilities are benchmarked to the same market interest rate and the spread between these two costs is positive, it will generate positive spread income (ignoring any cap risk and credit risk) regardless of changes in that market interest rate.

15. a. The surplus of an entity is the difference between the market value of it assets and the present value of its liabilities. Surplus management means managing the exposure of the surplus to changes in interest rates.

    b. The surplus of an entity may or may not be sensitive to changes in interest rates. A bank is a highly leveraged institution and so even small changes in interest rates can dramatically affect its surplus. In contrast, a highly funded pension fund—one with a large surplus—may not be materially affected by a change in interest rates compared to the effect on a bank.

16. a. Performance measurement involves the calculation of the return realized by a manager over a specified time interval. Performance evaluation involves the assessment of the observed performance.

    b. The two issues that performance evaluation addresses are: (1) assessing whether the manager added value by outperforming the established benchmark and (2) determining how the manager achieved the calculated return, using return attribution analysis.

CHAPTER 17

MEASURING A PORTFOLIO'S RISK PROFILE

SOLUTIONS

1. a. Since the distribution of annual returns for the HP Index is normal, a return greater than 14% is 9% above the average annual return of 5%. This is two standard deviations (9% divided by the standard deviation of 4.5%) above the average. From the normal probability distribution, Mr. Felder knows that approximately 96% of returns will fall within two standard deviations of the average. This means that there is a 4% probability (100% minus 96%) that the return will be outside this range. Since a normal distribution is symmetric, this means that half of 4%, or 2%, is the probability that the return for the year will be above 14%. So, Mr. Felder would tell the trustees that, based on his assumptions, there is a 2% probability of realizing a return above 14%.

   b. A return of 0.5% is 4.5% below the average. This is one standard deviation below the average value (−4.5% divided by the standard deviation of 4.5%). From the normal probability distribution, Mr. Felder knows that 68% of the outcomes fall within one standard deviation below and above the average. The probability is 32% that an outcome falls outside this range. Since a normal probability distribution is symmetric, this means that half of 32%, or 16%, is the probability that the return for the year will be less than 0.5%. Consequently, the probability that the return will be greater than 0.5% is 84% (100% minus 16%). So, Mr. Felder would tell the trustees that, based on his assumptions, there is an 84% probability of realizing a return greater than 0.5%.

2. Statements about the probability of an outcome, such as the return on a bond portfolio, depend on both the probability distribution and the standard deviation assumed. The assumption that the return distribution is normal means that, given the expected value (i.e., the average value) and the standard deviation, the consultant was able to determine the probability of realizing various returns cited in the consultant's report. With a higher standard deviation, the probability of realizing a given return increases.

3. Rather than using the traditional standard deviation, the target semivariance can be used. In the case of the bank, the target would be the target return identified by the bank's funding cost plus a spread. Thus, the target semivariance indicates the risk in terms of realizing a return less than the bank's funding cost plus a spread.

4. a. When returns are normally distributed, the variance and the semivariance are equivalent in terms of the rankings they provide with respect to risk. When a return distribution is not normal, the more appropriate measure of risk is the deviation below the expected value. The semivariance measures that exposure.

   b. There are three reasons (cited by Ronald Kahn) why semivariance is not commonly used. First, its statistical properties are not as well known as those of the standard deviation (variance) and so it is not an ideal choice for measuring risk which should be understood by all market participants. Second, computing target semivariance for a large bond portfolio is challenging. Third, if investment returns are reasonably symmetric, then no additional information is provided by the semivariance because most definitions of downside risk are simply proportional to standard deviation or variance.

5. a. Shortfall risk is the ratio of the number of observations below the target return to the total number of observations. When the target return is zero, shortfall risk is referred to as the risk of loss.

   b. One problem with shortfall risk as a risk measure is that the magnitude of the losses below the target return is ignored. Also, shortfall risk suffers from the same problems as the semivariance measure: "ambiguity, poor statistical understanding, difficulty of forecasting" (as described by Ronald Kahn).

6. a. To compute the portfolio's standard deviation, the variance and covariance for each pair of bonds must be estimated. There are two major problems in obtaining these estimates. First, as the number of bonds in the portfolio or the number of bonds considered for inclusion in the portfolio increases, the number of estimated inputs (variances and covariances) increases dramatically.

   The second problem is obtaining good estimates for the variances and covariances for each pair of bonds. Typically, historical data must be used. Time series return data for the bond market, particularly for certain types of bonds such as collateralized mortgage obligations, may not be readily available. In addition, even with time series data, the observed returns over time often have little meaning because the characteristics of the observed bond changes over time.

   b. Because of the problems with using historical data to estimate the standard deviation, bond portfolio managers have turned to multi-factor risk models. These models seek to analyze historical return data and to identify the key risk factors that explain bond returns. The risk of a bond portfolio is then measured in terms of its exposure to these risk factors.

7. The actual tracking error is 77.23 basis points as shown below:

Month in 2001	Portfolio return (%)	Benchmark SSB BIG return (%)	Active return(%)	Deviation from mean	Squared deviation
Jan	0.75	1.65	−0.90	−0.85	0.7282
Feb	0.40	0.89	−0.49	−0.44	0.1965
March	1.79	0.52	1.27	1.32	1.7336
April	−0.89	−0.47	−0.42	−0.37	0.1394
May	0.50	0.65	−0.15	−0.10	0.0107
June	0.72	0.33	0.39	0.44	0.1907
July	3.20	2.31	0.89	0.94	0.8773
Aug	1.95	1.10	0.85	0.90	0.8040
Sept	0.23	1.23	−1.00	−0.95	0.9088
Oct	1.20	2.02	−0.82	−0.77	0.5980

Month in 2001	Portfolio return (%)	Benchmark SSB BIG return (%)	Active return(%)	Deviation from mean	Squared deviation
Nov	−1.90	−1.38	−0.52	−0.47	0.2240
Dec	−0.25	−0.59	0.34	0.39	0.1495
Sum			−0.56	0.00	6.5607
Mean			−0.0467		
Variance					0.5964
Standard Deviation = Tracking error					0.7723
Tracking error (in basis points)					77.23

Notes:

Active return = Portfolio return − Benchmark Index return

Variance = (sum of the squared deviations from the mean)/11

Division by 11 which is number of observations minus 1

Tracking error = Standard deviation = square root of variance

8. One problem with using actual tracking error as a measure of future tracking error is that actual tracking error does not reflect the impact of the portfolio manager's current decisions on the future active returns. The manager can significantly alter key risk exposures of the portfolio (such as the portfolio's effective duration or sector allocations) to the extent that the actual tracking error calculated using data from prior periods would not accurately reflect the current portfolio factor risks. As a result, the actual tracking error has little predictive value and can be misleading with regard to future portfolio risks.

9. Forward looking tracking error is inappropriate for measuring historical performance because it reflects the current composition of a portfolio rather than the composition of the portfolio that resulted in the realized tracking error (called actual tracking error).

10. (a)

Bond	Market value	Percent	Duration	Percent × duration
1	10,000,000	29.41176%	7.2	2.1176
2	8,000,000	23.52941%	6.1	1.4353
3	4,000,000	11.76471%	1.1	0.1294
4	12,000,000	35.29412%	4.8	1.6941
Total	34,000,000	100.00000%		5.3765

Portfolio duration = 5.4

b. The contribution of bond 1 to portfolio duration is:

$$\frac{\text{market value of bond 1}}{\text{market value of portfolio}} \times \text{duration of bond 1} = \frac{\$10 \text{ million}}{\$34 \text{ million}} \times 7.2 = 2.1176$$

11. a. Spread duration is the risk exposure of a bond or bond portfolio to changes in the spread between non-Treasury and Treasury rates.

   b. Different spread duration measures depend on the measure of spread used. Specifically, one can measure spread in terms of nominal spread, zero volatility spread, or option-adjusted spread.

   c. This discrepancy can occur if the vendor of the analytical system and the dealer use different definitions of the spread. Without specifying the spread measure used, the spread duration measure is ambiguous and the reported values can be different.

12. a. Index effective duration $= 0.38(4.6) + 0.07(4.10) + 0.31(3.20) + 0.20(5.10) + 0.04$
    $(2.70) = 4.16$

    b. Index spread duration $= 0.38(0) + 0.07(3.90) + 0.31(6.10) + 0.20(5.40) + 0.04$
    $(5.80) = 3.48$

13. a. Portfolio effective duration $= 0.15(4.6) + 0.07(4.10) + 0.35(3.20) + 0.38(5.10) +$
    $0.05(2.70) = 4.17$

    b. Portfolio spread duration $= 0.15(0) + 0.07(3.90) + 0.35(6.10) + 0.38(5.40) + 0.05$
    $(5.80) = 4.75$

    c. A comparison of the risk exposure of the portfolio and the bond market index is
    provided below:

	Portfolio	Bond market index
Effective duration	4.17	4.16
Spread duration	4.75	3.48

   Both the portfolio and the bond market index have the same exposure to a small parallel
   shift in interest rates. The portfolio has greater exposure to changes in the spread as
   evidenced by its higher spread duration. The difference in the spread durations is 1.27.
   So, if spreads, on average, change by 50 basis points, for example, then the portfolio's
   value will change by approximately 0.64% more than the bond market index.

   d. A comparison of the risk exposure of the portfolio and the bond market index is
   provided below:

	Portfolio	Bond market index
Effective duration	3.76	4.16
Spread duration	4.75	3.48

   This portfolio has lower duration, and hence less exposure to a small parallel shift in
   Treasury rates than the bond market index. However, the portfolio still has greater
   exposure to changes in spread than the bond market index.

14. a. Reporting the differences between the percentage of holdings in the portfolio and the
    benchmark fails to capture the impact of these differences on the effective duration of
    the portfolio. To address this, Mr. Leone can calculate the contribution of each sector
    to effective duration. This is computed by multiplying the weight of the sector times
    the duration of the sector.

    b.

	Benchmark			Portfolio			Difference in portfolio vs. benchmark	
	% of bench.	Effective duration	Contr. to eff. duration	% of port.	Effective duration	Contr. to eff. duration	% of Holdings	Contr. to eff. duration
Governments	41.50	5.36	2.22	41.50	4.04	1.68	0.00	−0.55
Corporates	22.70	5.60	1.27	15.70	7.64	1.20	−7.00	−0.07
Mortgages	33.90	3.24	1.10	41.20	3.01	1.24	7.30	0.14
Total Fixed Rate ABS	1.90	2.68	0.05	1.60	2.54	0.04	−0.30	−0.01
U.S. Broad Market Index	100.00	4.64	4.64	100.00	4.16	4.16	0.00	−0.49

c. Based on the table in part (b), the following should be included in the memo:

- The interest rate risk exposure of the portfolio as measured by effective duration is less than that of the benchmark. So, for example, a 100 basis point parallel change in interest rates will change the portfolio's value by approximately 4.16% while the benchmark's value will change by approximately 4.64%.
- The difference in interest rate exposure between the portfolio and the benchmark is −0.49 which is primarily due to the difference in exposure to the government sector (contribution to effective duration) of −0.55. Thus, despite the fact that the portfolio and the benchmark have the same allocation to the government sector, this sector is the primary driver of the difference in interest rate risk exposure.
- Despite the significant difference in exposure to the corporate sector, this sector does not have a significant impact on interest rate risk.

d. The answer to the two questions are as follows:

Part i. Sector allocation and interest rate risk as measured by effective duration are the only two risks addressed. While the risks described are important, this is not a complete description of the major risks.

Part ii. The other risks that should be identified are differences in the risk profile with respect to: yield curve risk, spread risk, quality/credit risk, call and prepayment risk (particularly prepayment risk because of the overweight of the mortgage sector), and convexity risk (again, particularly with the overweight of the mortgage sector).

e. The completed table is:

	Benchmark			Portfolio			Difference in portfolio vs. benchmark	
	% of bench.	Effective duration	Contr. to eff. duration	% of port.	Effective duration	Contr. to eff. duration	% of holdings	Contr. to eff. duration
Governments								
U.S. Treasury	26.70	5.90	1.58	8.60	2.20	0.19	−18.10	−1.39
U.S. Agency	11.70	4.27	0.50	21.00	4.20	0.88	9.30	0.38
Foreign Govt/Supra	3.10	4.76	0.15	11.90	5.10	0.61	8.80	0.46
Total Governments	41.50	5.36	2.22	41.50	4.04	1.68	0.00	−0.54
Corporates								
Financial	8.40	4.60	0.39	5.20	5.10	0.27	−3.20	−0.12
Industrial	12.80	6.29	0.81	9.40	9.30	0.87	−3.40	0.07
Utility	1.50	5.36	0.08	1.10	5.40	0.06	−0.40	−0.02
Total Corporates	22.70	5.60	1.27	15.70	7.64	1.20	−7.00	−0.07
Mortgages								
FH&FN 30 Yr	21.20	3.18	0.67	12.20	3.10	0.38	−9.00	−0.30
GN 30 Yr	7.20	3.73	0.27	3.00	3.80	0.11	−4.20	−0.15
All 15 Yr	5.50	2.82	0.16	26.00	2.88	0.75	20.50	0.59
Total Mortgages	33.90	3.24	1.10	41.20	3.01	1.24	7.30	0.14
Total Fixed Rate ABS	1.90	2.68	0.05	1.60	2.54	0.04	−0.30	−0.01
U.S. Broad Market Index	100.00	4.64	4.64	100.00	4.16	4.16	0.00	−0.48

f. Based on further analysis of the index, the memo should include the following points

- As noted earlier, the major reason for the interest rate risk difference between the portfolio and the benchmark is the difference in contribution to effective duration in the government sector. While the holding in the portfolio for this sector is the same as the weight in the index, the contribution to effective duration results in a major reduction in the portfolio's effective duration relative to the benchmark's effective duration. With the more detailed sector analysis, we can say that this is due to a large decline in the contribution to effective duration in U.S. Treasuries and offset somewhat by an increase in effective duration due to an increase in exposure to U.S. Agency and Foreign government/supranationals.

- There is sector risk within the corporate and mortgage sectors. Corporates have less exposure to the financial sector and to the industrial sector. Despite the substantial underweights, the differential contribution to effective duration for the financial and industrial sectors is small.
- The mortgage sector in general is overweighted relative to the benchmark, due to the overweight in the 15-year products. That is, within the mortgage sector, 15-year products are overweighted relative to 30-year products. The allocation to the 15-year product contributes significantly to the differential in effective duration between the portfolio and the benchmark.
- The greater allocation to the mortgage sector requires a further investigation as to the impact of prepayment risk relative to the benchmark.

g. The additional information will be used to assess the impact of prepayment risk on the convexity of the portfolio relative to that of the benchmark. In general, it is known that mortgage passthrough securities, depending on their coupon rate, may expose the investor to negative convexity—the risk that, when interest rates fall, the gain is less than the loss that would be realized if interest rates increase. An analysis of the convexity of the mortgage sector in the benchmark and in the portfolio will quantify the convexity attributes.

h. The information on effective convexity indicates that the portfolio has less negative convexity than the benchmark, despite an overweighting of the mortgage sector. The reason for this can be determined from the allocation within the mortgage sector. The mortgage sector of the benchmark is exposed to negative convexity, which is approximately the same for the two 30-year product sectors but less for the 15-year products. Not only did the manager reduce exposure to the 30-year products, thereby reducing the negative convexity of the portfolio relative to the benchmark, but the manager also invested in 30-year products that exhibit less negative convexity than the products comprising the benchmark. The manager probably invested in low coupon 30-year passthrough securities which exhibit less negative convexity. In addition, the manager overweighted 15-year products (which have less negative convexity), and, the particular 15-year products in the portfolio have less negative convexity than the products in the benchmark.

i. In terms of interest rate risk, the portfolio is positioned well relative to the benchmark, for a rise in interest rates. The effective duration of the portfolio is lower. So, for example, for a 200 basis point rise in interest rates, the portfolio will decline in value by approximately 8.32% (4.16 × 2%) while the benchmark will decline by about 9.28%. Furthermore, recall that convexity is the adjustment to the duration estimate. The larger the negative convexity, the greater the percentage decline in value for a given change in interest rates. Hence, the lower negative convexity of the portfolio relative to the benchmark indicates better relative performance of the portfolio in a rising interest rate environment.

15. For securities that are callable or putable, the borrower has an option that can adversely impact the performance of a portfolio or a benchmark index. The risk associated with this adverse performance is referred to as optionality risk.

16. a. It is true that delta is a measure used in the options area. However, it is not only a measure to approximate the sensitivity of an option to a change in price (in the case of a stock option or a stock index option and effectively interest rate changes for options on bonds), but also for estimating the sensitivity of bonds with embedded options such as callable and putable corporate and agency debentures to changes in interest rates. Consequently, delta is a measure that attempts to quantify the optionality risk of a portfolio or a benchmark index.

    b. If the delta of the portfolio is greater than that of the benchmark index, then the optionality risk of the portfolio is greater than that of the benchmark index.

    c. The prepayment sensitivity measure seeks to quantify the prepayment risk of a portfolio or a benchmark index. Specifically, it a measure of how the portfolio's value changes when expected prepayments change. The report states "Prepayment sensitivity to a 1% increase in prepayments." This means that, if the prepayment rate for all the MBS in the portfolio increases by 1%, then the prepayment sensitivity measure indicates the approximate percentage change in the value of the portfolio. For Mr. Swensen's portfolio, for example, a 1% increase in prepayments will decrease the value of the portfolio by 1.15%. The benchmark index is less sensitive to changes in prepayments.

    d. Some MBS increase in value when prepayments increase (MBS trading at a discount and principal only mortgage strips) and some MBS decrease in value when prepayments increase (MBS trading at a premium and interest only mortgage strips). Those MBS that increase in value have a positive prepayment sensitivity measure and those MBS that decrease in value have a negative prepayment sensitivity measure.

17. An assessment of the risk profile of a portfolio relative to a benchmark index requires an analysis of the allocation to the MBS subsectors, referred to as MBS sector risk, because different MBS subsectors have different exposure to prepayment risk. Specifically, the sensitivity of an MBS to prepayments (and therefore to changes in interest rates) depends on the coupon sector. All other factors held constant (specifically, the degree of seasoning), low coupon MBS are less sensitive to changes in prepayments than high coupon MBS.

18. Predicted tracking error is decomposed into systematic risk and non-systematic risk.

19. Residual risk is the tracking error that remains after accounting for systematic risk.

20. Tracking error is measured in terms of standard deviations. Individual components of tracking error, such as tracking error due to systematic risk and non-systematic risk, cannot be added. Rather, the variances (which are the squared values of the tracking errors) can be added. Given the components of tracking error, the tracking error for the portfolio is the square root of the sum of the variances. (The implicit assumption in this calculation is that the correlation between the components of the tracking error is zero.) So, since systematic and non-systematic tracking error components are 90 and 30 basis points respectively, the predicted tracking error is:

$$[90^2 + 30^2]^{0.5} = (9,000)^{0.5} = 94.87$$

this is consistent with the reported tracking error.

21. Term structure risk is the exposure of a portfolio to the general level of interest rates in terms of exposure to a parallel shift in the yield curve and to a nonparallel shift in the yield curve.

22. a. The predicted tracking error due to non-term structure risk is found as follows:

Predicted tracking due to	Predicted tracking error	Square (variance)
sector risk	40	1,600
quality risk	15	225
optionality risk	3	9
coupon risk	2	4
MBS sector risk	12	144
MBS volatility risk	9	81
MBS prepayment risk	14	196
Variance		2,259

The square root of the variance is 47.53, which is the predicted tracking error due to non-term structure risk.

b. Predicted tracking error for MBS risk is found as follows:

Predicted tracking due to	Predicted tracking error	Square (variance)
MBS sector risk	12	144
MBS volatility risk	9	81
MBS prepayment risk	14	196
Variance		421

The square root of the variance is 20.52, which is the predicted tracking error due to MBS risk.

c. The tracking error due to systematic risk is

$$[100^2 + 47.53^2]^{0.5} = (1,2259.1)^{0.5} = 110.72 \text{ basis points}$$

23. a. Non-systematic risk is divided into those risks that are issuer specific and those that are issue specific.

b. Non-systematic risk is due to exposure to specific issues and issuers that is greater than the benchmark index.

CHAPTER 18

MANAGING FUNDS AGAINST A BOND MARKET INDEX

SOLUTIONS

1. The major difference is the degree to which the manager mismatches the risk factors in the portfolio relative to the benchmark index. As the mismatch increases, we move from indexing to active management. There is no duration mismatch in indexing and enhanced indexing whereas there can be intended mismatches in active management.

2. In an indexing and enhanced indexing strategy tracking error is very small. When a manager pursues a strategy of minor risk factor mismatches versus the index, there will be small tracking error and therefore this strategy is viewed as an enhanced indexing strategy.

3. a. Unlike equities, it is difficult to purchase all of the bonds in an index. The number of issues in a bond index far exceeds the number of equities in the S&P 500. This adds to the transaction costs associated with constructing an indexed portfolio. Moreover, some issues are difficult to obtain and trade infrequently.

   b. The index selected should reflect the liability structure of the fund. In particular, as discussed in Chapter 16, a starting point is an index with a duration that matches the duration of the liabilities so as to minimize the impact of changes in interest rates on the fund's economic surplus. The duration of the Lehman Aggregate Bond Index may not match the duration of the liabilities and therefore should not be used, even though that index is the benchmark for the active bond managers.

   c. Enhanced indexing differs from active management in terms of the extent of the divergence between the risk factors of the index and the risk factors of the constructed portfolio. Enhancement strategies are necessary to provide a net return equal to the index because the index does not incur expenses or transaction costs. In addition to expenses, a primary source of return shortfalls is the transaction costs associated with portfolio growth.

4. The logistical problems in implementing a pure bond indexing strategy are (1) prices for each issue used by the organization that publishes the benchmark index may not be execution prices available to the manager (i.e., prices at which the manager can transact in constructing and rebalancing a portfolio), (2) transaction costs that are not incurred by the index, (3) the large number of issues in the index makes it too costly to buy all of the issues, (4) problems unique to certain sectors in the bond market index that make replication difficult, in particular the mortgage sector with more than 80,000 agency

passthrough issues that are represented by generic issues, and (5) differences between actual reinvestment income that can be earned by the manager and the reinvestment income that is assumed to be earned on interim cash flows by the organization that constructs the index.

5. a. An inter-sector allocation strategy determines the allocation of a portfolio's funds among the major sectors of a bond market index.

   b. An intra-sector allocation strategy determines the allocation of funds among the subsectors of a major sector.

   c. Both inter- and intra-sector allocation strategies are aimed at benefitting from changes in spreads due to changes in credit spreads and spreads attributable to call and prepayment characteristics of a sector.

6. This statement is not correct. Forecasts about the direction of interest rates are also used to determine the allocation to products with call and prepayment features within subsectors of the major sectors of a benchmark index. For example, in the corporate sector, there are noncallable (bullet) bonds and callable bonds in the corporate sector. The latter subsector includes issues with low coupons relative to prevailing rates and issues with high coupons relative to prevailing rates. An expected decline in rates would call for a greater allocation to bullet and low coupon callable issues within the corporate sector. The same reasoning applies to the allocation decision within the mortgage sector.

7. Given the assumptions about the Treasury yield curve and the credit spread, the horizon yield is 6.15%. This means that the yield for this corporate bond declines over the 1-year investment horizon from 6.6% to 6.15%. The calculation of the 1-year total return is shown below.

   Step 1: Compute the total coupon payments plus reinvestment income assuming an annual reinvestment rate of 4% per year or 2% every six months. The semiannual coupon payment is $3.625. The future value is:

   $$\text{First coupon payment reinvested for six months} = \$3.625(1.02) = \$3.6975$$

   $$\text{Second coupon payment(not reinvested)} = \$3.6250$$

   $$\text{Total} = \overline{\$7.3225}$$

   Step 2: Next, compute the horizon price. The horizon yield is 6.15% (5.65% Treasury + 50 bp corporate spread). The 7.25% coupon 15-year corporate bond now has 14 years to maturity. The price of this bond, when discounted at 6.15% (a flat yield curve is assumed), is $110.2263.

   Step 3: Add the amounts in Steps 1 and 2. The total future value equals $117.5488.

   Step 4: Compute the following:

   $$\left(\frac{\$117.5488}{\$106.1301}\right)^{1/2} - 1 = 5.24\%$$

   Step 5: The total return on a bond-equivalent basis and on an effective rate basis are:

   $$2 \times 5.24\% = 10.48\%(\text{BEY})$$

   $$(1.0524)^2 - 1 = 10.76\% \text{ (effective rate basis)}$$

8. Given the assumptions about the Treasury yield curve and the decline in the credit spread, the horizon yield is 9.5%. The calculation of the 1-year total return is shown below.

Step 1: Compute the total coupon payments plus reinvestment income assuming an annual reinvestment rate of 5% per year or 2.5% every six months. The semiannual coupon payment is $5. The future value is:

First coupon payment reinvested for six month = $5(1.025) = $5.1250

Second coupon payment(not reinvested) = $5.0000

Total = $10.1250

Step 2: Next, compute the horizon price. The horizon yield is 9.5%. The 10% coupon 9-year corporate bond now has 8 years to maturity. The price of this bond, when discounted at 9.5% (a flat yield curve is assumed), is $102.7583.

Step 3: Add the amounts in Steps 1 and 2. The total future value equals $112.8833.

Step 4: Compute the following:

$$\left(\frac{\$112.8833}{\$95.7420}\right)^{1/2} - 1 = 8.58\%$$

Step 5: The total return on a bond-equivalent basis and on an effective rate basis are:

$$2 \times 8.58\% = 17.17\%(BEY)$$
$$(1.0858)^2 - 1 = 17.9\%(\text{effective rate basis})$$

9. In order to calculate total return, the value of the security at the investment horizon must be determined. A valuation model is used in this step of the total return calculation. If the valuation model is inaccurate, the estimate of the horizon price will be inaccurate and the total return will be incorrect.

10. The statement is incorrect. Total return analysis allows the analyst to change the OAS at the horizon date. However, a valuation model must be used to compute the horizon price based on the new OAS. Moreover, any yield curve shift can also be accommodated. The yield curve at the horizon date is a required input for the valuation model to compute the horizon price.

11. a. The top panel of Table A shows that the duration of the PAC barbell (4.10) is less than the duration of the 30-year FNMA 6% (4.53). Thus, if interest rates increase, a comparison of durations would lead us to conclude that the PAC barbell should outperform the collateral. The reverse is true if interest rates decrease.

b. Recall that different dealers and vendors of analytical services scale their convexity measures in different ways. The convexities in Table A—which were referred to as convexity measures earlier—are based on the scaling used by PaineWebber. Negative convexity is greater for the collateral (−1.72) than for the PAC barbell (−0.84). This means that, for large changes in interest rates, the collateral will underperform the PAC barbell.

c. The results in Table A suggest that it is only in the scenario where rates are unchanged, or the yield curve steepened, that the collateral outperformed the PAC barbell and the underperformance is slight (only 2 and 7 basis points, respectively). Thus, if a manager owns the collateral, the potential exists to enhance return by selling the collateral and purchasing the PAC barbell.

d. There are three important assumptions. First, it is assumed that the valuation model used to determine the horizon prices of the three securities (the collateral and the two PACs) does a good job of estimating price for each interest rate scenario. Second, it assumed that the OAS does not change. Third, it is assumed in the ±200 bp scenarios that the yield curve shifts in a parallel fashion.

e. The duration of the collateral is greater than the duration of the PAC barbell. Consequently, in declining interest rate scenarios, analysis of duration alone would lead one to expect that the collateral would outperform the PAC barbell. Due to the greater negative convexity of the collateral relative to the PAC barbell, this is not the case in Table A.

12. a. The total return comparison based on a 12-month investment horizon assuming a constant spread at the horizon date (i.e., a constant spread to the average life shown for the given scenario) indicates that if the rate change is between −50 basis points and +50 basis points, the 3-year nonagency MBS will outperform the 3-year HEL issue based on the underlying assumptions. Even if rates rise by 100 basis points, the nonagency MBS will outperform by 18 basis points. The nonagency MBS underperforms for a 150 basis point increase and for a decline in rates of more than 100 basis points. This is because of the fact that nonagency MBS has greater negative convexity than does the HEL issue.

b. Based on the probabilities, expected total return for the nonagency MBS (6.27%) is greater than the return for the home equity loan issue (5.94%). Therefore, the nonagency MBS is the preferred investment for an investor who agrees with these probabilities.

c. The critical assumptions are:
1. The yield curve shifts in a parallel fashion.
2. The spread to the average life is unchanged over the 12-month investment horizon.
3. The prepayment speeds are as expected.
4. The valuation model used to derive the horizon price provides accurate price forecasts.
For the probability analysis, it is assumed that the probabilities are correct.

13. If two positions have the same effective duration, then their respective percentage price changes will be equal for a small change in rates. However, if the two positions have different dollar values, the dollar price changes will not be equal. In a trade that does not attempt to benefit from changes in interest rates the objective is the neutralization of the trade against interest rate risk. Matching effective dollar durations accomplishes this for small changes in rates.

14. The market value of bond XYZ that must be purchased is computed as follows (where duration refers to effective duration):

$$\text{market value of bond XYZ} = \frac{\text{dollar duration of bond ABC}}{\text{duration of bond XYZ}/100}$$

Since:

$$\text{dollar duration of bond ABC} = \$1.2 \text{ million}$$
$$\text{duration of bond XYZ} = 7$$

then:

$$\text{market value of bond XYZ} = \frac{\$1,200,000}{7/100} = \$17,142,857.14$$

The par value of bond XYZ that must be purchased is equal to:

$$\text{par value of bond XYZ} = \frac{\text{market value of bond XYZ}}{\text{price of XYZ per \$1 of par value}}$$

Since the price of XYZ is $75 per $100 of par value, the price per $1 of par value is 0.75 and therefore:

$$\text{par value of bond XYZ} = \frac{\$17,142,857.14}{0.75} = \$22,857,142.86$$

15. Mr. Owens' response is unsatisfactory for two reasons.

    First, a portfolio manager must be concerned about risks associated with a benchmark index in addition to effective duration, spread duration, and key rate durations. In fact, the only risk Mr. Owens has focused on is term structure risk. He has ignored non-term structure risk. A multi-factor risk model provides a manager with information about exposure to these risks, as well as exposure to non-systematic risk.

    Second, a multi-factor risk model does more than simply describe the risk exposure of a benchmark index and a portfolio. It is used in constructing and rebalancing a portfolio, as well as for controlling risk relative to a benchmark index.

16. Ms. Radner should respond by indicating that scenario analysis can isolate some of the risk factors that affect portfolio return but fails to evaluate these risks simultaneously. In addition, scenario analysis does not assess how a bond swap might affect other risk factors. Moreover, substituting new bonds from the swap for bonds that will be sold results in a new tracking error which must be assessed as to its attractiveness relative to the current portfolio.

17. Altering the exposure of an actively managed portfolio to that of an enhanced indexing portfolio involves reducing the predicted tracking error to a level that is consistent with an enhanced indexing strategy. This can be accomplished using an optimizer to search for trades that would result in the greatest reduction in predicted tracking error per unit of bond swapped from the current portfolio. Mr. Lang would make their changes as soon as possible in order to reduce the predicted tracking error of the portfolio.

18. The manager can use a multi-factor risk model to create a portfolio with the desired predicted tracking error and risk exposure but constrain the optimizer to include in the portfolio the specific issues that the manager believes will be upgraded.

19. The consultant should tell the trustee that, while the three measures—Sharpe, Jensen, and Treynor—can be used to measure relative performance, none of these measures can be used to explain the reasons for inferior (or superior) performance.

20. a. The consultant should remind Trustee A that Order.com engages managers based on the likelihood that the manager will outperform the index for the reasons stated by the manager. Consequently, the performance must be evaluated relative to the skills that the manager claimed would produce the outperformance. Simply observing the difference between the manager's return and the return for the benchmark index is not sufficient to assess the skills that the manager claimed would produce superior returns. Return attribution analysis provides that information.

    b. Each manager outperformed the benchmark index after adjusting for management fees. While the Rollins Group had the largest differential over the benchmark index (102.5 basis points), the actual reason for the outperformance was inconsistent with the firm's claims. Rollins Group stated that it could identify undervalued issues and sectors. Yet, the return attribution analysis indicates that it underperformed the benchmark index by 51 basis points in selecting sectors and individual issues. This negative performance was offset by the fact that the portfolio was constructed to have a different interest rate exposure from that of the benchmark index, which lead to 106 basis points outperformance. Yet, the trustees were told that management would remain neutral relative to the benchmark index.

Consequently, the trustees should be concerned with the performance of the Rollins Group despite the superior "raw" performance relative to the other managers. The trustees should meet with the Rollins Group in order to determine whether there has been a change in the investment management style.

The M&M Company added 24 basis points using a strategy it had indicated it would use—adjusting the portfolio to have a different interest rate risk exposure compared to the benchmark index. However, this firm claimed that it could identify undervalued issues by using analytical models. Yet, with respect to the selection of individual issues, M&M underperformed the benchmark index by 11 basis points. The major portion of the return was due to sector/quality exposure that differed from that of the benchmark index; however, M&M had stated that its strategy was to remain neutral to the benchmark with respect to sector and quality. The trustees should discuss with M&M Company whether the firm has changed its investment style.

While Beta Associates had the lowest return relative to the benchmark index, it still outperformed the benchmark index after accounting for the management fee. Clearly, this firm outperformed for the reasons it had stated. The major reason for the outperformance was the selection of individual issues (44 basis points). In accomplishing this, the interest rate risk exposure was neutral to the benchmark index, consistent with the firm's claims.

21. a. Since the price per $100 par value is $95.46, this means that $500,000 par value [= $477,300/(95.46/100)] can be purchased.

b.

Assumed yield six months from now (%)	Price per $100 par value ($)	Market value ($)	Semiannual coupon payment ($)	Dollar return ($)	Annualized percent return (%)
9.00%	83.71	418,550	17,500	(41,250)	−17.3%
8.50%	87.42	437,100	17,500	(22,700)	−9.5%
8.00%	91.35	456,750	17,500	(3,050)	−1.3%
7.50%	95.54	477,700	17,500	17,900	7.5%
7.00%	100.00	500,000	17,500	40,200	16.8%
6.50%	104.75	523,750	17,500	63,950	26.8%
6.00%	109.80	549,000	17,500	89,200	37.4%

We illustrate here one of the calculations. Consider the 8% horizon yield. The corresponding horizon price is 91.35. So, for $500,000 in par value, the value of the bonds equals $456,750 [=$500,000 (91.35/100)].

The coupon interest is $17,500 (= $500,000 multiplied by the semiannual coupon rate of 3.5%). The total proceeds equals the value of the bonds ($456,750) plus the coupon interest ($17,500) which equals $474,250.

The dollar return is found by subtracting the initial investment of $477,300. The dollar return is then −$3,050. The semiannual rate of return is found by dividing the dollar return of −$3,050 by the initial investment giving −0.00639. Doubling this return gives an annual return of −0.01278 or −1.3% (rounded).

c.

Assumed yield six months from now (%)	Price per $100 par value ($)	Market value per $1 million par value ($)	Semiannual coupon payment ($)	Dollar return ($)	Annualized percent return (%)
9.00%	83.71	837,100	35,000	(108,274)	−45.4%
8.50%	87.42	874,200	35,000	(71,174)	−29.8%
8.00%	91.35	913,500	35,000	(31,874)	−13.4%
7.50%	95.54	955,400	35,000	10,026	4.2%
7.00%	100.00	1,000,000	35,000	54,626	22.9%
6.50%	104.75	1,047,500	35,000	102,126	42.8%
6.00%	109.80	1,098,000	35,000	152,626	64.0%

Once again, let's illustrate the 8% horizon yield scenario. There is now $1 million of par value invested. The value of the position is $913,500. The semiannual dollar coupon interest is $35,000 (= 3.5% semiannual coupon rate times the $1 million of par value). The total proceeds equals the dollar return (the value of the bonds plus the dollar coupon interest) reduced by the cost of borrowing $477,300. Since the borrowing rate is assumed to be 10.8%, the borrowing cost is $477,300 multiplied by 5.4%. The interest cost is therefore $25,774.20. This is the same interest cost for each scenario. The total dollar proceeds after the interest cost is then −$31,874. ($913,500 market value of position + $35,000 semiannual coupon interest—$25,774 interest cost on loan—$477,300 repayment of loan—$477,300 equity investment). Dividing by the equity investment of $477,300 and then multiplying by 2 gives an annual return of −13.4%.

d. The analysis below is based on a par value of $2,500,000.

Assumed yield six months from now (%)	Price per $100 par value ($)	Market value per $2.5 million par value ($)	Semiannual coupon payment ($)	Dollar return ($)	Annualized percent return (%)
9.00%	83.71	2,092,750	87,500	(309,347)	−129.6%
8.50%	87.42	2,185,500	87,500	(216,597)	−90.8%
8.00%	91.35	2,283,750	87,500	(118,347)	−49.6%
7.50%	95.54	2,388,500	87,500	(13,597)	−5.7%
7.00%	100.00	2,500,000	87,500	97,903	41.0%
6.50%	104.75	2,618,750	87,500	216,653	90.8%
6.00%	109.80	2,745,000	87,500	342,903	143.7%

e. The annual return for each case is reported below.

Horizon yield	No borrowed funds	Borrowed 477,300	Borrowed 1,909,200
9.00%	−17.3%	−45.4%	−129.6%
8.50%	−9.5%	−29.8%	−90.8%
8.00%	−1.3%	−13.4%	−49.6%
7.50%	7.5%	4.2%	−5.7%
7.00%	16.8%	22.9%	41.0%
6.50%	26.8%	42.8%	90.8%
6.00%	37.4%	64.0%	143.7%

The results clearly indicate that borrowing is advantageous in that it offers upside return greater than the return in the unleveraged case. The advantage increases as more is borrowed. However the loss increases as more leverage is used. This is the tradeoff when using leverage.

22. A repo is a transaction where a party borrows funds by using a security as collateral. A reverse repo is a transaction where a party lends funds with the loan collateralized by a security. Consequently, the borrower refers to the transaction as a repo and the lender refers to the transaction as a reverse repo.

23. A repurchase agreement can be used to lend funds (i.e., a high quality short-term investment or money market instrument) or as a financing vehicle (i.e., to borrow funds). The provision is unclear because, as stated, it suggests that the manager of the funds is permitted to use a repurchase agreement as either a short-term investment or a vehicle for financing. This may or may not have been the intent of the trustees of the pension fund.

24. When a repurchase agreement is used to create leverage (i.e., when it is used as a financing vehicle), it is risky because of the risk associated with leverage. In contrast, when it is used as an investment on a short-term basis, if properly structured, it is a high quality money market instrument.

25. a. The dollar interest cost is:

$$\text{dollar interest} = \text{amount borrowed} \times \text{repo rate} \times \text{repo term}/360$$

Since 97% of the market value can be borrowed:

$$\text{amount borrowed} = \$3,000,000 \times 0.97 = \$2,910,000$$

The appropriate repo rate is 7% and the term is one day. Therefore:

$$\text{dollar interest} = \$2,910,000 \times 0.07 \times 1/360 = \$565.83$$

b. Since this is a 30 day repo, the 30-day term repo rate of 7.3% is used. The dollar interest cost is:

$$\text{dollar interest} = \$2,910,000 \times 0.073 \times 30/360 = \$17,702.50$$

26. The Treasury security is not likely to be rich. One reason it offers a yield lower than that of similar maturity or similar duration Treasury securities is its greater liquidity since it is an on-the-run issue. However, the major reason it trades at a yield considerably less than that of otherwise comparable Treasury issues is that it is probably on special—that is, it is "hot" collateral. As a result, the issue offers attractive financing, and market participants are willing to pay more for this issue, thereby driving down its yield.

27. Because the security is on special, dealers are willing to offer cheaper financing in order to obtain the use of the collateral. Thus, for a given term for the repo, the repo rate will be less for this security than for generic collateral.

28. a. The lender's credit risk derives from the possibility that the value of the collateral declines and the borrower defaults. As a result, the lender then owns the collateral which has a market value less than the amount lent. Also, if the borrower holds the collateral, there is the risk that the collateral might be fraudulently used in another borrowing and/or the collateral might be sold without the lender's knowledge.

b. In a hold-in-custody repo, the borrower retains custody of the collateral. So, the risk derives from the possibility that the collateral will be fraudulently used in another borrowing and/or the collateral might be sold without the lender's knowledge.

c. A lender in a repo can protect itself in several ways. First, it can remove the risk of the collateral disappearing by using a tri-party repo. Second, the loan is for an amount less than the market value of the collateral. This difference is the repo margin or "haircut." Finally, the collateral is marked to market requiring that, if the margin declines below a specified amount, the borrower must either provide additional cash or transfer acceptable securities to make up a margin deficit.

29. a. Since the duration of the $200 million investment is 4, the portfolio's value will change by approximately $8 million for a 100 basis point change in rates. The duration of 5 for the $50 million of bonds purchased via a reverse repurchase agreement means that the value will change by approximately $2.5 million for a 100 basis point change in rates. Consequently, the portfolio's value will change by approximately $10.5 million ($8 million plus $2.5 million) for a 100 basis point change in rates. The change in value of the 1-month liability (i.e., the reverse repo) for a 100 basis point change in rates is zero. Therefore, we have

$$
\begin{array}{r}
\text{dollar duration of the bonds} = \$10.5 \text{ million} \\
- \text{dollar duration of the liabilities} = \$0 \\
\hline
\text{total change in portfolio value} = \$10.5 \text{ million}
\end{array}
$$

Relating the $10.5 million to the client's $200 million investment (not the $250 million invested by Mr. Reed) we find that the portfolio's value changes by 5.25% for a 100 basis point change in rates. Hence, the duration is 5.25.

b. Since the computed duration of the portfolio is 5.25, Mr. Reed has exceeded the maximum duration of 5 set forth in the investment guidelines.

CHAPTER 19

PORTFOLIO IMMUNIZATION AND CASH FLOW MATCHING

SOLUTIONS

1. For a coupon bond, the return that will be realized by holding it until the maturity date is unknown. This is because there is reinvestment risk. Therefore, the return over the investment horizon (which is equal to the maturity of the bond) is unknown.

2. The objective of a bond immunization strategy is to lock in a return irrespective of how interest rates change over the investment horizon.

3. a. The duration of this portfolio is greater than the investment horizon. Consequently, at the end of the investment horizon, the investor is forced to liquidate the issues in the portfolio that have not matured. The return on the portfolio over the investment horizon will depend on the value of the issues in the portfolio at the horizon date and the portfolio is therefore not immunized.

    b. Since the return depends on the value of the issues in the portfolio at the end of the horizon date, a rise in rates will reduce the value of these issues. The increase in reinvestment income generated for the portfolio by the rise in interest rates will partially offset the capital loss.

    c. If the duration of the portfolio is less than the investment horizon, this means that any bonds maturing prior to the investment horizon must be reinvested. The return on the portfolio will depend on the reinvestment rate and therefore reinvestment income. Consequently, the portfolio is not immunized because it depends on the reinvestment income.

    d. For a portfolio whose duration is less than the investment horizon, a rise in interest rates over the investment horizon will produce higher reinvestment income for both reinvested coupon payments and principal proceeds from maturing issues. Thus, a rise in interest rates will have a favorable impact on the portfolio's return.

4. The basic principle is to lock in a rate (or target value) by offsetting changes in reinvestment income with changes in market value when interest rates change. So, a rise in interest rates will decrease the market value of the bonds in the portfolio at the end of the investment horizon but will increase reinvestment income. A decline in interest rates will increase the market value of the bonds in the portfolio at the end of the investment horizon but will decrease reinvestment income. The objective is to select bonds where the offset is such that a rate can be locked in. This may be

accomplished for a parallel shift in the yield curve by matching the portfolio's duration to the investment horizon (i.e., duration of the liability).

5. The manager is incorrect in his assessment of the strategy as a buy-and-hold strategy. The portfolio must be periodically rebalanced. This occurs because the portfolio's duration will change over time and the change in interest rates. The change in the portfolio's duration will not be such that the new duration is equal to the remaining time to the investment horizon. Hence, it will be necessary to rebalance the portfolio periodically to adjust the portfolio's duration to equal the remaining time to the investment horizon.

    Moreover, the proceeds from maturing bonds, issues that have been called, and coupon income must be reinvested. The quality of the issues must also be monitored.

6. While it is true that the duration of the portfolio changes every day due to the passage of time and the change in interest rates, rebalancing the portfolio each day or each week would increase transaction costs. This could easily reduce the return over the investment horizon and discourage the use of such a strategy. In practice, however, rebalancing the portfolio to adjust its duration is done judiciously recognizing the trade-off between being matched to the remaining investment horizon and the higher transaction costs associated with rebalancing.

7. The statement is incorrect. There are in fact two other risks. First, even if the duration of the portfolio is matched to the duration of the liability, the portfolio is still exposed to a nonparallel shift in the yield curve. This risk is commonly referred to as immunization risk. Moreover, if there are callable securities in the portfolio, the portfolio is exposed to call risk.

8. While it is true that an investor can immunize a portfolio by buying zero-coupon bonds that mature on the horizon date, the problem is that the return that can be locked in may not be adequate. When a manager seeks to immunize a portfolio for a client, the manager is hoping to add value beyond what can be obtained by simply purchasing zero-coupon bonds that matures at the horizon date.

9. A cash flow matched strategy has less exposure to reinvestment risk and yield curve risk than a portfolio constructed using a multiperiod immunization strategy. Hence, a cash flow matched strategy has less risk of not satisfying the liabilities. However, typically it is initially more costly to set up a cash flow matched portfolio relative to a multiperiod immunized portfolio.

10. A condition for multiperiod immunization is not that the duration must match the longest maturity of the liability, but rather that the duration of the portfolio must match the duration of the liabilities. As long as a portfolio can be created with an average duration equal to the duration of the liabilities, then the manager can implement a multiperiod immunization strategy.

11. a. First, liabilities just like the cash flows of assets, should not be valued using a single interest rate. The interest rate should be unique to the time period when the liability must be paid. The appropriate rate for each liability is an appropriate spot rate. Second, the interest rate determined by an actuary is arbitrarily determined. It is not a market-determined rate.

    b. The argument in factor of using Treasury spot rates is twofold. First, spot rates not a single interest rate should be used. The spot rate is unique for each liability. Second, the present value when discounted at the Treasury spot rates effectively determines how much it would cost a plan sponsor to pay off the liabilities to which it has committed without incurring credit risk.

   c. There are at least three problems. First, as corporate spreads in the market increase (i.e., corporate bonds become riskier), the value of the liabilities decreases because a higher discount rate decreases the liabilities' present value (assuming the Treasury yield does not decline). Second, the yields on a corporate bond index yield curve are not spot rates and it is the spot rates that should be used to value liabilities (as well as assets). Finally, since there is credit risk there is risk that the liabilities will not be satisfied.

12. a. The safety net return is the minimum target return of 10%.

   b. The cushion spread is the difference between the immunized return of 12% and the safety net return of 10%. So the cushion spread is 200 basis points.

   c. Because the initial portfolio value is $50 million, the minimum target value at the end of 4 years, based on semiannual compounding, is $73,872,772 (= $50,000,000 $(1.05)^8$). (Note that the minimum target value is found by compounding at one half of the safety net return of 10%.)

   d. The rate of return at the time is 12% (the immunized rate of return), so the assets required at this time to achieve the minimum target value of $73,872,772 is the present value of $73,872,772 discounted at 12% on a semiannual basis. The required assets are therefore $46,348,691 (= $73,872,772/$(1.06)^8$).

   e. Since the initial value of the portfolio is $50 million and the assets required to achieve the minimum target value of $73,872,772 is $46,348,691, the initial dollar safety margin is $3,651,309 ($50,000,000 − $46,348,691).

   f. The cushion spread would be 100 basis points (12% − 11%). The minimum target value is $76,734,326 (= $50,000,000 $(1.055)^8$). The required assets to achieve $76,734,326 given an immunized rate of 12% is $48,144,065 (= $76,734,326/$(1.06)^8$). Therefore, the initial 100 basis points cushion spread translates into an initial dollar safety margin of $1,855,935 (= $50,000,000 − $48,144,065).

   g. The higher the minimum return specified by the client, the lower the initial dollar safety margin. This can be seen by comparing the initial dollar safety margin assuming a minimum return of 10% versus 11%. In part (e), the initial safety margin was found to be $3,651,309 when the minimum return is 10%. It is only $1,855,935 if the minimum return is 11% (part (f)).

   h. Six months from now, the bond is a 12% coupon 19.5-year bond. If market rates for this issue decline to 9%, the market value of the bonds would rise from par to 127.34 per $100 of par value. Consequently, the price of $50 million of these bonds would rise to $63,672,242. Coupon interest is $3 million (0.50 × 0.12 × $50 million). Thus the portfolio value at the end of six months is $66,672,242.

   i. The required assets are found by computing the present value of the minimum target value at 9% for 3.5 years. (The initial horizon is 4 years and six months later the remaining horizon is 3.5 years.) The required dollar amount is $54,283,815 (= $73,872,772/$(1.045)^7$).

   j. Since the portfolio value of $66.67 million is greater than the required assets of $54,283,815, the management firm can continue to manage the portfolio actively. The dollar safety margin is now $12,388,427 ($66,672,242 − $54,283,815).

   k. The market value of the bond would decline to $42,615,776. The portfolio value would then equal $45,615,776 (the market value of the bonds plus $3 million of coupon interest).

l. The required assets to achieve the minimum target value of $73,872,772 at the current interest rate (14.26%) would be $45,614,893 (= $73,872,772/(1.0713)^7$).

m. The required dollar amount is approximately equal to the portfolio value (that is, the dollar safety margin is almost zero). Thus the management firm would be required to immunize the portfolio in order to try to achieve the minimum target value (safety net return) over the investment horizon.

CHAPTER 20

RELATIVE-VALUE METHODOLOGIES FOR GLOBAL CREDIT BOND PORTFOLIO MANAGEMENT

SOLUTIONS

Note: Many of the questions are conceptual in nature. The solutions offered are one interpretation, and there may be other valid views

1. Relative value refers to ranking credit sectors, bond structures, issuers, and issues in terms of their expected performance over some future time period.
2. a. The dominant structure in the investment-grade credit market is the bullet structure with an intermediate maturity.
   b. There are three strategic portfolio implications of the bullet structure with an intermediate maturity:
      1. The dominance of bullet structures creates a scarcity value for structures with embedded call and put features, resulting in premium price for bonds with embedded call options. This "scarcity value" should be considered by managers in relative-value analysis of credit bonds.
      2. Because long-dated maturities have declined as a percentage of outstanding credit debt, there is a lower effective duration of all outstanding credit debt and, as a result, a reduction in the aggregate sensitivity to interest-rate risk.
      3. There will be increased use of credit derivatives, whether on a stand-alone basis or embedded in structured notes, so that investors and issuers can gain exposure to the structures they desire.
   c. High-yield issuers will continue to issue callable bond structures in order to have the opportunity to refinance at a lower credit spread should credit quality improve.
3. a. Yield curve placement is simply the positioning of a portfolio with respect to duration and yield curve risk. Trades involving yield curve placement are referred to as curve adjustment trades in the chapter. Sector and quality allocations refer to allocations based on relative value analysis of the different bond market sectors and quality sectors. Security selection involves the purchase or avoidance of individual issues based on some relative value basis.

b. For a manager who is evaluated relative to some bond index, the deviation of the portfolio from the benchmark in terms of yield curve exposure, sector exposure, quality exposure, and exposure to individual issues is the appropriate way to measure risk. The methodology for this is illustrated in Chapter 18.

4. a. Scarcity value means that an issue will trade at a premium price due to a lack of supply (relative to demand) for that issue. This is the same as saying that the issue will trade at a narrower spread. If investors want exposure to a first-time issuer, the spread can be narrower than otherwise comparable issuers.

   b. Analytical models for valuing bonds with embedded put options assume the issuer will fulfill the obligation to repurchase an issue if the bondholder exercises the put option. For high-yield issuers, there is the credit risk associated with the potential inability to satisfy the put obligation. Thus for high-yield issuers, the credit risk may override the value for a putable issue derived from a valuation model.

5. In general, the top-down approach involves beginning with a macro-economic outlook and making allocation decisions to sectors based on that outlook. With respect to credit in emerging markets, the top-down approach begins with the assessment of the economic outlook for emerging market countries and then basing the allocation of funds across emerging market credit issuers in different countries on that macroeconomic outlook. This is what Mr. Taylor means by "sovereign plus." The bottom-up approach focuses on the selection of corporate issuers in emerging market countries that are expected to outperform U.S. credit issuers. This is what Mr. Taylor means by "U.S. credits-plus."

6. a. Historical relations help a portfolio manager identify opportunities when current spreads are out of line and relative-value opportunities may be available. Liquidity considerations affect spreads and the ability to trade. Market segmentation means factors affecting supply and demand within sectors of the bond market due to impediments or restrictions on investors from reallocating funds across those bond sectors.

   b. Market segmentation may create relative value opportunities when spreads get out of line due to obstructions that prevent or impede investors from allocating funds to certain sectors due to regulatory constraints and asset/liability constraints. Market segmentation may affect the supply of bonds in a sector for the same reasons. In pursuit of the optimal timing to move into or out of a sector (industry category, maturity neighborhood, or structure) or individual issuer, historical analysis of spreads, based on mean-reversion analysis can help identify when spreads might revert to some "normal" equilibrium.

7. a. Spread curves show the relationship between spreads and maturity. They differ by issuer or sector in terms of the amount of the spread and the slope of the spread curve.

   b. Forward rates are derived from spot rates using arbitrage arguments. A forward spread, or an implied forward spread, can be derived in the same way. Also, forward rates were explained as basically hedgeable or breakeven rates—rates that will make an investor indifferent between two alternatives. For example, for default-free instruments a 2-year forward rate 3 years from now is a rate that will make an investor indifferent between investing in a 5-year zero-coupon default-free instrument or investing in a 3-year zero-coupon default-free instrument and reinvesting the proceeds for two more years after the 3-year instrument matures.

A forward spread can be interpreted in the same way. For example, a 2-year forward spread 3 years from now is the credit spread that will make an investor indifferent to investing in a 5-year zero-coupon instrument of an issuer or investing in a 3-year zero-coupon instrument of the same issuer and reinvesting the proceeds from the maturing instrument in a 2-year zero-coupon instrument of the same issuer.

The forward spread is a breakeven spread because it is the spread that would make the investor indifferent between two alternative investments with different maturities over a given investment horizon.

c. Because a forward spread is one that will make an investor indifferent between two alternatives, a manager must compare his or her expectations relative to the forward spread. Relative-value analysis involves making this comparison between expected spread and what is built into market prices (i.e., forward spread).

8. It was emphasized that yield measures are poor indicators of total return realized by holding a security to maturity or over some investment horizon. Thus, an asset manager does not know what a yield pick up of, say, 20 basis point means for subsequent total return. A bond manager can pickup yield on a trade (holding credit quality constant), but on a relative value basis underperform an alternative issue with a lower yield over the manager's investment horizon.

An example of this would be if at the beginning of the month, a portfolio manager sold the 5-year Ford issue at a spread of 140 basis points and purchased the 5-year General Motors issue at a spread of 150 basis points, for a yield pickup of 10 basis points. If the spread on the Ford issue continued to tighten throughout the month, while the General Motors issue's spread remained constant, the Ford issue would outperform the General Motors issue on a total return basis.

9. The reason suggested as to why heavy supply of new investment-grade credit issues will help spreads contract and enhance returns is that new primary bond valuations validate and enhance secondary valuations. In contrast, when new issuance declines sharply, secondary traders lose confirmation from the primary market and tend to require higher spreads on their bid offers.

10. a. The crossover sector refers to the sector with issuers whose ratings are between Ba2/BB and Baa3/BBB—by a major rating agency. These issuers are on the border between investment grade and high yield.

    b. A manager can purchase a below-investment grade issue which he believes will be upgraded to investment grade. If the manager is correct, then the issue will outperform due to spread narrowing resulting from the upgrade and also from increased liquidity as it becomes available to a broader class of investors.

11. A portfolio manager would consider implementing a credit-defense trade when they become increasingly concerned about geopolitical risk, the general economy, sector risk, or specific-issuer risk which could lead to widening credit spreads.

12. The motivation is to increase portfolio liquidity.

13. a. The European credit market has been consistently homogeneous having mostly high quality (rated Aa3/AA– and above) and intermediate maturity issues. So swap spreads were a good proxy for credit spreads. Because of the homogeneous character of the credit market in Europe, the swaps framework allows managers as well as issuers to more easily compare securities across fixed- and floating-rate markets. Moreover, in Europe, financial institutions such as commercial banks have been

much more willing to use swap methodology to capture value discrepancies between the fixed- and floating-rate markets.

    b. U.S. managers have embraced swap spreads for the MBS, CMBS, agency, and ABS sectors. This may gradually occur in the U.S. credit markets as well to help facilitate relative value comparisons across non-U.S. and non-credit sectors to U.S. credit securities.

    c. Individual investors understand the traditional nominal spread framework as a market convention. Moreover despite its limitations, this framework can be used across the entire credit-quality spectrum from Aaa's to B's. The disadvantage is that the nominal spread framework does not work very well for investors and issuers in comparing the relative attractiveness between the fixed- and floating-rate markets. This is the advantage of using the swap framework.

14. a. By buying ABC Corporation issue and entering into a 5-year swap to pay fixed and receive floating, the spread over LIBOR until the first reset date for the swap is:

Receive from ABC Corp. (6.00% + 120 bp)	7.20%
− Pay on swap (6.00% + 100 bp)	7.00%
+ Receive from swap	LIBOR
Net	LIBOR + 20 bp

        Since LIBOR is 5.70%, the manager is locking in a rate of 5.90% (= 5.70% + 20 basis points) until the first reset date.

    b. If the manager expects that interest rates will increase, total return performance will be better using the swap.

15. a. The manager is relying on primary market analysis. The manager believes that one of the reasons why the spread on single-A rated issues may be out of line in the fourth quarter of 1999 is due to the lack of single-A rated issues coming to market in that quarter. The manager expects that in the first quarter of 2000, there will be a surge of single-A rated issues that will come to market, resulting in a widening of spreads and thereby providing an opportunity to purchase single-A rated issues relatively cheaply versus BBB issues.

        The assumption is that the attractive level of the corporate spread for single-A rated issuers is driven principally by new issuance and not any structural issue or other factor that determines corporate spreads. Furthermore, it is assumed that once the market is cleared of the increase in supply of single-A rated issuers will narrow the spread and provide better performance relative to BBB rated issuers.

    b. The keys to this strategy are (1) that the cash flows will in fact remain strong, (2) that the spread for these health care issuers are not justified by the strong cash flow despite concerns with healthcare reform, and (3) that investors in the bond market will recognize this (by some time period), resulting in a decline in the credit spread for these issuers.

16. The motivation for this strategy is that while investment-grade issues may decline due to stronger-than-anticipated economic growth, a good amount of spread reduction has already occurred in above BBB rated sectors. Thus, on a relative basis, the decline in corporate spreads on investment grade bonds due to stronger-than-anticipated growth will be primarily in BBB rated sectors. The assumption is that spreads will contract more in the BBB rated sector.

17. This relative value strategy has two elements to it. First, there appears to be an allocation to single-A rated corporates versus lower-quality corporates. Hence, it

appears to be a credit-defense trade because of a concern with the economy slowing down. Moreover, there is an allocation within the single-A rated corporates to a sector—non-cyclical consumer non-durables—that is expected to outperform an alternative sector—cyclicals—should the economy slow down.

18. a. One can use mean-reversion analysis in this question as follows. For each issue, the number of standard deviations that the current spread is above the historical average (the mean spread for the past six months) is computed as:

Issue	Number of standard deviations above mean
A	$(110 - 85)/25 = 1.0$
B	$(124 - 100)/10 = 2.4$
C	$(130 - 110)/15 = 1.3$

Issue B has the largest deviation above the mean and is therefore the one more likely to contract. Actually, based on a normal distribution, the probability associated with realizing a specified number of standard deviation above the mean can be determined.

b. The assumptions are that (1) the spreads will revert back to their historic means and (2) there have been no structural changes in the market that would render the historical mean and standard deviation useless for the analysis.

19. Ms. Xu should first explain that callable bonds exhibit negative convexity when interest rates decline, while noncallable bonds exhibit positive convexity. This means that when rates decline, the price appreciation for a callable bond will not be as great as an otherwise noncallable bond. Since the management team expects a significant drop in interest rates in the next quarter, to better participate in the rise in bond prices, there was a shift to noncallable credit securities.

All mortgage passthrough securities exhibit negative convexity. However, low-coupon issues exhibit less negative convexity than high-coupon issues. That is, there will be greater price appreciation for low-coupon issues when rates decline. Given the anticipated decline in interest rates, the low-coupon issues will appreciate more and hence the reason for the shift to such issues.

20. Ms. Smith could sell retail issues and use the proceeds to purchase U.S. dollar-denominated corporate bonds of European issuers. This would be consistent with her expectation of underperformance of the retail sector and outperformance of the European corporate sector. She could make her purchases in the new issue market, if she believes new issues will be attractively priced.

Ms. Smith should use credit analysis to select which issues to buy or sell within each sector. She must consider the possibility of a risk premium in the European corporate sector, as some managers cannot purchase bonds in that sector. Seasonality may also be a factor, depending on the timing of her purchases/sales.

CHAPTER 21

INTERNATIONAL BOND PORTFOLIO MANAGEMENT

SOLUTIONS

1. a. The unhedged portfolio with 30% international bonds had both a higher return and a lower standard deviation for the 1985-1996 period than an all U.S. bond portfolio. (Accordingly, the Sharpe ratio, a measure of risk-adjusted return, was higher for the 30% international bond portfolio.)

   b. Yes, the results suggest that there are periods where an unhedged international bond portfolio with 30% international bonds underperformed a portfolio of only U.S. bonds. Specifically, for the period 1989-1992 the return was less and the standard deviation was greater for the 30% international bond portfolio resulting in risk-adjusted underperformance.

   c. The entire period (1985–1996) return for the hedged or 30% international bond portfolio was less than the U.S. bond portfolio period return. However, there was also a reduction in risk because the standard deviation for the 30% international bond portfolio was less than that of the U.S. bond portfolio. On a risk-adjusted basis, the Sharpe ratio shows the hedged international bond portfolio was superior to the U.S. bond portfolio.

      However, the results do vary depending on the period. For the periods shown in the consultant's report, the risk-adjusted return in the 1989–1992 period was higher for the U.S. bond portfolio.

2. A total-return oriented investor would be concerned primarily with the performance of the portfolio and may be less concerned with how the allocation is made among the countries comprising the index. This investor's major concern is absolute performance and may be less concerned about performance relative to the benchmark.

3. A short investment performance time horizon may encourage more short-term trading which could diminish the diversification benefit from international bonds as an asset class. Investors who emphasize the risk reduction benefits of international bond investment diversification should have a longer time horizon. Differences between economic cycles can be prolonged, and a longer horizon would provide enough time for a full economic cycle and thus the diversification benefit to be realized.

4. First, a manager operating in the global bond market must operate in the U.S. bond market plus 10 to 20 other markets, each with its own market dynamics. Second, with the exception of the market for mortgage-backed securities, changes in interest rates typically affect all sectors of the U.S. bond market in the same way; however, the

magnitude of the changes may vary. Like the equity market, where it is not unusual to have some industries or market sectors move in opposite directions, international bond markets may also move in different directions depending upon economic conditions and investor risk tolerances.

5. a. The conventional yield for the U.K. government bond is the yield quoted on a bond-equivalent basis. That yield is 5% in the question. The yield on an annual-pay basis if the conventional yield is 5% is:

$$(1 + \text{yield on a bond-equivalent yield}/2)^2 - 1 = (1 + 0.05/2)^2 - 1 = 5.06\%$$

   b. The bond-equivalent yield on the German government bond given a conventional yield of 5.6% is:

$$2[(1 + \text{yield on annual-pay bond})^{0.5} - 1] = 2[(1 + 0.056)^{0.5} - 1] = 5.52\%$$

6. When there are differences in how to calculate bond yield in two countries, the spread between the two bond's yields cannot be found by simply computing the difference in the conventional yields. The yield for one of the bonds must be adjusted to make it comparable to the yield on the other. In the question, the U.S. Treasury bond yield is a bond-equivalent yield based on semiannual coupon payments while the Spanish government bond yield is based on annual coupon payments. Consequently, the spread is not simply the difference between the two conventional yields of -100 basis points ($5\% - 6\%$). To compare the Spanish government bond yield to that of the U.S. government bond yield, the latter must be adjusted to the yield on an annual basis.

7. a. The forward exchange rate (equation (2) in the chapter) is

$$F_{US,A} = S_{US,A}\left(\frac{1 + c_{US}}{1 + c_A}\right)$$

   where

   $F_{US,A}$ = forward exchange rate between U.S. dollars and the currency of Country A
   $S_{US,A}$ = spot (or cash) exchange rate between U.S. dollars and the currency of Country A
   c_{US} = short-term interest rate in the United States which matches the maturity of the forward contract
   c_A = short-term interest rate in Country A which matches the maturity of the forward contract

   The relevant interest rate in both countries is the 1-year rate since that is the maturity of the forward contract. In the question:

$$S_{US,A} = 2 \quad c_{US} = 4\% = 0.04 \quad c_A = 10\% = 0.10$$

   Therefore,

$$F_{US,A} = 2\left(\frac{1 + 0.04}{1 + 0.10}\right) = 1.8909$$

   The 1-year forward exchange rate should be 1.8909.

b. A U.S. portfolio manager can exploit a 1-year forward exchange rate of US $2.1 for one unit of the local contract as follows: borrow in the U.S. for one year at the U.S. rate of 4% and enter into a forward contract to deliver the amount of the local currency (LC) one year from now as determined by the amount that will be available at the end of one year by investing at 10% in Country A. That is, the portfolio manager will sell forward the LC of Country A, or equivalently, buy forward U.S. dollars.

For example, suppose that $100,000 is borrowed by the U.S. portfolio manager. At the spot exchange rate of US $2 for one unit of the local currency, the manager will exchange the $100,000 for LC 50,000. The LC 50,000 will then be invested at 10% in Country A for one year, so that the amount available at the end of one year is LC 55,000. So, if the portfolio manager borrows $100,000, she will agree to deliver LC 55,000 one year from now at the 1-year forward exchange rate of US $2.1 for one unit of the LC.

Here is the outcome of this strategy at the end of one year:

From investment in Country A:
LC from investment in Country A   LC 55,000

From forward contract:
U.S. $ from delivery of LC 55,000 at forward rate $115,500

Profit after loan repayment:
U.S. $ available to repay loan $115,500
Loan repayment (principal plus 4% interest) $104,000
Profit $11,500

Assuming that the counterparty to the forward contract does not default, this is a riskless arbitrage because a $11,500 profit is generated with no initial investment. Therefore, a 1-year forward exchange rate cannot be sustained because it permits arbitrage profits.

c. A portfolio manager in Country A can exploit this pricing of the 1-year forward contract by (1) borrowing in the local currency in Country A, (2) exchanging to U.S. dollars at the spot rate, (3) investing in the United States, and (4) selling U.S. dollars forward or equivalently by buying the local currency of Country A forward. The amount that the portfolio manager will agree to deliver forward of the U.S. dollar is the amount that can be earned in the United States on the amount borrowed.

For example, suppose that the portfolio manager in Country A borrows LC 100,000 at a 10% interest rate. The manager can exchange this amount for US $200,000 at the spot exchange rate. This amount of U.S. dollars is then invested in the United States at an interest rate of 4% and will generate US $208,000 at the end of one year. So, in terms of the forward contract, the manager will agree to deliver US $208,000 one year from now and will receive LC 122,353 (US $208,000 divided by the forward exchange rate of 1.7) upon conversion to the local currency.

The outcome of this strategy at the end of one year is:

From investment in the United States:

US $ from investment in U.S.	US $208,000

From forward contract:

LC from delivery of US $208,000 at forward rate	LC 122,353
Profit after loan repayment:	
LC available to repay loan	LC 122,353
Loan repayment (principal plus 10% interest)	LC 110,000
Profit	LC 12,353

Once again, assuming that the counterparty to the forward contract does not default, this is a riskless arbitrage because a LC 12,353 profit is generated with no initial investment.

8. a. A manager can hedge a long position exposure to a currency by selling a forward exchange rate contract for that currency.

   b. Although cross hedging and proxy hedging sound similar, and even though they both include a third currency in the transaction, they are quite different. Cross hedging maintains foreign currency exposure, but shifts that exposure from the currency of country i in which the investment is made, to the currency of another country, say country j, using currency forwards. Proxy hedging reduces foreign currency exposure by hedging back into the home currency, but uses a currency forward in a second currency, that of country j, to hedge back into the home currency rather than the currency of country i in which the investment is made. The portfolio, however, is not a perfect hedge because it is exposed to movements between country i and country j currencies.

9. The interest rates and expected returns are as follows:

$$r_x = 4.0\%$$

$$c_x = 3.2\%$$

$$e_{US\$,x} = 5.1\%$$

$$c_y = 4.0\%$$

$$e_{US\$,y} = 4.6\%$$

$$c_{US} = 4.6\%$$

A summary of the calculations is provided in the table below:

	Hedged	Unhedged	Cross hedged	Proxy hedged
Expected Returns				
Cash	$c_{US\$}$ = 4.6%	$c_{US\$}$ = 4.6%	$c_{US\$}$ = 4.6%	$c_{US\$}$ = 4.6%
Excess Bond	$(r_x - c_x)$ = (4.0% − 3.2%) = 0.8%	$(r_x - c_x)$ = (4.0% − 3.2%) = 0.8%	$(r_x - c_x)$ = (4.0% − 3.2%) = 0.8%	$(r_x - c_x)$ = (4.0% − 3.2%) = 0.8%
Excess Currency		$e_{US\$,x} - (c_{US\$} - c_x)$ = 5.1% − (4.6% − 3.2%) = 5.1% − 1.4% = 3.7%	$e_{US\$,y} - (c_{US\$} - c_y)$ = 4.6% − (4.6% − 4.0%) = 4.6% − 0.6% = 4.0%	$(e_{US\$,x} - e_{US\$,y}) - (c_y - c_x)$ = (5.1% − 4.6%)− (4.0% − 3.2%) = 0.5% − 0.8% = −0.3%
	= 0.0%			
Total Return	= 5.4%	= 9.1%	= 9.4%	= 5.1%

The U.S. cash rate and the expected excess bond return in country i are identical for each of the strategies and equal to the expected hedged bond return. Thus we can begin with the hedged bond return and compare the excess currency returns (the third component of the equations) of the unhedged, cross hedged and proxy hedged strategies.

a. unhedged expected excess currency return = 3.7%.
b. unhedged expected total return = 9.1%
c. hedged expected total return = 5.4%
d. Based on the manager's expectations about the currency movement, the hedged expected return 5.4% is less than the 9.1% unhedged expected total return. Thus, the manager will not hedge currency X.
e. Expected excess currency return from cross hedging using Country Y's currency = 4.0%
f. Expected total return from the cross hedge = 9.4%
g. Since the expected return from the cross hedge of 9.4% is greater than both the unhedged expected total return of 9.1% and the hedged expected total return of 5.4%, based on the manager's expectations for the movement of currency X and currency Y, a cross hedge is the most attractive option.
h. Expected excess currency return for the proxy hedge strategy = -0.3%
i. Expected total return for the proxy hedge strategy = 5.1%
j. Based on the expectations for the currency movement, a proxy hedge strategy is unattractive. The proxy hedge strategy offers the lowest expected return of all the strategies considered in this question.

10. The interest rates and expected returns are as follows:

$$r_A = 3.3\%$$

$$c_A = 2.9\%$$

$$e_{UK,A} = -1.2\%$$

$$c_B = 4.2\%$$

$$e_{UK,B} = -3.5\%$$

$$c_{UK} = 4.6\%$$

A summary of the calculations is provided in the table below:

	Hedged	Unhedged	Cross hedged	Proxy hedged
Expected Returns				
Cash	c_{UK} = 4.6%	c_{UK} = 4.6%	c_{UK} = 4.6%	c_{UK} = 4.6%
Excess Bond	$(r_A - c_A)$ = (3.3% − 2.9%) = 0.4%	$(r_A - c_A)$ = (3.3% − 2.9%) = 0.4%	$(r_A - c_A)$ = (3.3% − 2.9%) = 0.4%	$(r_A - c_A)$ = (3.3% − 2.9%) = 0.4%
Excess Currency	= 0.0%	$e_{UK,A} - (c_{UK} - c_A)$ = −1.2% − (4.6% − 2.9%) = −1.2% − 1.7% = −2.9%	$e_{UK,B} - (c_{UK} - c_B)$ = −3.5% − (4.6% − 4.2%) = −3.5% − 0.4% = −3.9%	$(e_{UK,A} - e_{UK,B}) - (c_B - c_A)$ = (−1.2% + 3.5%)− (4.2% − 2.9%) = 2.3% − 1.3% = 1.0%
Total Return	= 5.0%	= 2.1%	= 1.1%	= 6.0%

a. expected unhedged excess currency return $= -2.9\%$.
b. unhedged expected total return $= 2.1\%$
c. hedged expected total return $= 5.0\%$
d. Based on the manager's expectations about the currency movement, the hedged expected return 5.0% is greater than the 2.1% unhedged expected total return. Thus, the manager will hedge currency A.
e. Expected excess currency return from cross hedging using Country B's currency $= -3.9\%$
f. Expected total return from the cross hedge $= 1.1\%$
g. Since the expected total return from the cross hedge of 1.1% is less than both the unhedged expected total return of 2.1% and the hedged expected total return of 5.0%, based on the manager's expectations for the movement of currency A and currency B, a cross hedge is unattractive.
h. Expected excess currency return for the proxy hedge strategy $= 1.0\%$
i. Expected total return for the proxy hedge strategy $= 6.0\%$
j. Based on the expectations for the currency movement, a proxy hedge strategy is attractive. The expected currency appreciation of Country A versus Country B is 2.3%, which is greater than the short-term interest rate differential between Countries A and B of 1.3%. The proxy hedge offers the highest expected total return of all the strategies considered in this question.

11. a. Forward rates—forward interest rates and forward exchange rates—indicate the expectations of the market. The forward rates indicate what currency exchange rate the manager can lock in today, thus it is a *hedgeable rate.*
    b. When making an allocation decision, a manager is expressing a view relative to the market or, more specifically, what the market has priced into the bonds and the currency of the country. Therefore, forward interest rates and forward exchange rates set the benchmark to determine whether or not the manager's outlook is materially different from that of the market.
    c. As explained in part (b), forward exchange rates indicate the expectations of the market for the country's currency and therefore provides a benchmark. If forward exchange rates indicate the currency will depreciate much more than the manager's outlook, and if the manager strongly believes in his or her forecast, he will want to increase exposure to the currency.

12. a. There is a 95 basis point or 0.95% three-month yield advantage by investing in the U.S. benchmark issue. This advantage can be offset if the U.S. dollar depreciates by more than 0.95% during the quarter or if there is a widening of the spread. The widening can occur in one of the following ways:

    - yields in country M can decrease, resulting in price appreciation of country M's government bond
    - yields in the United States can increase, resulting in a price decline of the U.S. Treasury bond

    A combination of the two can also occur.
    b. We can calculate how much the yield in country M must fall in order to eliminate the 0.95% yield advantage from investing in the U.S. government bond. Country M's yield must decline such that country M's government benchmark issue price

increases 0.95%. Since the duration of that bond is 6, for a 100 basis point change in yield the approximate percentage price change for the country M's government bond will be 6%. In general:

$$\text{change in price} = 6 \times \text{change in yield}$$

Letting W denote the spread widening, then we can rewrite the above as

$$\text{change in price} = 6 \times W$$

We want the increase in price caused by the spread widening to be 0.95%. Therefore,

$$0.95\% = 6 \times W$$

or

$$W = 0.95\%/6 = 0.158\% = 15.8 \text{ basis points.}$$

A decline of 15.8 basis points in country M's yield is the breakeven spread movement in country M that would eliminate the 3-month yield advantage from buying the U.S. Treasury issue.

c. The breakeven spread movement in U.S. yield is found as follows:

$$\text{change in price} = 4 \times W$$

We want the decrease in price caused by the spread widening to be 0.95%. Therefore,

$$0.95\% = 4 \times W$$

or

$$W = 0.95\%/4 = 0.238\% = 23.8 \text{ basis points.}$$

An increase of 23.8 basis points in the U.S. yield is the breakeven spread movement in the U.S. that would cancel the 3-month yield advantage from buying the U.S. Treasury issue. The breakeven spread movement in the U.S. of 23.8 basis points is much larger than the 15.8 basis points calculated for country M. The conservative course would be to use the minimum breakeven spread movement calculated using the country with the highest duration

d. The expected hedged return is:

$$[(r_\$ - c_\$) + c_M]/4 = [(7.0\% - 6.5\%) + 2.5\%]/4 = 0.75\%$$

e. When compared with the return on country M's 10-year government bond over the same period (3.2%/4, or 0.80%) the expected return on a hedged basis is a negative 0.05%. Thus, a portfolio manager in country M would have to expect a nominal spread *tightening* of at least 0.8 basis points $(-0.05\% = 6 \times W)$ for the trade to look attractive.

f. The manager's view must be that the dollar would either appreciate or depreciate versus country M's currency by less than the embedded forward rate. The embedded forward rate is obtained as follows:

$$f_{M,\$} = c_M - c_\$ = (2.5 - 6.5\%)/4 = -1.0\%$$

That is, the portfolio manager's view must be that the U.S. dollar will either appreciate or depreciate by less than 1%.

CHAPTER 22

CONTROLLING INTEREST RATE RISK WITH DERIVATIVES

SOLUTIONS

1. There are advantages of using Treasury futures contracts rather than cash Treasuries to alter the interest rate risk of a portfolio. They include:

   1. Despite the highly liquid Treasury market, transaction costs are lower in the Treasury futures market than in the Treasury cash market.
   2. Margin requirements are lower for futures than for Treasury securities; using futures thus permits greater leverage.
   3. It is easier to sell short Treasury futures than it is to short Treasury securities.
   4. Futures can be used to construct a portfolio with a longer duration than is available using cash market securities.

2. To obtain a portfolio duration of 11 where long-term Treasury bonds have a duration of 6 means that there must be bonds in the portfolio with a duration greater than 11. Zero-coupon bonds with a maturity greater than 11 years have the desired duration. However, this can also be accomplished by using leverage. Leverage can be used to increase the portfolio's duration. Alternatively, buying Treasury bond futures increases the dollar duration and the duration of the portfolio. By buying the appropriate number of futures contracts, a manager can increase the duration of the portfolio to 11.

3. a. Ms. Marcus wants to reduce the dollar duration of the portfolio. To do so, she must sell Treasury bond futures contracts. Thus, she will take a short position in the Treasury bond futures contracts.

   b. To determine the number of futures contracts it is first necessary to compare the current dollar duration without futures and the target dollar duration. We can compute these values for any basis point change in rates. Suppose that 50 basis points are used. Since the current duration is 5 and the market value of the portfolio is $200 million, for a 50 basis point change in rates the current dollar duration without futures is $5 million ($200 million × 5% × 0.5). The target dollar duration for a portfolio with a target duration of 3 is $3 million. Thus,

target dollar duration − current dollar duration without futures
= $3 million − $5 million = −$2 million

This means that the dollar duration of the futures position must be −$2 million in order to have a target portfolio duration of 3. We know that

dollar duration of futures position
= number of futures contracts × dollar duration per futures contracts

Since we know that

dollar duration of futures position = −$2,000,000

and

dollar duration per futures contracts = $5,000
then − $2,000,000 = number of futures contracts × $5,000

therefore

number of futures contracts = −400

Ms. Marcus should short (sell) 400 futures contracts to alter the portfolio's duration to 3.

4. The dollar duration for the futures contract is

$$\frac{\text{dollar duration of the CTD issue}}{\text{conversion factor for the CTD issue}} = \frac{\$6,000}{0.90} = \$6,666.67$$

5. Interest rate risk management involves altering the portfolio's duration to match the target duration. When hedging, the manager sets a target duration of zero. Hence, hedging is a special case of interest rate risk management.

6. The primary factor a manager should consider when identifying which futures contract to use in controlling a portfolio's interest rate risk is the correlation between the price on the futures contract and the interest rate that creates the underlying risk that the manager seeks to eliminate. However, correlation is not the only consideration when a large transaction is necessary to attain the target duration. Liquidity of the futures contract becomes important in such situations.

7. a. The target price for a hedge is the price that the manager seeks to lock in by hedging.
   b. If the target price is too low when hedging a future sale, the manager may decide not to hedge. If the target price is too high when hedging a future purchase, the manger may decide not to hedge.

8. When hedging using interest rate futures, the outcome of the hedge depends on what happens to the basis (i.e., the difference between the spot price and the futures price). The uncertainty in the outcome of a hedge is that when he initiates the hedge, the hedger does not know what the basis will be at the time the hedge is removed, except at the settlement date of the futures contract. So, the price that will be locked in will be between the current price and the futures price. The answers given by Ms. Alvarez

and Mr. Granger reflect those two extreme values. Ms. Alvarez, by hedging overnight, effectively locks in the current price, since under most circumstances, the basis will not change much in a day. In contrast, when Mr. Granger plans to remove the hedge at the delivery date of the futures contract, he is locking in the futures price because of convergence. So, both are correct with respect to the time period over which they plan to hedge.

9. a. Basis risk is the uncertainty about the value of the basis at the time the hedge is removed. (The basis is defined as the difference between the spot price and the futures price.) The outcome of a hedge depends on what happens to the basis at the time the hedge is removed.

   b. For a given investment horizon, hedging substitutes basis risk for price risk because the manager is exchanging the uncertainty of the price of the hedged security (i.e., price risk) at a future date for the uncertainty of how the basis will change (i.e., basis risk) at that future date when the hedge is removed.

   c. A manager will hedge because he or she believes that basis risk is less than price risk.

10. A cross hedge in the futures market occurs when the security to be hedged is not deliverable on the futures contract used in the hedge. For example, a manager who wants to hedge the sale price of a corporate bond or a mortgage-backed security might hedge with a Treasury note futures contract. Because non-Treasury securities cannot be delivered in satisfaction of the contract, the hedge is a cross hedge. Another example of cross hedging is when a manager wants to hedge a rate that is of the same quality as the rate for an available futures contract, but with a different maturity. For example, it is necessary to cross hedge a Treasury bond, note, or bill with a maturity that does not qualify for delivery on any futures contract. Thus, a cross hedge occurs when the security to be hedged differs from the futures contract specification in terms of either quality or maturity.

11. The two key relationships in a cross hedge of mortgage passthrough securities using Treasury note futures are:

   1. the relationship between the cheapest-to-deliver (CTD) issue for the Treasury note futures contract and the futures contract.

   2. the relationship between the mortgage passthrough securities to be hedged and the CTD issue for the Treasury note futures contract.

12. a. The target price for hedging the CTD issue is the product of the futures price and the conversion factor for the CTD issue:

$$106 \times 1.16 = 122.96$$

   b. Given the coupon rate and maturity of the issue, the yield to maturity is 7.8% if the CTD target price is 122.96.

   c. Since the yield spread for the corporate bond is assumed to be constant at 100 basis points, the target yield for the corporate bond would be 8.8%.

   d. The corresponding target price for the corporate bond for the target yield of 8.8% is 91.62. (This is calculated using the standard pricing formula. Note that because of interim values that may be rounded, one might obtain values for the target price from 91.59 to 91.62.)

   e. First the price for the CTD one month from now must be determined. Given a yield of 7.0% for the CTD issue, a coupon rate of 10%, and a remaining maturity of 21 years and 11 months, the price at the settlement date is 133.3580. (This price is used to compute the duration of 10.4 in the information set.)

Given the duration of 10.4 and the price of 133.3580 at the settlement date, the dollar duration per $100 par value for a 50 basis point change in interest rates is:

$$(10.4\%/2) \times \$133.3580 = \$6.935$$

Per $100,000 par value of the CTD issue, the dollar duration at the settlement date is

$$(\$100,000/100) \times 6.935 = \$6,935$$

f. First the price of the corporate bond one month from now must be determined. Given a yield of 8%, a coupon rate of 8%, and a remaining maturity of 29 years and 11 months, the price one month from now is 99.9892. (The price of 99.9892 was used to calculate the duration of 11.3 in the information set.)

For the corporate bond the dollar duration per 50 basis point change in rates per $100 par value given a duration of 11.3 is

$$(11.3\%/2) \times \text{price of corporate bond at settlement date}$$

Since the price of the corporate bond at the settlement date is 99.9892, the dollar duration per 50 basis point change in rates per $100 par value is

$$(11.3\%/2) \times \$99.9892 = \$5.6494$$

For $20 million par value, the dollar duration per 50 basis point change in rates at the settlement date is

$$\text{dollar duration for corporate bond} = (\$20,000,000/100) \times \$5.6494$$
$$= \$1,129,878$$

g. The number of futures contract to short is

$$\frac{\text{current dollar duration without futures}}{\text{dollar duration for the CTD issue}} \times \text{conversion factor for CTD issue}$$

The current dollar duration without futures is the dollar duration of the corporate bond (as computed in part (f)), $1,129,878. The dollar duration for the CTD issue (as computed part (e)) is $6,935. Since the conversion factor for the CTD issue is 1.16, then

$$-\frac{\$1,129,878}{\$6,935} \times 1.16 = -188.99$$

Therefore, 189 Treasury bond futures contracts should be shorted.

13. In hedging a nondeliverable security with a Treasury futures contract, it is common to assume that the yield on the nondeliverable security is equal to the yield on the cheapest-to-deliver Treasury security plus a spread. However, this may be an inappropriate assumption in that the relative spread may change when yields increase or decrease. The yield beta is an empirical estimate of the relative change in the spread when yields change and is used to adjust the hedge ratio by multiplying the number of futures contracts (computed without regard to the yield beta) by the yield beta.

14. The dollar duration for the portfolio for a 100 basis point change in interest rates is approximately 5.2% times $1 billion or $52 million. So, for a 50 basis point change in rates, the portfolio's market value will change by about $26 million. Since the dollar duration for the Treasury bond futures contract is $4,000 for a 50 basis point change in rates, the number of futures contracts to *short* is

$$\frac{\$26,000,000}{\$4,000} = 6,500 \text{ contracts}$$

15. To compute the hedge ratio (the number of futures contracts to implement a hedge), first compute both the dollar duration of the bond to be hedged and the dollar duration of the futures contract. If these values are not computed correctly, the hedge ratio will not be correct. While the hedge may still reduce price risk, it may not eliminate the price risk exposure. This is the first reason suggested by Ms. Rosetta.

Evaluation of the outcome of a hedge begins with an assessment of how closely the price from the hedge came to the target price. But there is no evidence that Mr. Elmo computed a target price. If the hedge was removed prior to the settlement date of the futures contract, the basis could have been different from the target basis. This is the second reason offered by Ms. Rosetta.

Finally, in constructing a hedge an assumption is made about the relative change in the yield of the bond to be hedged and the yield for the bond underlying the futures contract. If the relationship is incorrectly assumed to be constant when yields change (i.e., a yield beta of one), then the performance of the hedge may not be as expected. If Mr. Elmo computed a yield beta but the estimated value was wrong, then the result may not be as expected. This is the third reason offered by Ms. Rosetta.

16. a. For the swap leg of the position the finance company will pay interest of 7.2%/4 or 1.8% per quarter. (Note that this approximate calculation ignores the exact number of days in the quarter

Each quarter the finance company receives 3-month LIBOR/4. (Again, note that the day count for each quarter is ignored.)

The quarterly interest payment on the funds borrowed by the finance company is (3-month LIBOR + 56 basis points)/4, or 3-month LIBOR/4 + 14 basis points.

As a result of the swap, the quarterly net payments are as follows:

Quarterly interest rate received

From consumer loan portfolio(12%/4)	= 3.00%
From interest rate swap	= 3-month LIBOR/4
Total received	= 3% + 3-month LIBOR/4

Quarterly interest rate paid

To borrow funds	= 3-month LIBOR/4 + 0.14%
On interest rate swap	= 1.80%
Total paid	= 1.94% + 3-month LIBOR/4

Quarterly Outcome

To be received	= 3.00% + 3-month LIBOR/4
To be paid	= 1.94% + 3-month LIBOR/4
Spread income	= 1.06%

Thus, regardless of the value of 3-month LIBOR, the finance company locks in a spread of 106 basis points each quarter.

   b. The assumption is that there are no defaults or prepayments.

17. From the perspective of the fixed-rate receiver, the position can be viewed as follows:

$$\text{long a fixed-rate bond} + \text{short a floating-rate bond}$$

The dollar duration of an interest rate swap for a floating-rate payer (fixed-rate receiver) is:

$$\text{dollar duration of a fixed-rate bond} - \text{dollar duration of a floating-rate bond}$$

The fixed-rate bond is effectively a bond with a coupon rate equal to the swap rate, a par amount equal to the notional amount, and a maturity equal to the remaining number of years of the swap.

   Since the dollar duration of a floating-rate bond is close to zero,

$$\text{dollar duration of a swap for a fixed-rate receiver} \approx \text{dollar duration of a fixed-rate bond}$$

Thus, the dollar duration of a swap for a fixed-rate receiver is approximately the dollar duration of the fixed-rate bond. This means that by adding a swap to a portfolio in which the manager pays floating (receives fixed) increases the dollar duration of the portfolio.

18. A protective put buying strategy is used by a manager who wants to hedge against a decline in bond prices due to an anticipated rise in interest rates.

19. The option strategy suggested by the trustee is a covered call writing strategy. The trustee is wrong to conclude that there are no costs. The fact that a bond for which a covered call was written is called away at the strike price of the call option does not mean that there is no cost simply because the bond is in the portfolio. The covered call writer is sacrificing the upside potential of that bond. Moreover, as the portfolio manager correctly notes, the strategy is not really providing the type of protection against a rise in interest rates that one would expect from a hedge. The only protection afforded by the covered call writing strategy is the recovery of only the loss in value equal only to the option premium received. That is, there is substantial downside risk which is only offset to the extent of the option premium received.

20. The collar is like the protective put buying strategy in that it reduces the possible losses on the portfolio if interest rates increase. Like the covered call writing strategy, the portfolio's upside potential is limited by the cost of the option. Like an unhedged position, within the range defined by the strike prices of the put and call options, the value of the portfolio varies inversely with interest rates.

21. The strike price that Mr. Zhao seeks for the corporate issue is 90.80. Since the issue has 20 years to maturity and a coupon rate of 8% paid semiannually, the corresponding yield to maturity is 9% (from the price/yield relationship).

   Since Mr. Zhao assumes that there is a 125 basis point spread between the corporate issue and the CTD issue, this gives a yield for the CTD issue of 7.75%. Since the coupon rate of the CTD issue is 7.75%, this means that the price for the CTD issue is par (100).

Given the price of 100 for the CTD issue, the strike price of the futures contract is found by dividing 100 by the conversion factor of the CTD issue. Since the conversion factor is 0.95, the strike price for the Treasury bond futures contract is 105.2632 (= 100/0.95).

22. The number of options to purchase is computed as follows:

$$\text{number of options contracts} = \frac{\text{current dollar duration without options}}{\text{dollar duration of the CTD issue}}$$
$$\times \text{ conversion factor for CTD}$$

For a 50 basis point change in rates, the market value of the portfolio will change by approximately 3.5% (one half of 7%). Since the current market value is $100 million, the current dollar duration without futures is $3.5 million. Then,

$$\text{number of options contracts} = \frac{\$3,500,000}{4,500} \times 0.9 = 700$$

23. a. The portfolio manager can purchase an interest rate cap. If interest rates rise so that the coupon rate on the floating-rate notes becomes capped, a payment will be made to the portfolio manager by the seller of the interest rate cap agreement. The cost of this protection is the premium paid for the interest rate cap agreement.

b. The portfolio manager can purchase an interest rate floor. If interest rates do decline below the bank's funding cost, the coupon rate on the floating-rate notes will decline but a payment will be made to the portfolio manager by the seller of the interest rate floor agreement. The cost of this protection is the premium paid for the interest rate floor agreement.

CHAPTER 23

HEDGING MORTGAGE SECURITIES TO CAPTURE RELATIVE VALUE

SOLUTIONS

1. Mr. McFee failed to communicate clearly what he intended to do. The client is correct that if Mr. McFee hedged all of the interest rate risk of the mortgage products in which he invested, then a return close to the short-term risk-free rate would be earned. However, that is not his strategy. The performance of the mortgage products in which he invests will depend on the movements of the level of interest rates and the mortgage spread (more specifically the option-adjusted spread). The purpose of the hedge is to eliminate the risk attributable to changes in interest rates so that the manager only has exposure to changes in the mortgage spread (i.e., OAS). That is, he does not seek to hedge spread risk. Mr. McFee is proposing to capture value from a change in the mortgage spread (not interest rates) that the market does not yet anticipate.

2. Ms. Sze should point out that while both mortgage passthroughs and Treasuries will appreciate when interest rates decline, the relative performance of the two sectors due to the expected decline in interest rates is what is important. Mortgage passthroughs exhibit negative convexity at levels of interest rates below the rate on the underlying mortgages while Treasuries, which are option-free securities, always exhibit positive convexity. Because of the negative convexity feature, while mortgage passthrough will appreciate in value, Treasuries would appreciate more for a given initial duration. Hence the recommendation to underweight mortgages and overweight Treasuries.

3. There are investors who consider mortgages to be market-directional investments that should be avoided when one expects interest rates to decline. However, when properly managed by separating mortgage valuation decisions from decisions concerning the appropriate duration of the portfolio, mortgage securities are not market-directional investments. The ability to separate the value decision from the duration decision hinges critically on proper hedging. One must offset the interest rate-driven changes in the duration of mortgage securities to prevent the portfolio drifting adversely from its target. Hedged improperly, the portfolio's duration will be shorter than desired when interest rates decline and longer than desired when interest rates rise.

4. Volatility risk can be managed by buying options or by hedging dynamically. Hedging dynamically is selected when the volatility implied in option prices is high and it is believed that future realized volatility will be lower than implied volatility. When

implied volatility is low and it is believed that actual future volatility will be higher than implied volatility, hedging by purchasing options would be the better alternative.

5. Mortgage securities are particularly sensitive to changes in the level and twist in the yield curve. Using just duration hedges a mortgage security to changes in the level of interest rates but not to twists in the yield curve.

6. a. One can assess the convexity characteristic of the passthrough by looking at the change in price when rates are changed. The answer then depends on how much rates are changed. In the illustration, the price increase when rates decline is 1.205 (101.100 − 99.895) while the price decrease when rates rise is 1.940 (99.895 − 97.955). This means that the loss (in absolute value) is greater than the gain. This is a property of an instrument that is expected to exhibit negative convexity.

   b. The position in the two hedging instruments is found by using the following ten steps described in the chapter:

   Step 1: Compute the prices for the passthrough and hedging instruments for typical level changes in the yield. The information for Step 1 is provided in the question. It is summarized below:

Instrument	Price for	
	increase in yield	decrease in yield
Freddie Mac passthrough	97.955	101.100
2-year Treasury note futures	106.122	107.300
10-year Treasury note future	109.250	113.600

   Step 2: From the prices found in Step 1, calculate the price changes:

Instrument	Price change for	
	increase in yield	decrease in yield
Freddie Mac passthrough	−1.940	1.205
2-year Treasury note futures	−0.528	0.650
10-year Treasury note future	−1.940	2.410

   Step 3: Calculate the average value of the price change (using absolute values) for each instrument resulting from a level change:

$$\text{MBS price}_L = 1.573$$

$$\text{2-H price}_L = 0.589$$

$$\text{10-H price}_L = 2.175$$

   Step 4: Compute the prices for the passthrough and hedging instruments for typical twists in the yield curve. The information for Step 4 is provided in the question. It is summarized below:

Instrument	Price for	
	flattening	steepening
Freddie Mac passthrough	99.450	100.350
2-year Treasury note futures	106.104	107.268
10-year Treasury note future	110.850	111.790

Step 5: From the prices found in Step 4, calculate the price changes:

	Price for	
Instrument	flattening	steepening
Freddie Mac passthrough	−0.445	0.455
2-year Treasury note futures	−0.546	0.618
10-year Treasury note future	−0.340	0.600

Step 6: Calculate the average value of the price change for each instrument resulting from a twist in the yield curve:

$$\text{MBS price}_T = 0.445$$

$$\text{2-H price}_T = 0.582$$

$$\text{10-H price}_T = 0.470$$

Step 7: The change in value of the two-bond hedge portfolio for a change in the level of the yield curve is found as follows:

$$H_2 \times (0.589) + H_{10} \times (2.175)$$

Step 8: The change in value of the two-bond hedge portfolio for a twist of the yield curve is found as follows:

$$H_2 \times (0.582) + H_{10} \times (0.470)$$

Step 9: The two equations that equate the change in the value of the two-bond hedge to the change in the price of the mortgage security are:

$$\text{Level}: H_2 \times (0.589) + H_{10} \times (2.175) = -1.573$$

$$\text{Twist}: H_2 \times (0.582) + H_{10} \times (0.470) = -0.445$$

Step 10: Solve the simultaneous equations in Step 9 for the values of H_2 and H_{10}. This is done as follows:

Solve for H_2 in the "Level" equation:

$$H_2 = (-1.573 - 2.175\, H_{10})/0.589 = [-2.670628 - 3.692699\, H_{10}]$$

Substitute the above for H_2 in the "Twist" equation:

$$[-2.670628 - 3.692699\, H_{10}](0.582) + H_{10}(0.470) = -0.445$$

Solving we would find that:

$$H_{10} = -0.657657$$

To obtain H_2, we can substitute $H_{10} = -0.657657$ into the "Level" or the "Twist" equation and solve for H_2. Substituting into the "Level" equation we get:

$$H_2 \times (0.589) + (-0.657657) \times (2.175) = -1.573$$

$$H_2 = -0.242099$$

Thus, $H_2 = -0.242099$ and $H_{10} = -0.657657$

These values indicate that a short position will be taken in the two hedging instruments. The value of 0.242099 for H_2 means that the par amount in the 2-year Treasury note futures will be 0.242099 per \$1 of par amount of the mortgage security to be hedged. Since the par amount of the Freddie Mac passthrough to be hedged against interest rate risk is \$10 million, then 2-year Treasury note futures with a par amount of \$2,420,990 (0.242099 × \$10 million) should be shorted. Similarly, the value of 0.657657 for H_{10} means that the par amount in the 10-year Treasury note futures to be shorted will be 0.657657 per \$1 of market value of the mortgage security to be hedged.

7. The first assumption is that the yield curve shifts used in obtaining the prices that are used in computing the hedge are reasonable. In deriving the prices for a yield curve shift a prepayment model is used to obtain the mortgage price. Thus the second assumption that the prepayment model does a good job of projecting changes in prepayments when the yield curve changes. The third assumption is that the other inputs into the Monte Carlo simulation model for obtaining the new prices when the yield curve shifts are reasonable and can be expected to be realized in the future. The last assumption deals with the use of average price changes used in deriving the position in each hedging instrument. It is assumed that the average price change is a good approximation of how the mortgage security's price will change for small yield curve shifts assumed in deriving the prices.

8. a. A cuspy-coupon mortgage security is one in which the security is highly sensitive to small changes in interest rates. For example, a mortgage security whose coupon is 100 basis points higher than the current coupon is highly sensitive to small decreases in interest rates. For such securities, using the average price change will not provide the correct information for hedging.

   b. For cuspy-coupon mortgage securities, it is recommended that options be combined with other hedging instruments to hedge a position.

CHAPTER 24

CREDIT DERIVATIVES IN BOND PORTFOLIO MANAGEMENT

SOLUTIONS

1. A portfolio manager may be willing to assume credit risk if he or she has a positive outlook for the bond or the issuer. The portfolio manager may believe that the bond or issuer will be upgraded, resulting in a favorable price performance relative to other credits. The portfolio manager may have an expectation of other credit events which may have a positive effect on the bond or issuer such as an advantageous merger or acquisition by a strong credit. Finally, there are times in the economic cycle where banks may be willing to provide term loans to high-yield companies at more attractive rates than the bond markets, resulting in the calling of an outstanding issue at a premium to par or market value and thereby enhancing return.

2. When there is an actual or anticipated downgrade of an issue or issuer, the market will require a higher spread. There is also a risk because credit spreads will likely widen *before* there is a downgrade—and they may widen without a downgrade occurring. Credit spread risk is the risk that the market will require a higher credit spread.

3. Spread duration can be used. It is the estimated change in the value of a portfolio for a 100 basis point change in the spread. Spread duration must be properly estimated to focus only on a spread change due to credit risk.

4. The total return receiver realizes the cash flow from the reference obligation or basket of reference obligations which includes the change in the market value. The change in the market value can be attributable to a change in both the credit spread and the level of interest rates. Consequently, there is exposure to interest rate risk as well as credit risk.

5. A portfolio manager seeking exposure to a diversified portfolio of corporate bonds can purchase the individual bond issues in the market. This requires an upfront capital allocation and total transaction costs are relatively high. A more transactionally efficient way of realizing the total return from that diversified portfolio of corporate bonds is to enter into a total return swap as the total return receiver.

6. A portfolio manager who wants to short a corporate bond would find it difficult to do so in the corporate bond market. By shorting a corporate bond, the portfolio manager pays the total return. The same can be accomplished by using a total return swap as the total return payer with the corporate bond that the portfolio manager seeks to short as the reference obligation.

7. a. Since Mr. Martinez expects the credit spread to decline, he will be the total return receiver.

   b. Since the spread over the 12-year Treasury rate is 500 basis points and the bond is issued at par with a coupon rate of 11%, then the 12-year Treasury rate is 6%.

   c. The required market yield would be 10% for the reference obligation (6.5% plus 350 basis points). Thus the reference obligation would be priced as an 11-year 11% coupon bond trading at 10%. The price for this bond is 106.58 per 100 par value.

   d. The total cash flow is:

   Coupon payments total $1,650,000 (= 11% × $15 million)
   Change in market value:

initial price:	$15,000,000
market price one year later:	$15,987,000 (= 1.0658 × $15 million)
capital appreciation:	$987,000
Total swap payment to total return receiver:	$2,637,000 (= $1,650,000 + $987,000)

   e. The two payments are:

First swap payment paid: $15 million × 7.5%/2	=	$562,500
Second swap payment paid: $15 million × 8.5%/2	=	$637,500
Total payments	=	$1,200,000

   f. Mr. Martinez, the total return receiver, will receive payments of $2,637,000 and make payments of $1,200,000. The net payment received is $1,437,000.

8. a. A "scheduled term of five years" means that assuming the swap is not terminated as the result of a credit event prior to five years after the swap is initiated, then it is scheduled to terminate in five years.

   b. Since the market is 60 per 100 par and the par value is $25 million, the market value of the bonds is $15 million and this is the notional amount for the swap.

   c. The quarterly payment is determined as follows:

   quarterly swap premium payment

   $$= \text{notional amoung} \times \text{swap premium (in decimal)} \times \frac{\text{actual no. of days in quarter}}{360}$$

   Since the notional amount is $15 million and there are 90 actual days assumed in the quarter, then if the annual rate is 600 basis points (0.06), the quarterly swap premium payment made by the protection buyer would be:

   $$\$15,000,000 \times 0.06 \times \frac{90}{360} = \$225,000$$

   d. The swap is terminated and there are no more payments made by the protection buyer.

   e. Payment will be triggered only if restructuring is covered as a credit event in the credit default swap and, if it is covered, whether the definition selected includes the restructuring event.

f. Payment will be made only if obligation acceleration is covered as a credit event in the credit default swap. Today, obligation acceleration is usually not covered, but can be covered if the portfolio manager requests it.

9. a. The restructuring of a debt obligation involves changing its contractual terms so as to make it less attractive to the debtholder than the original terms. Examples of common restructuring provisions are a reduction in the interest rate, a reduction in the principal, lengthening the maturity of the obligation, postponement of an interest payment, and a change in the level of seniority of the obligation in the reference entity's debt structure.

   b. There are four choices for the treatment of restructuring in a credit default swap: (1) no restructuring; (2) "full" restructuring, with no modification to the deliverable reference obligations aspect; (3) "modified restructuring," which is typically used in North America; or (4) "modified modified restructuring."

10. The 1999 ISDA definition for restructuring, called full or old restructuring, provides the protection buyer with greater credit protection than the Restructuring Supplement Definition (modified restructuring). Hence, all other factors equal, a credit default swap using old or full restructuring should be would be more expensive.

11. a. The value of the binary credit put option is $0 because the credit rating of Company X is not below BBB.

    b. Because the issue is rated BB, the binary credit put option expires in the money. The payoff is $80 ($1,000 − $920).

    c. While this binary credit put option has a credit rating below BBB, its price is above par. Thus, the payoff would indicate a negative value of $10. However, because the option has a negative value, the option buyer will not exercise. Therefore, the payoff from the option is zero.

12. a. The trade recommendation suggested by Mr. Barnes does not make any sense. The total return swap and the position that the insurer should take in the trade suggested by Mr. Barnes (receiving the total return) would double the credit risk exposure and interest rate risk exposure, not reduce credit spread risk.

    b. The confusion here is that credit spread options can be written where the underlying is a credit risky bond with a fixed credit spread or where the underlying is a credit spread. When the underlying is a credit risky bond with a fixed credit spread, a put option provides protection against an increase in the credit spread. When the underlying is a credit spread, a call option provides this protection. Hence, Ms. Hepburn and Mr. Tracy could both be correct, it is just they were referring to a different type of credit spread option.

    c. The total return swap can be ruled out for the reason given in part (a). Both types of credit spread options would accomplish the objective sought by Mr. Rivers. Of the two types of credit spread options, the one in which the underlying is a credit spread should be preferred since the other assumes that market risk (i.e., interest rate risk) will not matter over the next six months.

13. The payout on a credit derivative in which the underlying is a credit spread should be based only on a change in the credit spread and not a change in the general level of interest rates. The risk factor is derived from the price sensitivity of a security to changes in interest rates. When the change in the credit spread is multiplied by the risk factor and the notional amount, the result is the change in value attributable to only a change in the credit spread.

14. a. Since the manager expects the credit spread to widen, the manager will benefit by purchasing a credit spread call option.

   b. The payoff for the credit spread call option is as follows:

   - if the credit spread at expiration is 200 basis points or less the payoff is zero
   - if the credit spread at expiration is greater than 200 basis points the payoff is

   $$\text{(credit spread at expiration} - 0.020) \times \$10,000,000 \times 6$$

   c. Because the option cost is \$120,000, the profit for the credit spread call option is

   $$\text{(credit spread at expiration} - 0.020) \times \$10,000,000 \times 6 - \$120,000$$

   If the credit spread is 300 basis points (that is, 0.030), the profit is:

   $$(0.030 - 0.020) \times \$10,000,000 \times 6 - \$120,000 = \$480,000$$

15. Before looking at the precise answers for parts (a) through (c), consider the difference between the credit spread call option in Question 14 compared to the credit spread put option in Question 15. In Question 14, the credit spread call option was written on the credit spread. As the credit spread widened, the credit option came into the money.

   Conversely, in Question 15, the credit spread put option is written on the underlying asset. As the credit spread widens, the value of the underlying asset declines, and the credit spread put option will come into the money. In Question 15, the credit spread is used to determine the strike price for the put option on the underlying asset.

   The key point of Questions 14 and 15 is to demonstrate that an investor can use both a credit call option and a credit put option to profit from widening credit spreads. The distinction is that the credit spread call option must be written on the credit spread, while the credit spread put option must be written on the underlying asset.

   a. The strike price is the present value of the future cash flow. The discount rate for computing the present value is the 5-year Treasury rate of 6.5% plus the credit spread of 250 basis points. So, the annual discount rate is 9% and the semiannual discount rate is therefore 4.5%.

   The coupon rate for the bond is 200 basis points over 6.5%, or 8.5%. The semiannual coupon payment is \$42.50.

   The first coupon payment of \$42.50 is not discounted because it is paid on the same day that the option matures, July 1. (That is, when evaluating as of July 1, it is not a future cash flow.) Since the bond is a 5-year bond, there are 10 coupon payments. However, there are nine remaining after July 1. The nine future coupon payments of \$42.50 per \$1,000 of par value are discounted at 4.5%. It can be shown that the present value of the nine future coupon payments is \$308.92.

   The present value of the maturity value of \$1,000 nine periods from now when discounted at 4.5% is \$672.90 [$= \$1,000/(1.045)^9$].

   Therefore the strike price is

   $$\text{strike price} = \text{current coupon} + \text{PV of future coupons} + \text{PV of maturity value}$$

   $$= \$42.50 + \$308.92 + \$672.90 = \$1,024.32$$

b. The payout is equal to:

$$\text{strike price} - \text{bond's value on July 1}$$

The bond's value on July 1 must be determined. It is assumed in the question that on July 1 the credit spread is 300 basis points and the 5-year U.S. Treasury note rate is unchanged at 6.5%. The discount rate is 9.5% and the semiannual discount rate is 4.75%.

The semiannual coupon payment is $42.50. Again, as of July 1, the first coupon is not discounted because it is paid on the same date as when the option matures. Since the bond is initially a 5-year bond, on July 1 there are 9 remaining coupon payments of $42.50. The present value of the 9 remaining coupon payments of $42.50 when discounted at 4.75% (the semiannual discount rate on July 1) is $305.47.

The present value of the $1,000 maturity value discounted at 4.75% nine periods from now is $1,000/(1.0475)^9 = $658.59

The value of the bond as of July 1 is therefore equal to:

$$= \text{current coupon} + \text{PV of future coupons} + \text{PV of maturity value}$$

$$= \$42.50 + \$305.47 + 658.59 = \$1,006.56$$

The payout is

$$\$1,024.32 - \$1,006.56 = \$17.76$$

c. The profit is equal to:

$$\text{strike price} - \text{bond's value} - \text{cost of the option}$$

Since the cost of the option is $10, the profit is

$$\$1,024.32 - \$1,006.56 - \$10 = \$7.76$$

16. The payoff for the credit spread forward contract is:

$$\text{payoff} = [\text{credit spread at maturity} - \text{contracted credit spread}] \times \text{risk factor}$$
$$\times \text{notional amount}$$

The following is known

credit spread at maturity of the forward (December 31) = 3.5%

contracted credit spread = 3.0%

risk factor = 3.25

notional amount = $500,000,000

Therefore,

$$\text{payoff} = [0.035 - 0.03] \times 3.25 \times \$500,000,000 = \$8,125,000$$

17. a. For a credit spread forward, the payoff at the maturity date would be:

    [credit spread at maturity for Credit Index − forward credit spread] × risk factor

    × notional amount

    By buying a credit spread forward contract, the payoff is positive if the credit spread at maturity for the Credit Index increases above the forward credit spread. If a manager is seeking to protect against a widening of the spread, a credit spread forward should be purchased.

    If the credit spread does widen, then there will be a decline in the value of the portfolio. However, this will be offset (fully or partially depending on how good the hedge is) from a payoff of the credit spread forward purchased.

    b. The payoff to the credit spread forward would have been:

    $$(0.06 - 0.035) \times 2.5 \times \$500 \text{ million} = \$31,250,000$$

    c. If credit spreads had narrowed by 50 basis points, the portfolio manager would have paid (as indicated by the negative sign) at the maturity date of the credit spread forward:

    $$(0.03 - 0.035) \times 2.5 \times \$500 \text{ million} = -\$6,250,000$$

    Note, however, that while the portfolio manager would have owed $6.25 million on the credit spread forward, the market value of the manager's cash portfolio would have increased.

    d. The payoff for a credit spread call option before deducting the cost of the option is:

    [credit spread at maturity for Credit Index − strike Credit Index] × risk factor

    × notional amount

    If the credit spread increases relative to the strike Credit Index, the payoff for a credit spread call option will be positive (before deducting the cost of the option). For a credit spread put option there would be no payoff if the Credit Index widens. Thus, the manager would purchase a call option on the Credit Index.

    e. The payoff for the credit spread call option after deducting the cost of the option is:

    $$(0.06 - 0.035) \times 2.5 \times \$500 \text{ million} - \$10 \text{ million} = \$21,250,000$$

    f. With a forward credit spread, the payoff is symmetric; that is, if the spread widens the manager receives a payoff but if it narrows the manager must make a payment. The disadvantage of a credit spread call option is that if the spread widens there is a payoff but the payoff must be reduced by the cost of the option. The advantage is that if there is a narrowing of the spread, the most that the option buyer can lose is the cost of the option.

    g. Option-adjusted spread is used in order to neutralize the effects of embedded optionality associated with corporate bonds. The OAS accounts for the individual bond characteristics such as sinking funds, call provisions, and other early retirement covenants.

18. a. The credit derivative used in a synthetic collateralized debt obligation is a (basket) credit default swap.
    b. The collateral manager is the credit protection seller.
    c. The collateral manager will invest in low risk securities.
    d. Since there are no payouts to the protection buyer, the collateral manager earns the return on the portfolio of low risk securities plus the swap premium fee received from the credit default swap.

19. a. In a synthetic CDO, there is protection against multiple financial obligations. Hence a basket default swap would be used.
    b. When there is a credit event requiring a payment by the collateral manager to the credit protection buyer, there is a reduction in the return to the CDO bondholders.

20. a. The subordinate basket default swap seller will make payments as follows:

    first reference entity to default: $7 million
    second reference entity to default: $10 million (maximum payout for a reference entity)
    third reference entity to default: $8 million (maximum aggregate payout on swap)

    The payments total to $25 million. The swap will terminate after the third reference entity defaults.

    b. The basket default swap seller will make payments as follows:

    first reference entity to default: no payment since the $25 million threshold is not reached; losses of $18 million needed to reach threshold ($25 million − $7 million).
    second reference entity to default: no payment since $25 million threshold is not reached; losses of $8 million needed to reach threshold ($25 million − $7 million − $10 million).
    third reference entity to default: threshold of $25 million reached; first $8 million of the third reference entity to default is needed to cover the threshold. The balance of the third reference entity to default after the threshold is covered is $2 million ($10 million − $8 million).
    fourth reference entity to default: the threshold is reached and there is still $23 million ($25 million—$2 million) that can be paid out. However, the maximum that can be paid on any reference entity is $10 million and that is the amount paid for the fourth reference entity's loss.

    The total payments are therefore $12 million. Since there only four reference entities covered by the swap, the swap terminates after the fourth reference entity defaults.

ABOUT THE
CFA PROGRAM

The Chartered Financial Analyst® designation (CFA®) is a globally recognized standard of excellence for measuring the competence and integrity of investment professionals. To earn the CFA charter, candidates must successfully pass through the CFA Program, a global graduate-level self-study program that combines a broad curriculum with professional conduct requirements as preparation for a wide range of investment specialties.

Anchored by a practice-based curriculum, the CFA Program is focused on the knowledge identified by professionals as essential to the investment decision-making process. This body of knowledge maintains current relevance through a regular, extensive survey of practicing CFA charterholders across the globe. The curriculum covers 10 general topic areas ranging from equity and fixed-income analysis to portfolio management to corporate finance, all with a heavy emphasis on the application of ethics in professional practice. Known for its rigor and breadth, the CFA Program curriculum highlights principles common to every market so that professionals who earn the CFA designation have a thoroughly global investment perspective and a profound understanding of the global marketplace.

www.cfainstitute.org

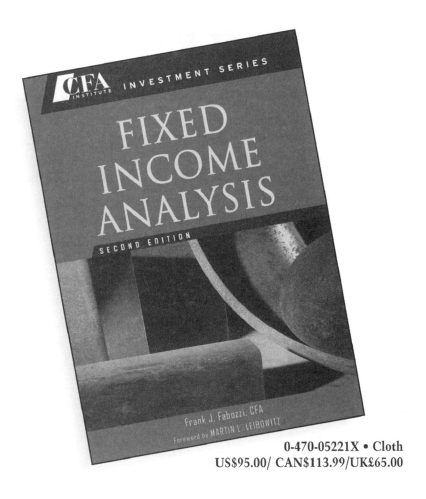